D1593081

The
Physical
Attractiveness
Phenomena

PERSPECTIVES IN SOCIAL PSYCHOLOGY

A Series of Texts and Monographs • Edited by Elliot Aronson

A Continuation Order Plan is available for this series. A continuation order will bring delivery of each new volume immediately upon publication. Volumes are billed only upon actual shipment. For further information please contact the publisher.

The Physical Attractiveness Phenomena

Gordon L. Patzer

Loyola Marymount University
Los Angeles, California

PLENUM PRESS • NEW YORK AND LONDON

Library of Congress Cataloging in Publication Data

Patzer, Gordon L.

The physical attractiveness phenomena.

(Perspectives in social psychology)
Bibliography: p.
Includes index.
1. Interpersonal attraction.   2. Interpersonal attraction—Cross-cultural studies.
I. Title.   II. Series.
HM132.P369   1985   302'.13   85-6593
ISBN 0-306-41783-9

© 1985 Plenum Press, New York
A Division of Plenum Publishing Corporation
233 Spring Street, New York, N.Y. 10013

Printed in the United States of America

Preface

Physical attractiveness phenomena permeate society with somber ramifications. Correspondingly, practical applications of physical attractiveness phenomena are extensive. The consequence is that almost every person can benefit from knowledge about research on physical attractiveness. Such research material provides valuable information for persons established in their careers, as well as those preparing for a career. Similarly, parents at all stages of their life cycle should be cognizant of how physical attractiveness impacts the psychological and physiological development of children. Because no one is isolated from physical attractiveness phenomena, knowledge of this material should be imperative for everyone.

This book consolidates research that specifically addresses physical attractiveness. The first summary was a classic review presented over 10 years ago (Berscheid & Walster, 1974). Since then the research literature has continued to grow, but no comprehensive review has again been published. Even though research summaries have been presented in a compilation of psychological abstracts (Cash, 1980), and in a discussion of stereotyping literature (Adams, 1982), the study of physical attractiveness phenomena is due for a comprehensive account and an analysis of the extensive, divergent research.

Research on physical attractiveness is conducted in a variety of disciplines and has produced findings that span the continuum of human life. Both the scientific community and the general public have expressed substantial interest in this research, and to accommodate these diversities of interest, *The Physical Attractiveness Phenomena* structures the expanse by collecting and synthesizing the massive body of research. A critical element of this structuring is the identification of the components that form a framework to organize past research and to encourage greater efficacy for future investigations.

In addition to a structured comprehensive update, this book reflects the topic's maturity by providing a different approach throughout. For example, the first chapter introduces the framework and fundamentals, whereas the second chapter is directed at measurement issues—a new consideration for physical attractiveness research. Knowledge typically associated with this research is dealt with in Chapters 3 and 4. However, the difference is that Chapter 3 discusses the interpersonal realities pertaining to stereotyping but Chapter 4 focuses on interpersonal reciprocations that are important in the daily lives of every person (i.e., romantic attraction, nonintimate liking, and employment dynamics). A stimulating contrast is the content of Chapter 5, which isolates the intrapersonal realities of physical attractiveness. Chapter 6 takes a new direction by dealing with the determinants of physical attractiveness. Because attempts to persuade are so universal in today's society, Chapter 7, which may be seen as a departure in treatment from most of the book, illustrates the research process by detailing a specific study of the relationship between communicator physical attractiveness and persuasive communication effectiveness. Chapter 8 not only offers an innovative cultural and societal perspective of physical attractiveness but also a review of cross-cultural research verifying that the information presented throughout is not limited to any one particular culture. This chapter concludes with a consideration of the progression that people are making in relation to physical attractiveness phenomena. Finally, Chapter 9 discusses physical attractiveness phenomena as they pertain to science and theory and proposes a comprehensive theory that is intended to provide understanding and to generate further theory-driven programmatic research.

Persons from practically every profession can benefit from knowledge about physical attractiveness phenomena, and many university courses can use this book as supplemental reading. It can be useful in understanding the past and influencing the future. Such an understanding may be especially relevant for courses within the broad categories of education, sociology, political science, business, and psychology. Furthermore, a thorough understanding of physical attractiveness phenomena can enhance professional competence of persons who are preparing for, as well as those already established in, careers related to education, politics, psychology, law, medicine, and management. In fact, every person who interacts with another, regardless of frequency or intensity, will gain valuable information from reading *The Physical Attractiveness Phenomena*.

Contents

Chapter 3 · Interpersonal Realities   42

Chapter 4 · Interpersonal Reciprocations   81

Chapter 5 · Intrapersonal Realities 115

Chapter 6 · Determinants of Physical Attractiveness 140

Chapter 8 · Cultures and Societies 225

Chapter 9 · Science and Theory 245

Chapter 1

Introduction

PHYSICAL ATTRACTIVENESS IS MORE THAN MEETS THE EYE

Physical attractiveness is the most visible and most easily accessible trait of a person. Physical attractiveness is also a consistently and frequently used *informational cue*. These facts may be the reason physical attractiveness is so important and its influence so pervasive in the lives of almost every person in today's society.

Scientific study of the effects of physical attractiveness began in the mid-1960s. The cumulative product of that research offers strong documentation about physical attractiveness as represented by facial appearance. The findings reveal that physical attractiveness plays a dramatic, but covert, role in an individual's interpersonal interactions, in how others perceive and respond to the individual, and even in the individual's personality development. Generally, the more physically attractive an individual is, the more positive the person is perceived, the more favorably the person is responded to, and the more successful is the person's personal and professional life.

This book discusses the scientific research on which these empirical findings are based. Therefore, the focus is on the specific topic of physical attractiveness. Collectively, the research and its subsequent findings may be summarized as the physical attractiveness phenomena. The phenomena are not mere speculation. Rather, they are based on documented facts that persons of different levels of physical attractiveness are perceived differently and are treated differently such that higher physical attractiveness is given overwhelmingly preferential treatment.

The physical attractiveness phenomena reflect an encompassing term, which is consistent with a general physical attractiveness stereotype that states, "What is beautiful is good." Consequently, this past stereotype provides a basis of proven fact that higher physical attractiveness is

1

advantageous to an individual, whereas lower physical attractiveness is correspondingly disadvantageous. This expression, coined by Dion, Berscheid, and Walster (1972, p. 285), is included in and exceeded by the physical attractiveness phenomena. Extension beyond this stereotype includes characteristics of power, pervasiveness, and subtleness.

People refuse to acknowledge the impact of physical attractiveness. But when these same people are placed into an experimental design, which camouflages the issue of physical attractiveness, their actions are to the contrary. The material presented in this book deals primarily with adults, but the findings are consistent with, and often parallel to, research with children. The information that follows represents work conducted with adherence to normally accepted practices of scientific investigation, usually under the auspices of university researchers.

FRAMEWORK

The physical attractiveness phenomena exist within a broader framework of general research principles and issues. As part of a larger scheme, the research conforms to generally accepted standards of scientific study. Although the physical attractiveness research is a distinct entity, it is not isolated from more global research disciplines. The physical attractiveness phenomena are interdisciplinary, but they exist primarily within the boundaries of social psychology.

Physical attractiveness involves matters unique to itself. This first chapter presents four general factors that surround the physical attractiveness phenomena: (a) explanation of cited research, (b) relationship of physical attractiveness research with other appearance research, (c) importance of the physical attractiveness variable, and (d) resistance by the general public and scientific communities. Three major fundamentals of the physical attractiveness phenomena are also identified: (a) pervasiveness, (b) subtleness, and (c) socialization.

Demarcation

This book is primarily restricted to recent research that involves facial appearance. Such an approach represents the distinct direction which physical attractiveness research has taken since the mid-1960s. Consequently, unless specifically stated, the discussion throughout this book excludes extreme face or body deformity, and is limited to a normal continuum of facial appearance possessed in the general population. Although definition remains elusive, physical attractiveness is dependent on a global evaluation based on a person's face. This explanation is admittedly abstract; however, practically all research utilizes this explanation, and it has proven to be operationally successful. (A thorough discussion of physical attractiveness measurement is presented in Chapter 2.) Because the boundaries associated with facial physical attractiveness are necessarily loosely defined, this book includes other selected research that enhances the immediate discussion.

Person Perception

Physical attractiveness is firmly entrenched in person perception. This relationship is readily understood when person perception is defined as the process by which a person perceives and thinks about other persons, their characteristics, their qualities, and their internal traits (Taruiri, 1954). In person perception, inferences are drawn from observations. Consequently, these two entities are interdependent because research demonstrates that physical attractiveness acts as an informational cue that affects person perception.

Person perception includes, but certainly is not limited to, current physical attractiveness research. In fact, current physical attractiveness research represents only one aspect of general appearance study which began much earlier and which has taken many forms. The earliest approach involved a "constitutional psychology" that associated body characteristics with criminal activities (Lombroso, 1891) and personality traits (Kretschmer, 1925; Sheldon, 1940). This early phase was followed by study of social interactions as a function of body characteristics (Goffman, 1963). Goffman's work provided an important precedent for a substantial portion of physical attractiveness research. However, its focus on negative stigmata limits its generalizations because it provides a valuable analogy only to lower physical attractiveness but not to higher levels. The reader interested in research with body characteristics is referred to a summary by Adams (1982).

Societal Importance

For society, and the human race in general, understanding of physical attractiveness is mandatory. This imperative for physical attractiveness research was probably first implied by Charles Darwin who, in 1871, stated that "no excuse is needed for treating this subject in some detail" (Darwin, 1952, p. 578). Darwin expanded his statement by quoting the German philosopher Schopenhauer who, in regard to physical attractiveness, had written that

the final aim of all love intrigues, be they comic or tragic, is really of more
importance than all other ends in human life. What it all turns upon is nothing
less than the composition of the next generation. . . . It is not the weal or woe of
any one individual, but that of the human race to come, which is here at stake.
(cited in Darwin, 1952, p. 578)

The importance of physical attractiveness in society did not begin with
Darwin's call for study. Rather, his statement was the result of the
observation that physical attractiveness has continuously played a significant role throughout the history of the human race. Anthropological
writings document the notion that high value was associated with physical
attractiveness since the beginning of history. Based on evidence from a
variety of sources, it is not difficult to identify artifacts that reveal attempts
to enhance individual physical attractiveness.

The attention given physical attractiveness is not only a contemporary
occurrence. Although the beginning of the physical attractiveness phenomena is impossible to verify with our current research technology, the
importance of physical attractiveness appears to be timeless. Supportive
evidence is apparent by the attempts of members of early populations to
alter their appearance. Paraphernalia related to individual physical attractiveness are readily found in every culture, ranging from the graves of Cro-
Magnon man, through the tombs of ancient Egypt, to the caskets of
present-day burials. The anthropological discipline appears to leave little
doubt about the respect that the human race has had for physical
attractiveness. For example, the anthropologist Harry Shapiro states: "so
universal is this urge to improve on nature (i.e., appearance or physical
attractiveness) that one is almost tempted to regard it as an instinct"
(Shapiro, 1947, p. 456).

The possible controversy regarding the innate or the environmental
origins of physical attractiveness is not of major concern in contemporary
study. Nor does modern study explore when human beings began to be
concerned about physical attractiveness. The anthropological writings
suggest that "the endeavor to embellish the appearance and personal
charms belongs to the most ancient cultural expressions of man" (Fiser &
Fiserova, 1969, p. 92). Even among animals, natural selection favors the
more physically attractive (Burley, 1981). Although these anthropological
and biological issues are interesting, the focus of this book is on the role of
physical attractiveness of humans in our contemporary society.

Communication and Physical Attractiveness

Central to contemporary society is communication. In fact, the
importance of communication cannot be overemphasized because everyone

in today's society is a communicator. Consequently, form of communication (verbal or nonverbal), setting of communication (personal or nonpersonal), and intent of communication (persuasion, commerce, explanation, courtship, or expression) have all received considerable attention and recognition of their value. Extending the focus on communication a step further, it is apparent that much, if not most, communication is between persons who are, or have been, visible to each other. Therefore, a thorough understanding of physical attractiveness is crucial because a communicator's appearance is the first and most obvious element observed in almost all (visual) communication. The conclusion must be that physical attractiveness is a major component of successful communication, for there are few, if any, communication situations that do not ultimately involve visual contact between the participants. As an illustration, four of the most common and important communication interactions in our society are (a) interpersonal relations with significant others in our lives, (b) business interactions and transactions, (c) commercial marketing communications and advertising, and (d) politicians and political campaigns.

Resistance of the Public

Despite relevance to everyday life, knowledge about physical attractiveness is at times resisted by the public. When such counterproductive response is expressed, it is typically in the form of indifference, disagreement, or anger. Indifferent people tend to feel that the importance of physical attractiveness is common knowledge and that dissimilar treatment is either not inherently bad or that it cannot be changed. These people are wrong. Although some aspects of the physical attractiveness phenomena are consistent with common thought, the dimensions that physical attractiveness exerts throughout our lives exceed all limits of common knowledge. Also, differential treatment results in serious implications that are disadvantageous for those lower in physical attractiveness, and advantageous for those higher. The second response, disagreement, is difficult to acknowledge, because such a response is not legitimate in light of the quantity and quality of scientific research documenting physical attractiveness phenomena. Finally, those persons who express anger appear to be questionning the morality of such research or are overly sensitive to the physical attractiveness of themselves or a loved one. The general response to persons within either of these categories should be that extensive, objective research documents serious consequences based on differences in physical attractiveness. Furthermore, failing to recognize the facts will not lessen the atrocity of such discrimination but will serve to aggravate that bias which already exists.

Reluctance of the Scientific Community

Interesting questions pertaining to physical attractiveness are endless. How is person perception influenced by physical attractiveness? Are those of higher physical attractiveness treated differently from those of lower physical attractiveness? Is physical attractiveness an asset or liability? Are those of different physical attractiveness levels also psychologically different? Are those lower in physical attractiveness physiologically different from those higher in physical attractiveness? Such questions are of interest to social and biological scientists, physicians of plastic and reconstructive surgery, decision makers in advertising and marketing, and people in general. Despite the interest, answers to such questions have relied more on folklore and conventional wisdom than on scientific evidence.

Some scholars have offered explanations for what appears to be a topic avoided in systematic scientific research. These explanations range from a "morphology neglect" (i.e., the study of surface characteristics) to subscription to one of America's most honorable but naively idealistic philosophies: that philosophy being a hesitancy to suggest any form of genetic determinism in the relationship between physical appearance factors and personal characteristics. The sentiment for an egalitarian society has stifled research that may suggest an undemocratic situation in which those persons who possess higher physical attractiveness are, somehow, better than those persons lower in physical attractiveness.

Prior to the early 1960s, physical attractiveness was a characteristic that was not addressed in systematic social science research. However, the importance of physical attractiveness is evidenced by folklore which often attributes personality traits as a function of height, weight, hair color, eye color, and length of nose.

The study of perceptions and responses has developed slowly. Even slower has been the development of study pertaining to the potential differences between individuals of lower and of higher physical attractiveness. Probably the first empirical examination of physical attractiveness was performed by E. Aronson, a social psychologist at Stanford University. This pioneering researcher has offered an explanation for the delay of science in pursuing physical attractiveness research:

> It is difficult to be certain why the effects of physical beauty have not been studied more systematically. It may be that, at some level, we would hate to find evidence indicating that beautiful women are liked better than homely women— somehow this seems undemocratic. In a democracy we like to feel that with hard work and a good deal of motivation, a person can accomplish almost anything. But, alas (most of us believe), hard work cannot make an ugly woman beautiful.

Because of this suspicion, perhaps most social psychologists implicitly would prefer to believe that beauty is, indeed, only skin deep—and avoid the investigation of its social impact for fear that they might learn otherwise. (Aronson, 1969, p. 160)

Despite past neglect, the physical attractiveness research, which began in the mid-1960s, has grown, prospered, and produced intriguing results. Since that statement by Aronson, attitudes have changed and physical attractiveness has become a topic that continues to receive considerable research attention. The research is of admirable quantity and quality and has been performed within universally accepted standards for both social and biological sciences. This research has revealed significant results that have confirmed the expected and often discovered the unexpected. The research is far from complete, but it has found causal relationships between physical attractiveness and a host of variables discussed throughout this book.

FUNDAMENTALS

Fundamental features of the physical attractiveness phenomena include pervasiveness, subtleness, and a socialization process. However, the foundation of the physical attractiveness phenomena is a stereotype that prevails throughout society. The essence of this physical attractiveness stereotype is expressed in the phrase that "what is beautiful is good" (Dion et al. 1972). Its existence is documented by research showing that those persons of higher physical attractiveness are perceived to possess more socially desirable traits, live better lives, and have more successful marriages and occupations than their counterparts of lower physical attractiveness (Dion et al., 1972). A massive national survey found that physically attractive persons are believed to obtain more happiness, have more sex, and receive greater respect than those of less physical attractivess (Berscheid & Walster, 1972). In general, their lives are assumed to be more socially exciting and active (Bassili, 1981).

Effects of physical attractiveness appear relatively universal for both males and females. Gender-specific research indicates that as the physical attractiveness of both males and females increases, perceptions of social desirability increases regardless of gender (Gillen, 1981; Gillen & Sherman, 1980; Tanke, 1982). Gillen (1981) specifically reports that females with higher physical attractiveness are perceived to possess greater femininity, whereas males with higher physical attractiveness are perceived to possess greater masculinity.

Persons higher in physical attractiveness are perceived to have more positive characteristics overall, as well as happier and more fulfilling lives (Dion, 1972). Physically attractive persons are perceived to be more intelligent, sensitive, kind, interesting, sociable, and more likely to attend college than their counterparts of lower physical attractiveness (Clifford & Walster, 1973; Smits & Cherhoniak, 1976; Walster, Aronson, Abrahams, & Rottman, 1966). Similarly, the less physically attractive a person is, the less the person is liked (Byrne, London, & Reeves, 1968; Korabik, 1981) and the less the person is preferred as a working, dating, or marriage partner (Blood, 1956; Brislin & Lewis, 1968; Huston, 1973; Stroebe, Insko, Thompson, & Layton, 1971; Tesser & Brodie, 1971). Once married, the spouse of higher physical attractiveness is generally viewed more favorably than the counterpart of lower physical attractiveness (Hartnett & Secord, 1983). For example, the spouse of higher physical attractiveness is perceived "as significantly more poised, interesting, sociable, independent, warm, exciting, and sexually warm than the unattractive spouse" (Brigham, 1980, p. 371).

In a study on the effects of physical attractiveness on impression formation, male and female judges were asked to indicate their impression of stimulus persons on seventeen dimensions (A. G. Miller, 1970a). Persons of higher physical attractiveness were evaluated as more curious rather than indifferent, complex rather than simple, perceptive rather than insensitive, happy rather than sad, active rather than passive, amiable rather than aloof, humorous rather than serious, pleasure seeking rather than self-controlled, outspoken rather than reserved, and flexible rather than rigid. The consequences of higher physical attractiveness are positive, whereas the consequences of lower physical attractiveness are negative.

Researchers consistently report that people do not behave in a manner consistent with the adage, You cannot judge a book by its cover. Based merely on physical attractiveness, people do formulate comprehensive notions about an observed person. Furthermore, these people exhibit different nonverbal behaviors in the form of either positive or negative responses. Usually, such responses, if they are not verbal, are in the form of smiles or frowns, specific looks, gestures, and head movements. The exact implication of such general social approval and disapproval may represent social acceptance and unacceptance of a person and/or behavior.

Whatever the implications, physical attractiveness is a determinant of differential attention. Experimental research shows that persons of higher physical attractiveness receive a significantly greater frequency of positive looks and smiles than do those of lower physical attractiveness (Kleck & Rubenstein, 1975). A. G. Miller observed that a consistent pattern emerges that of the unattractive person being associated with the negative or undesirable pole of the adjective scales and the highly attractive person being judged significantly more positively. (1970a, p. 242)

Pervasiveness

The physical attractiveness phenomena are not restricted to certain age groups. In fact, research across the developmental spectrum reveals that the physical attractiveness phenomena are pervasive across ages as well as situations (Dushenko, Perry, Schilling, & Smolarski, 1978). Although most of the physical attractiveness research has dealt with young adults, there is substantial research dealing with persons from early infancy to later elderly stages in life.

At the earliest stage, newly born infants were found to receive different treatment consistent with the physical attractiveness phenomena (e.g., Power, Hildebrandt, & Fitzgerald, 1982). Some research has involved infants 4 and 8 months old (Hildebrandt & Fitzgerald, 1978), 3 to 13 months old (Hildebrandt & Fitzgerald, 1979a), and even infants 3 months of age (Hildebrandt, 1980). The coverage of infants was extended by having teachers rate older children of school age (Lerner & Lerner, 1977). In this research the children of higher physical attractiveness were rated more likely to possess higher academic ability, to have better social relationships, and to be better adjusted. Similarly, parents were found to expect physically attractive children to be more popular, more successful socially, and to have better attitudes (Adams & LaVoie, 1974a). Even the young children themselves were found to rate children of higher physical attractiveness as being more friendly and social than children of lower physical attractiveness (Dion, 1973).

The effects go beyond childhood. Middle-aged persons are perceived as more honest, more sociable, having higher self-esteem, and possessing higher vocational status as a function of their physical attractiveness (Adams & Huston, 1975). Likewise, a study investigating couples aged 64 to 86 years old, reported results consistent with the physical attractiveness phenomena (Peterson & Miller, 1980).

The reason that physical attractiveness phenomena are so pervasive may be due to the physical attractiveness construct itself. The power of physical attractiveness, and the subsequent physical attractiveness phenomena, may be a consequence of the fact that no other personal characteristic is so readily observable with the exception of such variables as race and sex. When people first meet, their physical attractiveness is the most obvious and immediately accessible trait. The immediate and easily obtained informational cue provided by physical attractiveness remains important beyond the initial impression and into the long-term impression and relationship. The fact that one may be intelligent, educated, wealthy, and/or highly competent is probably more informative than physical attractiveness, but such information is not so readily available. Even when these less visible characteristics are known their perceived value is influenced, and even overpowered, by the early impression gained from physical attractiveness. Regardless of the social inequalities and moral ramifications, physical attractiveness certainly appears to open doors for those fortunate enough to possess this characteristic. Furthermore, once through these doors, the effects of physical attractiveness continue.

Subtleness

A disturbing feature of the physical attractiveness phenomena are their apparent subtleness. To verify the subtlety one need only consider the adage, Actions speak louder than words. Specifically, people adamantly state that another person's physical attractiveness has no effect on them, their perceptions, or their behavior. However, the experimental research literature shows that the average person drastically underestimates the influence physical attractiveness has on him or her (Efran, 1974; Hudson & Henze, 1969; Miller, H. L. & Rivenbark, 1970; Perrin, 1921; Tesser & Brodie, 1971).

Regardless of whether this subtleness is due to defensiveness, ambivalence, or ignorance, its existence is well documented. Relevant documentation can be cited at a global/societal level or a specific/individual level. On the societal level, people in the United States are obsessed by physical attractiveness. This obsession is apparent as people strive incessantly, beyond rationality, to improve their physical attractiveness. Huge amounts of time, money, and effort are spent on beauty aids, exercise books, and ultimately for cosmetic surgery. Although expenditures for physical attractiveness are immense, we refuse, in large part, to acknowledge the notion of the physical attractiveness phenomena. This same society, which endlessly pursues physical attractiveness, continues to contradict itself by explicitly subscribing to the honorable "democratic belief that physical appearance is a peripheral and superficial characteristic with little influence on our lives" (Berscheid & Walster, 1972, p. 43).

On the specific individual level the contradiction is equally obvious. College students who were openly asked to list characteristics desirable in a date normally placed physical attractiveness at the bottom (Hudson & Henze, 1969). However, experimental and observational studies confirm that both choice of and attraction to a date are predominantly a function of the date's physical attractiveness. For example, an early computer dance and dating situation revealed that physical attractiveness was the only predictor for liking a date (Walster *et al.*, 1966). This preference was shown to be superior to intelligence, social skills, and character of the partner even after interaction.

Socialization

Discrimination based on physical attractiveness probably excels prejudicial discrimination based on sex, race, or religion. Regardless of context or age of participants, society tends to view the physically attractive as inherently better than those of less physical attractiveness. This implicit stereotype has produced an environment with serious implications for such far-reaching activities as employment, helping behavior, dating and mating, election of politicians, and even personality development.

The consequence is differential treatment throughout life for those who differ merely in their physical attractiveness. The major dissimilarity between discrimination based on physical attractiveness versus sex or race discrimination is that the latter are legislated against whereas the former is not—yet. The major similarity is that sexism and racism have their origins in childhood as does social stereotyping based on physical attractiveness. Consequently, the stereotyping involved with the physical attractiveness phenomena continues to be bred into future societies as well as continuing to function within our current society.

The early years of a child are not spared from the physical attractiveness phenomena. Literally from birth, infants are introduced to the realities of physical attractiveness variances. The newly born, who are evaluated as higher in physical attractiveness, receive more smiles, touching, and attention than those infants evaluated as lower in physical attractiveness (Hildebrandt, 1982; Langlois & Stephan, 1981).

This early experience serves to imprint the discriminative treatment based on physical attractiveness. It also serves as the beginning of a continuing socialization process for indoctrination and progression of physical attractiveness phenomena. The most innocent nursery stories involve evil witches who are ugly, whereas the good characters are beautiful. Phrases abound to reinforce ideas that ugly is sin and pretty is virtue, and that ugly ducklings strive to be beautiful royalty. Throughout childhood the individual receives the same social messages which are delivered both explicitly and implicitly through books, movies, television, and advertising. The messages must have an impact because, by the age of 3, children are cognizant of the physical attractiveness phenomena. For example, children as young as three years old are more likely to select a photograph of a peer who is of higher physical attractiveness than of lower (Dion, 1977).

The concepts of physical attractiveness held by these young children are well developed and consistent with the general adult population. Boys and girls at the ages of 3 and 4 equate appearance of elderly ages as lower in physical attractiveness and younger adult ages as higher in physical attractiveness (Downs & Walz, 1980). Children of both sexes, at ages 5 and 6, even associate negative personality characteristics for those lower in physical attractiveness and positive personalities to those of higher physical attractiveness (Moran, 1976).

Extensive reviews of this research provide support that the physical attractiveness phenomena are just as pervasive and applicable to the lives of infants and children as they are to adults (cf. Hildebrandt, 1982; Langlois & Stephan, 1981). A disturbing fact of this finding among youth is that these are the formative years from which time on the encounters with the physical attractiveness phenomena will increase. The experiences will maintain an impact through socialization and throughout the human life cycle—passed and sanctioned from generation to generation.

These three major fundamentals (pervasiveness, subtleness, socialization) display the contradictions that abound with regard to the physical attractiveness phenomena. However, these contradictions are most striking when actions are compared to words. The reason for the irony involved with the physical attractiveness phenomena is perhaps explained by the following:

> It seems somewhat reprehensible to acknowledge publicly that people select friends or employees as much, if not more, for their appearance than their personality traits or skills. It is very much like marrying for money. No one wants to admit how often that occurs. Perhaps we still wish to believe that individual achievement is more important than being born beautiful or handsome. (Waters, 1980, p. 11)

SUMMARY

Physical attractiveness research is so exciting because its observations of reality often disconfirm logic and common sense and confirm empirical proposals. Experience shows many situations in which physical attractiveness was assumed insignificant until proven highly significant. Yet people consistently (and adamantly) report that physical attractiveness is unimportant to how they perceive and respond to others.

The evidence does not support what people say. People do "judge a book by its cover" despite their claims to the contrary. Proof is provided by scientific study. These measurements show that people can severely underrate the influence of attractiveness. This contradiction is noted by many researchers, and was formally acknowledged by the following statement: "It appears that they are either not fully aware or not fully honest about how important physical attractiveness really is to them" (Miller & Rivenbark, 1970, p. 702).

People respond in a number of negative ways when confronted with the topic of physical attractiveness research. They tend to dislike the entire idea of physical attractiveness research, they tend to be defensive about the topic, they express that it is unethical or improper research, they refuse to consider the importance and possible influence of physical attractiveness, and they attempt to ignore the proven effects of physical attractiveness. The problem with such reactions is that ignorance of the person's environment is promoted. Such ignorance does not make the physical attractiveness phenomena disappear, nor does such action minimize the impact of physical attractiveness on our lives and within our interpersonal relations. In fact, it maximizes the impact.

The basic study of physical attractiveness, as it subsequently relates to the physical attractiveness phenomena, is multidisciplinary. Some of these disciplines include anthropology, sociology, and psychology. Other scientific inquiry comes from cosmetic and apparel industries, and advertising and marketing personnel. The medical profession involves two domains. First, the relatively small amount of work done by medical researchers concerned with the physiological and biological implications of physical attractiveness. Second, the important and substantial amount of empirical study done by medical specialists involved with plastic and reconstructive surgery. Although all of the above studies, as well as others, contribute to the knowledge regarding the physical attractiveness phenomena, their contributions vary on a continuum from minor to major. Even though all the related endeavors are valuable, it appears that social psychology is providing the critical (and, it is hoped, unifying) mass of substantive evidence about the function of physical attractiveness within contemporary society.

The following chapters will elaborate on the physical attractiveness phenomena. These chapters discuss (a) research procedures, (b) interpersonal and intrapersonal consequences of physical attractiveness, (c) determinants of physical attractiveness, (d) original research on the relationship between communicator physical attractiveness and persuasive communication effectiveness, (e) cross-cultural verification of the physical attractiveness phenomena, and (f) a discussion of the philosophy and history of science, followed by a proposed theory of the physical attractiveness phenomena. The chapters on interpersonal realities and interpersonal reciprocations may be considered the core of the physical attractiveness phenomena. The reason for this statement is that the early research on physical attractiveness focused on either the differential perceptions (along with subsequent differential expectations and treatments) or the dynamics of reciprocal interpersonal interactions.

The early research identified the existence of a stereotype that basically stated that anyone who is beautiful is good. The discovery of such a stereotype can be viewed as the kernel from which substantial research has grown and extended into other areas. Ongoing research continues to provide insight into the very complex and very important area of interpersonal interactions, and how these interactions are affected by individual physical attractiveness. The initial stereotype is so interesting and valuable that is is not unreasonable to expand its scope by describing it as a multitude of phenomena, namely, the physical attractiveness phenomena.

Chapter 2

Measurement of Physical Attractiveness

Beauty as we feel it is something indescribable: What it is or what it means can never be said. (Santayana, 1936, p. 201)

A direct relationship may not exist between physical attractiveness and most personal attributes. But people, either knowingly or unknowingly, make strong assumptions about these characteristics, based only on the informational cue provided by an individual's physical attractiveness. The end result of these assumptions is an advantage for those people who possess physical attractiveness and a disadvantage for those who do not. The importance of understanding the influence of physical attractiveness appears relevant for all interpersonal proceedings. However, physical attractiveness is essentially not a quantitative trait. Therefore, an important research issue is the manner in which researchers identify and manipulate the physical attractiveness variable in order to study its effects.

DEVELOPMENT

The measurement of physical attractiveness developed slowly because of the difficulty in measuring such a fluid and abstract concept. The earliest attempts remotely resembling these measurement efforts probably began with Perrin in 1921. Throughout the next 40 years attempts were made, but no real value resulted.

The early measurement studies were crude attempts to identify traits and characteristics which constitute physical attractiveness. For example, Perrin (1921) asked his subjects to think of their friends who are physically attractive and those friends who are physically unattractive. He then asked them to identify the characteristics which made each person representative of their physical attractiveness level. The data suggested that physical attractiveness is a matter of good grooming. Good grooming may influence

15

physical attractiveness but the problem is that Perrin expected people to be able to judge physical attractiveness of their friends and also to expertly analyze levels of physical attractiveness. Although gallant in his efforts, it is very doubtful that Perrin's subjects were able to fulfill his expectations.

Later researchers attempted less comprehensive experiments. These researchers found, for example, that wearing eyeglasses had a negative effect on physical attractiveness but a positive effect on perceptions of intelligence (Brunswik, 1939; Thornton, G. R., 1943, 1944). Other studies focused on facial components, such as facial expression (Munn, 1940), mouth curvature and eye gaze (Secord & Muthard, 1955; Secord, Dukes, & Bevan, 1954), eye contact (Exline, 1971), pupil size (Hess, 1965), and eyebrow position (Andrew, 1963; Keating, Mazur, & Segall, 1977). These specialized investigations of minute facial components were interesting but lacked the ability to capture the essence of physical attractiveness.

Unfortunately, physical attractiveness did not prove measurable by summing up the parts. The outcome was an evolution toward a more global measure of physical attractiveness. Initially, the measure appears as ambiguous as the physical attractiveness concept itself. However, this measure has turned the abstract concept of physical attractiveness into a powerful research construct.

The global measure of physical attractiveness negates the popular fallacy, Beauty is in the eye of the beholder. This common folklore regarding the uniqueness of physical attractiveness appears to be based on statements by scholars from an earlier time. The opening quote of George Santayana expresses the intrigue (and frustration) experienced throughout history concerning questions of physical attractiveness characteristics and dimensions. Likewise, in the 1800s, Darwin (1952, p. 577) wrote that he had observed no universal standard of beauty among people in different parts of the world. In a much later discussion about sexual behavior, Ford and Beach (1951) expressed a similar observation by proposing that physical attractiveness is bound by culture.

Although such views pertaining to beauty standards may still hold intuitive appeal, they are no longer valid in today's world. In fact, Darwin also proposed possible developments in which "each race would possess its own innate ideal standard of beauty" (1952, p. 577). Darwin's latter statement is more accurate because contemporary times evidence increasing agreement about physical attractiveness even between races. The reason for this diminished plurality is that modern communications technology, combined with widespread acceptance of fashions and lifestyles, is producing what some scholars (Berscheid & Walster, 1974) recognize as a "global village" approaching a universal standard of beauty or physical attractiveness. Similarly, although such views as Santayana's may still be plausible, they are not accurate. For, even conceding that beauty may be in the eye of the beholder, people's perception of another person's physical attractiveness can be accurately predicted.

The most common mistake is the assumption that physical attractiveness is an evaluation unique to each individual. Even though no objective or absolute answer exists to the question of who is physically attractive or what determines physical attractiveness, people do agree. Therefore, researchers use a *truth-of-consensus method* to measure physical attractiveness. This method is based on the premise that judgments of physical attractiveness are necessarily subjective, but that such judgments are formed through gestalt principles of person perception rather than single characteristics. Consequently, for research on the effects of physical attractiveness it is not critical whether a specific facial characteristic or the overall facial appearance is the determinant of physical attractiveness. If a substantial number of judges rate a stimulus person as high or low in physical attractiveness, then, for research purposes this stimulus person is interpreted as representative of that respective level of physical attractiveness.

This method grew out of a realization that is contrary to common sense and popular belief. In other words, research shows that people closely agree on the physical attractiveness level of a person. Despite the elusiveness of a definition for physical attractiveness, researchers have developed a reliable construct that works. People can distinguish points along a physical attractiveness continuum that are consistent from one time period to another and that agree with the judgments of others. The consequence of these facts is that judges can be accurately and validly used to gauge the physical attractiveness of stimulus persons.

MEASUREMENT PROCESS

The measurement process is conducted through either a forced distribution or a free category rating (i.e., no forced distribution). In the forced distribution procedure, judges are typically asked to sort a number of photographs into a forced normal distribution (e.g., Byrne, London, & Reaves, 1968; Miller, 1970a). Overwhelmingly, minor variations of the free category rating method are most frequently used. In the free category rating method, judges rate the stimulus persons along a continuum (see Kopera, Maier, & Johnson, 1971) that ranges from extremely low to extremely high physical attractiveness, very unattractive physically to very attractive physically, or some variation of these descriptions. The measurement process of the physical attractiveness construct for infants is similar to that of adults, the only difference being the scale used. Rather than using the semantic differentials of low and high physical attractiveness, the research on infants has employed a continuum assessing cuteness (e.g., Hildebrandt & Fitzgerald, 1978, 1979a,b, 1983; Power *et al.*, 1982).

A typical example of the free category rating method uses either hand-held photographs or slides of photographs projected onto a screen. The physical attractiveness of the stimulus persons, used in the later experimental manipulations, is established before the actual experiment begins. The procedure involves viewing a projected slide or a photograph of a face for a few seconds after which the judges rate the stimulus person. Bipolar scales, having from 5 to 11 points, are typically used to assess physical attractiveness. These ratings are then treated as interval data and used to calculate the mean score and standard deviation for each stimulus person. Stimulus persons with the appropriate mean score and the smallest standard deviation are selected to represent their respective physical attractiveness level. Once these multiple stimulus persons are selected, based on mean scores and standard deviation values, *t* tests are performed to ensure that significant differences *do not* exist between scores for photographs in the same levels of physical attractiveness. On the other hand, *t* tests are also performed to ensure that significant differences *do* exist between scores for photographs intended to represent different levels of physical attractiveness. Finally, to minimize experimental error, the presentation is counterbalanced and each selected photograph is presented an equal number of times within each experimental treatment. Ideally, the research design includes multiple stimulus persons to represent each physical attractiveness level under study.

A primary reason for multiple stimulus persons is to minimize any unique characteristics or unique effects that a specific stimulus person may possess. Despite the potentially misleading impact that a unique stimulus person could have on the results, especially at the extremes of the physical attractiveness continuum, this precautionary effort is practically never reported. Unfortunately, only a small number of studies use research designs that incorporate more than one stimulus person for each physical attractiveness level.

MEASURE QUALIFICATION

As an abstract dimension, physical attractiveness is commonly thought to be so unique that measurement is not feasible. Such thinking is only partially correct. Indeed, self-evaluation of physical attractiveness does appear impossible. Individuals tend to see themselves "through a dark glass" (Berscheid & Walster, 1974, p. 185), producing no agreement between self-ratings and ratings by observers. In contrast, there is high agreement among the physical attractiveness ratings made by observers. The research shows that the truth-of-consensus method yields an accurate measure of physical attractiveness. This accuracy is supported by high agreement among judges of another person's physical attractiveness (Adams, 1977b; Kopera *et al.*, 1971).

The researchers, who have attempted to qualify physical attractiveness measures, report high correlation values between judges. These correlations show that, despite the popular belief that for each judge the evaluation of beauty is unique, a high degree of agreement exists among both same-sex and opposite-sex judges. Also, the statistical reliability of physical attractiveness evaluations is very high such that a person who rates physical attractiveness at one time period again assigns equivalent ratings at a later time period. Finally, when the studies are viewed as a whole, comprising thousands of participants, the currently used physical attractiveness measures prove extremely worthy. These measures are consistent regardless of the judges' ages, geographic locations, education levels, and socioeconomic classes.

MEASURE RELIABILITY

The goal of measure reliability is to have consistent measurement results from independent origins. The reliability of physical attractiveness measures certainly disproves the common belief that it is not feasible to measure the physical attractiveness of persons. Despite the abstract dimension that physical attractiveness represents, the truth-of-consensus procedure yields a research construct which is highly reliable as well as utilitarian. To the extent that reliability is the same as agreement between measures, the physical attractiveness measures are very reliable. Based on the high agreement between judges, beauty is documented *not* to be in the eye of the beholder.

Significant agreement or reliability is consistently reported regardless of gender combinations. At the lower end, interjudge reliabilities are reported in the range of $r = .49$ to $r = .58$ for both male and female stimulus persons (Walster *et al.*, 1966). These statistics are impressive considering the circumstances of the study. The situation involved 752 stimulus persons (376 males and 376 females) who bought tickets to a computer-matched dance. Measures of physical attractiveness reliability were not the focus of the study but appeared almost incidental. Consequently, the data were compiled from four raters who were busy selling tickets while having only a brief moment to rate each of the 752 persons.

Later studies have reported more impressive reliability. Kaats and Davis (1970) reported an interjudge reliability coefficient of $r = .79$ between two judges. Using more judges, Berscheid, Dion, Walster and Walster (1971) attained an average interjudge correlation of $r = .70$ (Pearson r). Murstein (1972) reported a correlation of $r = .80$ (Pearson r) between male and female groups of judges, and a $r = .90$ correlation between groups of judges when sex of the judges was disregarded. Cavior and Dokecki (1971) found correlations ranging from $r = .82$ to $r = .98$ (Pearson r). Also, contrary to conventional wisdom, findings indicate that males and females do agree in their judgments of another person's physical attractiveness. Research repeatedly reports no significant differences between the ratings of physical attractiveness given by male and female judges (Baker & Churchill, 1977; Berscheid *et al.*, 1971; Joseph, 1977; Kopera, *et al.*, 1971; Murstein, 1972). A host of other studies can also be found reporting significantly high interjudge reliability (Byrne *et al.*, 1968; Cross & Cross, 1971).

Test–Retest

Probably the most popular method of establishing measure reliability is to correlate the measures obtained at two different points in time. Physical attractiveness measures subjected to this analysis should idealistically approach perfect correlations. If the physical attractiveness has not changed between the two time periods of measurement, the scores also should not change. Although perfect correlations exist theoretically, they never do realistically.

Assessing test–retest reliability involves substantial effort and potential problems; however, the benefits outweigh the costs. Unfortunately, physical attractiveness research appears to have neglected this empirically sound, well-accepted procedure. An exception to this neglect is an extensive study that I performed (Patzer, 1980), as well as a study by Adams (1978). Because of the importance of the test–retest reliability, and because of lack of attention given to it, a detailed presentation follows.

My test of reliability, which I shall describe, is from an experiment pertaining to the relationship between physical attractiveness and persuasive communication effectiveness (Patzer, 1980). The test–retest procedure spanned a 2-week time period. Although the primary factor of concern was the test–retest statistics, two other methods were also employed: a bipolar rating scale method and an assimilation–contrast grouping method. Each of the two methods was repeated 2 weeks apart, and no subject who served in the rating method served in the grouping method, and vice versa.

Measurement Procedures

There were substantial differences between the two methods used. First, the bipolar rating method required the subjects to view and rate only one stimulus person at a time, whereas the assimilation–contrast grouping method required the subjects to view and group all the stimulus persons at the same time. Second, the instructions and forms for each method differed accordingly. Third, different subjects were used for each method.

Bipolar Rating Method. The bipolar rating scale was a 7-point, labeled, continuum ranging from extremely low to extremely high physical attractiveness. The sexiness construct was also measured so there was a second identical scale that differed in only the anchor words. Sixty subjects (30 males and 30 females) used this bipolar rating scale to rate the physical attractiveness of both male and female stimulus persons. Once the rater completed the physical attractiveness ratings, he or she was given a rest for 10 minutes, after which the rater was given a different sequence of the same photographs and asked to rate them for each stimulus person's sexiness. For each rating the photographs were randomized separately for each subject. In addition, the first sex to be rated was randomly assigned to each subject. To attempt to capture the essence of both physical attractiveness and sexiness, the definitions of each concept were printed on the instruction sheets, the response forms, and were placed in front of the subject at all appropriate times.

Assimilation–Contrast Grouping Method. The grouping method pertaining to assimilation and contrast followed a 7-level distribution. Sixty subjects (30 males and 30 females) employed in this method were not the same individuals used in the bipolar rating scale method. Each judge was given all the photographs and asked to rank the stimulus persons by forming groups through comparison and contrast. To perform their task the subjects were provided a labeled form with equal intervals. The photographs of stimulus persons placed within a group were to represent the same levels of physical attractiveness, whereas the photographs placed in different groups were to represent different levels of physical attractiveness. These identical procedures were also employed for the sexiness construct. The judges were asked to form different groups in columns that ranged from extremely low to extremely high in physical attractiveness. However, a forced distribution was not used because subjects were permitted to use as many or as few groups as they deemed appropriate.

Once the judge finished the physical attractiveness grouping, he or she was given a rest for 10 minutes. Then the judge was given a different sequence of the same photographs and asked to group them for each stimulus person's sexiness. For each grouping the photographs were randomized separately for each subject. In addition, the first sex to be judged was randomly assigned for each subject. To attempt to capture the essence of physical attractiveness and sexiness, the definition of each concept was printed on the instruction sheets and was placed in front of the subjects at all appropriate times.

Test–Retest Results

Measures of reliability to construct a multimethod matrix were obtained through a test–retest administered 2 weeks apart. This method and this time period have been suggested as recommended procedures (Peter, 1979, p. 8). Some concern has been expressed for using a test–retest method because of subjects' memory (Churchill, 1979, p. 70). This concern is not critical here because of the large number of photographs used for each judgment process. Also, each administration presented the photographs in random order. Because of this design, it is unlikely that the subjects could recall their responses from 2 weeks earlier for so many stimuli.

Multimethod Results

The results of the multimethod procedure are presented in matrix form in Table 1 for the male subjects and in Table 2 for the female subjects. Nunnally (1967, p. 226) proposed that for basic research, reliabilities of .50 and .60 are sufficient, and that attempts to obtain values above .80 are a

Table 1. Reliability Coefficients for the Physical Attractiveness Construct Based on Responses from the Male Judges[a]

	Method 1 (Rating) Time 1	Method 2 (Grouping) Time 1
Method 1 (Rating) Time 2	.791 MP[b]	
	.744 FP	
Method 2 (Grouping) Time 2		.773 MP
		.609 FP

[a]Coefficient values are Cronbach's Alpha Reliability Coefficient (Hull & Nie, 1979, pp. 110–144).
[b]MP represents photographs of males. FP represents photographs of females.

Table 2. Reliability Coefficients for the Physical Attractiveness Construct Based on Responses from the Female Judges[a]

	Method 1 (Rating) Time 1	Method 2 (Grouping) Time 1
Method 1 (Rating) Time 2	.821 MP[b]	
	.776 FP	
Method 2 (Grouping) Time 2		.688 MP
		.686 FP

[a]Coefficient values are Cronbach's Alpha Reliability Coefficient (Hull & Nie, 1979, pp. 110–144).
[b]MP represents photographs of males. FP represents photographs of females.

waste of effort. In light of Nunnally's propositions the Cronbach Alpha Reliability Coefficients obtained in the current study (.61 to .82) are very high. Furthermore, these values indicate that the measures of the physical attractiveness construct were quite reliable for both methods. This reliability was exceptionally high for the rating method and somewhat lower for the grouping method.

Measure Reliability Conclusion

The results of both the test–retest analysis and the use of multiple methods are supportive and encouraging. Both of these analyses amplify the strength of reliability indicated by studies investigating the interjudge correlations for physical attractiveness measures. Furthermore, *a priori* assumptions of reliability surrounding the physical attractiveness construct have also received encouraging documentation. In short, the physical attractiveness construct, as used extensively in the research, is truly a strong and reliable research instrument. The variety and magnitude of demonstrated reliability add the necessary credence to the findings which make up the physical attractiveness phenomena.

SELF-MEASURES VERSUS OTHER MEASURES

The research results consistently show that physical attractiveness measures are affected by the familiarity level of the participants. The title of this section conveys the general dichotomy of measures. Actually, there are three broad categories of judges that can be cited: (a) individuals whose physical attractiveness is judged by themselves, (b) individuals whose physical attractiveness is judged by associates of varying degrees for familiarity ranging from spouses to casual acquaintances, and (c) individuals whose physical attractiveness is judged by strangers. All three of these judge categories yield different ratings.

Self Judges

Self-measures of physical attractiveness do not work. Only one published study focuses on the relationship between self- and other measures (Downs & Wright, 1982). The study used 37 police cadets ranging in age from 20 to 56 years old. The authors of this study concluded that these two rating sources yield dissimilar results. A few additional studies have also explored self-measures but as secondary issues of interest. Again, the correlations or agreement between self-ratings of a person's physical attractiveness and the ratings of the person's physical attractiveness by others are not statistically significant.

One doctoral dissertation collected a variety of statistics pertaining to self measures of physical attractiveness (Balban, 1981). Disguised as a study investigating self-concept, subjects were asked to rate themselves as to how others would judge their overall physical attractiveness. A 10-point scale was used with 1 being extremely unattractive, 5 being attractive, and 10 being extremely attractive. For the ratings by others, one male and one female served as judges.

Ratings by others yielded interjudge reliability of .89 for the entire sample. Separated by sex, interjudge reliability for the female subjects was .89 and for the male subjects it was .87. Separated by physical attractiveness level, the interjudge reliabilities for low, average, and high physical attractiveness were .81, .76, and .77, respectively. Compared to the high interjudge reliabilities, the correlations between self-ratings and ratings by others were very low. Overall the correlation between self- and other ratings was .22.

This dissertation found that self-ratings of physical attractiveness were dramatically inaccurate. It also found that inaccuracy is most frequently in the direction of overestimation as opposed to underestimation. Probing the data reveals some variations in the general overestimation. These variations were that overestimation was a function of the person's physical attractiveness. Specifically, those of higher physical attractiveness tended to be more accurate, whereas those of average and lower levels tended to be more inaccurate. Males and females who were high in physical attractiveness tended not to give self-ratings significantly higher than the judges. Both males and females of low or average physical attractiveness gave significantly higher self-ratings than the judges afforded them. Furthermore, the male subjects exhibited greater discrepancy between ratings by self and ratings by others than did the female judges.

This last finding contradicted a hypothesis that females possess greater overestimation than males. The explanation provided for this contrary finding was that females receive large quantities of feedback pertaining to their physical attractiveness. The feedback is also frequent, which permits the females to adjust their self-ratings to coincide with this information, thereby reducing overestimation relative to males (Balbon, 1981, p. 61). Rand and Hall (1983) have also reported that females are more accurate in their self-ratings of physical attractiveness than are their male counterparts. As did Downs and Wright (1982), the dissertation concluded that people do not see themselves as others see them, and that self-ratings are consistently overestimated, whereas underestimation is extremely infrequent (p. 58).

Verification that self-measures are poor measures is not difficult to find. For example, the correlations between self-rating and impartial judges are reported at .37 when sex is disregarded (Adams, 1977a). Analyzing the data by sex revealed values of .33 for men and .24 for women (Murstein, 1972). Correlations as low as .17 are also reported between self-ratings and ratings by others of a person's physical attractiveness (Stroebe *et al.*, 1971).

Other Judges

The category of other judges consists of two distinctly different groups. These two subcategories are (a) judges who are acquaintances of the stimulus persons and (b) judges who are strangers. Within the first subcategory there are also degrees of familiarity which no research has addressed.

Because no absolute measure of physical attractiveness exists, the judgment by strangers is logically the true measure. It is then reasonable to assume that judgments by strangers yield an objective impartial measure. Therefore, this measure of physical attractiveness can reasonably be employed as a standard against which other measures can be validly compared.

A consistent pattern emerges when these three physical attractiveness measures of self, acquaintance, and others are compared. These measures were reported by a study done with engaged couples (Murstein, 1972) and later in a study with husbands and wives (Murstein & Christy, 1976). Without fail, the order from highest to lowest is spouse, self, and other. In other words, impartial judges rate individuals the lowest, the self-ratings are somewhat higher, with the ratings by a person's spouse being the highest. An interesting question is which direction is the apparent causal relationship between selecting a spouse and perception of a spouse's physical attractiveness.

Assuming impartial judges present the correct physical attractiveness rating, it is accurate to state that most individuals overestimate their own physical attractiveness. Furthermore, individual's overestimate their spouses physical attractiveness even more. These findings disprove the common belief that people see their physical attractiveness as it actually is or less so. Representative data are presented in a University of Minnesota doctoral dissertation (Weiszhaar, 1978) which illustrates that these patterns are stable and replicable.

The dissertation research involved a total of 88 subjects: 40 husbands, 40 wives, and 8 impartial judges (4 males and 4 females). Physical attractiveness ratings were made on a 10-point scale with endpoints labeled as either very unattractive or very attractive. The mean values for the husband and the wife were similar. Specifically, the mean values given the husband were 3.6 for the judges, 5.4 for the self-measures, and 7.2 for the spouse/wife measures. The mean values given the wife were 3.6 for the judges, 5.1 for the self-measures, and 6.5 for the spouse/husband measures. These results by Weiszhaar (1978) are congruent with other studies using premarital couples (Murstein, 1972), and married couples (Murstein & Christy, 1976).

MEASURE VALIDITY

Two major themes are germane to measure validity. First, there is the issue of internal and external validity with regard to the overall research. Generally, the experimental design provides good internal validity at the expense of external validity. In other words, internal validity focuses on strict controls to assure that the results are due to the manipulation of the experimental variable. External validity focuses on the realism of the experiment and its generalizability to the broader population as a whole. In both cases the physical attractiveness research has done well. The findings in the laboratory experiments have involved solid internal validity, which permits conclusions that physical attractiveness has caused the resulting variances. External validity is achieved through the numerous field experiments that verified the findings of the internally valid experiments.

A second issue is measure validity. Does the physical attractiveness research actually measure the physical attractiveness construct? Construct validity is very difficult to establish, but it is important in order to ensure scientific progress. Although internal consistency is a measure of construct validity, it is inadequate. Internal consistency is a necessary condition, but it is not a sufficient condition for construct validity (Nunnally, 1978, p. 103). Campbell and Fiske (1959) have proposed measurement procedures for both convergent and discriminant validity but the physical attractiveness research neglects this important component. An exception to this neglect is an attempt reported by me (Patzer, 1980). Some other studies appear to have dealt with measure validity but not as a primary motivation. For example, Adams (1978) did not identify it as such, but he did perform a test of validity through the use of two rating methods, and still other research reported different meanings for "sex appeal" and "good looks" (Morse, Reis, Gruzen, & Wolff, 1974; Morse, Gruzen, & Reis, 1976).

The multimethod and test–retest procedures, performed in my 1980 study, pertained to both measure reliability and measure validity of the physical attractiveness construct. For each of the two time periods and for each of the two methods, multiple traits were assessed in an attempt to establish validity. Convergent validity was explored and confirmed by the high correlations exhibited through the two independent measurement methods of the physical attractiveness construct (see Tables 1 and 2).

Discriminant validity was explored by assessing the correlation between another measure proposed as different from physical attractiveness. The exploratory attempt to establish discriminant validity measured the two traits of sexiness and physical attractiveness. Each of these two traits was assessed under the same conditions during the same time and using the same methods as detailed earlier in the measure reliability procedures of my 1980 study.

The research literature gives little attention to the definition of sexiness and no attention to the definition of physical attractiveness. However, I provided definitions for these terms in my study (1980). I used a modified version of Freud's (1958) definition of sexiness and an original definition of physical attractiveness:

> *Sexiness.* The extent to which the appearance of a stimulus person arouses a sexual or an erotic idea in the observer's mind. With opposite-sex dyads this arousal may be directly related to oneself, and with same-sex dyads this arousal may be the observer's perceptions of others' reactions.

> *Physical Attractiveness.* The degree to which a stimulus person is pleasing to observe. (This definition is not meant to be representative of other research manipulations of physical attractiveness. It is only meant to be an attempt to provide a common standard reference for use by the raters in this study.)

To capture the essence of both physical attractiveness and sexiness the definitions of each concept were continually accessible by the subjects. For the rating method, the definitions were printed on the instruction sheets, on the response forms, and were placed in front of each subject during the entire time that the appropriate rating tasks were performed. For the grouping method, the definitions of each concept were printed on the instruction sheets and were placed in front of the subjects during the entire time to be used for all relevant grouping tasks.

Physical attractiveness and sexiness are different concepts but they may also be very similar constructs. Logically, a person can be high or low in physical attractiveness without being high or low, respectively, in sexiness. Despite this *a priori* assumption, the results of the study do not permit such conclusions about discriminant validity. The correlations based on this exploratory attempt did not yield evidence in favor of the discriminant validity for the physical attractiveness construct. In this instance, the traits of physical attractiveness and sexiness were very similar and highly interdependent.

MODERATE PHYSICAL ATTRACTIVENESS

The research has often neglected moderate physical attractiveness, and this lack reflects a limitation of the collective research efforts. As such, it is probably considered a unique aspect of issues related to the measurement of physical attractiveness. Whatever the reasons, the fact is that moderate physical attractiveness is not studied as fully as the extreme ends of the normal physical attractiveness continuum.

Measures of moderate physical attractiveness might not yield the magnitude of agreement among judges as do the high and low levels. Although the moderate level may be less distinctly defined, it is no less important. In fact, because it is likely to be the most prevalent level, it may be the most important. Despite the additional measurement difficulties that moderate physical attractiveness poses, intuitive appeals suggest that it may possess curvilinear properties as opposed to linear. Because of its importance and prevalence, the discussion of moderate physical attractiveness in this section goes beyond measurement concerns. The remainder of this chapter represents a summary of my earlier work (Patzer, 1979a).

Inattention

Numerous reasons may be postulated for lack of research attention given to the moderate level of physical attractiveness. First, it is more definite to rate physical attractiveness at the two extremes. The two extremes of low and high physical attractiveness are likely to result in greater agreement (lower variance and higher consistency) of rating scores than the moderate level of physical attractiveness.

Second, any effects or results produced as a consequence of manipulating physical attractiveness will be more dramatic. The initial basic research on physical attractiveness was concerned with discovering if physical attractiveness is an influential variable, so the purpose was simply to identify an effect. Therefore, if an effect exists, it is more easily recognized using the polar extremes than gradations of physical attractiveness between these ends.

Third, there is a practicality of limited resources. Because much of the physical attractiveness research uses an experimental factorial design, the manipulation of two treatments keeps the data collection and analysis more manageable than if a third treatment were employed. The need for additional subjects and the complexity of handling the data escalates rapidly when additional treatments are added to factorial designs.

Fourth, past research has assumed a linear relationship between physical attractiveness and its consequences. This linear relationship implies that moderate physical attractiveness levels probably produce effects somewhere between the effects resulting from stimulus persons of low and high physical attractiveness.

Because of these four reasons, as well as other reasons, the moderate level of physical attractiveness is usually not addressed in the research. The research that does explore moderate physical attractiveness, as well as the extremes, is discussed in the chapters that follow. That research is not highlighted unless it is relevant. Before progressing to the actual research, a hypothesis in favor of moderate physical attractiveness will be discussed. Specifically, the pros and cons will be presented for a general hypothesis that predicts the moderate level of physical attractiveness to have greater positive consequences than either low or high levels. These effects will be discussed as apposite to persuasive communication.

Pro Argument

Moderate physical attractiveness may be the best level. Support for such a hypothesis can be established from several directions. Although empirical data pertaining to physical attractiveness are not favorable, intuition, general truths, and theory all acclaim the value of moderation.

Intuition

It is reasonable to propose that in a persuasive communication situation the communicator of moderate physical attractiveness will be most effective. This effectiveness may be based on "Just an average guy" who the receivers can consider as "one of the gang" and with whom they can identify. Such perceived similarity between the receiver and communicator produces greater liking than perception of dissimilarity (ct. Byrne, 1971, pp. 23–57). This greater liking combined with the ability to identify is likely to affect perceptions of trustworthiness. Related to this situation is the communications research that has identified three variables as major determinants of source credibility: liking, perceived trustworthiness, and perceived expertise (cf. Finn, 1976; Giffin, 1967; McGuire, 1969). Intuitively, identification with a moderately, physically attractive communicator will influence the first two variables directly, and may, indirectly, influence the third through greater liking of the communicator.

The goal of most persuasive communications, especially those using the mass media, is to influence the greatest number of individuals as possible. Therefore, given the knowledge that "likes attract" and the identification assumption, the effective communicator should be similar to the largest segment of the receiving population. Assuming, and there is no basis not to, that the physical attractiveness of individuals in the general population represents a Gaussian distribution (i.e., a normal or bell-shaped distribution), the greatest number of receivers of any mass communication is the moderately physical attractiveness level. The reasonable conclusion is that persuasive communications using a communicator of moderate physical attractiveness will produce the greatest number of receivers who identify with the communicator.

General Truth

According to folklore, the best porridge was neither too hot nor too cold. Similarly, a logical foundation exists for a hypothesis predicting that a communicator of moderate physical attractiveness will be more effective than a communicator of either high or low physical attractiveness. This tentative hypothesis is consistent with two additional arguments.

First, because the moderate level of physical attractiveness is in the middle of two extremes, it is likely to be more favorable to at least some members of each extreme group than are members of one extreme to be favorable to the opposite extreme. Second, it is harmonious with states of nature, in both the social and biological sciences, which suggest a golden mean where too much or too little of anything is less than optimal. For example, in political life it is not the extreme right or extreme left candidate who is elected, but rather, the one who is practically always in the middle who gains some support from each of the opposing factions. Another example can be cited from economics. If a government's taxes are too heavy, business is forced to close which, in turn, results in insufficient revenue to operate government services, and if taxes are too light, the

outcome is again insufficient revenue to sustain an effective government—
a trade-off is necessary. Finally, an illustration related to the biological
sciences is that the most healthy person is normally not the one who
indulges in megadoses of vitamins, nor is the most healthy person the one
who lacks vitamin intake. Rather, the most healthy individual is the one
who is somewhere between these two extremes.

Information-Processing Theory

Information-processing theory offers some support for a hypothesis
that predicts communicators of moderate physical attractiveness will be
more effective than communicators of either low or high physical
attractiveness. This support is based on a theme that is repeated throughout the information-processing literature which is that suboptimal or
superoptimal stimulation causes a person to tune out. In other words, there
is a middle range of stimuli input which produces an optimal level of
information processing. Stimuli input below or above the thresholds of this
range cause inattention and a reduction of cognitive activity.

Information-processing research has identified an inverted U-shape
relationship between the amount of stimuli and the amount or level of
information processing that occurs. Information processing refers to the
number of alternatives considered, the amount of information that
decisions are based on, and in general, the cognitive processes. This
inverted U-shape is demonstrated in problem-solving experiments, in
which an optimal level or range of environmental complexity appears
(Streufert & Castore, 1968; Suedfeld & Streufert, 1966). The inverted U-
shape also exists for the level of involvement within a situation and the
subsequent level of information processing that occurs (Driver, 1962).
There is an optimal level of involvement below which few dimensions are
considered in forming an attitude, and likewise, above which few
dimensions are considered. The greatest level of information processing
occurs at a moderate level of involvement.

In searching for information, if an individual expects information to
be boring or uninteresting the individual will not seek it out (Hansen, F.,
1972). At the other extreme, if the individual expects the information to be
too complex or too difficult the individual will ignore it. As well as
information-processing theory, the "arousal principle" suggests that
information expected to be either too conflicting or too trivial will be
ignored, whereas information expected between these two extremes will be
attended to (F. Hansen, 1972, p. 169).

Numerous empirical studies confirm the statement that optimal levels
of stimulus input, for information-processing activity, are between any

two extremes (see F. Hansen, 1972, pp. 27–217; Schroder & Suedfeld, 1971; Schroder, Driver, & Streufert, 1967). In addition to the empirical findings, there is theoretical support for the inverted U-shape relationships found in information processing. Two such applicable theories are the adaption-level theory (McClelland, Atkinson, Clark, & Lowell, 1953) and the aspiration-level theory (Lewin, Dembo, Festinger, & Sears, 1944).

Adaption-level theory proposes that a stimulus event below or above expectations will be judged unpleasant, whereas a stimulus that is within a moderate range will be judged pleasant and will be attended to. Applied to the physical attractiveness and persuasive communication relationship, the adaption theory implies that the receiver will find a communicator of moderate physical attractiveness to be more pleasant, and subsequently, will attend most to this communicator and the accompanying communication. Aspiration-level theory suggests that an individual aspires toward that goal which is believed achievable. Therefore, the receiver will most likely aspire to meet and become friends with the communicator of moderate physical attractiveness. This aspiration is based on the person's expected chances that achieving this goal is more realistic than with a communicator of high physical attractiveness. Aspiring to this achievable goal results in the communicator of moderate physical attractiveness causing greater arousal and attention than either extreme.

In conclusion, information-processing theory can certainly be used to document the supremacy of moderation. Here, as with intuition, a reasonable hypothesis predicts that the greatest persuasive communication effectiveness will be with the communicator of moderate physical attractiveness.

Con Argument

The first part of this section presents the arguments that can be made for the superior effects of moderate physical attractiveness. To fully explore the impact of moderate physical attractiveness, the arguments against such a superior effect of moderate physical attractiveness are presented.

Information Processing—Moderate Stimuli

Information-processing theory is versatile. Without contradicting the information-processing theory cited earlier, an alternative interpretation does not support a hypothesis of superior effects for moderate physical attractiveness. It might be suggested that the stimuli persons previously used in the physical attractiveness research are all part of a moderate range.

In other words, the low and high levels of physical attractiveness normally manipulated do not necessarily represent suboptimal and superoptimal levels of stimuli and environment complexity, but the lower and upper levels within the optimal range. In fact, assuming this optimal range proposition, the high physical attractiveness levels may be nearing the optimal point within the optimal range. Considering this explanation, a hypothesis that does not predict greater effects, resulting from moderate physical attractiveness, agrees with the optimal range concepts so consistently discussed in the research literature on information-processing theory (Hansen, F., 1972; Schroder & Suedfeld, 1971; Schroder et al., 1967).

Information Processing—Unusual Stimuli

In addition to the above interpretation of moderate range stimuli, there is empirical support for the need of novelty and/or complexity. When children are given a choice between games with expected endings and games with unexpected endings, they choose to repeat the latter over the former (Charlesworth, 1964). This positive attraction to the unusual exists throughout one's lifetime (Berlyne, 1960).

People are attracted to and receive pleasure from novelty. This novelty may be described as *incongruous inputs*, because the new input is not the same as past inputs. These inputs, incongruent with the past, define the changes which occur in the environments of persons. One study found that subjects could not stand being in a total stable congruent environment more than three days (Bexton, Heron, & Scott, 1954). The authors interpreted the lack of tolerance as a person's inability to experience only very low levels of arousal. People faced with totally congruent environments search out new situations of any kind (Heron, Doan, & Scott, 1956) and remain attracted much longer to these new situations than to any situation that is already familiar (Berlyne, 1960, pp. 99–102).

Assuming the population represents a normal, bell-shaped distribution of physical attractiveness, the most frequently encountered persons in one's life will be of moderate physical attractiveness. As a result, persons of moderate physical attractiveness can be equated with the familiar and congruent stimuli, whereas persons of high physical attractiveness can be equated with the novel or incongruent stimuli discussed above. In short, the communicator of high physical attractiveness will cause greater stimulation and arousal within a receiver than a communicator of moderate physical attractiveness. This incongruence caused by the novel situation is the preferred stimuli, which causes the receiver to be more attracted, pay more attention, and to attend longer to the communicator of high physical attractiveness as compared to the communicator of moderate physical attractiveness. The conclusion is that the novelty aspects of information-processing theory suggest not proposing a hypothesis of superior effects for moderate physical attractiveness.

Self-Perception: Empirical Findings

As stated earlier, it is reasonable to assume that the physical attractiveness of the population represents a bell-shaped (i.e., normal) distribution. There is no intuitive, empirical, or theoretical basis to contradict this distribution assumption. However, limited empirical findings suggest that such assumptions are not appropriate for arguing a hypothesis in favor of moderate physical attractiveness.

The notion that "likes attract" may be accurate but not relevant. Logically, the largest portion of the population is moderately physically attractive, and consequently, the greatest number of the mass population will identify with these similar communicators. This identification or similarity effect is intuitively and empirically sound but it is not applicable to physical attractiveness.

People are optimistically oriented. Thus, individuals of moderate physical attractiveness do not view their own physical attractiveness accurately. They instead tend to view their own physical attractiveness at a level higher than reality. The empirical research related to self-ratings support the fact that people do perceive their own physical attractiveness significantly higher than it really is. Furthermore, even if people of moderate physical attractiveness know they are moderately attractive, American society motivates them to strive for better, to reach for a higher level, or to aspire for an ideal physical attractiveness level which is above the average. The result is that these individuals identify with levels of higher physical attractiveness. The notion that the physical attractiveness of the population represents a bell-shaped distribution may be valid. However, if the individuals in this population do not judge their own physical attractiveness accurately, the normal distribution assumption is of little value to this identification argument.

Considerable empirical research confirms that people misjudge their own physical attractiveness. Regardless of their appearance, when a self-reporting technique is used to measure physical attractiveness, persons consistently rate their own physical attractiveness near the high end of the continuum (Patzer, 1975). The inability of the self-report technique to assess physical attractiveness should be expected if we consider the high value placed on physical attractiveness in our society. To admit less than an above average level of physical attractiveness is apparently so threatening or so demeaning to an individual that the person will either deny or fail to recognize their own true appearance.

Additional studies can be cited to document the notion that people do not judge their own physical attractiveness realistically. Interjudge correlations are high, ranging from published reports of .70 Pearson r correlations (Berscheid *et al.*, 1971) to .98 Pearson r correlations (Cavior & Dokecki, 1971). However, correlations between self-ratings and ratings by others are extremely low. The reported Pearson r correlations between self-ratings and ratings by others range from .33 (Murstein, 1972) to .24 for women, and even as low as only .17 (Stroebe *et al.*, 1971). Based on these empirical findings, it is reasonable to state that even if the physical attractiveness of the population represents a normal distribution, the self-perceptions do not. Given the identification assumption, the greatest number of the population will identify with the higher levels of physical attractiveness. The reason is that greater numbers of the population perceive themselves as high, or certainly above moderate levels of physical attractiveness.

Self-Concept versus Self-Perception

An individual's self-concept and its development may offer an explanation for the above empirical findings. Considering the dynamics of self-concept and the apparent dynamics of the physical attractiveness phenomena, the lack of accurate self-evaluation of physical attractiveness is logical. Throughout a person's life experiences, knowledge accumulates in a manner that establishes the person's self-concept. Assuming the person realizes the importance of physical attractiveness phenomena, it is understandable that evaluations regarding one's own physical attractiveness would be an integral component of self-concept. Consequently, attempts would be made to defend against negative physical attractiveness information.

Markus (1977) alluded to this process in terms of self schemata. According to Markus (1977, p. 64), self schemata involve

> cognitive generalizations about the self, derived from past experiences that organize and guide the processing of self-rated information contained in the individual's social experience.

Specifically applied to physical attractiveness, the individual will protect his or her self-concept by accentuating self-ratings of physical attractiveness within acceptable limits. Accepting the power of physical attractiveness phenomena, this protection may extend to the point of exaggeration that eludes evidence. In other words, self-ratings of physical attractiveness are distorted in defense of a positive self-concept.

Self-deception is consistent with the self-concept theorists who contend that information about onself is biased in a predictable and favorable direction (e.g., Wylie, 1979). In an effort to sustain a positive self-concept much of the negative self information is screened out, whereas the information which is allowed in its interwoven to mesh comfortably with existing information about the self. Such psychological mechanisms serve to acquire information that is ego enhancing, and to minimize and alter information that is negative to the ego. As a result, it is of little wonder that, in general, self-evaluations and, in particular, self-evaluations of physical attractiveness tend to be less than objective or accurate. The effect of physical attractiveness on self-concept is consistent with research indicating that physical attractiveness possesses implications for a person's self-concept (Adams, 1977b).

Empirical Data

Empirical research opposes a hypothesis for superior effects due to moderate physical attractiveness level. This empirical research involves three unpublished studies that went beyong simply investigating the correlations between self-ratings and ratings by others. These three studies all incorporated the moderate level of physical attractiveness into their respective research designs.

First, three levels of sexual attitudes and three levels of physical attractiveness were used to investigate the effects of these variables on heterosexual liking (Patzer, 1973). For sexual attitudes, a curvilinear relationship occurred in which the moderate level clearly resulted in the highest level of attraction, followed in order by conservative and liberal sexual attitudes. However, the effects of physical attractiveness were linear with high physical attractiveness resulting in the greatest liking, followed in order by the moderate and low levels of physical attractiveness.

Second, another study (Patzer, 1975), which used four levels of sexual attitudes and three levels of physical attractiveness, examined two issues: (a) the receivers' perception of a stranger's sexual attitudes based solely on the stranger's physical attractiveness, and (b) the receivers' perception of a stranger's physical attractiveness when the stranger's sexual attitudes are known. The major finding relevant to this current section was that a linear effect of physical attractiveness resulted. Those strangers of low physical attractiveness were perceived liberal; strangers of moderate physical attractiveness were assumed to possess moderate sexual attitudes; and the strangers of high physical attractiveness were attributed either moderate or conservative sexual attitudes, depending on the receiver's sexual attitudes.

Third, three levels of physical attractiveness and two levels of expertise were used by Joseph (1977) to investigate the effects of these variables on opinion change. Mixed results were reported, and Joseph stated that

> among the study's other major findings, sources high in physical attractiveness were found to be more liked, more credible, and more similar to receivers than sources who were medium or low in physical attractiveness. (p. 221)

Furthermore, he stated:

> But the findings from the present study suggest that the strategy of using average-looking models to capitalize on the similarity–persuasion relationship may be a serious mistake because audience members (regardless of their physical attractiveness) perceive greater similarity with communicators who are beautiful than they do with communicators who are not. (p. 231)

This research on moderate physical attractiveness is in agreement with indirectly related research. Wylie and Hutchins (1965) found that distortion of self-evaluations is most likely when the trait being evaluated is important. These authors also reported that this distortion is greatest for individuals who are in the moderate range as opposed to either extreme. Although their research found this distortion effect at the moderate level of IQ scores as opposed to the extreme levels, a similar effect would not seem unreasonable for the physical attractiveness characteristic.

Summary

This last major section has focused on the moderate level of physical attractiveness. The first part presented the intuitive and information-processing arguments in favor of a hypothesis that the moderate level of physical attractiveness will be superior in persuasive communication effectiveness. The second part presented information processing and empirical research arguments against such a moderate physical attractiveness hypothesis. The conclusion is that it is definitely not justifiable to propose a hypothesis that a communicator of moderate physical attractiveness will be more effective than a communicator of high physical attractiveness.

Even though the conclusion that a hypothesis supporting superior effects of the moderate level of physical attractiveness is unjustified, a conclusion that this level is unworthy of investigation is also unjustified. In actuality, the effects of moderate physical attractiveness are unknown and the scant evidence against it is not, at this time, conclusive. Although a hypothesis of superiority is not appropriate, a serious scientific investigation is appropriate given the (a) strong intuitive appeal; (b) absence of theoretical attention; (c) uncertainty of the moderate range of physical attractiveness for optimal information processing; (d) lack of published research; (e) current practice of the mass media, such as advertisers, to use communicators of moderate physical attractiveness; and (f) current lack of knowledge about the moderate physical attractiveness dimension.

RESEARCH PROCEDURE: EXPERIMENTAL DESIGN

Before presenting some of the specific research findings regarding the physical attractiveness phenomena, it is important to mention the research procedure. Much of the research in the social sciences uses the survey method in which those selected are asked questions regarding the topic of interest. Such survey methods allow only correlational or association data, and trying to deduce cause-and-effect relationships is not possible, because the fact two events happen at the same time does not mean one causes the other. For example, the stock market appears to go up each time the hemline of women's dresses go up. Although these two events are actually correlated, it is obviously incorrect to conclude that the shortening of women's hemlines causes an increase in the stock market.

Post hoc ergo propter hoc (after this, therefore because of this) expresses the fallacy of logical reasoning which arrives at the conclusion that because B follows A, B is caused by A. If physical attractiveness research relies on survey data, erroneous cause-and-effect conclusions are probable. Methodological research shows that people are very often unaware, unable, or unwilling to state their true thoughts, feelings, or even actions. Therefore, simply asking people how physical attractiveness affects them will not provide information to accurately describe the effect of physical attractiveness. An example of the weakness of the survey research method is illustrated by the 1980 presidential election. A national survey of 53,000 households was conducted by the Census Bureau 2 weeks after the presidential election (Associated Press, 1981). Martin O'Connell, Census Bureau spokesman, reported that if as many Americans voted as said they did, the percentage of eligible voters would have been the highest since 1948. However, objective ballot records show it was the lowest. This unpublished study found substantial differences between actual behavior and behavior specifically claimed in a survey.

Because physical attractiveness is, apparently, a very subtle variable which involves emotional reactions, the survey method is not appropriate. Rather, the predominant procedure is the experimental method. Experiments are used because the researcher is able to disguise the purpose of the study, to get the truth, and to obtain cause-and-effect relationships, rather than simply correlational relationships. Four specific reasons can be cited for using the experimental research design in studying physical attractiveness: (a) past social science research demonstrates that this method/procedure is suitable to manipulate the physical attractiveness variable without jeopardizing the internal or external validity; (b) past research shows that physical attractiveness possesses a causal relationship with other variables; (c) the research also allows for analysis of interaction among variables; and (d) people are not aware or are not willing to acknowledge the influence of physical attractiveness upon them, and so the experimental procedure serves as a way of disguising the manipulation of the physical attractiveness variable. The end result is that experiments, as opposed to surveys, allow researchers to conclude with confidence that the dynamics of physical attractiveness phenomena are actually caused by physical attractiveness.

The collective body of physical attractiveness research is extremely rich in research design. The heavy reliance on the experimental design is rounded out by creative use of laboratory and field experiments. Within each of these two categories there are a variety of settings, procedures, and subjects. Where appropriate, manipulation checks of the physical attractiveness variable are always conducted. These manipulation checks indicate no interaction effects in the totally successful manipulation of the physical attractiveness variable serving as an independent variable. The physical attractiveness research also utilizes nonobtrusive research designs in which observation has substantiated the results of other research methods.

MEASUREMENT LIMITATIONS

There are limitations in the physical attractiveness research, but they are minor relative to the strengths. A serious criticism which may be directed toward this research is its lack of robust examination of its primary component, namely, the physical attractiveness construct. Researchers appear unwilling to mass a rigorous analysis of the physical attractiveness construct. This complacency may be due to the satisfactory measure that the truth-of-consensus procedures produce. However, no attempts seem to have been made to improve on these measurements. Without such scrutiny, the major component of the entire physical attractiveness research is somewhat of an unknown.

The technology exists, but it has not been applied to the physical attractiveness research. Measure reliability could be established by at least conducting test–retest procedures of the stimulus persons' physical attractiveness ratings. Measure validity is more difficult, but could be attempted through construction of a multimethod–multitrait matrix.

An even more serious shortcoming is the lack of a definition for physical attractiveness. The construct is admittedly difficult to define, but is not a less than perfect definition better than no definition at all? When no information is provided, in the form of a definition, the researcher can make no valid assumptions about what the raters are using as a reference point. Similarly, the raters themselves are in an ambiguous state attempting to determine what is the appropriate rating criteria. Also, what should definitions be for related constructs, such as cuteness, sexiness, unattractiveness, and the like? There is a serious need for researchers to provide definitions, and even for entire research articles to solely address issues of definition. For example, what are the implications and what are the resulting differences when raters are provided no definition versus definitions of various types?

Another concern is that the process of identifying physical attractiveness levels for experimental treatment manipulations may have become too cavalier. That is, the judgment of two raters cannot be as accurate in defining the physical attractiveness of a stimulus person as the collective responses of a substantially larger number. Likewise, measures of attractiveness are being equated with measures of physical attractiveness, and distinctions are not being made between facial attractiveness and physical attractiveness. In addition, issues are not raised concerning the actual scale with which to measure physical attractiveness. Should the scale be labeled and what are the proper bipolar adjectives for the endpoints? Is there a difference in semantic meaning between a continuum ranging from low or high physical attractiveness (or some variant of low and high) versus a continuum ranging from very unattractive physically to very attractive physically? Can the adjective *physical* be dropped or should it be stressed when meaning physical attractiveness? Is low physical attractiveness the same as the lower end of physical unattractiveness? These scale differences pose important questions about the raters' cognitive processes required to perform the judging and, subsequently, the potential variances in the data.

Despite the excellent work done in the physical attractiveness research, there are a few important basic questions that need investigation and answers. Surely, an impressive building constructed on a weak foundation will not last long, and, likewise, impressive research findings based on an unknown construct may also falter. Maybe these criticisms are too idealistic, and, in time, perfection will be approached. Progress appears forthcoming. Recently, an entire published article addressed the appropriateness of the physical attractiveness measure being used in this research (Lucker, Beane, & Guire, 1981).

A summary statement about the limitations of the physical attractiveness research must be that the positive factors far outweigh the negative. Construct validity and reliability may not be sufficiently examined but the physical attractiveness variable has not contaminated the research. The truth-of-consensus method has extracted a very powerful and useful research tool from an abstract and difficult element. Finally, the extensive use of the experimental design has permitted identification of the true responses to differences in physical attractiveness. However, the experiments have too often used only the two extremes of physical attractiveness and infer a linear relationship for the middle or average range. Therefore, this chapter has included a discussion of the moderate level of physical attractiveness in detail.

Chapter 3

Interpersonal Realities

Research findings clearly, repeatedly, and consistently show people do not behave in a manner consistent with the adage, You can't judge a book by its cover. Based merely on an individual's physical attractiveness, people formulate complex, elaborate, and comprehensive ideas about another person. Research in the area of physical attractiveness and interpersonal realities has produced four general findings:

1. Greater social power is experienced by those of higher as opposed to lower physical attractiveness.
2. All other things being equal, individuals of higher physical attractiveness are better liked than those of lower physical attractiveness.
3. People of higher physical attractiveness are assumed to possess more positive and favorable characteristics than their counterparts of lower physical attractiveness.
4. Those higher in physical attractiveness have different effects on others and receive different responses from others than those lower in physical attractiveness.

This chapter on interpersonal realities and the next chapter on interpersonal reciprocations may be considered the core of the physical attractiveness phenomena. The early research on physical attractiveness certainly focused on these two topics. From that early research the identification of a stereotype emerged which contends that anyone higher in physical attractiveness is better than anyone lower. Because a huge portion of the physical attractiveness research deals with interpersonal consequences, two chapters are devoted to reporting this information. The first of these two chapters presents the research findings concerning a host of interpersonal realities. The second chapter specifically presents those research findings that correspond with three of the more frequent, and more significant, occurring interchanges in our lives. The interactions discussed within the context of interpersonal reciprocations deal with romantic attraction, platonic liking, and employment exchanges.

EXPECTATIONS AND ASSUMPTIONS

A major area of interpersonal realities is the significantly different expectations and assumptions based on differences in physical attractiveness. In fact, the expectations and assumptions as a function of physical attractiveness may be the foundation, and possible explanation, for this chapter and most of the next chapter.

An early study on impression formation laid the foundation for investigation of expectations and assumptions based on physical attractiveness (Miller, 1970a). That research presented seventeen dimensions to male and female judges and asked them to indicate their impressions of stimulus persons for each characteristic. The more physically attractive the stimulus person the more he or she was evaluated as curious rather than indifferent, complex rather than simple, perceptive rather than insensitive, happy rather than sad, active rather than passive, amiable rather than aloof, humorous rather than serious, pleasure seeking rather than self-controlled, outspoken rather than reserved, and flexible rather than rigid. Similarly, the results of a national survey found that people believed that those who were higher in physical attractiveness were happier, had better sex lives, and received more respect than those of lower physical attractiveness (Berscheid, Walster & Bohrnstedt, 1973).

Physical attractiveness is affiliated with glamour (Bassili, 1981). A total of 332 subjects participated in three experiments designed to identify attributes that differentiate individuals of lower and higher physical attractiveness. Factor analysis of the data revealed a glamour effect. Specifically, persons of higher physical attractiveness were associated with greater excitement, greater emotional stability, and, generally, a more active and exciting social orientation. Because the stimulus persons were all casually attired, the author concluded that those higher in physical attractiveness elicit impressions of glamour and stated that "good looking individuals are thought to share many of the characteristics possessed by glamorous people" (p. 251).

Direct questioning discloses that these expectations and assumptions are subtle. People believe that physical attractiveness has no effect on them. They state that physical attractiveness is superficial and peripheral, and that it should not and does not influence our lives. But the research literature provides evidence to the contrary. Simple observation of the cosmetic, clothing, and advertising industries certainly offers additional verification of the insights gained through formal research.

People are either not aware or are not willing to admit any relationship between a person's physical attractiveness and perceived personal attributes. But when these same people are put into an experimental research design, they exhibit strong assumptions about personal characteristics and qualities based on physical attractiveness. These assumptions and attributions are so potent that there is a definite advantage for those who possess physical attractiveness, and a definite disadvantage for those who do not. Because of the subtle effect that physical attractiveness apparently has on people, the research has necessarily utilized experimental designs to secure accurate data. This chapter presents the significant interpersonal realities produced by physical attractiveness as identified and documented through strict, universally accepted standards of scientific research.

PSYCHOPATHOLOGY

The interpersonal realities of the physical attractiveness phenomena are not based on extreme levels of physical appearance. Rather, respective research has probed degrees within a normal range along the continuum of appearance. The physical attractiveness manipulations do not extend beyond the lower levels of typical appearance into such areas as disfigurement. However, perceptions are not limited to a corresponding range of ordinary personality differences.

Perceptions of psychopathology are accentuations and exaggerations of customary interpersonal realities of the physical attractiveness phenomena. The perceptions based on differences within the normal range of physical attractiveness go beyond the usual limits into the attributions of abnormality. The pattern of the physical attractiveness stereotype extends into the area of medical disturbances. Furthermore, the assumptions of psychologically related problems are present within both normal and abnormal populations, including the lay public and trained professionals.

Lay Public

Among the so-called normal population, the likelihood of a peer being perceived as mentally disturbed or mentally ill increases as the person's physical attractiveness decreases (Novotny, 1977). One study focused on the attribution of a neurological disorder such as epilepsy (Hansson & Duffield, 1976). One hundred nonprofessional subjects (50 males and 50 females) were asked to identify an epileptic person from among a group of stimulus persons. Among the male stimulus persons, a person of lower physical attractiveness was identified as the epileptic by 83% of the subjects. Among the female stimulus persons, a person of lower physical attractiveness was identified as epileptic by 69% of the subjects. This selection pattern was consistent regardless of decision time involved, personality differences between the subjects, or prior acquaintance with an epileptic.

A later study assessed attribution of general psychological disturbance rather than a specific neurological disorder (Cash, Kehr, Polyson, & Freeman, 1977). The subjects were 144 males and females who were not professionally trained. These subjects observed interviews conducted with females whose psychological adjustment reflected either low or high levels, and whose physical attractiveness was either low, high, or unidentified. The physical attractiveness variable was manipulated through use of photographs, or lack thereof for the condition of no physical attractiveness information. Regardless of the level of maladjustment, those stimulus persons of higher physical attractiveness were perceived as less mal-adjusted, and received better prognosis than their counterparts of lower physical attractiveness. Greater maladjustment and worse prognosis was also attributed to the stimulus persons of lower physical attractiveness than to those persons whose physical attractiveness was not identified. Finally, the maladjusted stimulus persons who were high in physical attractiveness were attributed more favorable personal characteristics.

Two experiments similar to Cash et al. (1977) each produced similar results (Jones, Hansson, & Phillips, 1978). A total of 98 college students served as subjects in the two experiments that varied their instructions. One major difference was that subjects in the second experiment were instructed not to use physical attractiveness as a cue for psychopathology because it was unimportant. The results from both experiments showed that, regardless of the difference in instructions, the physical attractiveness of the stimulus person was negatively correlated with attributions of greater psychopathology based on lower physical attractiveness.

Perceived justification for psychological illness differs as physical attractiveness differs. A case report of a young female who tried to commit suicide was read by 90 male subjects (Pavlos & Newcomb, 1974). The case reports varied in their description of the stimulus person's physical attractiveness and in the medical prognosis of the stimulus person's cancer. The subjects were asked to rate the stimulus person's emotional adjustment and her justification for attempting suicide. First, the research found that perception of less justification for suicide was related to a perception of greater emotional unstableness. Second, the case report of a female afflicted with terminal cancer resulted in perceptions that the attempted suicide was more justified for the stimulus persons of higher physical attractiveness as opposed to lower physical attractiveness.

Professionals and Institutions

The same assumptions possessed by the lay public within the general population exists among helping professionals within their corresponding institutions. Although difficult to accept within the general lay population, the possible effects are harmless relative to the seriousness of such practices within the psychological helping environment. The general population's expectations of mental illness based on physical attractiveness is embarrassing and potentially serious. The effects of the general public's expectations may, at worst, be contributing factors to causing mental illness to emerge especially among those so predisposed. In any case, these expectations can not be good or even neutral. Even more deplorable is the notion that, once mental illness does develop, the patient, from this point on, is further subjected to discrimination based on physical attractiveness.

When a patient is admitted into a counseling situation, the professionals are found to give more favorable judgments, diagnoses, and prognoses as a function of the patient's physical attractiveness (Barocas & Vance, 1974). As patients, those lower in physical attractiveness tend to be less social, have more severe diagnoses, are hospitalized for longer periods of time, and receive fewer community visitors than the physically attractive patients (Farina, Fischer, Sherman, Smith, Groh, & Mermin, 1977). A specific study in this area focused on 77 acute adult schizophrenic patients (Martin, Friedmeyer, & Moore, 1977). With the physical attractiveness interest disguised, the judges revealed they considered the patients of higher physical attractiveness to be better adjusted than those of lower physical attractiveness.

Both the formal and informal treatment of patients may represent a pattern of judgments based on physical attractiveness. Consequently, the physical attractiveness of a mentally ill patient influences the quantity and quality of attention received from professionals. Also, the physical attractiveness of the patient is found to influence the intensity of the therapy given by staff members. The implications for the patient of lower physical attractiveness is grim, for, both degree of attention and intensity of therapy are important factors in the healing process of emotional disorders (Cavior, 1970). Added to this treatment factor is the fact that individuals low in physical attractiveness are often not even accepted for therapy, or if they are, they are placed in group therapy more frequently than those of either medium or high physical attractiveness (Cavior, 1970).

EDUCATIONAL MILIEU

One of the most influential periods in human life is the time spent in school. During this time, the individual learns many social messages in addition to the formal academic information. One social message that is continually presented is that persons of different levels of physical attractiveness are treated differently by those in authority. The physical attractiveness research provides educational data that are consistent with physical attractiveness phenomena. In other words, those higher in physical attractiveness generally elicit more positive expectations and receive preferential treatment over those of lower physical attractiveness.

The effect of higher physical attractiveness on positive evaluations of children is well documented (Adams & Cohen, 1976; Clifford, 1975; Kehle, Bramble, & Mason, 1974). This effect is also reported for the relationship between a child's physical attractiveness and evaluation of the child's social status and behavior (Adams & Cohen, 1976; Adams & LaVoie, 1974a, 1974b; LaVoie & Adams, 1974; Vaughn & Langlois, 1983). Even parents tend to exhibit different expectations of children depending on the child's physical attractiveness. The more physically attractive the child, the more popular, the more likely to succeed, and the greater personal and social success the parents expect the child to experience (Adams & Crane, 1980; Adams & LaVoie, 1975).

Even though the physical attractiveness research within education is focused on young school children, its results agree with other research documenting the physical attractiveness phenomena. In addition to the child subjects is one study that used university level students and still reported congruent results (Singer, 1964). Other research involving educational settings shows that peer perceptions, interpersonal relations, and liking are all influenced by the physical attractiveness phenomena among children (Dion, 1973; Dion & Berscheid, 1974), college students (Dion et al., 1972), and for both middle-aged and older teachers (Adams & Huston, 1975).

Because of the overwhelming emphasis on early childhood, this area is correspondingly represented. The research in this section presents a thorough discussion of physical attractiveness phenomena as they impact on children within the educational environment. Overall, this book gives only passing mention to the physical attractiveness research involving young children, except for this immediate section pertaining to physical attractiveness and education. It is important to present some detail here because the childhood educational experience is a crucial stage in the human life cycle. These years and this environment may establish the person's future relationship with physical attractiveness phenomena.

The physical attractiveness research pertaining to children is not limited to only the educational process. Other authors provide the interested reader with a quite thorough coverage of the entire spectrum of physical attractiveness research pertaining to children, especially as it is applicable to child development (Hildebrandt, 1982; Langlois & Stephan, 1981).

The research pertinent to physical attractiveness and education can be categorized into three areas. The first category centers on teachers' perceptions, teachers' expectations, and teachers' treatment of children with regard to their educational abilities. This first area represents the majority of research on the role of physical attractiveness within education. A second category, given scant research attention, examines the reverse of the first category. In other words, this research assesses the school children's perception of teachers who differ in physical attractiveness. The third category represents research attempts beyond perceptions into actual realities. In this third category, a few studies try to determine if actual educational performance differs according to the physical attractiveness of the child.

Children's Endowment

A child's endowment of physical attractiveness influences perception of scholastic abilities. These effects begin at birth and continue throughout elementary school. Perceptions of abilities emerge from hospital nurses, parents, peers of school children, and teachers at all levels of experience. Premature infants represent the earliest age investigated (Corter, Trehub, Bonkydis, Ford, Celhoffer, & Minde, 1975). Ratings of intellectual abilities and development were elicited from nurses who regularly attended to the needs of these infants. The data revealed a significant correlation ($r = .90$) between the premature infant's physical attractiveness and evaluations about likely intelligence.

Education programs are inadequate for training teachers to be aware of unique student characteristics. In practice, there appears to be little impact of such training on the expectations and behaviors of teachers, according to Adams (1978, p. 29). Within a few years after infancy the child moves into a preschool environment replete with the physical attractiveness phe-nomena. In an extremely well-controlled study, preschool teachers were interviewed with regard to initial teacher expectations based on a child's physical attractiveness, sex, and race (Adams, 1978). Those preschoolers receiving the less positive ratings were, respectively, boys, children of lower physical attractiveness, and black students, as compared to the girls, children of higher physical attractiveness and white students. Those children of high physical attractiveness, as compared to those of low, were believed to be significantly higher in intellectual ability, greater in academic achievement, more socially outgoing, and to possess greater athletic ability.

The author concluded that a preschool child's physical attractiveness has a strong influence on the initial expectations of preschool teachers. He suggested that children are likely to be stereotyped consistent with physical attractiveness phenomena as early as 3 or 4 years old. The article ends with an alarming note that growing research shows that "stereotyping leads to the internalization of the stereotyped personality image by the target person" (Adams, 1978, p. 39). A similar study published several years later reported similar findings for preschool children aged 3, 4, and 5 years (Stohl, 1981). Those children perceived as possessing higher physical attractiveness were also perceived as being more attentive, friendly, and relaxed by preschool teachers.

Regardless of whether the judges are teachers or parents, the expectations of preschool children are the same. Two related studies consisted of preschool children (39 boys and 35 girls), 55 mothers, 36 fathers, and 20 teachers of these preschool children (Adams & Crane, 1980). A series of experimental tasks were conducted to assess expectations about behavior held by the parents and teachers of these children. The parents and teachers consistently expressed expectations congruent with the physical attractiveness phenomena; that is, the more positive behavior was expected from the children of higher physical attractiveness. The article noted that parents and teachers serve as strong socialization agents for the physical attractiveness phenomena.

Student Teachers

According to Clifton and Baksh (1978), it is reasonable to assume that the more experienced teacher will be the more objective teacher. Thus, student teachers may be less objective and more influenced by such student factors as physical attractiveness. To test this potential relationship, a study was designed to assess the amount of influence that student physical attractiveness has on teachers possessing varying lengths of training and experience. Educational and social ability measures were collected using a standard report card with an attached photograph that represented a student of either high or low physical attractiveness. The subjects were 687 student teachers (357 females and 330 males) with 16% in their second year, 17% in the third year, 43% in the fourth year, and 23% in the fifth year.

The evaluations given by the student teachers were statistically significant for every measure of educational and social potentials. Without exception, the students higher in physical attractiveness were perceived more favorably than those lower in physical attractiveness. The dependent variables were (a) the students' IQ, (b) their social relationships with peers, (c) their parents' attitude toward their work, (d) the amount of probable lifetime educational achievement, and (e) their self-concept. The hypothesis that level of education would affect teacher objectivity with regard to student physical attractiveness was clearly disproved. The authors stated that contrary to their expectations

> student-teachers who were more advanced in their education were just as easily persuaded that they could make meaningful evaluations of pupils on the basis of very superficial information as student-teachers who were less advanced in their education. (Clifton & Baksh, 1978, p. 43)

Parallel research used 141 student teachers to evaluate perceived social and academic attributes of seventh grade boys (Tompkins & Boor, 1980). The results were not significant for academic attributes, but the physically attractive students were rated significantly higher than the less physically attractive students on every social attribute measure.

Experienced Teachers

Tompkins and Boor (1980) suggested that the physical attractiveness of students may affect expectations of student teachers more than experienced teachers. This tentative hypothesis has neither theoretical nor logical support. Furthermore, no existing empirical data even permit such inferences. Although no research directly examines these potential differences, an infinitely more eminent hypothesis about experienced teachers has been addressed. This empirical research documents the fact that experienced teachers hold expectations about students in agreement with the physical attractiveness phenomena.

Research encompassing large numbers of teachers in a wide variety of research designs repeatedly reports that teachers hold more favorable expectations of students who are high in physical attractiveness. These expectations are most likely an outgrowth of the teachers' first impression which, in normal educational administration, is based on the child's school record and physical appearance. Early research in this area presented the school records and photographs of fifth graders to 404 working teachers (Clifford & Walster, 1973). The stimulus children were either male or female with low or high physical attractiveness. Responses by the teachers exposed significantly higher evaluations of the physically attractive student as compared to his or her counterpart. These evaluation differences dealt with (a) the child's intelligence, (b) the parent's interest in the child's education, (c) the child's likely eventual educational attainment, and (d) the popularity of the student with peers.

Adams and Cohen (1976) pursued teacher expectancy research by increasing the type of information usually provided with physical attractiveness. The subjects were 490 public school teachers (180 males and 310 females) in eight different school systems. The teachers all had at least a four-year college degree and averaged 5½ years of teaching experience. Characteristic of the first author's research, this study applied the strictest standards to its procedure. The procedure included cumulative folders for each subject, which were printed to approximate the official school folders. The folders contained standard information about the student's slightly above average academic performance, a report card for kindergarten through second grade, and medical data for a healthy child. The variable information in each folder included (a) home background representing middle or lower class, (b) negative or positive comment of the child's general ability, and (c) a photograph of either a boy or a girl of either high or low physical attractiveness. An enclosed evaluation form was made up of five items: creative ability level, intellectual ability level, ultimate educational training likely to attain, educational placement, and quality of teacher–student interactions.

The student's physical attractiveness yielded significant influence on teachers' expectations. The data also indicated differing expectations of teachers as a function of the child's sex, family background, and reported general ability. The higher the student's physical attractiveness, the higher were expectations of creativity, intelligence, educational level, and ultimate educational attainment. Despite these expectations, the teachers stated that physical attractiveness of the student would not affect their teacher–student interactions. The authors concluded that the results confirm those of Clifford and Walster (1973), who also reported varied teacher expectations due to student physical attractiveness. The suggestion was that the physical attractiveness phenomena exist to such a degree as to affect differences in expectations which, in turn, translate into differences in interactions between teachers and students. Empirical data published 8 years later supported this notion of interaction differences. In addition to reporting teacher expectations consistent with earlier research, Martinek (1981) reported that teachers truly are more receptive to ideas from students of higher physical attractiveness.

The majority of relevant research data supports the above two studies. However, several studies can be cited that do not offer such persuasive data. Yet, these same studies still insinuate that teacher discrimination might favor elementary students who possess higher physical attractiveness (Adams & LaVoie, 1974a; Feeg & Peters, 1979; Felson, 1980; LaVoie & Adams, 1974). Ross and Salvia (1975) reported teachers systematically rate less physically attractive children less favorably than the more physically

attractive children. This systematic difference includes expectations for
future academic and social development. DeMeis and Turner (1978) found
that this teacher expectancy effect is highly consistent among teachers (i.e.,
high interjudge reliability).

It is not unreasonable to believe, given the strong evidence of the
physical attractiveness phenomena within education, that dire behavioral
consequences take place. With all the teacher expectancies operating
according to student physical attractiveness, issues pertaining to teacher
behavior need attention. Surprisingly, there is practically no such research.
Even though scientific research designed to investigate if and how teacher
expectations translate into teacher behavior is difficult, it needs to be
accomplished. Despite the methodological problems, some research has
attempted to infer behavior by measuring behavioral intent, and still other
research has attempted to assess actual behavior.

One study dealing with behavioral intent assessed likely teacher
behavior when dealing with misbehavior (Rich, 1975). Subjects were 144
female elementary teachers presented with a situation of misbehavior
committed by a child. Each presentation included a photograph of either a
male or female child of either high or low physical attractiveness. Subjects
were asked to evaluate the student's blame, personality, and punishment
for the misdeed. First, like other research findings, those higher in physical
attractiveness were attributed more favorable personalities. Second, the
same misdeed attributed to students of lower physical attractiveness was
considered less undesirable when attributed to students of higher physical
attractiveness. A similar procedure found that student teachers are equally
influenced by the combinations of student misbehavior and student
physical attractiveness (Marwit, Marwit, & Walker, 1978).

The only research attempting to assess actual teacher behavior are
three studies reported in the early 1970s. The first two studies (Adams &
Cohen, 1974; Rist, 1970) employed observational research techniques.
Unfortunately, no real information can be gained from the limited scope
and confounding problems inherent in their specific methodologies. The
third study, which involved postevent analysis (Barocas & Black, 1974),
examined the effects of student physical attractiveness on referrals for
psychological assessment, speech, reading, and learning disabilities. Fifty
undergraduate college students judged the physical attractiveness of 100
third grade students referred for help. Photographs of the 54 males and 46
females were used for establishing their physical attractiveness. The results
were that the greatest referrals were made for children of higher physical
attractiveness. The article concluded that children of higher physical
attractiveness receive greater attention which yields more judicious notice
and response to their problems.

Critical Note

It is somewhat difficult to understand why so little research attention addresses actual teacher behavior as a function of student physical attractiveness. It is even more difficult to understand because research has produced powerful findings regarding teacher expectations. The lack of research certainly cannot be due to the insignificance of this very important question. Therefore, one possible reason centers on methodological problems. To obtain causal data an experimental design must be employed. But if actual behavior is desired, there are necessary manipulations that are ethically unacceptable. Experimental designs are not necessarily ruled out because surrogate measures could be obtained by going beyond mere expectations into simulated teacher–student behavioral interactions. An alternative may be an observational technique. Efforts could be made, even though ethical and logistical problems exist, by unobtrusive observation in naturalistic settings. A final avenue is postevent analysis such as conducted by Barocas and Black (1974). Although only correlational data can be obtained, it would be a beginning from which reasonable and insightful inferences about actual behavior may be made.

Regardless of the methodological problems, the lack of research attention in this area of actual teacher behavior is deplorable. Research attempts should be made for, surely, imperfect information is better than no information. Possibly the delay in this research is analogous to the delay suggested by Aronson, in which social science seemed to hesitantly begin exploration of the physical attractiveness variable.

Aronson, then a Stanford University professor, wrote that social science is fearful to confirm preferential treatment based on physical attractiveness (Aronson, 1969, p. 160) and that to do so is to acknowledge that amid our democratic philosophies there operates a very undemocratic practice of birthrights. It is feasible that Aronson's statement on general physical attractiveness research is equally applicable to this specific physical attractiveness research within education. The thought that the innate physical attractiveness of young school children determines their treatment by teachers is frightening. However, it is more frightening to think that by ignoring a problem it either does not exist or will disappear. The only way the inequities of the physical attractiveness phenomena can be minimized is to first identify them.

Teachers' Endowments

The ratings of teachers by students are consistent with the physical attractiveness phenomena. Teachers endowed with higher physical attractiveness are evaluated more favorably on a variety of competency variables. The findings are consistent among the four studies that comprise the physical attractiveness research on teacher evaluations by students. There is good quality in the experimental procedures and in the variety of subjects of these studies. Three of the studies used a range of elementary students to evaluate teachers of their respective level, and the fourth study used college students to evaluate professors.

The elementary students in one experiment consisted of sixty 9-year-old students and sixty 13-year-old students as subjects (Chaikin, Gillen, Derlega, Heinen, & Wilson, 1978). After viewing a videotape of a teacher, the subjects were asked to provide numerous evaluations. Higher evaluations were associated with teachers of higher physical attractiveness. This pattern emerged for all three ratings, competency of the teacher, ability to stimulate students, and ability to motivate students.

The knowledge about effects of teacher physical attractiveness was expanded by including the variables of teachers' sex and age (Irilli, 1978). The subjects were 144 third grade students. These students were given a teacher's photograph and asked to complete a 21-item questionnaire that referred to the teacher. Age and sex of the teachers did not significantly influence the students' evaluations but physical attractiveness of teachers did. More positive evaluations were given for teachers of higher physical attractiveness and more negative evaluations for teachers of lower physical attractiveness. Teachers of higher physical attractiveness were evaluated as superior teachers who were more fun, more interesting, and more willing to play games with the students. The students also expressed that they would experience more comfortableness with the teachers of higher physical attractiveness. Surprisingly, there were no interaction effects between the teachers' sex, age, and physical attractiveness variables. Instead, the students' evaluation differences of the teachers were a function of the single visual cue provided by physical attractiveness.

The results have been replicated, regardless of grade level in school. A total of 150 subjects were asked to evaluate seven dimensions of teacher performance (Goebel & Cashen, 1979). The experimental design allowed for control of the teachers' age, sex, and race, as well as physical attractiveness. Regardless of student level, younger teachers received higher evaluations than older teachers. Interactions between teachers' sex and physical attractiveness indicated that those teachers receiving the lowest evaluations were teachers of lower physical attractiveness who were also middle-aged females and older males. The physical attractiveness variable produced a significant main effect. Teachers of higher physical attractiveness were evaluated significantly more positive on all performance measures by all student education levels.

College students exhibit a pattern analogous to elementary students. In the judgment of their respective students, the physical attractiveness of a college professor is similar to that of an elementary teacher. A photograph of a stimulus person described as a psychology college professor was evaluated by college students (Lombardo & Tocci, 1979). The stimulus person was either a male or a female of either high or low physical attractiveness. After viewing the photograph, the subjects (60 males and 60 females) expressed their evaluations on a standard questionnaire. The significant effects included preference of both sexes for a male professor as opposed to a female, with a same-sex effect for male subjects giving the male professors the highest ratings of competency. The effects due to professor physical attractiveness were the same across professor sex and subject sex. The professor of higher physical attractiveness received significantly higher ratings of warmth, sensitivity, superiority, communication ability, and knowledge of subject material.

Student Performance

Teacher expectations vary according to variations in student physical attractiveness. Although teacher behavior is certainly of interest, student behavior is of primary concern. Considering the many teacher presuppositions, actual student behavior emerges as a pertinent issue. The research has addressed this behavior through measures of school achievement records. Coincidentally, such factual student performance information offers potentially valuable insight into the teacher–student relationship based on physical attractiveness.

If school performance is significantly correlated with student physical attractiveness, the question of *why* arises. A logical explanation is suggested by the combination of physical attractiveness phenomena and self-fulfilling prophecy. According to the self-fulfilling prophecy, students expected to perform better by their teachers will ultimately do so. The research is not conclusive, nor is the direction known, but a reasonable hypothesis is that students of differing levels of physical attractiveness do actually perform differently within the educational system.

The first study in this area is badly flawed by what may be described as poor measurement of the physical attractiveness construct (Clifford, 1975). It involved two stages in an attempt to independently assess behavior. First, an experiment examined teacher expectations based on student physical attractiveness. The greater the child's physical attractiveness, the greater was the perceived educational achievement variables, such as IQ, parent interest, peer relations, and self-concept.

The second stage produced correlational data in a test of the potential effects of physical attractiveness on educational performance. Subjects were 39 second graders, 45 fourth graders, and 48 sixth graders. Physical attractiveness of these subjects was determined from school photographs, which, apparently, were group photographs of the entire class. Those individuals selected were judged by 14 teachers unrelated to the subjects except that they taught the same grade levels at other schools. The problem with the measurement of the physical attractiveness construct was that the judges did not agree. Apparently, interjudge correlation was about .32, with the range being .23 for second graders to a high of .40 for the fourth graders. The author stated "there is relatively little consensus among teachers on judgement of individual attractiveness in a typical class" (Clifford, 1975, p. 207). Such lack of agreement (i.e., measure reliability) invalidates the study, because it can reasonably be assumed to explain the results but not the studied construct. Thus, a relationship was not found between student physical attractiveness and school performance.

Two later studies, with better measure reliability, found significant relationships between physical attractiveness and school performance (Murphy, Nelson, & Cheap, 1981; Salvia, Algozzine, & Sheare, 1977). The two studies are substantially different except that both used the same two types of school performance indicators. One measure was school grades, which may be more subjective than the other measure of scores from a standardized achievement test. The reason for these two measures is that standardized achievement test scores should be totally objective because there is no personal interaction between the test taker and the test scorer.

The only independent variable in the study by Salvia, Algozzine, and Sheare (1977) was the students' physical attractiveness. The subjects were 440 Caucasian students in the third and fifth grades. Physical attractiveness of the subjects was determined through evaluations of photographs by 7 graduate students majoring in special education. The standardized achievement scores were somewhat higher for those students rated higher in physical attractiveness, whereas the school grades (i.e., report cards) were significantly higher for those students higher in physical attractiveness.

Murphy, Nelson, and Cheap (1981) explored both sex and physical attractiveness variables as related to school performance. The subjects were 24 male and 17 female high school students. Physical attractiveness was determined through photographs evaluated by 20 undergraduate college students. Analysis of variance revealed significant main effects due to physical attractiveness and sex for both academic achievement and sociability. The school measures (i.e., grade point averages) were significantly correlated with physical attractiveness. The suggestion of the study is that actual evaluations by teachers may be similar to the teacher expectancy research. The authors stated that both academic performance and student's physical attractiveness does affect teacher evaluations.

Self-Fulfilling Prophecy

The final word concerning the role of physical attractiveness within education is alarming. Too much theory, logic, and empirical data show expectations produce self-fulfilling prophecy. If teachers expect different behavior from students of different physical attractiveness, the students sense these messages, process the subtle cues, and develop accordingly to conform to the expectations. The result is very favorable for those students of higher physical attractiveness but very unfavorable for those lower in physical attractiveness.

General social psychological research offers data that support a relationship between expectations of others and ultimate corresponding behaviors by the target person (e.g., Aronson & Carlsmith, 1962; Dailey, 1952; Zajonc & Brickman, 1969). Specific research on teacher expectations offers data that support a relationship between teachers' expectations and ultimate student behavior (cf. Rosenthal & Jacobson, 1968). Subsequent research is not unanimous, but Adams and Cohen (1976) state that extensive summaries of both laboratory and naturalistic research reveals strong support for student–teacher relationships leading to a self-fulfilling prophecy (cf. Brophy & Good, 1974; Rosenthal, 1971a, 1971b).

A major *Psychology Today* article (Rosenthal, 1973) has summarized the research investigating the relationship between student performance and teacher expectation. That article shows that teachers' expectations are powerful determinants of students' learning, performance, development, and achievement. These studies, unrelated to the physical attractiveness phenomena, report that conscious and unconscious treatment influences IQ points, sports accomplishments, mathematics skills, and academic performance. Rosenthal's research shows that favorable expectations have a positive effect on students, but unfavorable expectations have a negative effect. Special recognition is demonstrated by the fact that teachers often unconsciously work harder with a child they believe is bright. Consequently, the (perceived) bright child is treated better, whereas the (perceived) less bright child faces a double handicap—less intelligence or less ability combined with expectations and treatment which further promote these inferior qualities. This body of research has established that students live up or down to their teachers' expectations and subsequent treatment. This self-fulfilling prophecy is especially portentous in light of the physical attractiveness phenomena within the educational process.

SOCIAL DEVIANCE

Social deviance and minor transgressions are not immune from the physical attractiveness phenomena. Persons whose behavior is socially deviant are responded to differently depending on their physical attractiveness. Social deviance may be viewed as a continuum ranging from minor misdeeds to criminal acts. Throughout this continuum runs the common thread of punishment and the threat of punishment. Consequently, social deviance, minor misdeeds, crimes, and courts could be discussed under one heading. However, for clarity, the physical attractiveness research regarding social deviance will be categorized into two sections. The first section will discuss relatively minor anomalies, and the next section will discuss the more serious deviations which may be described as crimes. This division is logical from a punishment perspective. The first category involves simple administration of punishment by individuals, but the second category involves complex administration of punishment by courts, juries, and institutions.

Children

Children who commit the identical misdeed but who differ in physical attractiveness elicit different responses from adults. Female subjects were provided with a written description of a child's offensive behavior (Dion, 1972). Attached to each description was a photograph of a child who was either high or low in physical attractiveness. When the misdeed was attributed to a child of low physical attractiveness the behavior was viewed as more serious and more likely to be a part of the child's permanent character. On the other hand, the same behavior attributed to a child of high physical attractiveness was viewed as less serious, probably transitory, and as atypical of the child. Subjects were also asked to contemplate future behavior. The child of lower physical attractiveness was predicted to display more negative behavior and to commit offensive misdeeds more frequently.

A somewhat similar study by the same author yielded similar results (Dion, 1974). In addition to the physical attractiveness variable, the child's sex was examined as a factor for different adult responses, and actual adult behaviors, rather than perceptions, were examined. Also, instead of manipulating mischief, mistakes were manipulated for a child's performance on a picture-matching task. The subjects (52 white females and 44 white males) administered punishment based on the incorrect responses of each child. The punishment was to take 1 to 5 pennies away from the child for each error. The data permitted the conclusion that subjects were more lenient when punishing a child of higher physical attractiveness than lower.

Involuntary responses by adults are no different than voluntary responses. Two experiments were directed at the involuntary behavior of adults in response to a child's physical attractiveness (Berkowitz & Frodi, 1979). In both experiments, the subjects were deliberately provoked by a confederate of the experiment. In an attempt to assess involuntary responses, as displayed in the form of displaced aggression, the subjects were required to discipline a child after being provoked. In the first experiment, a 10-year-old girl of either high or low physical attractiveness was paired with 56 female subjects. The subjects appeared to vent more aggression on the girl of low physical attractiveness by administering greater punishment.

The second experiment paired 40 subjects with a 10-year-old boy. The boy was either high or low in physical attractiveness with either a noticeable stutter or with normal speech. Both of the manipulated variables elicited involuntary aggression. The boy who stuttered and the boy with low physical attractiveness received more severe discipline than their counterparts. These results of biased punishment are consistent with a series of studies on teachers' responses to transgression of students who differed in physical attractiveness (Marwit, 1982).

Adults

Adults, as well as children, are vulnerable to perceptions of social deviation as a function of their physical attractiveness. The only difference may be that adults and children do not usually exhibit the same type of deviations. Adult subjects were involved in two experiments conducted to test the hypothesis that persons of lower physical attractiveness are more likely to be perceived as socially deviant (Unger, Hilderbrand, & Madar, 1982). Photographs of stimulus persons were sorted into *socially acceptable* and *socially deviant* categories. The first experiment had 60 male and 60 female subjects sort photographs of female stimulus persons. The second experiment replicated the first but the stimulus persons were males. As hypothesized the less physically attractive were judged to be the more socially deviant. For example, both males and females of lower physical attractiveness were perceived as more likely to be politically radical. Females of lower physical attractiveness were more likely to be identified as homosexual, whereas males of lower physical attractiveness were more likely to be identified with occupational aspirations stereotypically feminine.

Misdeeds committed by children may be viewed as mild forms of social deviancy when compared to misdeeds by adults. Likewise, minor misdeeds by adults may be viewed as somewhat analogous to very mild forms of crime. As the magnitude of adult misdeeds increases, they begin to enter the realm of crime with the possibility of corresponding punishment. If crime does, in fact, represent a different location on a continuum of social deviance, then these expressed expectations hold important implications for the physical attractiveness variable within crime and courts.

CRIME AND COURTS

Substantial research exists in the area of physical attractiveness and its relationship within the legal system. Results indicate that physical attractiveness is a variable that is not neutral but that possesses powerful and complex implications for criminal activities. Topics of research include both civil (noncriminal) and criminal cases. The criminal cases span a wide spectrum from burglary and swindling to rapes and murders. Experimental manipulation is discouraged because of the seriousness of the circumstances, and research, therefore, has necessarily relied on mock juries and legal simulations. Postevent analysis of actual cases could be performed, but the value of the results is difficult to ascertain due to confounding variables. However, one pioneering effort (Stewart, 1980) has been performed by using observational, postevent analysis of the parties in actual trials. Regardless of approaches, the research has commonly focused on the effects of physical attractiveness for defendants and victims in criminal cases. Limited exceptions have examined its effects in civil cases for both plaintiffs and defendants. Finally, the physical attractiveness research has concentrated on the role of physical attractiveness in the decisions of juries. Such an emphasis is justified in light of our punishment system which rests primarily with jury members, and a few other prominent characters, who must all rely on less than perfect information when making their decisions. A limitation of this research is that the simulated jury settings have not fully reflected the deliberation stage of actual court procedures.

Antecedent Conditions

Preconceptions are distinguishable before evidence is evaluated. General research introduces the notion that physical attractiveness phenomena are as applicable to court and crime settings as they are to other interpersonal interactions. This position is advanced by specific research that finds that the less physically attractive are expected to be the more socially deviant (Deitz & Byrnes, 1981; Michelini & Snodgrass, 1980; Unger *et al.*, 1982). Those lower in physical attractiveness are also expected to be more vulnerable to sinister outside influence (Miller, Gillen, Schenker, & Radlove, 1974). Among all of these antecedent conditions is the belief that jury judgments should be objective, based only on the facts, and not influenced by a person's physical attractiveness (Efran, 1974). Yet one study involving 896 subjects found that physical attractiveness had significant effects on jurors' decisions (Feild, 1979).

The state of nature is a paradox, because the antecedent conditions, before a criminal suspect is judged, are contradictory. On the one hand, there is strong evidence of subtle predispositions based on physical attractiveness, and, on the other hand, there is the desire to have judgments based on the facts and not on physical appearances.

Predisposition

Evidence in support of subtle predispositions may be readily extracted from research pertaining to obedience or submission to malevolent pressures. Milgram's obedience paradigm was used to examine the relationships between persons of different levels of physical attractiveness and obedience to male authority (Miller *et al.*, 1974). The subjects were 120 males and 120 females in two experiments. The variables of interest were prediction and perception of obedience to authority as a function of sex and physical attractiveness of stimulus persons.

The first experiment assessed association between harmful obedience and physical attractiveness. Subjects were shown slides of male and female stimulus persons of either high or low physical attractiveness. The subjects were then asked to predict each stimulus person's response when confronted with Milgram's "dilemma of obedience to authority." For their prediction, the subjects indicated the amount of electrical shock that the stimulus person would probably deliver to an innocent person when requested to do so by a person of authority. Stimulus persons of lower physical attractiveness were predicted to deliver higher, more harmful, electrical shock in obedience to authoritative requests. The second experiment presented stimulus persons whose behavior was described as extremely obedient or extremely defiant in an earlier setting of the Milgram paradigm.

The conclusion of the study was that the physically attractive are perceived as more caring, more responsible, and more independent. Those higher in physical attractiveness were seen as more internally motivated and more resistant to control by others. The implication is that people of higher physical attractiveness are considered less likely to commit negative, harmful behaviors. Subsequently, they may be less likely to be assigned guilt and punishment when accused of crime.

Ramifications of differential legal actions based on physical attractiveness are disturbing. The foundation of our democratic society is equal and fair treatment for all, and the need for this equality is highlighted in our legal system which often culminates in the courtroom. But once in the courtroom, the physical attractiveness variable maintains its role in plain sight of everyone. Defense attorneys certainly recognize the capacity of physical attractiveness as they advise their clients to maximize their appearance through grooming, posture, behavior, and dress. Subjective experience has no doubt established that such subtle and legal tampering with juries increases the likelihood of favorable treatment for the defendant of higher physical attractiveness.

Jurors are apparently influenced by these tactics, for they appear unable to be impartial to the physical attractiveness of defendants. Both for legal crimes and social offenses, the physically attractive are treated more leniently (Jacobson & Berger, 1974; Piehl, 1977) and are assigned less harsh punishment (Aronson, 1969; Cavoir & Howard, 1973; Cavoir, Hayes & Cavoir, 1974; Efran, 1974; Friend & Vinson, 1974). Even in civil cases, simulated court settings reveal that plaintiffs of higher physical attractiveness are given more favorable judgments and are awarded larger amounts of money (Stephan & Tully, 1977).

Contradictions

Despite ideals for objectivity based on facts, subjectivity based on physical attractiveness may often influence legal judgments. An opinion survey of 108 college students showed that these subjects (who certainly are potential jury members) believe in legal objectivity (Efran, 1974). Seventy-nine percent of the subjects said that jurors' decisions should be influenced by the character and history of defendants. Ninety-three percent said that physical attractiveness of defendants should not influence jurors' decisions. It is reasonable to interpret these expressed opinions to mean that people believe they are not and would not be influenced by a defendant's physical attractiveness if they served as jurors.

Motivated by these survey data, Efran conducted an experiment to analyze the agreement between these idealistic beliefs and actual behavior. The sample for the experiment involved 66 different subjects selected from the same population as the survey. Consequently, there is no reason to believe that the two samples should possess statistically different beliefs. The experimental procedure to test this notion was a simulated court procedure in which potential jurors (i.e., the subjects) were presented with case summaries of a defendant. Attached to each case summary was a photograph of a defendant of either high or low physical attractiveness.

Contrary to behavioral intentions expressed by the survey data, the experimental data exposed actual behavior by the potential jurors to be significantly influenced by the defendant's physical attractiveness. Those defendants of higher physical attractiveness received statistically different evaluations of (a) less certainty of guilt and (b) less severity of recommended punishment. Consistent with a liking–leniency explanation posed by Michelini and Snodgrass (1980), these data revealed greater liking for defendants of higher physical attractiveness. Regardless of explanation, the fact remains that preferential treatment occurred in this circumstance of the legal process.

Recognition

The recognition that physical attractiveness may be a potential determinant of penalty severity was already alluded to in the 1940s:

> Even social workers accustomed to dealing with all types find it difficult to think of a normal pretty girl as being guilty of a crime. Most people, for some inexplicable reason, think of crime in terms of abnormality of appearance, and I must say that beautiful women are not often convicted. (Monahan, 1941, p. 103)

One potential explanation for this leniency of punishment is offered by a "reinforcement–affect model" of attraction (Byrne & Clore, 1970). This model proposes that beauty has positive reinforcement values which lead to relatively more positive affective responses toward a person who possesses higher physical attractiveness. Because we like a physically attractive person more, and liking a defendant increases evaluation of his physical attractiveness (Landy & Aronson, 1969; Michelini & Snodgrass, 1980), we would expect physically attractive defendants to be punished less than defendants of lower physical attractiveness.

Interactions

The research regarding this behavior/punishment dimension represents interactions. Some research demonstrates that physical attractiveness is a disadvantage within legal situations. This disadvantage is due to evaluators who view the offense of a physically attractive person as taking an undue advantage of his appearance. Also, the punishment varies as the crime varies. The physically attractive are punished more severely for crimes involving embezzlement and swindling (Sigall & Ostrove, 1975). Interaction effects also depend on the evaluator's own high or low physical attractiveness. When the evaluator is lower in physical attractiveness, the offender of higher physical attractiveness is treated more harshly than the offender's counterpart (Dermer & Thiel, 1975).

Beneficial Circumstances

The hypothesis that higher physical attractiveness is beneficial to an individual within the legal process is supported from two standpoints. First, the physical attractiveness phenomena are supported by the fact that general preferential treatment is well documented for higher physical attractiveness. Second, empirical research can be cited so as to arrive at the same conclusion. However, two of these studies, establishing the benefits of higher physical attractiveness, indicate that favorable effects may be moderated.

Regardless of the proposals, direct evidence reveals an overall bias of inequitable benefits. Those lower in physical attractiveness are expected to perform more offensive behavior than those higher in physical attractiveness. Once an offensive behavior is performed, the identical behavior by persons of lower physical attractiveness is considered more serious than the behavior exhibited by the counterpart of higher physical attractiveness. The result is differential punishment based on difference in physical attractiveness.

The research advocating a beneficial hypothesis begins with appraisal of the perception of transgressions. Perceptions of transgressions interact with physical attractiveness when the intentions of the offender and the consequence suffered by the victim are considered (Nesdale, Rule, & McAra, 1975). Manipulation of physical attractiveness was conducted through descriptive as opposed to visual means. The stimulus person was described as a male of either high or low physical attractiveness. The 128 female subjects read a transcript which described an aggressor with either good or bad intentions and a victim who experienced either mild or severe aftereffects. Significant implications for physical attractiveness resulted. The aggression committed by a person of higher physical attractiveness was evaluated less unfavorably. Intentions did not affect evaluations of the aggressor high in physical attractiveness, but the aggressor of lower physical attractiveness with bad intentions was judged to be more likely to aggress again in the future.

Judges of different ages are not affected differently by a defendant's physical attractiveness. Gray and Ashmore (1976) used 133 subjects who ranged in age from 29 to 82 years old. The data from their experiment verified that defendants of higher physical attractiveness received less severe punishments for a specific crime than did the defendants of lower physical attractiveness. This difference in sentence recommendations did not differ as a function of the judges' ages. Solomon and Schopler (1978) used 60 male college students under the age of 29 years and also reported that defendants of higher physical attractiveness received less punishment.

Moderations

Group discussion may moderate individual bias due to defendant physical attractiveness (Izzett & Leginski, 1974). A fictional case (the same as was used by Landy & Aronson, 1969) concerned an accidental automobile homicide that implied negligence. The same case, except for a defendant who was either of low or high physical attractiveness, was presented to 50 subjects. The procedure involved three steps: (a) subjects recommended a sentence, (b) subjects made a public statement and then discussed the sentence, and (c) subjects again recommended a sentence. In the first step, the sentences were significantly longer for the defendants of lower physical attractiveness as compared to higher. After group discussion, the sentences for defendants of higher physical attractiveness remained unchanged, but the sentences of defendants of lower physical attractiveness were now significantly more lenient. A shift in favor of lower physical attractiveness is understandable considering the basic premises of the physical attractive phenomena. People are neither aware nor willing to admit dispensing treatment as a function of lower physical attractiveness.

Increasing the factual information may lessen prejudice against defendants of different physical attractiveness levels (Baumeister & Darley, 1982). The hypothesis was that bias in favor of higher physical attractiveness would decrease as the jurors knew (and remembered) more about the facts of the case. The experiments involved a hypothetical drunk-driving arrest. The defendant's physical attractiveness was either high or low, and driving speed and intoxication level were either explicitly stated or left ambiguous. After receiving the case, the subjects were asked to recommend the appropriate sentences, and then to recall facts of the case from memory. As the subjects' knowledge about the factual information of the case increased, their preferential treatment in favor of the higher physical attractiveness decreased. The study concluded that increasing factual information shifts judgment from the person to the crime.

Interactions

Some circumstances may reverse the effects of higher physical attractiveness from beneficial to detrimental. In a study by Piehl (1977), the scenario was a street accident caused by a traffic offender who varied in physical attractiveness. The study's major point of interest was the length of imprisonment recommended by the 44 female and 46 male subjects. If the accident did not cause a fatality, the defendant of higher physical attractiveness was given more favorable treatment than the defendant of lower. But if the accident caused a fatality, the defendant of lower physical attractiveness then received more favorable treatment.

Defendant's physical attractiveness also interacts with the victim's history of being a victim (Storck & Sigall, 1979). After observing a hypothetical aggression, 40 female subjects recommended a level of punishment. The manipulated variables were (a) the aggressor's physical attractiveness and (b) whether the victim was being victimized for the first time or had been victimized in the past. In the experimental treatment of the victim who had a history of victimization, the aggressor of higher physical attractiveness was recommended less punishment than the aggressor of lower physical attractiveness. When no such history existed, the aggressor of lower physical attractiveness was recommended less punishment than the physically attractive counterpart.

Type of crime determines whether physical attractiveness is a benefit or detriment for the defendant (Sigall & Ostrove, 1973, 1975). Crimes of burglary and swindle were investigated and defined as either unrelated or related to physical attractiveness, respectively. An interaction was hypothesized between defendant physical attractiveness and type of crime. The defendant's physical attractiveness was either high, low, or unknown (achieved by providing no information to the subjects). Subjects (60 males and 60 females) were presented with a criminal case and then asked to recommend punishment. When the crime was unrelated to physical attractiveness (i.e., a burglary), the defendants higher in physical attractiveness were recommended more lenient sentences. When the crime was related to physical attractiveness (i.e., a swindle), the defendants lower in physical attractiveness were recommended the more lenient sentences. A study, 5 years later, reported similar results between defendant physical attractiveness and crimes of swindle and burglary (Smith & Hed, 1979).

Civil Cases

Civil cases, as well as criminal, are addressed by the physical attractiveness research. In these cases, the prosecutors were replaced by plaintiffs, and the punishment did not involve penal sentences but rather financial damages and monetary awards. Whatever the modifications, effects of physical attractiveness did not change.

Civil case plaintiffs of higher physical attractiveness were awarded larger sums of money than their counterparts of lower physical attractiveness. A hypothetical civil case involved a plaintiff suing for personal damages (Stephan & Tully, 1977). Plaintiff's physical attractiveness, sex, and age were manipulated as independent variables in a 2 X 2 X 2 factorial experiment, with the subjects' sex being a two-level blocking variable. The 124 subjects were asked to determine responsibility for liability and financial damages. Effects of the sex variable were demonstrated by female jurors who were not affected by plaintiff sex, whereas the male jurors tended to award smaller amounts to female plaintiffs and larger amounts to male plaintiffs. Reaction due to age was nonsignificant; however, effects due to physical attractiveness produced a significant main effect. In determining liability and in awarding money, the plaintiff of higher physical attractiveness received more favorable judgments.

Because typical civil cases involve two opposing individuals, the physical attractiveness of each party does not function in isolation. In Kulka and Kessler (1978), the case was a noncriminal (i.e., civil case) automobile trial which manipulated physical attractiveness of the plaintiff and defendant. Rather than the usual written synopsis, the 91 subjects were exposed to videotaped presentations. The authors believed this audiovisual technique made the simulation more realistically approximate the actual courtroom dynamics. Although the presentation technique was an excellent extension and complement to existing research, the authors did not mention that it was, in fact, a trade-off for greater external validity at the possible expense of less internal validity.

The physical attractiveness variable was reported to have significant consequences consistent with the physical attractiveness phenomena. More judgments and greater amounts of money were awarded to the plaintiff when the dyad was a plaintiff of higher physical attractiveness and a defendant of lower physical attractiveness. Fewer judgments and smaller amounts of money were awarded for damages when the dyad was a plaintiff of low physical attractiveness and a defendant of high physical attractiveness. The authors concluded that the beneficial effects of physical attractiveness were not unanimous, which implies that they may be dependent on the perceptions of the seriousness of the crime.

Reality

In general, higher physical attractiveness is beneficial for those accused of criminal conduct. Regardless of whether the research designs were experiments or unobtrusive observation, the differential benefits were uniform. These research designs, with one exception, have utilized experimental procedures: the one exception to experiments with laboratory simulations being an observational field study. This exception can be viewed as an invaluable extension of research findings. The collaboration of results encourages generalization from laboratory simulations to the realities of the real world courtroom.

Realistic experimental manipulations can only be approximated when dealing with consequences as severe as lifetime imprisonment and possibly worse. Therefore, Stewart (1980) used an unobtrusive, observation procedure in an attempt to bridge the gap between internal and external validity. For this study, the defendants were actual litigants appearing in criminal court for offenses described as varying from mild to serious. The defendants were described as 42 white and 32 nonwhite persons between 22 and 25 years of age. Differences due to physical attractiveness were significant. Those higher in physical attractiveness received less harsh sentences, whereas those lower in physical attractiveness received more harsh sentences. Seriousness of crime and race of defendant were confounding factors, but multiple regression analysis demonstrated a significant relationship between physical attractiveness and conviction or acquittal of the defendant.

Rape

Crimes of rape have drawn a substantial amount of physical attractiveness research. This criminal act has produced a unique research focus directed toward the victim's physical attractiveness. For this crime, higher physical attractiveness is beneficial for the defendant but may be beneficial or detrimental for the victim. Consequently, the research also examines perceptions of the victim's responsibility in provoking the rape as a function of her physical attractiveness.

The physical attractiveness phenomena impact both parties within rape dyads (Jacobson, 1981). A criminal case of rape was presented to 60 male and 60 female subjects. The physical attractiveness variable was fully manipulated so that the assailant and the victim were presented as either low or high in physical attractiveness. After reading the case, the subjects were asked to specify their (a) belief of the defendant's alibi, (b) sympathy for the defendant, (c) sympathy for the victim, and (d) the recommended length of prison sentence for punishment.

The defendant and the victim of higher physical attractiveness were shown greater sympathy than their counterparts of lower physical attractiveness. Notwithstanding physical attractiveness, assailants were more likely to be found guilty with a victim of higher physical attractiveness. Provided the same case scenario, the assailants of lower physical attractiveness were found guilty by 82% of the jurors, but those of higher physical attractiveness were found guilty by only 57%. The sentence terms for a guilty verdict differed from 10 years of imprisonment for the assailant higher in physical attractiveness to 14 years for the assailant of lower physical attractiveness.

The victim's physical attractiveness carries implications for punishment of her assailant. Three hundred subjects were used in an experiment to probe the influence of a rape victim's physical attractiveness (Thornton, 1977). The subjects were placed in a jury simulation in which the hypothetical case presented a rape victim of either high or low physical attractiveness. The results did not indicate significant main effects for perceptions of the victim. In other words, perceived credibility of the victim and perceived responsibility of the victim for provoking the rape did not differ as her physical attractiveness differed. The assailant's punishment did vary as the victim's physical attractiveness varied. The assailant was given a significantly longer punishment when the victim was high in physical attractiveness as compared to low.

Physical attractiveness affects perception of the rape victim after her incident (Calhoun, Selby, Cann, & Keller, 1978). A hypothetical rape case was presented to 45 female and 28 male subjects. The variables of interest were the physical attractiveness of the victim and the sex of the subject. Both independent variables yielded significant main effects but no interactions. Responsibility for the rape was more likely to be attributed to the victim by the male subjects than by the female subjects. After the incident, judges of both sexes expressed greater social acceptance for the victim of higher rather than lower physical attractiveness. Despite the greater social acceptance, the victim of higher physical attractiveness was perceived as being more likely to provoke the rape than her counterpart, and this may hold implications for conviction or acquittal of a defendant.

Rape victims may represent a unique niche among crime victims. Victims of higher physical attractiveness were hypothesized to pose a disadvantage for some crimes (Seligman, Brickman & Koulack, 1977). The experiment to test this hypothesis used six experimental treatments with 48 male and 48 female subjects. The independent variables were low or high physical attractiveness, and the type of crime was either rape, mugging, or robbery.

The subjects completed a questionnaire after reading a criminal case. The case given each subject involved one of the possible six experimental conditions. Contrary to the hypothesis, victim's physical attractiveness yielded two significant effects for the crime of rape but not for robbery or burglary: the victims of higher physical attractiveness were seen as more likely candidates to be raped, and the victims of lower physical attractiveness were perceived as more likely to provoke their own rape.

Verdict

It is not unanimous, but the verdict has to be in favor of the physical attractiveness phenomena. The evidence documents that physical attractiveness is a powerful and complex factor within the legal process. Research data from examinations of the defendant's physical attractiveness reveal overwhelming evidence in favor of higher physical attractiveness. General patterns of preferential juridic judgment appear, initially, to be disrupted by rape crimes. However, this complication is actually caused by reassigning the physical attractiveness focus from the defendant to the victim.

An exception to the general relationship between physical attractiveness and legal decisions can also be cited in an area unrelated to crimes of rape. An early study reported that jurors may overcompensate for feared prejudice against defendants of lower physical attractiveness (Friend & Vinson, 1974). In an attempt not to exhibit prejudice, the jurors may resort to reverse prejudice. This reverse discrimination is the explanation that Friend and Vinson gave for their data which disclosed that mean sentences of 5.48 years were conferred on defendants of low physical attractiveness, whereas those of higher physical attractiveness were given mean sentences of 8.40 years.

The conclusion must be that physical attractiveness phenomena represent a variable that is not neutral. Rather, it is a variable likely to be of significant power and of disturbing proportions within our legal system. Despite a few minor exceptions, the defendants of higher physical attractiveness are treated more favorably by potential jurors than are those defendants of lower physical attractiveness. Furthermore, preferential treatments are corroborated by observational data from actual defendants subjected to the consequences of actual legal decisions.

HELPING BEHAVIOR

Helping behavior represents a serious and important dimension of human life. The need for help is an activity which cannot be predicted and which can touch any person's life at any time. The dynamics of helping behavior consist of two parties: the help seekers and the help providers. To be consistent with this division, the physical attractiveness research presented in this section is divided accordingly. To accomplish this separation is difficult because the two entities are interdependent.

Seekers

Regardless of whether the individual is in control of his or her negative circumstance, the differences due to physical attractiveness are the same. In other words, if the predicament is in the form of committing a crime, or if the unfavorable predicament is simply bad luck over which the person has no control, the physical attractiveness of the person will influence the treatment by others. Even when those low in physical attractiveness experience some sort of unfortunate predicament over which they have no control, they receive less sympathy and less help than do those higher in physical attractiveness (Shaw, 1972). Likewise, for those in need of help, those higher in physical attractiveness receive more help, whereas those lower in physical attractiveness receive less. For example, in the same situation, the person of high physical attractiveness may recieve actual physical help as opposed to the person of low physical attractiveness who may, at most, receive verbal assistance for the same need (Moss & Page, 1972).

Bystanders react differently when the emergency involves a person low as opposed to high in physical attractiveness (Piliavin, Piliavin, & Rodin, 1975). A field experiment involved New York subway passengers ranging from 6 to 72 years of age. Manipulations were the stimulus person's physical attractiveness and the personal costs to the helper. Procedure was for a male stimulus person to fall in a subway car, either in the middle of a run (i.e., low helper cost) or at the end (i.e., high helper cost). Helping and speed of helping were dependent variables measured for each of the 166 trials spread over many time periods. Placement of the emergency did not affect results; however, the conditions with higher physical attractiveness produced greater and faster help.

Self-Disclosure

Helping behavior received by a stimulus person interacts between the person's physical attractiveness and the person's level of self-disclosure. A field experiment with 216 male subjects used a female stimulus person to ask directions (Harrell, 1978). The stimulus person's physical attractiveness was manipulated by varying facial characteristics such as hair and cosmetics, and body characteristics such as clothing. The results reported more time was spent helping the stimulus person of higher physical attractiveness than the stimulus person of lower physical attractiveness. No main effects for self-disclosure were indicated, but an interaction occurred. The greatest amount of help (i.e., giving directions) was given by subjects to the physically attractive stimulus person who self-disclosed (i.e., gave name as opposed to not).

Wilson (1978) also reported the least help was offered to stimulus persons of lower physical attractiveness who self-disclosed. In addition to manipulating self-disclosure, Wilson used two different tasks. A female stimulus person of either high or low physical attractiveness approached male subjects for help. One task asked 30 subjects for directions, and the other task asked 40 subjects to mail a letter. Regardless of the task, significantly more help was reported when the stimulus person was of higher physical attractiveness and self-disclosed.

A later study expands the methodology of earlier work (Kleinke & Kahn, 1980). Five experiments with a total of 540 subjects employed a variety of experimental treatments. These treatments included male and female stimulus persons who were either of low or high physical attractiveness, several topics for potential self-disclosure, and three magnitudes of self-disclosure. For self-disclosing conditions, females of highest magnitudes were more favorably evaluated than those of low or moderate magnitudes, especially when the topic dealt with sexual attitudes or parental suicide. When the topic dealt with aggressive feelings of competitiveness, the females of highest self-disclosure were less preferred than those females of moderate self-disclosure. For the males the results were quite different. Those males least preferred exhibited high self-disclosure. Regardless of sex, the general conclusion was that self-disclosures by persons of low physical attractiveness were evaluated less favorably than self-disclosures by persons of high physical attractiveness.

Conduct

The helping behavior of both males and females appears equally affected by physical attractiveness. Forty subjects (20 males and 20 females) participated in a study on interpersonal attraction and help volunteering behavior (Mims, Hartnett, & Nay, 1975). The research purpose was disguised by asking subjects to evaluate participants in a videotaped debate. The debaters were either low or high in physical attractiveness and displayed behavior described as either nice or obnoxious. After viewing the videotape, the female stimulus persons of either high or low physical attractiveness asked the audience for volunteers to help with a task. The stimulus female persons of higher physical attractiveness were able to get volunteers more readily than their counterparts, regardless of the person's conduct or subject's sex.

Detached

Helping behavior is influenced even when no personal contact is made. Without even meeting or seeing the person, male stimulus persons of high physical attractiveness received more help (Benson, Karabenick, & Lerner, 1975). In this study, the male stimulus persons of higher physical attractiveness received more help than their counterparts of lower physical attractiveness. This pattern of help was the same regardless of the subjects' sex. The procedure employed to collect these data centered on a stamped letter left in a telephone booth. Accompanying the "forgotten" or "lost" letter was a message that stated an urgency for its delivery. Also contained in the letter was an application and a photograph of the applicant. The data showed that when the application letter contained a photograph of a person of higher physical attractiveness the letter was more likely to be mailed by the finder.

Moving from total detachment to at least distant vision, a female stimulus person was placed in a distress situation (Athanasiou & Greene, 1973). The research involved placing a lady in a stalled car on a highway. By manipulating the appearance of a single stimulus person, the same person was used in both conditions of low and high physical attractiveness. Initial contact was limited to a brief distant glimpse as the subjects traveled past at highway speeds. Females in the high physical attractiveness condition resulted in more male motorists stopping and offering help than the lady in the condition of low physical attractiveness. The outcome was probably predictable, but that does not make it any less morally disconcerting.

Severity

Severity of the need or emergency interacts with the help seeker's physical attractiveness (West & Brown, 1975). A field experiment design involved 60 male subjects who were approached for help as they walked past a building. The person seeking help was female of either low or high physical attractiveness, and who appeared in either a low or high need of help. Need of help was manipulated by the severity of the emergency. In this case the person claimed she had been bitten by a rat. As she spoke, she visually displayed her hand wrapped in either a clean handkerchief or a bloodstained handkerchief. Help was defined in terms of amounts of money donated. The severity manipulation resulted in more help for the high emergency condition (i.e., bloodstained handkerchief) than in the low emergency condition. An interaction resulted between manipulations of physical attractiveness and level of severity. Help was not affected by physical attractiveness in the conditions of low severity emergency.

However, in the high severity of emergency condition the physical attractiveness of the stimulus person did significantly affect helping behavior. When the stimulus person was high in physical attractiveness, the money donated was greater than when the stimulus person was low in physical attractiveness.

Providers

The previous section reported research related to how physical attractiveness affects the public's offer to help. Turning that situation around, one study investigated the question of how the physical attractiveness of helpers influences those seeking help. In other words, does a helper's physical attractiveness enhance or inhibit contact by those needing assistance?

Two competing positions are relevant to answering the question of helper's physical attractiveness. One, if physical attractiveness phenomena apply in this situation, the person in need of help may ask the physically attractive person first. This action is predicted because higher physical attractiveness apparently represents greater value, kindness, and knowledge than does lower physical attractiveness. The second position is that the person (helper) of lower physical attractiveness is expected to be approached first. This action is proposed because the physically attractive person is likely to represent greater value, which may imply a greater social distance between the average help seeker and help provider. Therefore, the seeker may possess a feeling of probable rejection when asking for help from the physically attractive person.

Physical attractiveness is a relevant variable for both help seekers and help providers. Apparently, the physical attractiveness of a help provider has an impact on the help seeker (Stokes & Bickman, 1974). To test the effect of physical attractiveness of a help provider, an experiment was designed with 80 subjects and two stimulus persons of either high or low physical attractiveness.

Among the reported results a pattern was displayed by three relevant findings. First, less help was sought from providers of high physical attractiveness as compared to low. Second, fewer subjects approached providers of higher physical attractiveness. Third, subjects communicated quicker, and with less hesitancy, with the help providers of lower physical attractiveness as compared to their counterparts. Possible explanation of these differences was suggested by the subjects (i.e., help seekers) who reported feeling greater uneasiness and more uncomfortableness when in the presence of the help providers of higher physical attractiveness. The authors concluded that, "While a 'what is beautiful is good' stereotype may in fact exist, it also appears that under certain circumstances 'what is beautiful is unapproachable' may also be correct" (Stokes & Bickman, 1974, p. 292).

Professionals

Helping behavior is not restricted to chance occurrences. Its dynamics embody accidental, unorganized assistance, as well as planned, structured interaction. The former classification pertains to help seekers and help providers in an unplanned, informal milieu. The latter classification contains the same characters but in a formal setting with professional help providers.

Research examining the relationship between physical attractiveness and professional helping behavior is a serious topic that has not received extensive attention. The efforts center on the role of physical attractiveness within the healing professions. Three divisions or subtopics make up these endeavors. First, the greatest amount of attention is directed at perceptions about professional psychological helpers who vary in physical attractiveness. Second, a comparable amount of effort reverses the direction to observe professional psychological helpers with regard to help seekers who vary in physical attractiveness. Third, a small amount of research examines physicians who serve patients of lower and higher physical attractiveness.

Psychological Help Providers

Evidence supports the physical attractiveness phenomena for providers of psychological help, but it is not unanimous. The conflicting data consist of two studies that do not exactly represent psychotherapy. One study asked 64 high school counselors to predict eventual education and occupation of students (Mercado & Atkinson, 1982). Using photographs and customary school profile information, no significant differences were displayed for students of lower and higher physical attractiveness. The other study assessed interpersonal attraction by female undergraduates who played the role of a counselor (Lewis, Davis, Walker, & Jennings, 1981). Within this situation, no significant differences were exhibited for clients of lower and higher physical attractiveness.

Mental Health Practitioners. Practicing mental health professionals are not immune to the physical attractiveness phenomena. They are shown to select patients of higher physical attractiveness for intensive individual therapy, whereas patients of lower physical attractiveness are selected for group psychotherapy (Bringmann & Abston, 1981). Variation of prognoses may explain these selection decisions. However, prognosis is also dependent on physical attractiveness (Barocas & Vance, 1974). A field study observed 15 counselors (11 males and 4 females) working with 155 clients (75 males and 80 females) who came to a counseling center for personal problems. Prognosis was unrelated to either sex of the counselor or the client. But both prognosis and interview performance were significantly correlated with retrospective ratings of physical attractiveness by the counselors.

Origins. The impact of physical attractiveness may originate with variables underlying prognosis and subsequent treatment. Initial perceptions offer explanation for the apparent association between a help seeker's physical attractiveness and the actions taken by the providers of psychological help. Schwartz and Abramowitz (1978) reported that clients lower in physical attractiveness are perceived as more likely to prematurely terminate therapy than their counterparts of higher physical attractiveness. Their research involved 32 male graduate students who were trainees in clinical and counseling psychology. Each subject was queried after viewing a 4.5 minute excerpt from a videotape of a simulated intake session.

Perceptions of self-concept and liking for the client also provide possible origins. Graduate students (13 males and 3 females) in clinical psychology rated the self-concept of participants in videotaped interviews (Hobfoll & Penner, 1978). The participants (i.e., stimulus persons) were male and female, whose physical attractiveness was rated earlier by independent judges. The primary finding was that both male and female stimulus persons of higher physical attractiveness were perceived as possessing more healthy self-concepts than their counterparts. Sharf and Bishop (1979) examined intake counselors in their natural environment. Among the variables investigated was the relationship between the counselors' liking of a client and the client's physical attractiveness. Data were based on 507 clients (332 females and 175 males) who received help at a university counseling center. The relevant finding was that these intake counselors expressed greater liking for those clients who were higher in physical attractiveness.

Psychological Help Seekers

People who seek psychological help are influenced by the helper's physical attractiveness. The perceived effectiveness is determined by expected factors such as technical skills, and by factors such as attire (Kerr & Dell, 1976) and physical attractiveness (Zlotlow & Allen, 1981). Vargas and Borkowski (1982) used 80 subjects to role-play clients with social skill problems. Each subject viewed three videotaped counseling sessions involving a male client and female counselor. Regardless of the skill displayed by the counselor, perceived effectiveness was positively associated with her physical attractiveness.

Dominance. Significant physical attractiveness effects, independent of counselor's skill, are not unique (Vargas & Borkowski, 1982). Physical attractiveness is shown to supercede other variables such as the counselor's technique of employing profanity (Paradise, Cohl, & Zweig, 1980) and the counselor's sex (Cash & Kehr, 1978). Paradise *et al.* (1980) concluded that regardless of counselor sex or use of profanity, those higher in physical attractiveness were judged to possess more favorable professional and personal characteristics. These counselors were also perceived as more likely to achieve successful outcomes for a variety of counseling problems.

Cash and Kehr (1978) focused on possible sex effects. The counselors were males and females whose physical attractiveness was either low, high, or unknown. Ninety-six female subjects were exposed to simulated counseling interviews that were tape recorded. Dependent measures included (a) attributions about the counselor, (b) perceived facilitative conditions, (c) motivations for the counselor to continue the work, and (d) expectations about the counseling outcome. No difference due to counselor sex was evident in the multivariate analysis of the data. Consistently, less positive judgments were expressed for counselor traits and facilitative conditions when he or she was lower in physical attractiveness. Those counselors lower in physical attractiveness were also perceived as less committed to their work and less likely to achieve satisfactory outcomes.

Impressions. The superiority conferred to those of higher physical attractiveness may represent underlying premises. Data from 160 clients, who evaluated their counselors, revealed that those counselors of higher physical attractiveness were judged as more intelligent and to have greater empathy (Kunin & Rodin, 1982). Similarly, Cash and Salzbach (1978) reported that counselors of higher physical attractiveness were judged more positive on a host of behavioral dimensions, such as regard, empathy, and genuineness. Finally, Carter (1978) found that more positive outcomes are expected with counselors of higher physical attractiveness.

Two similar studies done by different authors in different years produced extremely similar results (Cash, Begley, McCown, & Weise, 1975; Lewis & Walsh, 1978). Both studies asked approximately 30 males and 30 females to view a videotape involving a counselor of either high or low physical attractiveness. Each study then asked the subjects to express (a) their impressions of the counselor on 12 personal traits, and (b) their expectations for the counselor's ability to deal with 15 personal problems.

Some interactions occurred, but the general results were consistent for both studies and for both sexes. Control groups who listened to the tapes, but were not aware of the physical attractiveness of the counselors, did not differ in their responses. The other subjects rated the counselor of higher physical attractiveness more positively on intelligence, friendliness, assertiveness, trustworthiness, competence, warmth, professionalism, assertiveness, interest, relaxation, and likability. Correspondingly, the counselors of higher physical attractiveness were expected to be more successful when dealing with specific personal problems, such as anxiety, shyness, career choice, sexual functioning, and inferiority.

Quasi Behavior. Considering all the impressions and expectations surrounding psychological helpers, a reasonable hypothesis pertaining to actual behavior must be in the same direction. Although the research is extremely scant, it does suggest that greater self-disclosures are made to individuals of higher physical attractiveness. These self-disclosures are made regardless of whether the persons are general acquaintances (Brundage, Derlega, & Cash, 1977) or professional counselors (Kunin & Rodin, 1982). Kunin and Rodin manipulated counselor's sex, physical attractiveness, and status, as well as the client's sex. Status was manipulated through variations in education and experience, and levels of low and high physical attractiveness were presented through photographs. Therapy clients were role played by 160 college students. Among the results were data revealing that subjects actually disclosed more when the counselor was higher as opposed to lower in physical attractiveness.

Medical Domain

Four limited probes of the medical field have suggested behavior relevant to the physical attractiveness phenomena. These restricted efforts have reported no significant physical attractiveness effects for either nurses (Gillmore & Hill, 1981) or first and second year medical students (Silvestro, 1982). However, significant effects are reported for both responses made by patients (Young, 1980) and behaviors displayed by physicians (Hooper, Comstock, Goodwin, & Goodwin, 1980).

Patients. Two experiments were conducted to determine the effect of a physician's physical attractiveness on self-disclosure by patients (Young, 1980). Ninety-eight subjects (49 males and 49 females) indicated their willingness to disclose and discuss personal symptoms with a specific male physician. Manipulation of low and high physical attractiveness was performed with photographs. Physical symptoms were manipulated to deal with the genital regions, mental illness, and nonprivate body parts. Notwithstanding the subjects' sex, the primary finding was a significantly greater willingness to discuss and to disclose problems with a physician of higher physical attractiveness, as opposed to lower.

Medical Doctors. The study of physician's behavior has dealt with patient appearance rather than the specific variable of physical attractiveness (Hooper *et al.*, 1980). Tentative generalizations may be permissible because overall appearance is probably a surrogate measure of physical attractiveness. All observations regarding appearance, as well as age, ethnicity, and sex, were performed by two trained persons over a 3-month period. To approximate an unobtrusive approach, data were collected at a (teaching) clinic with a one-way window that permitted scrutiny of typical patient–physician interactions. Although the physicians were aware of the study, attempts were made to record normal behaviors.

Treatment based on physical attractiveness was statistically significant. The authors stated that "ratings of physician behaviors, made by a trained observer, varied with the sex, age, appearance, and ethnicity of the patient" (p. 11) and that each variable "acted independently in influencing physician behavior" (p. 12). Specifically, all ratings of the physician's behavior improved as the patient's physical attractiveness increased. These ratings included interviewing, nonverbal attention, courtesy, information giving, empathy, physician initiated interruptions, and interaction time. However, only four were statistically significant: (a) interviewing, (b) physician initiated interruptions, (c) nonverbal attention, and (d) courtesy.

Physical attractiveness, or at least physical appearance, was shown to influence a medical doctor's interactions with patients. This study documented the impact by identifying patient characteristics which have a measurable influence on the behavior of medical doctors. Such an impact is typically neglected (and refuted), even though psychiatrists have long recognized that certain patient characteristics can trigger unconscious behaviors in a physician (Freud, 1959). The importance of patient physical attractiveness is implied by the authors who concluded that "obvious though this may seem, medicine has managed to ignore, almost entirely, the fact that patient characteristics influence physician behavior" (p. 15).

CONCLUSION

Interpersonal realities represent the most well-developed segment of the physical attractiveness research. However, important information still remains to be discovered. Overall, additional categorical headings are necessary to document the extent of physical attractiveness phenomena. Generally, each of the existing and future headings/categories present an opportunity to also test interactions. For example, do some factors (e.g., age and occupation) interact with the physical attractiveness phenomena identified in this chapter? Are expectations and assumptions situational? How does a person's actual intelligence or interpersonal skills interact with his or her physical attractiveness? More specific questions are also unanswered. For example, what are the characteristics of teachers, clergy, attorneys, governmental policy makers, and the like? Who are most and least affected by their clientele's physical attractiveness? With regard to crime and courts, there is virtually a void of research addressing the reality of legal dynamics. An interesting query here may be the relationship between physical attractiveness and those persons now on death row. The list of questions is unlimited, so despite the extensive progress reported in this chapter, much more work remains.

In summary, this chapter has verified the three fundamentals indicated in the first chapter. Specifically, the fact that physical attractiveness phenomena are subtle, powerful, and pervasive. Despite failure to acknowledge the impact, objective research results verify that there is scarcely a major interpersonal activity that resists the pervasive coercion of this variable. This chapter provides a comprehensive documentation of physical attractiveness research that addresses human involvements which are not strictly mutual interchanges. The next chapter expands these involvements by discussing the reality of physical attractiveness within reciprocal interactions. Regardless of the thoroughness reflected in these two chapters, the addressed topics are probably a small portion of likely avenues to be traveled in the future.

Chapter 4

Interpersonal Reciprocations

Contemporary life revolves around mutual interchanges. Three of the most common interactions basic to everyone's life are romantic attraction, nonintimate friendship, and vocational employment. These three topics are presented together in one chapter because of a shared similarity in that each involves reciprocal interactions commonly experienced in every person's life.

The interpersonal realities of the previous chapter form the foundation for the physical attractiveness research in this chapter. Much of the material in these two chapters may be viewed as interdependent. Consequently, there are problems of categorization between and within the chapters. Even though the divisions in this chapter may be questioned, they are appropriate because each of the three major topics may be viewed as representing a different location on a spectrum of interpersonal reciprocations. Germane to everyone's life is the first topic that deals with the physical attractiveness phenomena as they pertain to romantic attraction. Within romantic attraction, the entire sequence from romantic preferences to dating and to mating is presented. Being that not all interpersonal interchanges are romantically orientated, the second section covers nonintimate friendships. The last topic is a natural complement to the first two because it represents one of the three most significant activities in life. Also, the employment presentation is a logical extension of nonintimate liking because employment decisions before and during employment are influenced by feelings of liking.

ROMANTIC ATTRACTION

Romantic attraction is important because it normally precedes eventual mating, and because it is relevant for both the human race, in general, and for individuals, in particular. The universal interest of romantic attraction underscores the value of efforts to identify those variables which influence such interactions. Research regarding the attraction that ultimately leads to a committed relationship has come from a host of disciplines. Probably an accurate synopsis is that romantic attraction is complex and continues to elude thorough understanding. Without diminishing the complexity of romantic attraction and the subsequent bonding of individuals, one important variable is the physical attractiveness of the individuals.

Research on the role that physical attractiveness plays within romantic attraction can be categorized by three sequential stages that correspond with the natural progression involving (1) the time prior to and including the first meeting, (2) a period of dating, and (3) a period of marriage or some equivalent committed relationship. The role of physical attractiveness would seem to decline as the romantic process evolves. However, even if so, the importance of physical attractiveness could not be minimized because without early encounters the latter would never occur. Regardless of such logical debate, the discussion of marriage and physical attractiveness presents the actual research findings, which pertain to romantic attraction, as extending well beyond the point of committed bonding. Finally, after each of the above three stages are discussed, an additional discussion disregards the sequential stages by summarizing specific sex differences demonstrated throughout the duration of romantic attraction.

Logically, the effects of physical attractiveness on interpersonal attraction may be expected to diminish over the duration of the relationship. But the research findings do not support this notion of subsiding effects and reveal instead enduring effects of surprising strength. Physical attractiveness remains a major determinant of mutual romantic attraction regardless of the elapse of time, the number of meetings, and even competing negative information.

An extreme situation is appropriate to illustrate the importance that physical attractiveness has for romantic attraction. For it is at the extreme that physical attractiveness appears to supercede all other aspects of a romantic attraction. The example is an actual case taken from the files of psychotherapy. In this case, the male patient describes his female friend as a chronic alcoholic, lesbian, psychotic, and a castrating bitch with whom he continues to maintain a "romantic relationship" because of her high physical attractiveness (Robertiello, 1976). Many dynamics may be occurring here, but one fact is that continuance of the relationship has served more than intrapersonal companionship needs. That is, both males and females who associate with partners of higher physical attractiveness are accorded other interpersonal compliments. These persons are regularly attributed more positive traits, such as greater confidence, sociableness, and likability (Sigall & Landy, 1973; Strune & Watts, 1977). Before initiating a relationship, the individuals must first encounter one another, yet, even at this premeeting stage, the physical attractiveness variable exerts its influence.

Prior to Meeting

Because there must always be a first encounter for later encounters to follow, the importance of the initial encounter cannot be overemphasized. Components which determine the first encounter then become important by their own power to increase and decrease the probability of such meetings. The physical attractiveness phenomena suggest that physical attractiveness may be a personal characteristic that is operating even before the first meeting occurs.

Preferences

The research shows a definite physical attractiveness predisposition before the initial meeting ever takes place. In one study with manipulations of physical attractiveness, attitude similarity, intelligence, and population, 48 males were asked to indicate their desire to date a stimulus female person (H. K. Black, 1974). The male subjects' desire to be both friends and/or to date was substantially greater for the female higher in physical attractiveness as compared to her counterpart. In another study, male subjects again exhibited a significantly greater likelihood of asking a female for a date when she was of higher physical attractiveness versus lower (Pellegrini, Hicks, & Meyers-Winton, 1979). A third study involved the rating of a potential dating partner by 60 male and 60 female subjects (Stretch & Figley, 1980). Manipulation of the stimulus person's physical attractiveness and social status were accomplished through use of a bogus tape recording and snapshot. Subjects' responses revealed both a more favorable personality and a significantly greater desire to date the potential partner of higher physical attractiveness.

Idealistic desires to date may differ from intentions to date. When placed in a somewhat more realistic situation, males may consider their likelihood of acceptance based on the target female's physical attractiveness (Huston, 1973). Seventy-two males were involved in an experiment with three levels of physical attractiveness and two levels of acceptance or rejection by the potential date. The males selected the more physically attractive female when assured of acceptance, but not otherwise. When asked about the likelihood of female acceptance, the males estimated those females of higher physical attractiveness would be less likely to accept them as a date. Furthermore, the males' self-ratings of their physical attractiveness related to their estimates of their chances of acceptance for a date.

The results of female subjects mirror those of male subjects. A study with 138 female subjects found that self-ratings of physical attractiveness were negatively related to perceived desirability of a potential male date (Hagiwara, 1975). In other words, the perceived desirability of a male date decreased as the self-ratings of the females physical attractiveness increased. The perceived likelihood that females will be accepted by males is similar to the findings with male subjects (Shanteau & Nagy, 1979). Three experiments concluded that females use both physical attractiveness and probability of acceptance in indicating their desire to seek a date with a male target person. If only physical attractiveness is provided, females indicate significantly higher desire to potentially date the male who is higher in physical attractiveness versus lower.

Still, in the category of considerations before the first meeting, similar results are reported for both male and female subjects by Nida and Williams (1977). This study used 148 females and 168 males as subjects in an experiment to assess the role of physical attractiveness within romantic attraction. By asking preferences for marital partners, the research focused on the time period before any meetings occurred. Both male and female subjects preferred the physically attractive significantly more than the counterpart of lower physical attractiveness for a marriage partner.

To emphasize the importance of physical attractiveness in the desirability of dating partners, race was introduced as a rival characteristic (Allen, 1976). An attempt was made to explore if physical attractiveness or if race had a greater impact on dating choices made by white subjects. The subjects were white university students (43 males and 35 females) and the stimulus persons were either black or white with either high or low physical attractiveness. Results, in at least this instance, were that physical attractiveness rivaled race in determining dating desirability. Although none of the subjects was willing to actually accept a date, the female subjects gave race more weight than physical attractiveness, but the male subjects gave physical attractiveness more weight than race.

Behaviors

Perceptions and desires consistently determine the role of physical attractiveness before the first meeting. The desires set the stage and the actions need to be confirmed. Although actions and intentions are often different, they appear the same before the initial meetings within romantic attraction. The behaviors of individuals are similar to the preferences identified above (Crouse & Mehrabian, 1977). Forty male and 40 female subjects were used to study the actual behavior of individuals in the presence of stimulus persons who varied in physical attractiveness. Interactions took place for 5 minutes in a waiting room. During this time, the stimulus persons behaved in a standardized manner with all conversations recorded and later analyzed. The authors concluded that even though physical attractiveness did not affect affiliative behavior in this situation, the stimulus persons of higher physical attractiveness were the most preferred for potential dates and marriage partners.

Explanations

In addition to the general physical attractiveness stereotype, some research offers specific explanation for romantic attraction preference. One hundred male and female subjects viewed a videotape of an interaction between a couple described as a boyfriend and a girlfriend (Meiners & Sheposh, 1977). The experimental treatments were variations of the physical attractiveness and intelligence of the female partner. The dependent variable was evaluation of the male partner. Although intelligence manipulations affected a few select perceived attributes of the male, physical attractiveness significantly affected each of the ten dependent measures. If mere association of a romantic partner affects perceptions of the individuals, these perceptions are likely to influence the role that physical attractiveness seems to play even before romantic interactions occur.

Another explanation for the physical attractiveness preference pertains to rewards. Mathes and Edwards (1978) investigated whether the findings that women of higher physical attractiveness receive greater rewards from men than the reverse, can be generalized to men receiving rewards from women. The researchers used 36 male and 36 female subjects in opposite-sex and same-sex social exchanges. The results showed that men and women of higher physical attractiveness received greater rewards in social exchanges than their counterparts of lower physical attractiveness. However, this effect occurred only within opposite-sex as opposed to same-sex exchanges. The explanation offered for this discrepancy deals with rewards related to erotic pleasure. The authors went on to test and conclude that the reason for these greater social awards was that the physical attractiveness of the other person provided greater erotic pleasures.

The conclusion must be that even before the first meeting, physical attractiveness plays a role within romantic attraction. Furthermore, this role is consistent with the advantageous and disadvantageous dynamics expressed in the physical attractiveness phenomena. Expectations and preferences are possessed, which, in turn, influence the desire to selectively meet only certain individuals within the context of potential romantic attraction. Explanation of this finding may lie with the general physical attractiveness stereotype or with a theory of social reward exchanges. The selectivity may also reflect an interdependency between physical attractiveness and self-confidence. For example, individuals whose self-ratings of physical attractiveness are higher tend to view the entire romantic interaction more positively, and more attainable than their counterparts of lower physical attractiveness (Pellegrini, Hicks, & Meyers-Winton, 1980).

Dating Stage

The early physical attractiveness research, as related to romantic attraction, focused on the dynamics which can be categorized as the dating stage. This research deals with situations that are beyond expectations and preferences revealed in feelings held prior to the first meeting. This section picks up from the point where the couple has at least met. Research of the dating stage, therefore, deals with the role of physical attractiveness once the individuals have spent some time interacting.

Time Variations

The first study to test the attraction effect of physical attractiveness used couples paired at a computer dance (Walster et al., 1966). After a period of several hours, the subjects filled out comprehensive questionnaires. Regardless of the subjects own physical attractiveness, the most important determinant of liking the partner was the partner's physical attractiveness. A similar study, using a computer dating service, was performed several years later (Curran, 1973; Curran & Lippold, 1975). Based on the results of 150 subjects the study reported that the most significant predictor of romantic attraction was the individual's rating of the partner's physical attractiveness. This early identification of a relationship between physical attractiveness and dating is supported by other research documenting the importance of physical attractiveness in dating and marriage (e.g., Berscheid et al., 1971; Brislin & Lewis, 1968; Byrne, Ervin & Lamberth, 1970; Curran, 1973; Huston, 1973; Murstein, 1972; Shepherd & Ellis, 1972), in sensations of love (Critelli, 1975; Peplau, 1976), and in sex appeal (Cavior, Jacobs & Jacobs, 1974).

Variations of interaction durations have not produced variations in results. These interactions have ranged from hours to months. At the shorter extreme are subjects (61 males and 61 females) who became acquainted in literally a few minutes (Bailey & Schreiber 1981). The focus was on how the acquaintance's rating of physical attractiveness would affect desire to date the partner after this interaction exercise. Each subject was asked to rate his or her own physical attractiveness and that of their partner, and to estimate how their partner would rate the subject's own physical attractiveness. Subjects were later given bogus scores about the partner's rating of the subject's physical attractiveness. The subjects were then asked to indicate their liking and desire to date the other person. The partners who were liked most and desired most were those who either supported or accentuated the subjects own self-rating of their physical attractiveness.

The results were the same immediately after interaction as they were a month later. In a unique research design, male subjects were paired with female confederates who were either high or low in physical attractiveness (Kleck & Rubenstein, 1975) After an initial brief interaction, the individuals separated from 2 to 4 weeks. After these 2 to 4 weeks, the subjects were questioned with regard to themselves and their partners. The higher the physical attractiveness of the partner, the more the subjects reported that they thought about her in the interim, the more they continued to feel they liked her, and the more they tended to remember details about her appearance.

The early finding by Walster *et al.* (1966) was extended 10 years later by varying the number of interactions (Mathes, 1975). This study involved a computer date with one encounter. After this one encounter, the only reliable predictor of dating desirability was the partners perceived physical attractiveness. Mathes questioned if the personality information that surfaces after the first encounter would not assume a dominant role in the romantic attraction, that is, nonvisual information would cancel or override the physical attractiveness effect experienced in the initial encounter. Twenty-six couples were involved in a series of five encounters. Based on data from these couples, Mathes concluded that even though personality plays a role, the physical attractiveness variable has a continuing and undiminishing effect on romantic attraction.

Actual Experience

In addition to experimental data, research has probed natural dating relationships through unobtrusive techniques. These various surveylike designs identified that differences in physical attractiveness correspond to differences in dating practices and experiences. Analysis of survey data revealed a positive correlation ($r = .61$) between the physical attractiveness of females and their dating experience during the past year (Berscheid *et al.*, 1971). Not focusing on a single year, women of higher physical attractiveness were found to date more, have more friends, be in love more, and have more sexual experiences than women of average or lesser physical attractiveness (Kaats & Davis, 1970).

These actual relationships are not limited to females, but are replicated in research using both sexes. Regardless of sex, physical attractiveness is correlated with those who date with low frequency and those who date with high frequency (Glasgow & Arkowitz, 1975). Physical attractiveness is also positively correlated with experiences and sexual experiences for both males and females (Curran & Lippold, 1975). Using data from 91 middle-class adolescents involved in a longitudinal study on sexual attitudes, it was found that those lower in physical attractiveness were less likely to have a steady dating partner than their counterparts of higher physical attractiveness (Chess, Thomas, & Cameron, 1976).

Dating Progression

While in a dating relationship, the physical attractiveness of the partners may affect the behavior of each individual. Measures of physical attractiveness, romantic love, and dominance were obtained from 123 dating couples (Critelli & Waid, 1980). The relative differences in physical attractiveness appeared to produce significant effects within the relationship of individual couples. The person who considered the other to be more physically attractive tended to have greater love for that partner. This person also indicated greater submission to a partner who was relatively higher in physical attractiveness as opposed to lower.

Actual differences yield similar effects. Instead of dealing with the perceptions of partners, other research has considered the impact of actual discrepancies of physical attractiveness within couples. Feingold (1982a) reported that the physical attractiveness of couples who begin their romantic relationship shortly after meeting tend to have discrepancies of smaller magnitude. Those romantic relationships which begin slower after meeting tend to have greater discrepancy of physical attractiveness between the partners. These findings were based on a sample of 49 couples who were described as either "dating steady" or "in love." The fast pace was defined as those couples whose romances began within 3 months of meeting. The slower pace was defined as those couples whose romances began after knowing each other for at least 8 months before beginning to date.

Progression of romantic relationship, or lack thereof, may be determined by the physical attractiveness of the partners. Interpersonal dating problems associated with physical attractiveness range from jealousy to eventual breakups. Physical attractiveness of individual partners was assessed for 123 couples (White, 1980). These couples were described in various stages of their relationship: (a) casually dating, (b) seriously dating, (c) cohabiting, or (d) engaged to be married. For the first two stages of casually and seriously dating, the partner with relatively higher physical attractiveness tended to have more friends of the opposite sex. Those partners of higher physical attractiveness also tended to worry less about their partner's potential involvement with another person. This worry is consistent with a different study that examined the potential relationship between jealousy and physical attractiveness (Shettel-Neuber, Bryson & Young, 1978). A positive correlation was reported between expressed jealousy and the physical attractiveness of a third person tangently associated with an existing relationship.

Jealousness may be justified because physical attractiveness plays a surprisingly strong role in determining commitment during dating (Kramer, 1978). Sixty-one dating couples were asked questions about their (a) commitment to their partners, (b) amount of time spent with the partner, (c) amount of time spent arguing, (d) length of their relationship, (e) partner's physical attractiveness, and (f) desire to maintain the relationship with their partner. The most important factor for the commitment level was amount of time spent together. The second most important factor in commitment level was the perceived physical attractiveness of the partner.

Two studies suggest that physical attractiveness may play a direct role in the eventual breakup of romantic relationships. In White's (1980) research with 123 couples, a 9-month follow-up study was done with the first two groups, casually dating and seriously dating. This follow-up revealed that physical attractiveness was predictive of the dating progress. In another exposition, a 2-year longitudinal study examined the factors that predict breakups of romantic relationships that do not progress to eventual marriage (Hill, Rubin, & Peplau, 1976). The study focused on dating relationships among college students. It found that desire to breakup was seldom mutual and that the female partner was more likely to perceive premarital problems and also more likely to initiate the breakup than was the male partner. Among a number of factors identified, differences in the partners' physical attractiveness were recognized as a significant factor in contributing to relationships that ended.

Marriage

The physical attractiveness phenomena appear pervasive throughout romantic attraction. Their influences begin in the stage even prior to the first meeting, continue during the dating stage, and remain evident throughout marriage. The importance of physical attractiveness does not seem to diminish from the dating to the marriage stage. Weiszhaar (1978, p. 97) stated that "it can be concluded that physical attractiveness is important to the marriage relationship, at least for the first fifteen years.''

Marital Satisfaction

The role of physical attractiveness within marital satisfaction is exhibited across marriages. The role is the same regardless of the length of marriage or the ages of the couples. Based on his review of the research literature and the data from his University of Minnesota dissertation, Weiszhaar (1978) found that the accentuation of the partner's physical attractiveness is associated with marital satisfaction. He reported that

> results of this study support the hypothesis that individuals who accentuate the physical attractiveness of their spouse to a larger extent have greater marital satisfaction than those who accentuate the physical attractiveness of their spouse to a lesser extent. (p. 98)

An uncommon approach to examining the relationship between physical attractiveness and marriage satisfaction involved a scientifically controlled survey with readers of *Psychology Today* (Berscheid *et al.*, 1973). The subjects of this study were asked to complete a 109-item questionnaire about the body. Two thousand questionnaires were selected from a pool of over 62,000 respondents. The 2,000 questionnaires were randomly selected, but controlled for sex and age distributions that matched the national population distribution. Among the findings, marriages appeared less stable when the physical attractiveness of the partners was not similar and more stable when the partners represented similar levels of physical attractiveness.

To examine the breadth of the relationship between physical attractiveness and marital adjustment, couples described as middle-aged were selected as subjects (Murstein & Christy, 1976). The subjects were 22 middle-class couples who averaged 15.4 years of marriage. Measures of physical attractiveness were assessed by (a) judges, (b) self-ratings, and (c) spouse ratings. Marital adjustment was measured by the Locke-Wallace Marriage Adjustment Scale. The results were mixed but it was reasonable to conclude that physical attractiveness was an important aspect of marital adjustment in this study of middle-aged couples. Another finding was that the individuals comprising each couple were very similar (i.e., matched) in their physical attractiveness.

An extension beyond middle age involved the relationship between physical attractiveness and marital adjustment among older couples (Peterson & Miller, 1980). Subjects were 32 middle-class couples who ranged in age from 64 to 86 years old. A procedure, similar to that of Murstein and Christy (1976) was used to examine middle-aged couples.

The results indicated that couples were matched for physical attractiveness and that physical attractiveness correlated with marital adjustment among these elderly couples.

If public intimacy of married couples can be gleaned from marital adjustment, then a relationship between physical attractiveness and adjustment is indirectly supported (Harrell, 1979). Harrell analyzed public intimacy of married couples by using an unobtrusive observation research approach. Subjects were 558 married couples observed within a field setting. The results showed that the more physically attractive the couple, the more likely they were to exhibit intimacy between themselves in public.

Matching Hypothesis

An area of research suggested earlier deals with the physical attractiveness of the marriage partners relative to each other. The evidence seems conclusive that a significant similarity of physical attractiveness exists between partners within marriage, regardless of age or duration. Looking back at the dating stage, this similarity may appear inconsistent because men place more importance on the partner's physical attractiveness than do women. Idealistically, men do prefer the best-looking women over the less attractive women. However, the *matching* hypothesis (Berscheid & Walster, 1974) states that men expect a greater probability of rejection by women who are high in physical attractiveness, as opposed to women who are low in physical attractiveness. Consequently, according to the matching hypothesis, men prefer partners close to their own levels of physical attractiveness.

Research conducted in four singles bars investigated an *idealistic strategy* hypothesis which opposes the matching hypothesis (Glenwick, Jason, & Elman, 1978). Idealistic strategy predicts that more physically attractive women would receive more frequent approaches by men in a singles bar than would less physically attractive women. An alternative hypothesis, such as the matching hypothesis or the realistic strategy, was also investigated. The study observed a wide range of physical attractiveness levels and found that physical attractiveness is not significantly correlated with approaches—supporting the matching hypothesis (Glenwick *et al.*, 1978).

Lasting Potency

The value of physical attractiveness continues beyond the initial encounter of men and women. Dating and marriage partners apparently make their selection based on a matching or realistic strategy. Individual facial photographs of 36 marriage partners were prepared, and intermixed (Shepherd & Ellis, 1972). These photographs were later given to 40 subjects (20 males and 2 females), asking them to sort the individual photographs into 9 levels of physical attractiveness. The researchers found a positive correlation between the physical attractiveness of the husbands and wives.

Another study (Murstein, 1972) investigated individuals who were either going steady or engaged. Using a similar procedure, this study revealed similar results, in that those individuals who were seriously dating tended to be at the same level of physical attractiveness. The existence of this matching hypothesis of physical attractiveness, in serious dating and marriage, is well supported in the research literature (see Cavior & Boblett, 1972; Stroebe et al., 1971).

Similarity between the physical attractiveness of partners might be expected because personality similarity among marriage partners was identified as early as the 1930s (Schiller, 1932; Schooley, 1936). The best verification of a matching hypothesis for physical attractiveness is revealed in marriages, and especially in those of substantial duration. Support for this relationship is offered in a number of studies with a number of research designs. One study selected two dissimilar samples of married couples (Price & Vandenberg, 1979). One sample was defined as young, recently married, and between 19 and 31 years old. The other sample was older married couples, not recently married, and between 34 to 64 years old. Both samples were Americans of European ancestry, consisting of 55 couples from mainland United States and 72 couples from Hawaii. The data support the matching hypothesis, and document that it is stable within and across generations. The matching hypothesis of physical attractiveness between couples was reported for both middle-aged couples married an average of 15.4 years (Murstein & Christy, 1976) and for older couples aged 64 to 86 years old (Peterson & Miller, 1980).

Divorce

Physical attractiveness plays a role throughout dating and marriage up to the end in the case of couples that do not last. Research in this area deals with both extramarital affairs (Hartnett & Secord, 1983) and divorces (Brigham, 1980). Hartnett and Secord presented 128 subjects (64 males and 64 females) with one of four vignettes. Half of the time, the husband or wife was either low or high in physical attractiveness and was having an outside affair. Both independent variables of cheating and physical attractiveness produced significant perception effects, as well as inter-actions. The authors concluded, it appears that, when individuals have affairs, their physical attractiveness affects not only how they are perceived but also the perception of their spouses and the other parties to the affairs. (p. 310)

Brigham dealt directly with divorce. Two-page profiles of divorcing couples were presented to 279 subjects (161 females and 118 males). The profiles presented a marriage of 5 years, with no children, which was ending due either to incompatibility, adultery by the husband, or adultery by the wife. Perceptions were assessed for both during and after the marriage. In the marriage, the spouse of higher physical attractiveness was seen "as significantly more poised, interesting, sociable, independent, warm, exciting, and sexually warm than the unattractive spouse" (p. 371). Sex differences, specifically related to the wife, were that those of higher physical attractiveness were perceived as (a) having greater opportunity and temptation for extramarital affairs, (b) not as likely to divorce a second time, and (c) more vain than her counterpart of lower physical attractiveness. Results showed that an individual's physical attractiveness did not significantly influence either responsibility for the divorce or recommendations for subsequent financial settlement. However, postdivorce perceptions were significantly affected. The divorced spouse of higher physical attractiveness was seen as having an easier time finding a new spouse (especially for wives), and more likely to remarry regardless of it being the wife or the husband.

Sex Differences

There are definite sex differences within the relationship between physical attractiveness and romantic attraction. Females are more concerned with their own physical attractiveness than males are concerned with their own physical attractiveness (Wagman, 1967). However, males consider physical attractiveness of their partner to be more important than females consider it for their partner (Coombs & Kenkel, 1966). This greater emphasis that males place on a partner's physical attractiveness is consistent with other research indicating a higher correlation between dating popularity and physical attractiveness for females, but the lack of such a correlational relationship for males (Berscheid et al., 1971). Similarly, the Wall Street Journal concluded that in Japanese marriages, "the men are all looking for good-looking women and the women are all looking for men who can support them well" (Lehner, 1983, p. 1).

Research has directly addressed the sex differences with regard to the role that physical attractiveness plays in determining heterosexual attraction (Miller & Rivenbark, 1970). For their study, 177 males and 177 females were asked to judge the importance of physical attractiveness in interpersonal situations. The male subjects considered physical attractiveness to be significantly more important than the female subjects did.

The greater importance of physical attractiveness for females is reflected by the correspondingly greater emphasis in our society. This greater emphasis of feminine physical attractiveness, as opposed to masculine physical attractiveness, is apparent in the mass media, business organizations, and commercial products. Examples of commercial products are evident in advertising, mass media entertainment, and the appearance industries such as cosmetics, fashion, and clothes. Overall, physical attractiveness is more consequential for evaluation of females than it is for evaluation of males (Bar-Tal & Saxe, 1976a,b).

Dating Experience

Different values placed on physical attractiveness as a function of gender, generalize to the dating stage of romantic interactions. Berscheid *et al.* (1971) monitored the dating activity of college males and females during an entire year. For females a correlation of $r = .61$ was reported between physical attractiveness and dating experience, but for males this correlation was only $r = .25$.

A later study examined the stage, antecedent to actual meeting with intent to date (Krebs & Adinolfi, 1975). The focus here was on the relationship between physical attractiveness and social contact with the opposite sex dyads. The difference due to physical attractiveness varied similarly between males and females. Physical attractiveness and social contact with the opposite sex was correlated ($r = .45$) for females and was not significantly correlated ($r = .08$) for males. This study also revealed no significant differences between the dating popularity of males of higher and lower physical attractiveness. The authors concluded that males are able to compensate for low physical attractiveness in themselves. However, because physical attractiveness is a much greater factor in the appeal to the opposite sex for females, corresponding nonappearance compensations are not feasible.

Social Mobility

For females, a significant relationship exists between physical attractiveness and upward social mobility (Elder, 1969; Illsley, 1955; Taylor & Glenn, 1976; Udry, 1977). To arrive at this conclusion one study examined social rank of the husband in comparison to the woman's premarital social level (Elder, 1969). The more physically attractive the woman the more upward mobile she was, as measured by her husband's social class and her premarital social class. In addition, the likelihood of marriage to a man of higher social class was dependent on the woman's physical attractiveness, but independent of the woman's educational achievements.

It appears that the important assets for men are the person's status, wealth, and potential status, but for women, the important asset is their physical attractiveness. Intelligence for men is a major determinant of occupational mobility (Elder, 1968), but for women physical attractiveness is more important than intelligence (Elder, 1969). Also, the more a man's social status exceeds that of his wife's, the more likely his wife will be exceptionally high in physical attractiveness (Elder, 1969). Finally, Elder found that 20 years after graduation, a woman's physical attractiveness in high school is positively correlated with the status of the man she married.

The woman's role in society has changed dramatically, but the role of a woman's physical attractiveness has remained constant. In an update to the research of the late 1960s, the relationship between social mobility and physical attractiveness was again examined in the late 1970s (Udry, 1977). This later research included interviews with over 6,000 black and white women. These interviews focused on upward mobility through marriage, as a function of both education and/or physical attractiveness of the female. The survey data were controlled to allow for close comparison with earlier research. This updated study found that physical attractiveness, as well as education, is significantly related to attaining status through marriage, regardless whether the woman is black or white. The data indicated some interactions between the variables. For example, the physical attractiveness and mobility relationship for white women was strongest for those lower educated as opposed to higher educated. But this relationship for black women was stronger for the higher educated as compared to those of lower education.

Marital Satisfaction

Sex differences within marital relationships also differ with regard to the relationship between physical attractiveness and satisfaction with the marriage. Such a difference is probably expected because our culture certainly places greater emphasis on female as opposed to male physical attractiveness. Within the marriage domain, research reports a number of differences between marriage partners.

Bailey and Price (1978) collected information from couples they defined as married either long term (about 5 years) or short term (about 1 year). They reported that wives expressed concern that their husbands agree with the self-ratings of the wives physical attractiveness. Husbands, however, did not express a similar concern about their wives perceptions of the husbands self-ratings of physical attractiveness.

Similar inequities occur with regard to marital satisfaction. Murstein and Christy (1976) reported that marital adjustment is not equally correlated with a parity of physical attractiveness of the partners. For males, marital satisfaction was correlated with a perception that the partner was substantially higher in physical attractiveness than the husband, but females did not express a corresponding pattern. Similarly, an examination of elderly couples found that the husbands' marital adjustment was more highly correlated with a mate's physical attractiveness than it was for the wives' marital adjustment (Peterson & Miller, 1980).

These differences within marriage dyads seem to generalize to the ratings of the partner's physical attractiveness. Terry and Macklin (1977) reported that females exaggerate the similarity of their marriage partner's physical attractiveness. But the males minimize the similarity of their marriage partner's physical attractiveness by exaggerating her physical attractiveness.

NONINTIMATE LIKING

Interpersonal reciprocations are not limited to romantic interactions. In fact, the greater portion of all relationships are outside the romantic realm. These differences often translate into assumed values or relevance for physical attractiveness. In other words, physical attractiveness may logically be assumed as important to romantic attraction but of negligible value for nonromantic relationships. However, the reality is that the role of physical attractiveness, in determining nonromantic attraction, is no less prominent than in romantic attraction. Furthermore, these effects are reported for both same-sex and opposite-sex friendships.

The first published study reported a significant correlation between liking and physical attractiveness (Perrin, 1921). Much later a more stringent experimental design was used to investigate the effect on interpersonal attraction (Byrne et al., 1968). This experiment found that physical attractiveness was the most influential variable in determining nonintimate attraction between strangers. Likewise, after examining a host of physical and nonphysical characteristics, it was concluded that physical features "are the best predictors of the attraction response" (Lyman, Hatelid, & Macurdy, 1981). Many other studies have found the same positive relationship between physical attractiveness and interpersonal attraction (see Brown & Eng, 1970; Coombs & Kenkel, 1966; Korabik, 1981; Krebs & Adinolfi, 1975; McWhirter, 1969; Moss, 1969; Roff and Brody, 1953; Stroebe et al., 1971; Thornton & Linnstaedter, 1975, 1980).

Measures of weak liking may be equivalent to disliking. A conference paper used a continuum ranging from disliking to liking, rather than a continuum from weak to strong liking (S. D. Mahoney, 1978). This study involved 160 subjects (80 males and 80 females) with stimulus persons who were either high or low in physical attractiveness and who either exhibited behavior described as pleasant or unpleasant. After viewing a videotaped interview, the subjects were asked to indicate their liking or disliking for the stimulus persons. In this instance, an interaction occurred between physical attractiveness and type of behavior. When the behavior was unpleasant, the stimulus person was disliked in both conditions of physical attractiveness. But in the pleasant behavior condition, only the stimulus person of lower physical attractiveness was disliked, whereas the stimulus person of higher physical attractiveness was liked.

Interaction Variations

These positive effects of physical attractiveness on nonintimate liking are widely demonstrated. They include situations with (a) face-to-face interaction both inside and outside of the laboratory, (b) using photographs in a variety of circumstances, and (c) various lengths of exposure between the persons (Byrne et al., 1970). This relationship has proved consistent, beyond simple exposure to photographs, up to periods of prolonged interaction among participants within time frames of various lengths of exposure (e.g., Byrne & Clore, 1970).

The research regarding nonromantic interpersonal attraction has often dealt with initial encounters. Under these conditions, physical attractiveness is shown to play a significant role in liking of the person. But what are the effects of physical attractiveness when the people are no longer strangers? Again, the research shows that the effect of physical attractiveness persists even after person-to-person interactions occur. This persistence is not only important during the initial phases of interaction, but maintains its influence regardless of accumulated interaction time and additional information about the persons (Byrne & Clore, 1970; Kleck, Richardson, & Ronald, 1974; Levinger, 1972). One study found that friendship choices following two weeks of intense social interaction were strongly and positively related to the physical attractiveness of the individuals involved, who in this study were children (Kleck et al., 1974).

Other research focusing on the relationship between physical attractiveness and liking has varied the number of interactions instead of the length of a single interaction. Although interaction was not used, frequency of exposure was varied to be either 1, 2, 5, 10, or 25 times (Pheterson & Horai, 1976). The results showed that the greater the exposure frequency, the greater the magnitude of liking was expressed. The data also showed that the stimulus persons of higher physical attractiveness were liked better regardless of exposure frequency.

Personality

Research with personality and physical attractiveness has involved personality characteristics of both the subjects and stimulus persons. The focus of this section is on the assumed personality traits of the stimulus persons. However, significant interaction effects are revealed for personality characteristics pertaining to subjects. For example, both subjects who are higher sensation seekers (Horai, 1976) and who score higher on machismo measures (Touhey, 1979), as opposed to their counterparts, are those who most like stimulus persons of higher physical attractiveness rather than lower.

Some research has used the two main independent variables of liking and a measure of personality or character. Such research direction offers an explanation in addition to the identification of the relationship between liking and physical attractiveness. McKelvie and Matthews (1976) used photographs of 24 female stimulus persons. Stimulus persons were either high or low in physical attractiveness and were described in terms of either a favorable or unfavorable character. Subjects were 20 males and 20 females who rated their liking for each stimulus person. Both physical attractiveness and the attributed character influenced liking significantly. Statistical interactions occurred for the male subjects who were more influenced by physical attractiveness than the female subjects. On the other hand, females were more influenced by the character attribution than were the male subjects.

Similarly, Smits and Cherhoniak (1976) investigated liking as a function of physical attractiveness and friendliness. Thirty-six males were presented with a photograph of a woman of low or high physical attractiveness, accompanied with an autobiographical statement communicating either a friendly or unfriendly person. The data were analyzed through analysis of variance and multivariate analysis of variance. Higher physical attractiveness produced higher ratings of personality and friendliness. Physical attractiveness was also positively correlated with ratings of social attractiveness.

A third research effort, with implicit explanation direction, was two studies testing the halo effect of physical attractiveness (Lucker, Beane, & Helmreich, 1981). Subjects were 310 males and females and the stimulus persons were 24 males and females. The second study was a replication which yielded findings congruent with the first study. Their results were that physical attractiveness was found to be strongly related to liking, sexiness, and perceived femininity or masculinity as appropriate.

Nonromantic liking is associated with personal characteristics which are both physical and nonphysical. Despite an apparent interdependency between physical attractiveness and personality, as related to liking, the reasonable conclusion is that physical attractiveness may be the most persistent and predominant determinant of liking. Research consistently shows that people of higher physical attractiveness are afforded greater liking and more positive personal characteristics. But, a 1980 study (Timmerman & Hewitt) reported that liking was not correlated with attributions of more positive personality characteristics. This study utilized 167 subjects ranging in age from 16 to 56 years old. The measurements involved rating and rank ordering of stimulus persons on a number of personality dimensions.

Similarity of Attitudes

The relationship between physical attractiveness and nonintimate liking may be related to the effect that physical attractiveness has on perceived similarity. Perceived similarity is both logically assumed and empirically shown to determine liking (Byrne, 1961, 1971; Byrne & Nelson, 1964; Byrne, Griffitt, Hudgins, & Reeves, 1969; Kaplan, 1972; Scott, 1973). A 1973 article (Insko, Thompson, Stroebe, Shaud, Pinner, & Layton) published results supporting a causal link between similarity and liking. Therefore, research investigating the relationship between physical attractiveness and perceived similarity is certainly germane to the relationship between physical attractiveness and liking. The physical attractiveness research includes numerous circumstances verifying a physical attractiveness influence on perceived similarity. Apparently the higher the physical attractiveness of another person the more people perceive the person's nonappearance characteristics as similar to their own.

Research focusing on the relationship between similarity and physical attractiveness has studied both attitudes and personalities. A 1975 experiment tested a hypothesis that people perceive (opposite-sex) strangers of higher physical attractiveness to have attitudes more similar to their own attitudes (Schoedel, Frederickson, & Knight, 1975). Support for this hypothesis was revealed through the analysis of variance tests of both the first experiment and a follow-up experiment. This study was later expanded by Mashman (1978). A 15-item questionnaire was used by 220 subjects (99 males and 121 females) to assess the subjects' own attitudes and their perceptions of the attitudes possessed by stimulus persons. The stimulus persons represented three levels of physical attractiveness (low, moderate, and high) and were paired in opposite-sex dyads with the subjects. The major result was a monotonic increasing relationship between perceived attitude similarity and physical attractiveness of the stranger (i.e., stimulus person). The physical attractiveness of the stimulus person was not manipulated by the subjects' perceptions, but was rated earlier by judges unrelated to the similarity questionnaire phase of the experiment. Details of the results indicated that the effect of physical attractiveness on attitude similarity was greater for lower as opposed to higher physical attractiveness, and it was also greater for female as opposed to male subjects.

A positive relationship between physical attractiveness and perceived attitude similarity exists among younger people. Cavior and Dokecki (1973) reported factors which contribute to nonintimate liking among elementary and secondary school students. Subjects were 58 students who knew each other and 60 students who did not know each other. The study examined the variables of physical attractiveness, perceived attitude similarity, and academic performance as they contribute to interpersonal attraction among adolescents. Academic performance was found to be negligibly related to interpersonal attraction. Positive correlations were reported for both physical attractiveness and attitude similarity for both grade levels investigated. Likewise, positive correlations were reported, for both grade levels, between physical attractiveness and perceived attitude similarity. The study concluded that the causal direction appeared to be from physical attractiveness to liking for those of highest and least physical attractiveness, whereas the causality was interactive for persons of moderate physical attractiveness.

The first author of this 1973 study was also involved in a 1975 study which used a naturalistic setting as opposed to the laboratory (Cavior, Miller, & Cohen, 1975). Using 23 tenth graders and 24 twelfth graders who knew each other, the study examined physical attractiveness, attitude similarity, and length of acquaintance as they contributed to nonintimate liking among adolescents. The attitude similarity in this study involved measures of both perceived and actual attitudes. Of most significance to the physical attractiveness phenomena is that regression analyses of the data supported the general hypothesis that physical attractiveness and perceived attitude similarity are positively correlated.

As an extension of the attitude similarity research, one study has focused on personality similarity (Miller & Maruyama, 1981). Sixty-six subjects rated both themselves and stimulus persons on personality characteristics described as negative, neutral, and positive. Stimulus persons were represented by photographs of females of either high, low, or moderate physical attractiveness. The higher the physical attractiveness of the stimulus persons, the greater was the perceived similarity of positive personality characteristics.

Similarity of Physical Attractiveness

The romantic attraction research and the nonintimate liking research share the dynamics of physical attractiveness similarity. Both of these types of attraction reflect a matching hypothesis of physical attractiveness. Several studies have identified significant matching of physical attractiveness among opposite-sex couples in dating and marriage (Murstein, 1972; Peterson & Miller, 1980; Price & Vandenberg, 1979). An extension of the romantic attraction research examined if matching occurs within non-romantic attraction (Cash & Derlega, 1978). To disguise the physical attractiveness interest, subjects were asked to indicate their willingness to participate in a psychological project dealing with written communication. In addition, these subjects were asked to give names of close friends who would be willing to participate also. Twenty-four male and 24 female subjects were randomly selected from a much larger population of volunteers. Once selected, both the subjects and their friends were asked to rate their degree of friendship and to pose for a full-length, front-view, smiling photograph.

The rating of physical attractiveness was also disguised. Raters were one male and one female who did not know the purpose of their physical attractiveness ratings. The ratings used a 7-point scale, the judges worked independently, and the 96 photographs of stimulus persons were randomized for each rater. Interjudge reliability was statistically significant at the .001 level ($r = .751$). The data analysis revealed a significant relationship between the physical attractiveness and liking of these nonintimate, same-sex friends. A final analysis was a chi-square test which indicated significant similarity of physical attractiveness between close friends of the same sex for both males (at the .02 level) and females (at the .05 level). The authors concluded that their results were a valuable extension of related research reporting similar results with opposite-sex dyads in romantic attraction.

EMPLOYMENT

Employment is, for all but a select few, a necessity within our society. Practically every person's adult life is related to employment practices as either an employee or an employer. Consequently, the dynamics surrounding employment interactions are of widespread importance to individuals as well as to society. A vital component in these interpersonal reciprocations of employment is the physical attractiveness of those persons involved. For example, research efforts have identified significant relationships between physical attractiveness and both hiring decisions for job applicants and compensation during employment. A substantial amount of this research has focused on either the perception of personal characteristics deemed important for employee success or it has dealt with evaluation of product quality related to creative work.

The physical attractiveness phenomena apply to evaluations of competence, ability, performance, and final task outcome. Both males and females expect those higher in physical attractiveness to do better work than those lower in physical attractiveness. Furthermore, once completed, this work is rated more highly than the identical work performed by those of lower physical attractiveness (Berscheid & Walster, 1972). Objective verification of such employment discrimination is indirectly offered by a study of political elections. Efran and Patterson (1974) found that actual political candidates of higher physical attractiveness received significantly more votes than their counterparts of lower physical attractiveness. They concluded that physical attractiveness "is an important attribute which interacts with the political system" (pp. 355–356).

Quality of Product

The classic study in the area of product quality involved judgments pertaining to writing quality (Landy & Sigall, 1974). Two essays were used, one had been previously judged to be of good literary quality and the other had been judged to be of poor literary quality. A photograph of a female (stimulus) person of either high or low physical attractiveness was attached to each essay. Sixty male readers (i.e., judges/subjects) were presented with these stimulus persons posing as authors of the essays. The judges evaluated both the essay quality and writer ability on a number of dimensions. Experimental treatments were physical attractiveness levels of either high, low, or no information. Both the authors' physical attractiveness and the essays' quality produced significant main effects. The essays with the "authors" of higher physical attractiveness were evaluated as having better ideas, possessing better style, being more creative, and generally being of higher quality than those essays with authors of lower physical attractiveness. The physically attractive authors were attributed higher intelligence, greater sensitivity, greater talent, and overall greater ability than their counterparts of lower physical attractiveness.

An interaction did occur between the essay quality and author physical attractiveness. When the essay was of poor quality, the authors of higher physical attractiveness, and their respective work, were rated substantially different from the authors of lower physical attractiveness and their work. The differences were not as great when the essay was of good quality. The authors interpreted this interaction as follows:

> If you are ugly, you are not discriminated against a great deal as long as your performance is impressive. However, should your performance be below par, attractiveness matters! You may be able to get away with inferior work if you are beautiful. (Landy & Sigall, 1974, p. 302)

By focusing on author physical attractiveness and writing ability, several research efforts have expanded the early work of Landy and Sigall (1974). Two experiments were conducted to assess the potential interaction between sex and physical attractiveness as they pertain to evaluation of an author's work (Kaplan, 1978). In the first experiment, 140 male and female subjects evaluated an essay supposedly written by a female of either low or high physical attractiveness. Although the female judges did not differ according to author physical attractiveness the male judges rated the authors of higher physical attractiveness as more talented. In the second experiment 120 male and female subjects evaluated an essay supposedly written by a male of either low or high physical attractiveness. This time the physical attractiveness of the male authors did not produce different evaluations of the author's talent according to physical attractiveness. The research article concluded that a poorly written essay by a female of higher physical attractiveness can still receive a favorable evaluation. However, a female writer of lower physical attractiveness must produce work of substantially higher quality to receive favorable evaluations of that work.

In addition to sex, race was examined in connection with physical attractiveness (Maruyama & Miller, 1980). Essays supposedly written by either a black or white author were evaluated by 530 male subjects in three experiments. Both black and white authors were evaluated more favorably when they were higher in physical attractiveness. Anderson and Nida (1978) also reported a positive correlation between author physical attractiveness and evaluations of writing ability. However, their data revealed that authors of higher physical attractiveness received the highest evaluations from members of the same sex, regardless of whether the subjects were males or females. Bull and Stevens (1979) published results consistent with other research reporting sex differences related to physical attractiveness. These authors reported that the ratings of male authors were not significantly correlated, but the ratings of female authors were positively correlated with their physical attractiveness.

Evaluations of artistic ability are no different than evaluations of writing ability. Instead of an author and an essay, an artist and a painting were used as stimulus materials (Murphy & Hellkamp, 1976). The variables manipulated were the physical attractiveness of the artist, the personality of the artist, and sex of the judges. Four paintings were evaluated by 32 male and female subjects (equally divided for each of the four paintings). Personality manipulation was achieved through a tape-recorded message intended to portray either a warm or a cold person. To minimize potential order bias, the presentations of both the artist and painting manipulations were counterbalanced. The results found no differences due to sex of the evaluators. Both a warm personality and higher physical attractiveness produced more favorable results than their respective counterparts.

Outcome Responsibility

Physical attractiveness research has examined some personal traits that may be only indirectly related to employment. The research is applicable because it holds important implications for actual employment biases, perceptions, and decisions. Generally, the higher the person's physical attractiveness, the more the person is viewed as responsible for successful outcome and good work. On the other hand, the lower the person's physical attractiveness, the more the person is viewed as responsible for unsuccessful outcome and poor work (Hill & Kahn, 1974). Attribution of outcome responsibility was examined through an experimental design with 72 male and 72 female subjects (Seligman, Paschall, & Takata, 1973, 1974). They reported a significant interaction in that females of higher physical attractiveness were perceived as more responsible for a good outcome than were females of lower physical attractiveness. Likewise, a bad outcome was perceived to be the responsibility of females of lower physical attractiveness.

Turkat and Dawson (1976) investigated the relationship between attributions of responsibility and outcome of a chance event. The variables of interest were the sex and the physical attractiveness of the stimulus person. Forty-eight subjects (males and females equally represented) read a story in which a chance event ended with either a negative or positive outcome. An individual in the story was described as either male or female who was either low or high in physical attractiveness. After completing the story, the subjects were asked to indicate the individual's responsibility for the outcome. The results found no support for a sex difference among the stimulus persons. Attribution of responsibility did differ as the stimulus persons' physical attractiveness differed. When the chance events had a positive ending, the stimulus persons of higher physical attractiveness were assumed responsible, but when there was a negative ending the stimulus persons of lower physical attractiveness were attributed the responsibility.

Sex-Typed Tasks

Some research may be viewed as indirect examinations that still allow generalizations to actual employment dynamics. For example, individuals of lower physical attractiveness are assumed to have less internal locus of control, but the reverse is true for those of higher physical attractiveness (Cash & Burns, 1977; Miller, 1970b; Rotter, 1966).

More direct research was performed by Hill and Lando (1976), who were concerned with physical attractiveness, sex, and performance of sex-typed work activities. They found that the physical attractiveness of the stimulus persons had a greater impact than the sex of the stimulus persons. For both general personal characteristics and specific performance evaluations those higher in physical attractiveness were rated more favorably than those lower. Thornton and Linnstaedter (1975) used only female stimulus persons to examine sex-typed tasks. They also reported that evaluation of a stimulus person's competence and preference as an employee was more positively correlated with the person's physical attractiveness than was the relationship between the person's sex and the traditionally sex-typed nature of the job.

A relationship between physical attractiveness and employment appears to exist. Up to this point the research reveals that work involving creative input is perceived to represent higher talent and quality when done by those of higher physical attractiveness. Similarly, there is an indication that people prefer employees of higher physical attractiveness. In general the lay public has expressed more favorable evaluations of competency and work quality of those who are higher in physical attractiveness as compared to lower. The next step is to determine if these physical attractiveness phenomena generalize to cases of actual employment.

Job Applicants

If high physical attractiveness can open doors, low physical attractiveness can close them. Evaluations of competency and work quality performed on the job may be irrelevant because those of lower physical attractiveness may never receive an opportunity to demonstrate their capabilities. Even among the professionally trained evaluators, judgments pertaining to employment potential may be tainted by the applicant's physical attractiveness.

Physical attractiveness is sometimes accepted as relevant for successful functioning in some capacities. One study focused on how the physical attractiveness of an applicant influences employment selection for a position where it is considered relevant to the job (Beehr & Gilmore, 1982). This relevancy question was examined through a two-step procedure. First, four management-trainee job descriptions were presented to the subjects. Second, rather than assuming physical attractiveness relevancy, each subject individually indicated his or her own perception of the importance of physical attractiveness in that position. Unfortunately, the study used college students in place of actual personnel professionals as the subjects, and no significant differences were identified. The lack of significance in this study may be attributed to the subjects or to the questions raised by the authors about the validity of their study and its measurement scales. Despite this lack of significance, the authors concluded that if the interviewer believes physical attractiveness is an important job attribute, then being higher in physical attractiveness is a direct advantage to the applicant. The authors' conclusion is supported by the following research that reports significant employment differences due to physical attractiveness.

Information Order

The effects of physical attractiveness on employment practices may be moderated by the sequence in which information about an applicant is presented. The influence of physical attractiveness may be determined if it is observed before work performance or vice versa. Because typical employment procedure involves face-to-face interviews before hiring, research pertaining to sequence questions is especially relevant. Four experiments, with 720 subjects, addressed the question of presentation order as it impacts on the relationship between physical attractiveness and attributions of ability (Benassi, 1982). These data showed that persons of higher physical attractiveness levels received consistently higher attributions regardless of performance. The conditions of lower physical attractiveness and of no physical attractiveness information received consistently lower attributions. The most important finding of this study, for employment, was that the advantage enjoyed by high physical attractiveness was most prominent when presented before performance. When performance was observed before physical attractiveness, attributions given to those higher and lower in physical attractiveness were not significantly different. The conclusion is that if the applicant is given a chance, by being hired, the effects due to physical attractiveness could be lessened.

The notion that employment decisions due to physical attractiveness may be minimized through the presentation sequence is promising, but this sequence is difficult to put into practice. The difficulty is especially pronounced at the application stage when the applicant has not yet had an opportunity to prove him or herself. For existing employees, organizational superiors could possibly design evaluation procedures which allow evaluation of work performance without knowledge of the employees physical attractiveness. The problem is that such procedures are difficult to implement except for a very large organization. But even then, the remote possibility only applies to select work tasks.

For the application stage, one study did attempt to minimize the effect of physical attractiveness on this employment decision (Cann, Siegfried, & Pearce, 1981). Subjects were 96 male and 148 female college students involved in an experiment which attempted to minimize hiring decisions based on sex and/or physical attractiveness. The subjects were forced to postpone a hiring decision until they had evaluated specific qualifications. To accomplish this postponement the application credentials were submitted and evaluated before the subjects were presented with the applicants who were male or female of either low, moderate, or high physical attractiveness. The results revealed that evaluation of the specific employment qualifications were influenced by the order of presentation. However, the hiring decision continued to be dependent on sex and physical attractiveness. The fact that physical attractiveness appeared to play a determining role, regardless of order presentation, is consistent with the commonly held notion that interviewers make their cognitive decisions within a few moments of the interview.

Relevancy of Sex

The finding that the effects of physical attractiveness interact with the sex type of position is not unique (Cash, Gillen, & Burns, 1977). Another study at Yale University used both male and female subjects to explore the impact of physical attractiveness in response to female applicants (Heilman & Saruwatari, 1979). The experiment involved the evaluations of applicants for both managerial and clerical positions. For the male applicants, physical attractiveness was advantageous for both types of positions. For the female applicants, physical attractiveness was advantageous for only the clerical positions.

These advantages and disadvantages were consistent for ratings of the applicants' qualifications, hiring recommendations, starting salary suggestions, and rankings of hiring preferences. The effects of physical attractiveness and its interaction with sex-typed positions is consistent across studies. An experiment found that both males and females of higher physical attractiveness were preferred as employees over their counterparts (Marvelle & Green, 1980). Furthermore, both male and female job candidates of higher physical attractiveness were only preferred when they were evaluated for positions traditionally viewed as sex-appropriate.

Bias based on sex and physical attractiveness is not limited to sex-typed jobs. The effects of both sex and physical attractiveness within employment decisions were fully manipulated for both applicants and interviewers (Dipboye, Arvey, & Terpstra, 1977). Subjects were 110 male and female university students used to simulate professional interviewers. For both the applicant and the interviewer, physical attractiveness involved unobtrusive ratings by two impartial judges. Physical attractiveness manipulations represented low, moderate, and high levels. Independent variables also included description of the applicants' qualifications, represented as either high or low quality. The dependent variables included recommendations to hire and recommendations for starting salary.

All the independent variables pertaining to the stimulus persons (i.e., applicants) yielded significant results. Highly qualified applicants, male applicants, and applicants of higher physical attractiveness were each significantly preferred over their counterparts. The variables for inter-viewer sex and interviewer physical attractiveness did not yield a significant influence or interaction. Among the findings was that stimulus persons of lower physical attractiveness received the most negative bias when their qualifications were low as opposed to high. The authors stated that despite possible limitations of the study, it was reasonable to conclude that prejudices based on sex and physical attractiveness do exist within employment decisions. This study lends further justification to the conclusion that physical attractiveness is of sufficient importance within employment to warrant continuation of serious research attention.

Professional Employment Personnel

The first study in this area involved 30 professional employment interviewers (Dipboye, Fromkin, & Wiback, 1975). These interviewers served as subjects along with 30 college students who played the role of professional employment interviewers. Simulating an employment selec-tion process all 60 subjects rated and ranked résumés as appropriate for a managerial position. The résumés varied in only applicant sex, applicant physical attractiveness, and applicant academic standing. The physical attractiveness manipulation was accomplished by attaching a photograph of a stimulus person whose physical attractiveness was judged by other individuals prior to being attached to the résumés. Applicants who were males, as well as applicants with higher academic standings, were preferred over their respective counterparts. These applicants for a managerial position were most likely to be selected when they were higher in physical attractiveness as compared to lower.

Another study with experienced personnel consultants was reported a couple years later (Cash *et al.*, 1977). Again, résumés were presented to subjects, with a photograph of an applicant representing lower or higher physical attractiveness, or with no information (i.e., a résumé with no photograph attached). The subjects were 36 male and 36 female personnel consultants with practical, actual work experience. The sex manipulation was controlled by only changing the applicant's name on the résumé from John Williams to Janet Williams. The applicants of higher physical attractiveness were most likely to be hired unless the position was traditionally sex stereotyped. In other words, the higher physical attractiveness was selected if the position was traditionally sex appropriate such as a male applying for an automobile sales position or a female applying for a position as office receptionist.

Genuine Applicants

Regardless of whether the application process is simulated or real, the outcome is the same. Studies with both good internal and external validity have identified the importance of an applicant's physical attractiveness in the employment process. To achieve this validity actual practitioners were used in laboratory experiments, with some trade-off between internal and external validity. This trade-off was minimized by going beyond simulations with actual recruiters to a field experiment with nothing simulated. Résumés were sent to the appropriate personnel offices at major corporations and employment agencies in three major cities (Waters, 1980). The résumés were identical except for the photograph of the applicant. In an effort to control internal validity, as well as external validity, the same female was used for both physical attractiveness conditions. The difference was that the conditions of higher physical attractiveness presented a woman whose physical attractiveness was enhanced by a professional makeup artist. Those prospective employers who received the résumé with the applicant of higher physical attractiveness offered starting employment salaries of 8% to 20% more than those salaries offered to the applicants of lower physical attractiveness.

Employee Reality

The physical attractiveness of the applicant has received the majority of research attention within employment practices. This emphasis may be justified since one must pass through the application stage before becoming an employee. Transition from research performed with applicants to the applicants once they are employed, necessarily shifts from experimental designs to surveys with actual employees. The validity of these self-reporting surveys is always a concern. However, research response among the employed is very consistent, which suggests credibility. In addition, these data are realistic and serve as a complement to employment data collected through other means.

A survey of 498 students reported that they consider physical attractiveness an important factor in three areas of employment (Sweat, Kelley, Blouin, & Glee, 1981): securing a job, retaining the job, and promotion on the job. Respondents to the survey questionnaire, who possessed greater employment experiences, viewed personal appearance and physical attractiveness with greater importance for all three areas, as compared to those of less employment history.

Professional Men

The effects of physical attractiveness on actual professional employees has been probed for both males and females. Both Kaslow and Schwartz (1978) and Ross and Ferris (1981) investigated the role of physical attractiveness for professional employees within their natural employment milieus. A primary difference was that Kaslow and Schwartz centered on interpersonal dynamics specific to females, and Ross and Ferris centered on financial compensations specific to males. The latter study used only males for two related reasons. First, the effects of physical attractiveness are different for the sexes—typically greater for females (Bar-Tal & Saxe, 1976; Heilman & Saruwatari, 1979). Second, the firms sampled had disproportionately few female employees to allow any type of meaningful analysis.

The natural employment setting for professional men involved two public accounting firms (Ross & Ferris, 1981). Together these firms offered 368 potential subjects who were either accountants or managers. Because of the type of data collected, an experiment was ruled out in favor of cross-sectional field investigations. Major variables of study were physical attractiveness, attitude similarity, and social background. The physical attractiveness variable was defined as a combination of facial attractiveness, height, and weight. Major dependent variables were performance ratings and salaries.

Data collection was both subjective and objective. To control for potential extraneous variables, a host of information was collected, such as grade point average, quality of university graduated from, and years employed. Salary information and performance evaluations were secured from company records, and additional evaluations were received from employee supervisors through questionnaires. The employees completed self-reports for height, weight, and age, as well as numerous other questions. Physical attractiveness of the stimulus persons was established by three judges using a 5-level, Q-sorting procedure with photographs.

The results showed that one of the basic goals of rational administrative theory is not achieved in practice. Despite the intent for objective evaluations, physical attractiveness of these professional employees played a role in their employment activities. "Physical attractiveness was found to be related to many ratings of performance at both levels, and in both organizations" (Ross & Ferris, 1981, p. 628). Whether or not the employees were junior or senior executives, their physical attractiveness appeared to lead to better outcomes in terms of evaluations and salary.

Professional Women

Women in the work force receive considerable attention in the mass media and in scholarly writings. One issue pertaining to working women that is consistently recognized is the problem of irrelevant prejudices simply because of gender. Numerous studies have identified bias against working women who are highly competent (e.g., Fugita, Panek, Balascoe, & Newman, 1977; Hagan & Kahn, 1975; Sommers-Feldman & Kiesler, 1974; Spence & Helmreich, 1972).

The implications of being a female in the work force are amplified by her physical attractiveness. Professional women who are both high in competence and physical attractiveness pose complications in today's society. Male business associates often patronize or are sexually attracted, and female associates often respond with jealousy and contempt (Ancker-Johnson, 1975; Kaslow & Schwartz, 1978; "Women as Bosses," 1983; S. L. Paulson, personal communication, June 4, 1983). Such women have a double handicap because they must prove both their work commitment and their competence (Ancker-Johnson, 1975; Harris, 1970; Kollar, 1974; S. L. Paulson, personal communication, June 4, 1983). "In the business and professional world, the attractive woman has had to pay a heavy price for being well-endowed by nature with comeliness" (Kaslow & Schwartz, 1978, p. 313).

Professional males experience irrelevant encumberances due to their physical attractiveness (Ross & Ferris, 1981), but professional females sustain burdens due to both their sex and their physical attractiveness. Kaslow and Schwartz (1978) investigated professional women who were both successful and physically attractive. Eighty-four female college graduates were selected from across the country in a variety of vocations. To eliminate extraneous variables such as tokenism, only Caucasians served as subjects. The criteria for describing successful women were defined as "high status and success in chosen field of endeavor subsequent to graduation from college" (p. 314). Demographics included 13 Ph.D.'s, 3 M.D.'s, 1 J.D., 15 master's degrees, and 14 bachelor's degrees. Representatives were from, but not limited to, business, media, academia, and the helping professions. Data were collected through use of mailed questionnaires consisting of 10 open-ended questions.

The results revealed consistent positive and negative implications, as well as some inconsistencies. The major inconsistency pertained to exposure to job opportunities in which some women considered their high physical attractiveness as an advantage and others considered it a disadvantage. Overall, high physical attractiveness was seen as a valuable attribute for beginning interactions, initially accessing job opportunities, and the reason for their organization's selection for a position of high visibility.

Problems specific to each sex were reported. The problems with other females were with both associates of low physical attractiveness and wives of male associates. Jealousy and sabotage were reported as not uncommon. Problems with males included resentment of the woman's achievements, and sexual attraction. Women of higher physical attractiveness reported that "they look at me, rather than my product" (p. 413). Men treat these women as a date by insisting on paying the check, which they do not do with other women of lower physical attractiveness or with other men. High level decisions often exclude women because males exhibit paternalistic and protective attitudes, or they avoid close interactions because they fear their impulses. A significant problem reported was that male colleagues often desire a sexual–personal relationship rather than professional. Related, were the reports that a woman's friendliness is often misinterpreted.

Problems not specific to males or females were also reported. Over three-fourths of the women stated that they are the objects of serious gossip and insinuation. Because of the common belief that beauty and competence cannot exist together, physical attractiveness does seem to interfere with capabilities. Kaslow and Schwartz concluded that

> many colleagues assume that the attractive female professional has obtained her high-level position through seductiveness, manipulation, or because she has been sexually available. (1978, p. 315)

The professional competence and hard work of a successful employee is not given serious consideration when the person is a professional female of higher physical attractiveness.

Discrimination and Employment

The physical attractiveness phenomena do operate within employment regardless of chances to demonstrate competence. The problem is to minimize the impact of personal factors irrelevant to performing a job. Legislation is designed to eliminate discrimination based on sex, race, and religion throughout employment, and despite less than perfect success, the intent has been established. Assuming that behavior may at times precede attitude, equal rights legislation in employment practices may well be eventually followed by a corresponding change in equal rights attitude.

Equal employment rights for those of different levels of physical attractiveness is more difficult to legislate. Unlike sex and race, which may be easily tabulated, the very nature of physical attractiveness poses an intrinsic difficulty of measurement and tabulation. Because of the difficulties inherent within definitions of physical attractiveness, it is probably not feasible to expect legislation to force documentation of physical attractiveness levels within an organization. The result is that covert biases will continue to be translated into discriminatory behavior based on the physical attractiveness of the applicant and the employee. Surrogate measures are different because legislation against certain aspects of physical attractiveness can be cited. For example, societal reactions have forced lawsuits and formation of various activist groups to promote elmination of unnecessary discrimination based on a person's weight and height.

The issue of employment discrimination based on physical attractiveness is not easily resolved. Such discrimination may be morally questioned for serious societal ramifications, however, organizations may well be justified for financial and production implications. Given the physical attractiveness phenomena, those higher in physical attractiveness may well be more productive. Consequently, the practice of selecting visible personnel based on physical attractiveness may be beneficial to the organization.

Staffing based on physical attractiveness discrimination may even be justified for nonvisible positions. Congruent with both intrapersonal and interpersonal realities, people of differing physical attractiveness may differ in important employee attributes, such as motivation, confidence, and ability to interact with others. Similarly, managerial positions may best be staffed with attention given to physical attractiveness. The reasoning is that one's behavior is, at least in part, a function of how others respond. Therefore, if those higher in physical attractiveness are perceived as more competent, they may incorporate that perception by acting and becoming more competent. Ultimately, despite moral issues, employment practices that are biased in favor of higher physical attractiveness may be justified as an accurate assessment of reality.

CONCLUSION

This chapter has revealed the powerful implications of physical attractiveness for romantic attraction, nonintimate liking, and employment. The importance of physical attractiveness within interpersonal reciprocal interactions cannot be overemphasized. It is a fact that people of higher and lower physical attractiveness experience different personal interchanges throughout life. Either denying this fact or not knowing it will not diminish the significance of a person's physical attractiveness.

Reasonable speculation cannot disregard the potentially serious internal effects of the physical attractiveness phenomena. With all the interpersonal dynamics operating, as identified in these last two chapters, it is reasonable to speculate on the internal implications. Are people of differing levels of physical attractiveness actually different or are they just perceived and treated differently? If these people are not born with different internal makeups, does the differential treatment, literally from birth, affect their development? A final question is which causes which? Do differences in physical attractiveness cause intrapersonal differences, or do intrapersonal variations cause interpersonal differences related to physical attractiveness, or are these groups of variables merely correlated? Whatever the relationship, the next chapter reveals that interpersonal discrepancies are correlated with actual, intrapersonal variations between those of lower and higher levels of physical attractiveness.

Chapter 5

Intrapersonal Realities

According to Ovid, Pygmalion fell in love with his sculpture Galatea. Aphrodite, in an act of kindness to Pygmalion, then gave life to this beloved idealized sculpture. George Bernard Shaw's interpretation of the Pygmalion myth portrayed Henry Higgins's using language to transform a cockney flower girl into an elegant lady. Today, although the ability to produce the ideal mate does not exist, analogous to these situations is the fact that expectations can produce psychological and physiological characteristics in others. Such an ability is now often referred to as either the Pygmalion effect or the self-fulfilling prophecy, whereby people conform and internalize what others expect or prophesize for them. The Pygmalion effect is more than mere intuitive speculation in today's society. Its effects are well documented in both academic and on-the-job situations as well as inside and outside of laboratory settings. Science does not know how the process works, but it does know it occurs and that it possesses the power to hinder and to help the development of others (Rosenthal, 1973).

The issue of how people respond to another person's physical attractiveness was dealt with in the previous two chapters. The reality is that, despite what people claim, differences in physical attractiveness produce significant interpersonal differences. The current issue is the relationship between a person's physical attractiveness and that person's intrapersonal consequences. Causal data are typically not as feasible with intrapersonal variables as they are with interpersonal variables. Consequently, the valuable experimental design is limited to select areas within intrapersonal dynamics. The limitation is due to practical and ethical implications involved with fully manipulating the intrapersonal variables. Therefore, physical attractiveness research pertaining to intrapersonal consequences necessarily relies more heavily on survey designs that yield correlational data. The result is that only association can usually be established. Neither the causation nor the direction of influence can be deduced in these research findings that identify the relationship between physical attractiveness and intrapersonal realities.

A relationship between physical attractiveness and intrapersonal characteristics is supported both theoretically and empirically. The theory builds on the Pygmalion effect and combines with the physical attractiveness phenomena. If society holds different expectations for individuals of dissimilar physical attractiveness levels, those individuals are likely to internalize the respective expectations. The outcome is that people will yield to the self-fulfilling prophecy by actually evolving into disparate persons according to their physical attractiveness.

The empirical evidence may not offer an explanation but it does identify an association. Persons lower and higher in physical attractiveness are different psychologically and even physiologically. Although relevant research is sparse, it does yield an affirmative response documenting that the physical attractiveness phenomena carry implications beyond interpersonal responses, into intrapersonal characteristics, and possible intrapersonal development.

REALITY

It appears that the interpersonal realities, described in Chapters 3 and 4, translate into intrapersonal realities. Research literature documents that physical attractiveness of a person elicits different responses from both strangers and significant others in their lives. Additional research expresses that these responses may be internalized and subsequently influential in individual development (Adams, 1977b; Adams & Crossman, 1978, pp. 69–85; Adams & Read, 1983).

The environment is quite contrastive for those of lower and higher physical attractiveness. It is a pleasant, forgiving, supportive world for the latter and the opposite for the former. This fact proposes that a child of higher physical attractiveness may be maladjusted more than those of lower physical attractiveness because he is more pampered, favored, and spoiled. The appropriate research data, however, disclose that the reverse is true. Those lower in physical attractiveness are the ones whose personal life adjustments are less positive and less effective (Berscheid et al., 1971; Kirkpatrick & Cotton, 1951). For example, elementary school girls who are high in physical attractiveness are more successful at persuading peers than those lower in physical attractiveness (Dion & Stein, 1978). Unobtrusive observation of natural play revealed numerous distinctions for children who vary in physical attractiveness (Langlois & Downs, 1979). The behavior of the children (both males and females, ages 3 and 5 years old) was recorded for several categories of activity. Those children of higher physical attractiveness were less active and played with feminine toys more often than their counterparts. For the 5-year-olds those lower in physical attractiveness tended to exhibit more aggressive behaviors, such as hitting their peers.

Collectively, the physical attractiveness phenomena appear omnipotent. On one hand, interpersonal research documents that persons of higher physical attractiveness are assumed to possess more desirable attributes. On the other hand, intrapersonal research documents perceptions are often accurate in reality. For example, the more physically attractive persons date more often (Spreadbury & Reeves, 1979), have more friends, and have happier marriages (Kirkpatrick & Cotton, 1951). They experience less social anxiety (Adams, 1977a), possess and exhibit greater individuality (Krebs & Adinolfi, 1975), and are better adjusted socially (Lerner & Lerner, 1977). These few illustrations are expanded on in this chapter, which verifies that those of higher and lower physical attractiveness are not just perceived differently but actually are.

INTERPERSONAL OUTCOMES

Interpersonal interactions are not isolated from physical attractiveness. Contrasting physical attractiveness levels are associated with divergent interaction outcomes. The question is whether these associations reflect only perceptions or if they represent true experiences within individuals (i.e., intrapersonal realities). The answer is that people do experience discrepant social outcomes as a function of their physical attractiveness.

These discrepancies are identified through all major research designs. Supportive empirical data have been collected by survey, observation, and experiment. Another effort consisted of a longitudinal study begun over 50 years ago that recently reported (Runyan, 1980) that those higher in physical attractiveness remember their earlier years as more satisfying than those lower in physical attractiveness. This report was based on data from 45 men and 46 women selected to participate in a project that began in 1932 with a sample of 212 fifth and sixth graders. The implication is that different outcomes from social interactions are not only perceived by others but are actually experienced within the lives of individuals.

Such experiences are not necessarily uniform, because, generally, physical attractiveness is most important for females. In fact, actual interpersonal outcomes often vary significantly between the sexes. The best verification of such discrepancies was presented by the ambitious longitudinal study of Udry & Eckland (1983), which began in 1955 with a national sample of high school sophomores and was followed-up in a 1970 survey of 4,151 of the original participants. This 1970 survey obtained completed mailback questionnaires from 2,077 respondents who were all in their early 30s. Ten years later, these same respondents were investigated in an attempt to identify actual long-term consequences of physical attractiveness in adult life. This step involved six research assistants (three males and three females) who evaluated each respondent's physical attractiveness based on original high school photographs.

Overall, this longitudinal study offers further documentation of the actual intrapersonal reality experienced by males and females of differing physical attractiveness levels. It was found that, although physical attractiveness of males was not significantly different for household income, it was significant for female physical attractiveness. The authors stated that "the relationship is clear and nearly linear: the more attractive the female, the higher the household income" (p. 6). Because physical attractiveness in a woman is not related to her own income, this difference appears to be solely a function of the fact that a woman of higher physical attractiveness marries a "higher income-producing husband" (p. 11).

Several marriage-related facts are identified. First, both males and females of higher physical attractiveness marry earlier than their counterparts of lower physical attractiveness. Second, although no relationship exists between male physical attractiveness and those married or not, for females "the least attractive are ten times as likely never to have married as the most attractive" (p. 10). Third, "the more attractive the male is, the less educated his wife is," but "the more attractive the woman was in high school, the more highly educated the husband she gets" (p. 10).

Because the data for males are opposite to that of the females, the effects initially appear contradictory to the physical attractiveness phenomena. For example, males of lower physical attractiveness are more educated and possess higher occupational status, whereas no relationship exists for their physical attractiveness and income. However, males also benefit from higher physical attractiveness. More detailed analysis revealed that those at the lower and the higher levels of physical attractiveness had a similar job status. This equality existed despite the fact that standardized tests during adolescent years indicated higher verbal and math scores for those males lower in physical attractiveness. The authors interpreted these data to possibly mean that males of lower physical attractiveness "are socially handicapped in high school, which leads them to concentrate on educational achievement" (p. 9) and which results in positions of corresponding prestige, but with no greater earnings. On the other hand, males of higher physical attractiveness, "in spite of their ordinary showing on educational achievement, do nearly as well in job prestige as the most homely men" (p. 9).

Self-Fulfilling Prophecy

Intrapersonal characteristics may extend into reality through a process of self-fulfilling prophecy. This notion was investigated through an intricate experimental design done by Snyder, Tanke, and Berscheid (1977). Telephone tape recordings were made of interactive dyads between 51 males and 51 females. The males were led to believe that the females were either high or low in physical attractiveness, but the females were not aware of the designation or that physical attractiveness was even of experimental interest.

Analysis of the tape recordings was done by naive judges. Even though the female target persons were unaware of the male perceivers assumptions, and even though these assumptions were inaccurate, the female stimulus persons behaved in a manner consistent with the physical attractiveness phenomena. Those stimulus persons who were unknowingly perceived as high in physical attractiveness presented more friendly, likable, and socially desirable behavior than those persons unknowingly perceived as lower in physical attractiveness. An article in the *New York Times* paraphrased one of the research authors as saying that people will adjust their personalities to meet the expectations of others (Bennetts, 1978, p. 10).

Friends and Dates

Spreadbury and Reeves (1979) specifically tested two opposing theories pertaining to dating frequency among college women. The theories proposed that dating frequency was either a function of superficial physical characteristics (Waller, 1937) or deeper personality characteristics (Blood, 1955). Subjects were 323 undergraduate women who responded to 1,500 randomly mailed questionnaires. Self-rating data were collected for personality, physical attractiveness, dating frequency, and number of men dated. Data firmly supported predictive superiority for physical attractiveness as opposed to personality. In other words, physical attractiveness was significantly more predictive of dating behavior than personality. Several years later, Maroldo (1982) concluded that physical attractiveness was more important in love than any of the numerous personality variables she investigated.

Those self-rated as lower in physical attractiveness are also those who report significantly greater difficulty in interpersonal relationships (Mitchell & Orr, 1976). In this study, subjects were self-rated as either physically attractive, average, or physically unattractive. As compared to the physically attractive subjects, a significantly greater number of physically unattractive subjects reported that others judge their social skills as inadequate. The physically unattractive also reported higher levels of anxiety in situations prior to opposite-sex interactions.

These data are informative but may be questioned given the use of self-ratings. Considering the limitations of self-ratings, as discussed in Chapter 2, the remainder of this section will discuss true physical attractiveness manipulations as based on independent ratings by judges other than the subjects themselves.

Linearity

There is ample evidence of a linear relationship between physical attractiveness and intrapersonal reality. One such sample is a study that collected data pertaining to measures of sociometric status (Schunk & Selg, 1979). The physical attractiveness of individuals was analyzed with regard to group entropy and individual popularity. Correlational analysis indicated a monotonic increasing relationship between physical attractiveness and individual status.

Linearity was also demonstrated by another study with 56 male fourth graders and 48 male sixth graders (Lerner & Lerner, 1977). Physical attractiveness was assessed by 97 adults through the use of photographs representing the stimulus persons in standard poses. The individual's physical attractiveness was positively correlated with actual academic performance as measured by grade point averages as well as being correlated with social interactions. Further correlations were shown between the physical attractiveness of the children and their actual interpersonal adjustment. Measures of interpersonal adjustment were obtained through (a) responses given by peers and (b) observations made by teachers.

Although evidence does focus on a linear relationship, curvilinear data can also be cited. An example of these latter data is research that assessed natural interaction patterns among university freshman (Krebs & Adinolfi, 1975). Unobtrusive measures, taken after the event, identified social contacts of 60 males and 60 females. The social contacts were categorized as either rejection, acceptance, or unknown by their same-sex peers. Physical attractiveness of the stimulus persons was determined by independent judges. The curvilinear notion was based on the fact that those categorized as rejected, accepted, or unknown were described as most, less, and least physically attractive, respectively.

Quantity and Quality

Two related studies employed a diary technique to assess actual social interaction (Reis, Nezlek, & Wheeler, 1980; Reis, Wheeler, Spiegel, Kernis, Nezlek, & Perri, 1982). Both studies focused on the role of physical attractiveness within social interaction. The procedure was to use a recording technique that required subjects to tabulate every interaction of 10 minutes or longer. The interest in the physical attractiveness variable was disguised and measured by independent judges located at another university.

The primary question of the first study centered on the effect of physical attractiveness on social interaction in terms of both quantity and quality (Reis *et al.*, 1980). The procedure involved 35 males and 35 females who volunteered to participate in "a research project on social interactions" (p. 606) for 8 months of their first year in college. The quantity of social interactions based on physical attractiveness was significant for males but not for females. For males of higher physical attractiveness the quantity of social interactions was positively related for opposite-sex encounters but negatively related for same-sex encounters. Specific data for these males revealed that those higher in physical attractiveness had opposite-sex social interactions that were more mutually initiated. Males and females of higher physical attractiveness spent greater quantities of time in conversation as opposed to activities with others. The importance of physical attractiveness increased as the interaction time increased. Despite common thought that the importance of a person's physical appearance decreases during the duration of an association, this study reported "that satisfaction showed a tendency to be increasingly positively correlated with attractiveness over time" (p. 165).

The primary issue of the second study (Reis *et al.*, 1982) centered on the sex differences revealed in the first study. The significant social interaction effects for males but not for females was thought to be based on a "marketplace economy effect." Basically, this effect was that first-year female students can be more selective in their opposite-sex interactions because they typically interact with males of all four years. This second study involved 43 males and 53 females who were university seniors. Social interactions were recorded in the same manner but for time spans of 7 to 18 days during November.

The results of the second study were not different from those of the first. Males of higher physical attractiveness experienced a greater quantity of social interactions than did their female counterparts. The authors explained these sex differences as not due to a marketplace economy effect but due to a difference in aggressiveness. Although males of higher physical attractiveness were more aggressive, females of higher physical attractiveness were less aggressive. Those more physically attractive males were more assertive and less fearful of women and, accordingly, were more likely to approach women. The more physically attractive females were less assertive, more distrustful of the opposite sex, and more likely to wait to be approached. Quality, as well as quantity, was also more favorable. That is, the social interactions by females of higher physical attractiveness were reported as "more satisfying, pleasant, intimate, and disclosing" (p. 993).

In summary, social relationships are influenced by the physical attractiveness of the participants. Those lower and higher in physical attractiveness do actually have different interaction behaviors and experiences. As an intrapersonal reality, it can be concluded that those higher in physical attractiveness, as opposed to those lower, have more favorable social relationship interactions.

Social Power

Social power is positively correlated with physical attractiveness. The explanation may begin with the fact that physical attractiveness serves as a cue whereby others evaluate a person (Adams & Huston, 1975; Dion, 1972; Dion, Berscheid, & Walster, 1974). Individuals who are physically attractive enjoy greater acceptance and popularity among others (Dion & Berscheid, 1972; Kleck, Richardson, & Ronald, 1974). Because acceptance and popularity are important elements of social power, persons of higher physical attractiveness should therefore be more successful in their influence than persons of lower physical attractiveness (Dion & Stein, 1978). The general sentiment is that if competency is measured in terms of social power to influence, those who are higher in physical attractiveness are significantly more competent than those who are lower (Dion & Stein, 1978).

Helping Behavior

An indirect measure of social power may be the ability to receive greater aid when seeking help. The entire help-seeking section of Chapter 3 presents documentation that those of higher physical attractiveness are able to secure greater help. Those higher in physical attractiveness have been shown to be able to solicit more volunteers, help, compliance, money, and physical effort, as well as more verbal assistance (Benson, Karabenick, & Lerner, 1976; Mims, Hartnett, & Nay, 1975; Tedeschi, Schlenker, & Bonoma, 1975; West & Brown, 1975). Overall, those individuals of higher physical attractiveness are able to elicit greater aid than those lower in physical attractiveness.

Helping behavior research has also manipulated surrogate measures of physical attractiveness. These measures involve unusual shortness and fatness (Miller, 1970a) and physical deformity (Kleck, 1968, 1969; Kleck, Ono, & Hastorf, 1966). Soble and Strickland (1974) used an interviewer who appeared to have either a deformed back or a physically normal back. The female interviewer met with 116 middle-class housewives for an initial interview. In each interview she requested a follow-up, but for 58 of the subjects she appeared with a normal back and for the other 58 with a deformed back. Compliance for the second interview was significantly lower when the interviewer appeared to have a deformed back versus a physically normal back.

Beyond passive attempts to influence, measured in terms of receiving help, more active attempts produced similar results. The help-seeking section cited that those higher in physical attractiveness were more successful in eliciting help and in recruiting volunteers (Mims et al., 1975; Wilson, 1978). Furthermore, once these people volunteer, they work harder for those of higher physical attractiveness (Kahn, Hottes, & Davis, 1971; Sigall, Page, & Brown, 1971).

The ability to influence honesty may be viewed as complementary to the ability to influence helping behavior. Regardless of classification, honesty was shown to be influenced by physical attractiveness (Sroufe, Chaikin, Cook, & Freeman, 1977). A stimulus person of either high or low physical attractiveness left money in a telephone booth. The subjects were 180 individuals who went to use the telephone after the stimulus person. Physical attractiveness was manipulated by altering the appearance of a single person. As a subject entered the booth, the stimulus person returned to inquire about the money. The subjects responded with socially desirable behavior (i.e., honesty) significantly more with the stimulus person of higher physical attractiveness.

Evaluation

Evaluation impact is accentuated by physical attractiveness. Sigall and Aronson (1969) found an evaluation from a person of lower physical attractiveness had significantly less influence than an identical evaluation from a person of higher physical attractiveness. The methodology involved male subjects with a female stimulus person made-up to appear either high or low in physical attractiveness. Care was taken to alter only the physical attractiveness of the stimulus person and not the credibility. The authors hypothesized that rewards and punishments from a highly valued evaluator (i.e., one of high physical attractiveness) would be more intense than those from an evaluator of low value (i.e., one of low physical attractiveness). Therefore, if a positive or a negative evaluation came from a source of lower value, the receiver was not likely to be greatly affected.

A manipulation check indicated that the physical attractiveness was successfully manipulated without affecting the person's credibility. Physical attractiveness did have an accentuating impact on evaluations. The evaluators liked most were those of high physical attractiveness who gave positive evaluations. The evaluators liked least were those of high physical attractiveness who gave negative evaluations. The evaluators who were between these liking extremes were those of low physical attractiveness, regardless of whether their evaluations were negative or positive.

There may be a greater desire to please a physically attractive person. The data from Sigall and Aronson (1969) revealed that the type of evaluation administered by a person of lower physical attractiveness is not important, as compared to their counterpart of higher physical attractiveness. Both rewards and punishments are increased with a person of higher, as opposed to lower, physical attractiveness. The authors summarized these results by stating that

> people like pretty girls who evaluate them positively and dislike pretty girls who evaluate them negatively, with unattractive girls falling in between these two extremes. On the other hand, people desire to be with pretty girls over ugly girls regardless of their evaluations. (Sigall & Aronson, 1969, p. 99)

Accentuated repercussions are likely to produce variations in magnitudes of effort expended for work. Sigall, Page, and Brown (1971) measured the effort expended by subjects during the initial trial of a task. These male subjects received either a negative or positive evaluation of their performance from a female of either high or low physical attractiveness. The subjects who received a negative evaluation from an evaluator of high physical attractiveness increased their effort on the second trial. But the subjects who received a negative evaluation from an evaluator of low physical attractiveness worked even less on their second trial.

Physically attractive females elicit greater effort expenditures and greater attention than their counterparts of lower physical attractiveness. The reaction and evaluation from a female of higher physical attractiveness appears to increase the value to a male receiver. Hartnett, Gottlieb, and Hayes (1976) proposed that lower performance may be due to distraction caused by higher physical attractiveness rather than evaluations administered by such persons. Donley and Allen (1977) refined these data by suggesting that performance differences due to an evaluator's physical attractiveness are, in part, a function of the type of task. They reported that task performance was highest when the evaluator was either low in physical attractiveness or the task was not ego involving. Task performance was lower when the condition was not ego involving and the evaluator was of high physical attractiveness. It is believed that in this latter example, the subjects attended to the physical attractiveness of the evaluator at the expense of their performance. Unfortunately, Donley and Allen did not fully rotate the sex manipulation by also using female subjects with a male stimulus person. These experiments have focused exclusively on the impact of a female stimulus person on male receivers, but other research does suggest an expanded hypothesis to include individuals of both sexes. For example, within dyads of opposite sex peers, both males and females of higher physical attractiveness are more successful in their influence attempts (Dion & Stein, 1978; Nida & Williams, 1977). However, recent research has begun to suggest that the medium of interaction (i.e., print, audio, video, and face-to-face) may play a role in the specific instances of influence effectiveness (Chaiken & Eagly, 1983; Newman, 1983).

Cooperation and Competition

Cooperative and competitive behaviors are affected by physical attractiveness. People of lower and of higher levels of physical attractiveness respond differently in situations of cooperation and competition (Kahn, Hottes, & Davis, 1971). Responses of participants were examined for a simulated interpersonal interaction that used a prisoners' dilemma game (i.e., a zero-sum situation). Four experimental conditions were employed: (a) both a male and female of high physical attractiveness, (b) both a male and female of low physical attractiveness, (c) a male of high and a female of low physical attractiveness, and (d) a male of low and a female of high physical attractiveness.

Sex and also physical attractiveness affected cooperation and competition. Males and females did not have different motives for cooperating but they did respond differently. Females were more cooperative with males than with other females as partners. Females of lower physical attractiveness were more influenced by male partners of higher physical attractiveness than were the female counterparts of higher physical attractiveness. The females of lower physical attractiveness expressed great interest in the exercise when paired with a male partner of high physical attractiveness, but not with male partners of low physical attractiveness. In fact, both females of higher and lower physical attractiveness responded poorly (i.e., did not cooperate) with male partners of lower physical attractiveness. The cooperation versus competition was not significantly affected for the males paired with partners of low and high physical attractiveness. However, males were most cooperative when paired with a female of the same physical attractiveness level as himself.

Influence Strategy

Persons of lower and higher physical attractiveness seem to possess inherently different influence strategies for persuasion. Seventy-seven fifth and sixth graders, ranging in age from 10 to 12 years old, attempted to persuade a partner to eat a bad-tasting cracker (Dion & Stein, 1978). Motivation for the subjects successful persuasion was in the form of monetary payment. Physical attractiveness of the subjects was rated independently by peer consensus of photographs. The pairings involved subjects of either high or low physical attractiveness who were unknown to each other.

The results supported the general physical attractiveness belief pertaining to intrapersonal realities. There was an imbalance of success between the levels of physical attractiveness and the variety of influence strategies employed. Overall, the physically attractive manipulators were most successful at influencing the behavior of the opposite-sex peers. This influence was greater for females with a male receiver than a male with a female receiver. The specific influence strategies employed were:

1. Males of lower physical attractiveness used direct, aggressive, and commanding behaviors, including physical threats. This finding is consistent with a 1974 study done by Dion and Berscheid which identified aggressive behavior as more characteristic of children of lower physical attractiveness.
2. Males of higher physical attractiveness were assertive but not aggressive. They attempted to coax, making use of reassurance and pleading tactics. These males were not successful with male targets for they appeared to evoke ambivalent reactions which reduced compliance.
3. Females of higher physical attractiveness were the least persistent and least forceful of the groups. They also made the fewest number of influence attempts, however, they were successful in influencing the opposite sex.
4. Females of lower physical attractiveness were more assertive but less successful than the females of higher physical attractiveness. This group, representing members lower physical attractiveness, were not significantly different in their success with the same-sex and opposite-sex partners.

The findings are interesting and consistent with the physical attractiveness phenomena. The theme of this chapter on intrapersonal differences has been verified for those who differ in physical attractiveness. The results clearly indicate that stimulus persons of different levels of physical attractiveness possess and exert different influence strategies within social interactions.

Capability

A general summation may be that the physical attractiveness phenomena apply to social power. Perceptual differences related to such characteristics as poise and sociability cause expectations of greater social competence for those higher in physical attractiveness (Dion, Berscheid, & Walster, 1972). An exception is faintly alluded to by one unpublished study (cited in Dion & Stein, 1978). It suggested that same-sex individuals of high physical attractiveness may elicit caution due to feelings of deceitful purposes.

Overall, the social power is in favor of those higher in physical attractiveness. Explanation for this situation may rest in the fact that communications of higher physical attractiveness are evaluated as more calm, popular, and desirable as an acquaintance. Consequently, the greater influence within social interactions may be due to the greater impact that high physical attractiveness has on its delivery of rewards and punishments (Barocas & Karoly, 1972).

PERSONALITY

Research has specifically addressed personality characteristics possessed by those of different physical attractiveness levels. The data have identified personality variations as a function of higher and lower physical attractiveness (Adams, 1977b; Shea, Crossman, & Adams, 1978). It is always difficult to conclude causality, but a strong relationship does exist between external physical attractiveness of an individual and the person's inner cognitive concepts. This association exists for adolescents (Lerner & Karabenick, 1974; Lerner, Venning, & Knapp, 1975), college students (Adams, 1975; Lerner, Karabenick, & Stuart, 1973; Lerner, Orlos, & Knapp, 1976), and adults (Berscheid, Walster, & Bohrnstedt, 1973). Sex differences exist in that the physical attractiveness of females exerts much greater power in all directions. For example, the contrast in self-concepts between females of lower and higher physical attractiveness is significantly greater than the contrast exhibited for their male counterparts (Adams, 1975; Lerner & Karabenick, 1974).

The overall data support a general presupposition that interpersonal perceptions reflect actual intrapersonal realities within the recipient. The data's consistency indicates that individuals may internalize differential treatments so that positive responses translate into positive personalities, whereas negative responses translate into negative personalities. Association of personality and physical attractiveness is very evident at the extreme level of institutionalized persons; however, lack of experimental data prohibits determination of causation.

Institutionalized Persons

The relationship between physical attractiveness and severe personality or mental disorders has received some attention. Physical attractiveness of female patients hospitalized for mental disorders was examined in two related studies (Farina *et al.*, 1977). The first study involved psychiatric patients, university employees, and shoppers. Ratings of physical attractiveness were performed through photographs and face-to-face interactions. Results were the same regardless of the rating technique, and despite the subjects' lack of awareness about the mental status of the stimulus persons. The psychiatric patients were rated significantly lower in physical attractiveness than individuals in nonhospitalized control groups.

The second study focused on the physical attractiveness of psychiatric patients within their hospital. Based on a sample of 40 subjects, those lower in physical attractiveness experienced more negative consequences. For example, those lower in physical attractiveness showed less social ability on standardized tests, received more severe diagnoses, were hospitalized longer, and received fewer outside visitors. Similar intrapersonal patterns were reported in a study with adolescent females admitted to a state hospital (Edgemon & Clopton, 1978). Measures of 24 characteristics revealed significant positive correlations between physical attractiveness and personality for those admitted for psychological problems. Napoleon, Chassin, and Young (1980) also dealt with female psychiatric inpatients. They concluded that their data suggested persons of lower physical attractiveness were predisposed to a host of negative social outcomes, even to the extent of incurring mental illness.

Outside of these three efforts, the entire research in this chapter pertains to intrapersonal differences within the general population. This disparity within the population does not diminish the importance of recognizing that certain individuals of different levels of physical attractiveness possess subsequent personal characteristics that go well beyond mere perceptions. For instance, people who rate themselves as high in physical attractiveness also hold themselves in higher self-regard, consider themselves more likable, outgoing, confident, and generally more competent than those of lower physical attractiveness (Adams, 1977a, 1977b).

Personal Traits

Researchers report that for both sexes a positive relationship exists between physical attractiveness and personality characteristics. Formal personality tests reveal that females of higher physical attractiveness are more understanding, more achievement oriented, have greater endurance, and are more independent, whereas males of higher physical attractiveness are more aggressive and dominant than those of lower levels (Krebs & Adinolfi, 1975). The logical explanation for these personality traits is related to an interactive process, according to Adams (1977b). As persons of different levels of physical attractiveness interact within society, the differing impressions that others hold are reflected back as valuable information. This feedback causes the person to react and to modify his or her self-concept accordingly. The result is intrapersonal personality differences that may be caused, or at least influenced, by the physical attractiveness of the person.

In one study, numerous measures of personality and physical attractiveness were assessed (Adams, 1977a). As a validation procedure, the correlations between ratings of physical attractiveness were calculated and averaged (.67). For the males, facial physical attractiveness and good general appearance were associated with healthy self-concepts and positive functioning in social settings. For the females, facial physical attractiveness, good general appearance, and a thin body type were all important characteristics. Those females with lower weights and good facial physical attractiveness were more resistant to peer influences, more self-accepting, less fearful of being evaluated, and viewed themselves as more physically attractive. Self-perceptions of facial physical attractiveness and general appearance were not significantly different for the sexes, that is, these variables were equally valuable for both males and females.

This study showed a significant relationship between physical attractiveness, personality characteristics, and social behavior. It is likely that the physical attractiveness of an individual leads to an internalization of the self-concept resulting from peer pressure and peer response influences. The data indicated that for both those lower and higher in physical attractiveness, the individual internalized the corresponding stereotypes. Also, those lower in physical attractiveness tended to possess greater external control orientations (as opposed to internal motivations)— emotionality, perceptions of not being liked, social distress, and anxiety.

Personality as a function of physical attractiveness may interact with sex (Mathes & Kahn, 1975). Mathes and Kahn used 211 subjects to examine the relationships between physical attractiveness and happiness, psychological health, and self-esteem. Measures of physical attractiveness were obtained by independent judges, and the personality traits were determined by self-completed personality inventories.

Physical attractiveness of females was positively correlated with self-esteem and happiness and negatively correlated with neuroticism. Physical attractiveness of males was not significantly correlated with the variables in this study. The authors interpreted their findings to mean that our society still considers the physical attractiveness characteristic to be more important for women than for men. Women possessing high physical attractiveness are able to obtain greater outcomes of higher values than men can obtain. Furthermore, those preferential outcomes for physically attractive women make them happier, psychologically healthier, and prouder of themselves. All of which may yield different outlooks on life for women of different levels of physical attractiveness. One example is a sense of humor in which those lower in physical attractiveness showed significant preference for cartoons admiring females of high physical attractiveness (Wilson & Brazendale, 1974). Furthermore, women of higher physical attractiveness found risqué cartoons less funny than their counterparts of lower physical attractiveness (Wilson, Nias, & Brazendale, 1975).

Self-Concept

An intrapersonal consequence of physical attractiveness may well be a commensurate self-concept (Adams, 1977b). This dependence of self-concept on physical attractiveness is especially pronounced in those who are at the extremes of the physical attractiveness continuum. The reasoning is based on the notion that among the many ways of describing oneself, we tend to use the descriptions which are most distinctive (McGuire & Padawer-Singer, 1976). As social environments change, distinctive characteristics diminish as others emerge. Characteristics which distinguish an individual will receive the most attention by that individual. McGuire and Padawer-Singer (1976) found that people describe themselves in terms which most set them apart from their peers. In other words, a person of tall height will not describe himself or herself as tall when surrounded by peers of equal or greater height.

Self-concept develops through social interaction. This process involves communication of attitudes, expectations, and behaviors between people. Subsequently, an individual adopts a role congruent with societal messages. The result is a mirrored self-image, according to those subscribing to this symbolic interaction process (Gergen, 1972; cf. Kuhn, 1972). Support of this view is provided in a review of over 1,000 studies dealing with self-concept (Wylie, 1979). These studies conceded that self-concept, and self-esteem, were more a function of subjective self-perceptions than any objective demographic characteristics. Wylie concluded that it was not objective reality but subjective interpretation of events that determined behavior and ultimately self-concept.

Specific Subjectivity

Internal states of mind and external body characteristics form an integral unit. Personality and self-concept are not independent of physical attractiveness. When people state that they are either satisfied or dissatisfied with themselves, they are not saying that the person and body are two separate entities. In fact, self-judged physical attractiveness is one of the major components of self-image (Fisher, 1973; Smith, P. A., 1962).

Physical attractiveness is then a specific self-concept characteristic that is vulnerable to subjective perception. That is, those who have a high public self-consciousness are also those who are very aware of their physical appearance qualities. This premise, pertaining to public self-consciousness, is based on two studies by Turner, Gilliland, and Klein (1981). In the first study, 103 subjects were administered a standard self-consciousness scale. Those measuring high public self-consciousness were able to evaluate specific physical features in significantly less time. The second study employed 99 female subjects from two different geographical locations. Those with high public self-consciousness were also those evaluated as possessing high physical attractiveness.

People generally process information selectively (Treisman, 1964). A specific intrapersonal peculiarity involving selectivity relates to how those of lower and higher physical attractiveness form self concepts. Specifically, an information-filtering process, which protects and enhances an individual's self-concept, varies according to physical attractiveness. Seventy-two subjects, observed in a naturalistic environment, tended to approach or avoid self-awareness as a function of their physical attractiveness (McDonald & Eilenfield, 1980). Unobtrusive measures compared approach and avoidance of these subjects who were classified as either high, low, or moderate in physical attractiveness. The data revealed an increasing linear relationship between physical attractiveness and selective exposure to self-awareness. In other words, those of higher physical attractiveness sought greater self-awareness, whereas those of lower physical attractiveness did not.

Physical Characteristics

The effects of physical attractiveness upon self-concept begin early in life. Simmons and Rosenberg (1975) found that among adolescents those who thought they were less good looking (i.e., less physically attractive) had lower self-esteem than their counterparts. These authors also reported that self-perceived physical attractiveness was significantly related to beliefs about being liked by the opposite sex. Starr (1982) examined 67 subjects described as young adults (aged 19 to 31 years old) with cleft lip or palate. Each subject was administered a scale to measure physical attractiveness and self-esteem. Subjects higher in physical attractiveness scored significantly higher in self-esteem than those lower in physical attractiveness. No differences in self-esteem were indicated between sex or educational level for these subjects. The author implied that the results advance a notion of causality between self-perception of physical attractiveness and self-perception of self-esteem.

A positive relationship between physical attractiveness and self-concept is reported consistently (Adams, 1977a; Lerner & Karabenich, 1974; Lerner et al., 1973; Lerner et al., 1976). Later research has used three gradations of physical attractiveness to explore self-concepts. It similarly reported that subjects of higher physical attractiveness yield the highest self-esteem scores as compared to those of lower or average physical attractiveness (Balban, 1981). Still other research has focused on specific body components as related to physical attractiveness and self-concept.

Self-concept is integrally related to body satisfaction as a function of physical attractiveness. Such satisfaction was disclosed through 2,000 questionnaires randomly selected from a total of over 20,000 responses to a survey published in a national magazine (Berscheid et al., 1973). Those who expressed satisfaction with their face and body where also those who viewed themselves as most conscientious, assertive, likable, and to have the most favorable heterosexual relationships.

Some research examines only one sex, whereas other research reports data for both. A study using only female subjects reported that women who are higher in physical attractiveness are most likely to describe themselves as likable, intelligent, physically attractive, a good date, and feminine (Kaats & Davis, 1970). However, men tend to be more satisfied with their appearance and less concerned about their weight than women (Berscheid et al., 1973). Somewhat related results were obtained through stepwise regression to evaluate differential contributions made by specific body qualities (Mahoney & Finch, 1976a). The conclusion pertaining to self-esteem was that the male's satisfaction with voice and chest is most important, but for women, self-esteem is largely determined by their overall physical attractiveness.

Independence and Confidence

It is difficult to determine causal direction among the relationships between physical attractiveness and measures of independence and confidence. Both males and females of higher physical attractiveness possess greater internal control and greater resistance to peer pressure (Adams, 1975; Adams, 1977a). But the cause of such independence may be due to the fact that those higher in physical attractiveness also have greater self-acceptance (Adams, 1975). Conversely, they may gain greater confidence because those higher in physical attractiveness also demonstrate higher achievement scores, intelligence scores, self-esteem scores (Clifford, 1975; Maruyama & Miller, 1975), and grade point averages (Lerner & Lerner, 1977).

Independence and confidence can be inferred from research using surrogate measures, as well as direct measures. One indirect measure of confidence may relate to expressed liking. McWhirter (1969) pursued this attraction effect by manipulating the physical attractiveness of both male subjects and female stimulus persons. He reported that the males of highest physical attractiveness were most attracted to females of high physical attractiveness. However, the males of lowest physical attractiveness were most attracted to the female stimulus persons in the middle range of the physical attractiveness dimension. The interpretation of these findings is applicable to a maximization strategy for success in dating, which is an analogous measure of confidence. The latter measure illustrates a difference of confidence between the levels of physical attractiveness whereby those higher in physical attractiveness are more confident.

Diversity in independence and confidence is associated with many characteristics. It is not limited to self-rated physical attractiveness but includes physical attractiveness ratings by independent judges. Both self-ratings and ratings by others were used in an inspection of expected outcomes (Abbott & Sebastian, 1981). The subjects were 60 women who indicated their likely success in both social and nonsocial tasks. Subjects higher in physical attractiveness (based on both self-ratings and ratings by others) were significantly more likely to expect success than those lower in physical attractiveness. These intrapersonal expectations of success were especially prominent for social tasks that included interpersonal liking. For nonsocial tasks that involved manipulative, skilled, or intellectual abilities, high physical attractiveness was less predictive of expected success.

Locus of control varies according to physical attractiveness. Adams (1977a) collected both self-ratings of physical attractiveness and objective ratings by independent judges. Factor analysis of the data revealed that males higher in physical attractiveness demonstrated greater internal locus of control as well as greater self-acceptance, sensation seeking, ability to resist peer pressure, and a more healthy self-concept. The same data revealed that both higher physical attractiveness and lower body weight, for females, were associated with greater self-acceptance, greater resistance to peer influence, and less fear of being evaluated.

Locus of control and physical attractiveness may have a curvilinear relationship (Anderson, 1978). The specific motivation was to test the reality of interpersonal perceptions pertaining to a positive relationship between physical attractiveness and internal locus of control. Independent measures of physical attractiveness were compared with locus of control scores for 28 male and 35 female subjects. The control scores were determined by Rotter's Internal–External Locus of Control scale. As hypothesized, these data revealed that the greatest internal locus of control was displayed by subjects of moderate physical attractiveness.

Social Skills

There may be justification for the perceptual differences identified in the chapters on interpersonal consequences. The justification may rest on the fact that people of disparate physical attractiveness levels, who are perceived to possess unequal social skills, may actually do so (Guise, Pollans, & Turkat, 1982). Reis *et al.* proposed a mediational process where

as a result of a person's physical attractiveness, differential levels of social competence are acquired . . . these in turn affect social participation. (1982, p. 992)

Whatever the process, the variances are substantial.

Subconsciousness

Social skills are positively correlated with physical attractiveness even when appearance is not visible. To identify this relationship, two studies conducted social interactions over the telephone. In one study the subjects, presumed to be of higher physical attractiveness, exhibited more socially appealing behavior (Snyder *et al.*, 1977). Telephone conversations were arranged between males and females, with the latter being of average physical attractiveness and not aware of the research interest in physical attractiveness. Each male was told that their female telephone partner was of either high or low physical attractiveness. At no time was any of the physical attractiveness information verbally conveyed to the females. Independent judges, who later analyzed tape recordings, identified the females as acting more friendly, likable, and sociable under the condition that the male subjects thought they were high in physical attractiveness. This study documents that social behavior can be subconsciously and effectively shaped in a manner consistent with the physical attractiveness phenomena.

The other telephone interaction also involved unseen participants (Goldman & Lewis, 1977). The subjects (60 males and 60 females) engaged in a 5-minute telephone conversation with each of three opposite-sex partners. After each interaction, the participants evaluated the social skills of their partner. Physical attractiveness of the participants was determined by three judges independent of the telephone interactions. The subjects neither conveyed any physical attractiveness information, nor were they aware of the research interest in physical attractiveness. Those stimulus persons rated more likable, more socially skillful, and less anxious were also those rated higher in physical attractiveness by independent judges.

Self-Disclosure

Heterogeneous social skills may offer partial explanation for the findings that those lower in physical attractiveness were actually less social and subsequently more socially isolated (e.g., Krebs & Adinolfi, 1975; Reis et al., 1980; Reis et al., 1982). Even though no physical attractiveness information was exchanged in the above telephone studies, other relevant information could be communicated. Those higher in physical attractiveness tended to be more open and more likely to self-disclose to others (Cash & Soloway, 1975). Specific research reveals that those of higher physical attractiveness actually self-disclose to a greater degree (Pellegrini, Hicks, Meyers-Winton, & Antal, 1978). Ninety-six subjects (48 males and 48 females) participated in an interview with an opposite-sex listener (i.e., stimulus person). The stimulus person was a male or female whose physical attractiveness was either minimized or maximized. Physical attractiveness of subjects was determined as either high or low by independent judges. More intimate self-disclosure was significantly greater for those subjects of higher physical attractiveness as compared to lower. Like the next study described, more intimate self-disclosures were also given to a stimulus person of higher physical attractiveness.

Those of higher physical attractiveness may naturally elicit greater self-disclosure from others (Brundage et al., 1977). Ninety-six female subjects were asked to write a self-description to be given to an unknown male they would soon meet. Before writing, the subjects were shown a photograph of a stimulus person who represented either high or low physical attractiveness. Self-disclosure was more intimate with the stimulus person of higher physical attractiveness than lower.

Nonverbal Demeanor

It is logical that social skills, associated with physical attractiveness, may represent underlying factors not readily visible. Consequently, it is appropriate to consider the impact of nonverbal behavior. Because underlying factors may be unconscious, and even subliminal; assertiveness, personal space, and nonverbal facial messages have been explored. It appears that people of higher physical attractiveness incorporate psychological, social, and behavioral attributes more effectively than those lower in physical attractiveness. A series of two experiments, using two different rating methods, tested the hypothesis that the assertiveness of American females is positively associated with their physical attractiveness (Jackson & Huston, 1975). The data showed that subjects high in physical attractiveness were more assertive as demonstrated by their quicker and stronger responses to impolite social treatment.

Proximity of participants was probed as it pertains to social skills associated with physical attractiveness. Experiments were conducted to examine the relationship between physical attractiveness and personal space (Kmiecik, Mausar, & Banziger, 1979; Powell & Dabbs, 1976). Powell and Dabbs used laboratory and field experiments. In the laboratory experiment, subjects (30 males and 30 females) entered a room to view posters of persons either high or low in physical attractiveness. Distances between where the subjects stopped to view the poster and the location of the poster were used as measures to reflect customary personal space between the stimulus person and the subject. In the field experiment, 102 sidewalk pedestrians (both males and females) were stopped for an interview. The interviewer was a male or female of either high or low physical attractiveness. Distances between the interview dyads were recorded and analyzed through use of a camera located on a nearby rooftop. Overall, the results were minimal. The only significant effects were for female subjects who stood closer to both male and female interviewers of higher physical attractiveness.

Kmiecik et al. (1979) used 120 subjects in a field experiment. Their procedure involved approaching pedestrians about to cross an intersection (i.e., intruding into the subjects' personal space). They found that physical attractiveness caused significant behavioral reactions pertaining to personal space. Specifically, personal space intruded on by stimulus persons of higher physical attractiveness caused the subjects to cross the intersection at a slower speed, but lower physical attractiveness caused faster speed.

Two articles reported that those of higher physical attractiveness possessed greater nonverbal communication skills (Brideau & Allen, 1980; Larrance & Zuckerman, 1981). The ability or accuracy to send nonverbal cues as a function of facial physical attractiveness and voice likability was examined by Larrance and Zuckerman. Both audio and visual recordings were made of 60 subjects (30 males and 30 females) who served as communication senders. Six judges (3 males and 3 females) used videotapes and audio tape recordings to analyze the facial and vocal qualities of the communicators. The data indicated that greater accuracy of nonverbal social skills was exhibited by those communicators of higher physical attractiveness as well as those with more likable voices. The data also revealed that the communicators of higher physical attractiveness were most accurate with nonverbal cues that represented studied as opposed to spontaneous expressions. The authors pointed out that this difference represented a controllable skill that had been developed.

The greater nonverbal abilities possessed by those higher in physical attractiveness may be due to development that depends on social inter-actions. Larrance and Zuckerman concluded that the faces of those higher in physical attractiveness may constantly be a focus of attention. This attention then encourages those of higher physical attractiveness to make the most effective use of facial qualities in nonverbal communication. Brideau and Allen (1980) reported that females of higher physical attractiveness had greater nonverbal communication skills than females of lower levels but that males did not differ. These authors concluded that development of greater nonverbal skills is consistent with other research documenting that physical attractiveness is a social variable of more importance for females than males.

PHYSIOLOGICAL EFFECTS

The consequences of the physical attractiveness phenomena include physiology as well as psychology. General indications support a juxta-position of external physical characteristics and states of internal arousal. When defined in terms of blood pressure, internal states of arousal are believed to be affected by a variety of psychosocial stresses (Lazarus, 1978; Rose & Levin, 1979). The medical literature in this field includes one published article designed to explore the relationship between physical attractiveness and blood pressure (Hansell, Sparacino, & Ronchi, 1982).

This article reported the results of a series of four studies. Collectively, the studies involved over 1,000 subjects who ranged in age from 14 to 76 years old. Blood pressure readings were taken 3 to 10 times per person. Physical attractiveness measures were obtained from independent judges using a 9-point bipolar scale. Precautions were taken to minimize confounding and extraneous variables pertaining to the blood pressure measures. Controls were carefully executed for those who took the readings, the equipment used, the time and location of the readings, and the subjects characteristics, such as posture and level of activity.

Those of lower physical attractiveness had significantly higher blood pressure. However, an interaction of sex and physical attractiveness occurred in the first studies with a sample of 283 females and 369 males. In two of the four studies, females of higher physical attractiveness had lower blood pressure (both systolic and diastolic) than their counterparts of lower physical attractiveness. However, no significant differences were revealed for males in these two studies. Based on the differences of blood pressure among younger females, the researchers expanded into another study that involved adults. Their fourth study used 594 municipal employees (441 men and 153 women) with average ages of 40 years for males and 35 years for females. The results with these adults did not reveal a significant difference in blood pressure due to physical attractiveness.

The authors concluded that the effects of physical attractiveness on blood pressure were most prominent among younger people as compared to older. They also summarized that the greatest impact is on younger females. This differential impact is consistent with other research that has identified physical attractiveness to be of greater importance for females than males. Younger females with physical attractiveness rated to be in the top 50%, had significantly lower blood pressures than their counterparts rated in the bottom 50%. The authors stated that for adolescent females "the results of the four studies reported here document the existence of an association between physical attractiveness and chronic blood pressure" (p. 120).

PROSPECTIVE HORIZON

The interpersonal landscape is established, but the intrapersonal territory remains undeveloped. Intrapersonal investigations represent a few early attempts to exceed the boundaries of perceptions and assumptions. Future exploration into the actual experiences of individuals of higher and lower physical attractiveness are likely to yield rich findings. Discoveries that delineate intrapersonal realities will equal, or exceed, current interpersonal endeavors. The reason for this intense value is that such findings will have greater repercussions. The differences will submit to formal measurements that will force society to confront serious human issues pertaining to the physical attractiveness phenomena.

Intrapersonal traits appear to parallel interpersonal perceptions. However, our knowledge of physical attractiveness is not yet sufficient to identify the causal element, or even if one exists. Consequently, answers are not available to two germane questions: (a) Do internal personal qualities, within individuals, explain the variance of interpersonal interactions as they pertain to physical attractiveness? (b) Do treatments by society, as they pertain to physical attractiveness, explain the variance of internal personal qualities within individuals?

The latest, and possibly most exciting dimension of physical attractiveness phenomena is the potential interdependencies between physical attractiveness and physiological composition of individuals. There are ethical and societal issues to be dealt with if a person's physical attractiveness is confirmed to produce corresponding intrapersonal characteristics. At this moment, however, early signals are emerging which indicate that an individual's physical attractiveness is an underlying factor influencing psychological and physiological measures.

Chapter 6

Determinants of Physical Attractiveness

This book documents the physical attractiveness phenomena. Because of the very powerful and serious implications, this treatise necessarily includes antecedents of physical attractiveness. Certainly a basic anterior issue pertains to underlying determinants of the physical attractiveness variable. To contend with the difficult abstract nature of the physical attractiveness construct, research manipulations rely on a gestalt approach to measurement and definition. Commonly referred to as the truth-of-consensus method, it employs a global approach. For example,

> if a significant number of "judges" designate a person as physically attractive, then that person is defined as physically attractive. Whether it was the dimple on the chin which the judges were responding to, whether more redheads than brunettes were classified as attractive, is not typically a matter of concern. (Berscheid & Walster, 1974, p. 181)

For research purposes the gestalt approach has worked well and continues to be the best available solution. But beyond this solution there is still the need to identify ingredients of physical attractiveness.

Twenty years ago it was stated that our society knows less about the physical attractiveness variable pertaining to people than it does for fish (Hochberg, 1964, p. 112). Since that time, the situation may have changed in favor of the people. Although social science has not completed its work, substantial knowledge has accumulated about specific determinants as well as about physical attractiveness in general. Contrary to the suggestion that attempts to identify the ingredients of physical attractiveness present insurmountable barriers (Huston & Levinger, 1978), progress is being made. Efforts continue to pursue identification and definition of the underlying dimensions of physical attractiveness. Recently, an unpublished master's thesis has attempted to assess the separate roles that the face and body have in determining physical attractiveness (Jones, 1982).

140

Determinants of physical attractiveness are not restricted to physical body characteristics, nor are they restricted to tangible factors possessed by the person. The determinants of physical attractiveness, which have been currently identified, include many parts and dimensions of the body, tangible enhancements such as clothes and cosmetics, perceptual distortions such as reputations and accomplishments, and even environmental factors. All these factors contribute to the evaluation of physical attractiveness, but their significance is not the same. In fact, research implies a hierarchical ordering of body dimensions that contribute to physical attractiveness.

HIERARCHICAL RANKINGS

Body dimensions do not contribute equally to physical attractiveness. In fact, there is a two-level hierarchical system that is sequential. On the first level are such encompassing body components as the face and physique. On the second level are subcomponents such as the face's nose and mouth.

Because variations in methodologies make it difficult to compare relevant research, identification of a sole hierarchy is not practical at this time. This difficulty is due primarily to the wide range of dimensions studied in each effort. At one extreme, an article has reported only one dimension (Miyamoto & Dornbusch, 1956) and, at the other extreme, a study used 46 dimensions (Secord & Jourard, 1953). Between these two extremes are scales involving 12 dimensions (Jourard & Secord, 1954), 20 dimensions (Mahoney & Finch, 1976a), and 25 dimensions (Berscheid et al., 1973). The most recent study, which used more substantial methodology was a doctoral dissertation consisting of 44 dimensions (Budge, 1981).

The dissertation focused on an importance ranking of body dimensions as they contribute to the evaluation of physical attractiveness. A second focus pertained to the level of agreement for ideal dimensions. The stimulus persons involved in this research were 37 males and 38 females with a mean age of 22 years. However, before the formal study was conducted, about 600 subjects (equally divided between sexes) contributed over a 5 year period. These prestudy subjects were asked to describe their level of physical attractiveness by using body dimensions they deemed significant contributors. Based on the product of these 5 years, combined with similar conclusions from other work (Lerner et al., 1977; Mahoney & Finch, 1976b), a collection of 44 body dimensions were considered relevant to the definition of physical attractiveness.

Using a 7-point scale, stimulus persons were evaluated on each of these 44 dimensions. The evaluation procedure employed 5 male and 5 female judges to rate the stimulus persons in a live setting. Three general findings were produced based primarily on *t* tests and factor analyses. First, the author concluded that the data supported the hypothesis that both sexes agree on ideal traits for both males and females. This finding is further evidence that beauty is not an assessment unique to any one observer.

Second, relatively few characteristics determine physical attractiveness, and only 6 of the 44 dimensions examined contributed substantially. Regardless of the stimulus persons' sex or the judges' sex, these six factors accounted for about 75% of the variance in the physical attractiveness evaluations. Similarly, one factor alone accounted for about 50% of the total variance for all sex dyad combinations.

Third, even these relatively few characteristics are not equal. The most important body component in determining physical attractiveness is the face. With regard to dimensions, there is a slight difference in ranks for male and female stimulus persons. The ranks for male stimulus persons, regardless of judges' sex, were, first, face (accounting for about 50% variance) and, second, weight and weight distribution (accounting for about 10% variance). The ranks for female stimulus persons, regardless of judges' sex, were, first, weight and weight distribution (accounting for about 50% variance) and, second, face (accounting for about 10%). The conclusion suggested by Budge (1981) is that the face is the most important component of a person's physical attractiveness for both judges and stimulus persons of either sex.

SEX DIFFERENCES

Similarities between the sexes are greater than the dissimilarities. Both males and females agree on the relative importance of body components as they determine physical attractiveness. There is also high agreement with regard to corresponding rankings for an individual's own physical attractiveness. Such agreement between self and other is probably expected because the formulation of attitudes are no doubt interactive.

Two different studies, with two different perspectives, indicated only minor differences with regard to the importance of specific components. Both studies attempted to dissect global ratings of physical attractiveness into minute details. Although the objectives were the same, the approaches were different. The approaches employed either self-evaluations (Mahoney & Finch, 1976b) or evaluations by others (Budge, 1981). Both studies used multidimensional scales and factor analysis to identify components of physical attractiveness. Because different dimensions were used in each study, it is difficult to directly compare the two. Yet, some comparison is beneficial.

Self-Evaluations

Self-evaluations displayed some dissimilarity as well as similarity, for the most important factors for each sex (Mahoney & Finch, 1976b). Five factors were significant for determining physical attractiveness for females. The order of importance was (1) weight, (2) face, (3) height, (4) legs, and (5) extremities. Six factors were significant for determining physical attractiveness for males. The order of importance was (1) face, (2) legs, (3) weight, (4) torso, (5) voice/hair, and (6) height.

Other Evaluations

Evaluations by others produced data similar to self-evaluations. Comparison of their evaluation procedures is difficult but their results appear similar. Evaluations by others also displayed some dissimilarity for the most important factors for each sex (Budge, 1981). For each male and female combination, six factors were significant for determining physical attractiveness.

The factors for each of the four sex combinations are presented in order of importance. Combining female stimulus persons and male judges yielded factors labeled (1) weight/weight distribution, (2) face, (3) height, (4) hands, (5) figure, and (6) teeth. The female stimuls persons with female judges indicated factors of (1) weight/weight distribution, (2) face, (3) facial complexion, (4) legs/height, (5) hands, and (6) face profile. Combining male stimulus persons and female judges yielded factors labeled (1) face/features, (2) weight/weight distribution, (3) hair, (4) body profile, (5) shoulders/arms, and (6) height/voice. The male stimulus persons with male judges indicated factors of (1) face, (2) weight/weight distribution, (3) legs, (4) shoulders/arms, (5) complexion/hands, and (6) hair/head.

Body Peculiarities

Minor variations do exist between males and females with regard to determinants of physical attractiveness. A fundamental difference is the greater emphasis consistently placed on female physical attractiveness. This difference may be one of the reasons that both male and female judges possess better defined stereotypes of ideal physical attractiveness for females than for males (Korthase & Trenholme, 1982). Some of these variations are not really comparable between the sexes because of inherent biological differences. Research within these areas may best be used to explore speculation of cultural stereotypes. For example, the bust size of females is a body component often thought to be very important in the determination of female physical attractiveness. However, research has failed to indicate a parallel reality, at least when other factors are also considered.

The importance of the female bust in determining physical attractiveness has not proven statistically significant. Factor analysis performed by Budge (1981) indicated that neither male nor female judges considered the female bust to be important enough to yield very high loadings on any of the factors. The highest rating was given by male judges where the female bust received a .58 factor loading that explained 3.4% of the total variance. However, these data may be qualified by the fact that the busts of females involved in this study were rated as quite favorable on the respective attractiveness scale. Therefore, if the presence of extremes leads to greater awareness, the lack of such extremes may explain the lack of indicated importance. Regardless of these qualifiers, the lack of importance is congruent with other research showing that bust size is not as important a factor in determining physical attractiveness as popular thought maintains (Berscheid et al., 1973; Horvath, 1979, 1981; Mahoney & Finch, 1976a).

Unless breast size is unusually small or large, it apparently is not a significant determinant of physical attractiveness. However, it is shown to be associated with perceptions of internal qualities. A series of four experiments were conducted to assess first impressions of females as a function of bust size (Kleinke & Staneski, 1980). In the first experiment, 135 male and 135 female subjects read written descriptions of female stimulus persons. After reading the descriptions, which suggested either small, medium, or large bust sizes, the subjects were asked to evaluate a variety of characteristics pertaining to the stimulus persons. The authors stated that their results agreed with other research that has paired subjects of both sexes with silhouette figures representing female stimulus persons. The results of this first experiment indicated a golden mean in that too small or too large was not as favorable as moderate. Stimulus persons, rated highest in personal appeal and liking, were those with medium bust sizes as compared to either small or large.

The other three experiments in this series employed photographs. To minimize effects due to potential extraneous variables, the photography was manipulated so that the same stimulus person was used in each of the experimental treatments for busts of small, medium, and large sizes. After viewing the photographs, each of 147 male and 141 female subjects evaluated the stimulus person. No significant differences were revealed for liking or personal appeal evaluations. This lack of significance was attributed to the fact that with photographs, more information than breast size was considered by the subjects. Consequently, facial physical attractiveness could have overridden the effects of focusing primarily on bust size. The other evaluated traits were positive for those with small bust sizes and negative for those with large bust sizes. Those with small bust sizes were perceived most intelligent, competent, modest, and moral; whereas those with large bust sizes were perceived as relatively unintelligent, incompetent, immodest, and immoral.

THE FACE

The face is the most frequently used component in the physical attractiveness research. Although exceptions exist, this research has relied heavily on experimental manipulations of the face as the indicator of physical attractiveness. With rare exceptions has the face not been the primary, if not the only, factor representing physical attractiveness or lack thereof.

The face is interesting, enduring, and informative. Consistent use of the face in evaluating physical attractiveness is justified because of its unique and powerful properties which appear to make it omnipotent and omnipresent. Currently, billions of dollars are spent annually on enhancing the face through the applications of cosmetics and reconstructive surgery. Despite the best of efforts, the face cannot be obliterated but only altered. Even the aging process does not transform the face beyond recognition.

Formal discussion of the face may not be abundant but it exists in a variety of writings. Abraham Lincoln once stated in a campaign speech that, based on the appearance of his face, no one ever expected him to be president (Rubenstein, 1983). Mr. Lincoln's statement can now be interpreted given the fact that the face serves as an informational cue. As such, the physical attractiveness of one's face is used by observers to assume substantial and wide-ranging information.

General Facial Research

The use of the face as an indicator of nonfacial qualities began long ago, continues today, and will project into the future. As late as 1870, a person's criminal nature was assumed to be recognizable through assessment of facial components. This belief was advanced by an Italian physician named Cesare Lombroso who attempted even to differentiate between types of crimes committed based on facial components. Fifty years later, Lombroso was supported by Ernst Kretschmer, the German psychiatrist. Kretschmer stated that "the face is a visiting card of the individual's general constitution." He believed that the entire person is represented in the face. In fact, the "science" of phrenology developed under the assumption that facial features coincide with personal traits (cf. Liggett, 1974, pp. 180–257).

On a less formal scale, the face continues today to be viewed as a comprehensive document. Although not openly confessed, the face, as a measure of physical attractiveness, is assumed to yield a plethora of personal information. Among this information are assumptions that the face is an accurate indicator of specific personal attributes. Current training practices of personal bodyguards and general law enforcement personnel includes careful scrutiny of faces in the crowd. The belief is that the face can be used as a window to observe impending danger. This belief may be supported by a host of research attention on the indicative value of physical qualities. Such research includes a focus on the relationship between personality attributes and specific facial components such as eyebrows (Keating, Mazur, & Segall, 1977), facial expression (Darwin, 1872; Feleky, 1914; Munn, 1940), eye contact (Exline, 1971), pupil size (Hess, 1965), as well as body language (Fast, 1970), and even personal space (Sommer, 1969).

The future role of the face is likely to continue in its importance. Despite the uncertainty of prediction, popular literature foretells the continuing assumptions about personal information regarding the face. George Orwell (1949, p. 29) wrote that facial expression will be so important, and correspondingly accurate, that the wrong appearance (i.e., "facecrime") will result in punishment.

The power of the face as a stimulus is not limited to adults. A review of the relevant research literature discloses that the unique impact of the face exists in early infancy (cf. Hopkins, 1980). Infants 3 and 4 months old give greater attention and fixate longer on faces than other similar nonface stimuli (Koopman & Ames, 1968). This pattern is even suggested with infants as young as 4 days (Fantz, 1966). The early impact of the face is probably due primarily to the eyes. During the first 2 months, infants do not smile in response to a real face that has the eyes hidden, but they do smile in response to a face mask with eyes represented by only dots (Ahrens, 1954; Spitz & Wolf, 1946). By the age of 4 weeks, infants may begin to establish actual eye contact. Close scrutiny of infants indicated that they scan a face until they locate the eyes, at which time the infant exhibits a substantial change in focus (Wolff, 1963). But as the infant ages, the facial components necessary to hold interest require more than only the eyes of a face. During maturation, the attention capability of infants increases, and, correspondingly, more parts of the face are needed and are processed before a response is elicited from the infant (Bower, 1977).

In 1872, Charles Darwin probably began discussion of the role of the face within humans in his well-known book *The Expression of the Emotions in Man and Animals*. Since that time, substantial amounts of scientific writing have focused on facial expression. This work was carefully categorized and presented in a relatively recent book *Darwin and Facial Expression* (Ekman, 1973). The chapters of the book correspond to the major categories of facial expression study: (a) facial expression of emotion in nonhuman primates, (b) facial expressions of infants and children, and (c) cross-cultural studies of facial expression.

Facial expression is certainly an important topic, but it is only indirectly related to physical attractiveness phenomena. Even though that material is not presented in this book, it can provide valuable supplemental information that may be interdependent with facial physical attractiveness. Larrance and Zuckerman (1981) investigated the relationship between facial physical attractiveness and the ability to send nonverbal signs of emotion. Videotapes of 60 senders were evaluated by six judges who concluded that higher physical attractiveness enhanced the accuracy of transmitting facial expressions. Such specific physical attractiveness research is germane to physical attractiveness phenomena, but it may also be more appropriate within the topic of general facial expressions.

A more relevant book, *The Human Face* (Liggett, 1974), goes beyond facial expressions and documents the extreme importance placed on this body feature throughout recorded history. The face is shown to be a very valuable asset within all cultures at all times. The book is a comprehensive treatment of the human face that is both historical and cross-cultural. Even though the book is a general discussion, it is invaluable as a supplement to this section. Most relevant is the fact that it established the extreme importance that has, and continues to be, placed on the physical attractiveness of the human face.

Cultural values pertaining to specific aspects of physical attractiveness may be moderated, but they are never extinguised. The chapter, in the aforementioned book, on primitive facial elaborations discusses early practices of artificially deforming the skull to increase beauty. Somewhat parallel to this early practice may be a contemporary article published in 1981 that investigated the current relationship between head shape and perceptions of physical attractiveness (Alley, 1981). Three experiments manipulated morphological changes in head shape during development. Stimulus materials were drawings of infants' heads. The 25 subjects perceived physical attractiveness (i.e., cuteness) to decrease as the head shape grows through its early developmental periods.

Specific Facial Research

Practically all the physical attractiveness research centers on the face. Physical attractiveness research involves a number of variables (e.g., body type, perceptual distortions, and association) but visual presentation of the face is overwhelmingly the most frequently manipulated stimulus. Likewise, the face itself involves a number of variables (e.g., head shape, facial and head hair, and accessories such as eyeglasses), but the overall face is practically always the manipulated stimulus. Two examples of face-related characteristics that were researched but are not commonly manipulated are complexion and age. These two variables are reported in this section but are not discussed elsewhere because complexion and age are not necessarily limited to the face.

Although complexion involves the skin of an entire body, it is predominantly displayed as a facial characteristic. As such, the research indicates that complexion may be an ingredient of physical attractiveness and that there are distinct sex differences. Over 1,000 Caucasians (approximately 500 males and 500 females) participated in a study to determine preference between the sexes (Feinman & Gill, 1978). Females expressed significantly greater preference for men with dark eyes, dark hair, and dark complexion, whereas the males significantly preferred females with light eyes, light hair, and light complexion. Feinman and Gill also stated that these color preferences are held by both white and black people in the United States. However, variations in preferred complexion color may occur across cultures and countries. For example, in Japan light skin color is preferred for both sexes, and Japanese females especially prefer males with light colored skin (Hulse, 1967).

Age is not strictly a facial characteristic even though it may be predominantly displayed in the face. As a facial component, age is an ingredient of physical attractiveness (Korthase & Trenholme, 1982). Therefore, research was conducted to determine if older faces are perceived as more or less physically attractive than younger faces. The stimulus materials were photographs of males and females in either an age category of 31 to 38 years old or 14 to 16 years old. Sixty subjects were asked to sort these stimulus persons, first, according to physical attractiveness and, second, according to age. As perceived age increased, perceived physical attractiveness decreased.

Artificial additions to the face affect physical attractiveness. The investigated accessories include both beards and eyeglasses. Statistical averages showed that, usually, beards did not have a constant significant effect on one's physical attractiveness (Feinman & Gill, 1977; Freedman, 1969; Kenny & Fletcher, 1973). In other words, beards did not consistently raise or lower physical attractiveness.

Wearing eyeglasses did have a negative or detrimental effect on both observers' perceptions and on self-ratings of physical attractiveness (Berscheid & Walster, 1974; Terry & Brady, 1976; Terry & Kroger, 1976; Terry & Zimmerman, 1970). Wearing eyeglasses had a negative effect on personality (Manz & Lueck, 1968) and physical attractiveness, but in the past tended to have a positive effect on perceptions of intelligence by observers (Brunswik, 1939; Thornton, G. R., 1943, 1944). Times have changed and this latter research pertaining to intelligence is questionable in light of today's fashions, for this research is now 40 years old and possibly dated.

Hierarchy of Importance

Components of the face do not contribute equally to evaluations of physical attractiveness. There is a hierarchy in that some components are of greater importance than others. It is difficult to conclude the exact ordering because different research efforts are not easily compared. The difficulty arises from divergence in the methodologies used and the components examined.

Attention. An early study employed a methodology that assumed attention paid to specific facial components reflected their relative importance in determining physical attractiveness (Yarbus, 1967). To determine importance under this assumption, the subjects were not queried about ordering importance but simply scrutinized very closely. A pupilometer recorded eye movements of a person observing a photograph of another person's face. When people are presented with a face, they scan the total stimuli and then return repeatedly to focus on the eyes and mouth.

Memory. Identification of determinants was also attempted through recall measurements (Davis, Ellis, & Shepherd, 1977). Instead of recording eye movements, components of a stimulus person's face were manipulated. Subjects were presented with a photograph of a stimulus person, had it removed from their presence, changes were made, and then had it re-presented. Based on their memory, subjects were asked to indicate their recognition of new facial components. Assuming that recognition could be equated with importance, the authors concluded that the mouth and eyes were the most important features in determining physical attractiveness. A third study using similar procedures of memory and recognition tests supported the importance of mouth and eyes (Seamon, Stolz, Bass, & Chatinover, 1978).

Ratings. The hierarchy of importance for facial components appears to be mouth, eyes, facial structure, hair, and nose. This hierarchy was supported by three different articles which used three different procedures to collect data: (1) self-ratings (Terry & Brady, 1976), (2) ratings of dissected photographs by independent judges (Terry & Davis, 1976), and (3) ratings of intact photographs by independent judges (Terry, 1977). The three articles varied methodologies through systematic research effort performed by the same first author. Despite the similarity, the variation of components studied caused some difficulty in direct comparison of results.

The first two articles allowed close comparison because the same facial components were investigated from two different perspectives. Both studies measured importance by correlating the ratings of specific facial components with ratings of overall facial physical attractiveness. Self-ratings of 45 female stimulus persons were used in the initial study (Terry & Brady, 1976). The mouth was first ($r = .54$), followed by eyes ($r = .51$), hair ($r = .49$), and nose ($r = .47$). To make the information more substantial, the second study went beyond self-ratings into ratings by others (Terry & Davis, 1976). Photographs of stimulus persons were dissected and the isolated components evaluated individually by 25 male and 25 female subjects. The hierarchy of importance was identical, with mouth ($r = .53$) being of greatest importance, followed by eyes ($r = .44$), hair ($r = .34$), and nose ($r = .31$).

The third article attempted to extend the other methodologies by using the data from intact photographs (Terry, 1977). Photographs of stimulus persons were presented to 25 male and 25 female subjects. These subjects used a 10-point scale to rate seven specific components as well as overall physical attractiveness for each stimulus person. Comparing the results with the previous two studies, the ordering was first mouth ($r = .72$), followed by eyes ($r = .68$), and nose ($r = .61$). An addition of different components produced an ordering of: expression ($r = .76$), which is actually a combination of mouth and eyes, mouth ($r = .72$); eyebrows and complexion (both at $r = .69$); eyes ($r = .68$); chin ($r = .64$); and nose ($r = .61$). The author concluded that despite the supremacy that is assumed to be held by the eye component, it actually holds a position secondary to that of the mouth in determining physical attractiveness. He qualified this statement by suggesting that a confounding factor showed the eye to be the most important component unless it is altered by eyeglasses.

Body Parts. Further insight into the hierarchy of importance of facial components can be gleaned from a comprehensive consideration of body parts (Budge, 1981). Even though the face was not focused on, a portion of the data provided interesting results concerning such a heirarchy. The data were analyzed through factor analysis and reported by sex for each of four judge and stimulus person dyads. Those results specifically pertaining to the face are detailed in the following four paragraphs.

Males judging males produced six factors that accounted for 77.1% of the total variance. Of these six factors, three included face components. Factor 1 was labeled face and accounted for 49% of the total variance. The highest factor loadings reported were overall facial appearance (.78), smile (.69), face (.66), eyes (.63), teeth (.59), and nose (.58). Factor 5 accounted for 4.5% with facial complexion (.74) being the only facial component. Factor 6 accounted for 3.7% and included hair (.77), head shape (.53), face (.47), and hair color (.47).

The sex dyad of female judges and male stimulus persons produced six factors that accounted for 78.1% of the total variance. Of these six factors, four included some components of the face. The Factor 1 was labeled face and features and accounted for 45.7% of the total variance. The relevant face components were nose (.79), lips (.78), skin texture (.77), facial complexion (.75), profile (.68), smile (.66), forehead (.59), and chin (.56). Factor 2, with 14.2%, included only two face components—face (.96) and overall facial appearance (.93). Factor 3, with 5.9%, included hair (.81), hair color (.75), and head shape (.52). Factor 4, with 4.5%, included only teeth (.63) as a face component.

The factors for the female stimulus persons were not identical but sufficiently similar for the author to call them "remarkably similar" (p. 21). Males judging females produced six factors which accounted for 79.4% of the total variance. Of these six factors, only two involved components of the face. Factor 2 was labeled face and accounted for 10.9% of the variance. This face factor included overall facial appearance (.82), forehead (.81), lips (.78), face (.77), facial complexion (.76), nose (.72), head shape (.71), smile (.68), chin (.67), eyes (.67), skin texture (.66), and teeth (.66). Factor 6, with only 2.5%, had teeth (.56) as the only loading.

The sex dyad of female judges and female stimulus persons accounted for 76.2% of the total variance with six factors. Of these six factors three involved components of the face. Factor 2, with 8.5%, was labeled face and included teeth (.76), smile (.75), lips (.73), eyes (.63), face (.60), forehead (.56), and overall facial appearance (.50). Factor 3, with 5.8%, included facial complexion (.84), skin texture (.83), and overall facial appearance (.52). Factor 6, with 3.6%, consisted of nose (.66), profile (.47), and chin (.47).

Attempts to construct a hierarchy of importance for facial components are difficult for three reasons. First, facial components, as well as all body components, are evaluated within a context of all other components. Second, the relevant research is difficult to compare because manipulated variables differ between studies. Third, both global measures (e.g., facial appearance and profile) and specific features (e.g., lips and eyes) are treated the same within individual studies. Despite these problems and limitations, the research reveals serious attempts to identify the relative contributions of individual components that determine physical attractiveness. Among this research appears to emerge a tentative conclusion that a reasonable hierarchy of importance for facial components is the mouth area, followed closely by the eye region, followed by hair, and nose.

Infant Dimensions

Research efforts go beyond investigations of a hierarchy of importance. These efforts have attempted to identify the specific dimensions of each component which will determine the evaluation of that component. The work begins by trying to identify the actual dimensions of physical attractiveness, or cuteness in the case of infants. Hildebrandt and Fitzgerald (1979a) used 50 photographs of infants, ten photographs representing the ages of 3 months, 5 months, 7 months, 11 months, and 13 months. Each photograph of an infant was first rated for cuteness and then subjected to a physical measurement of 14 different facial features. The authors concluded that perceived cuteness could be predicted as a function of quantitative measurements. Those infants perceived as most cute were those most likely to have a large forehead, large eyes, and large pupils with short and narrow features.

Another study on infant physical attractiveness focused specifically on the pupil size of the infant's eye (Kirkland & Smith, 1978). Four photographs of the same infant's face were shown to 10 female supermarket shoppers. The subjects were asked to select the most (physically) attractive infant, however, the subjects were not informed that the only difference was pupil size of four levels. To assure uniformity of stimulus persons, the pupils of the photographed infants were altered by mechanical means and then reproduced. Reproductions appeared natural and showed either dilated or constricted pupils which were either highlighted or not. The subjects selected the infant's photographs with highlighted constricted pupils as most physically attractive.

Study of infant physical attractiveness carries valuable potential for the physical attractiveness phenomena. In light of the research that shows differential treatment for children during their early formative years, a worthy goal is to minimize such treatment based on a child's physical attractiveness. Such goals are consistent with an ethological approach to child development that contends different infant stimuli elicit different adult responses (Sternglanz, Gray, & Murakami, 1977). Loosely interpreting ethological theory (e.g., Eibl-Eibesfeldt, 1970; Lorenz, 1943), adults may give preferential treatment to those infants of higher physical attractiveness, and the correspondingly opposing treatment to infants lower in physical attractiveness. A logical quest is then to discover what characteristics determine physical attractiveness.

Existing research on specific components as they determine infantile physical attractiveness was done in response to a general hypothesis by Konrad Lorenz in 1943. This hypothesis was that specific characteristics of infants elicit specific caretaking behaviors in human adults. One study examined adult preferences as a function of forehead height and forehead curvature of infants (Huckstedt, 1965). The manipulations involved four variations normally displayed in profiles of infants. Distinct preferences were indicated with those profiles most preferred being described as infantile shape as opposed to adult shape. These results are consistent with the work of Alley (1981) who found that the head shape viewed as most physically attractive was reflective of younger infants.

The general hypothesis by Lorenz has also received support from research manipulations of eye characteristics (Sternglanz et al., 1977). Subjects were 692 white middle-class college students. Stimulus materials were line drawings developed into slides which varied infants' eye height, eye width, eye height and width, iris size, and vertical variations in the eye position. After viewing each slide, the subjects rated the stimulus persons for physical attractiveness on a 7-point scale. Despite the authors' note of possible confounding due to necessary chin and forehead size manipulations, they concluded that significant differences did occur in support of an ethologically based hypothesis. They also concluded that specific facial features which create different responses could be isolated even though they were extremely subtle.

Adult judges were able to assign ratings of different physical attractiveness to experimental treatments with different infantile characteristics. Generally, the higher physical attractiveness ratings were given to those infants with most "babyish" characteristics, regardless of the judges' sex. Specifically, the higher ratings of physical attractiveness were given to babies with large eyes as opposed to small, small chins and large foreheads as opposed to large chins and small foreheads, less eye width as opposed to greater eye width, higher eye height as opposed to lower eye height, and iris size of moderate to large size as opposed to smaller. The data revealed no significant differences in responses on any of the features as a function of the judges' sexual activity, experience with children, social class, or religion. Minor significant difference, of no practical magnitude, occurred between male and female judges for feature position and eye width. The authors suggested the data may hold implications for eliciting and inhibiting aggression related to battered children.

Adult Dimensions

Adults also hold physical attractiveness preferences for specific dimensions of each facial component of other adults. Two related studies assessed the determinants of physical attractiveness for facial components

(Wagatsuma & Kleinke, 1979). The first study used 40 white females to arrive at definitions of physical attractiveness for both male and female stimulus persons. The subjects were asked to use a 6-point importance scale to rate the following types of components (i.e., dimensions):

- Hair texture: straight, wavy, kinky, frizzy
- Hair color: black, dark brown, light brown, blonde
- Face shape: heart, oval, pear, squarish
- Nose profile: pug, hawk, Roman
- Nose width: wide, medium, narrow
- Mouth: full lips, average lips, thin lips
- Skin tone: fair, rose, tan, light brown, chocolate

The characteristics of the stimulus persons rated highest in physical attractiveness (i.e., most important) were:

- Heart- and pear-shaped faces for females and square-shaped faces for males
- Pug nose for females and Roman nose for males
- Narrow nose and full lips for females
- Dark-brown and light-brown hair for males
- Fair and rose skin tone for females and tan skin tone for males

The second study compared the ratings of physical attractiveness components of American judges with those of Asian judges. Subjects were 10 Asian females and 20 Caucasian females, all American born. The stimulus persons were all female and were rated using the same scales as employed in the first study. The characteristics which the judges rated highest in physical attractiveness (i.e., most important) were:

- Straight hair for Asian judges and frizzy hair for American judges
- Black and dark-brown hair for Asian judges more than for American judges
- Hawk noses and Roman noses for American judges more than Asian judges
- Wide and narrow noses for American judges and medium nose width for Asian judges
- Fair skin for Asian judges more than for American judges

Research on the dimensions of facial components has utilized both unstructured and structured techniques. The unstructured technique consists of creating components (McCullers & Staat, 1974; Sternlicht, 1978), whereas the structured technique deals with existing components (Wagatsuma & Kleinke, 1979). Both methods reported that finer features were associated with higher physical attractiveness and broader features were associated with lower physical attractiveness. Ratings of existing components found that finer features were evaluated as higher in physical attractiveness, at least for female stimulus persons (Wagatsuma & Kleinke, 1979).

For unstructured creation of facial components, subjects were asked to draw persons of either low or high physical attractiveness. One study used moderately retarded adults and concluded that drawings of people representing lower physical attractiveness tend to possess exaggerated facial components (Sternlicht, 1978). A similar procedure used black and white college students who were instructed to draw males and females of lower and higher physical attractiveness (McCullers & Staat, 1974). The persons drawn to represent higher physical attractiveness tended to have finer facial features, whereas those representing lower physical attractiveness tended to have broader facial features. This pattern of features was consistent regardless of subjects' race, and was cited by the authors as consistent with the common belief that black individuals who possess more "white physical features" are perceived as higher in physical attractiveness.

Lay Perspective

Attempts to identify the values of specific facial components that determine physical attractiveness are not new. Nor are these attempts limited to social scientists. Surprisingly, much of the early descriptions by philosophers, writers, and artists agree with current descriptions produced by social science researchers.

The very earliest recorded work with physical attractiveness centered on definitions of beauty (Liggett, 1974, p. 140). These early efforts proposed beauty to be a function of mathematical proportions. Plato was one among the ancient Greeks whose idea of beauty was based on proportion. Plato believed that beauty always had a break one-third of its length. This view meant that the most beautiful face would have eyes one-third from the hairline. Medieval artists believed beautiful faces consisted of areas divided up into one-sevenths. Thus, the nose covered two-sevenths of the face for optimal beauty. Analysis of work by Leonardo da Vinci reveals his attention to mathematical proportions for beautiful physical traits.

Contemporary scholarly thought centers not so much on detail but on the total. However, this gestalt approach is not fully subscribed to, especially when the physical attractiveness of women is considered. Despite its abstract nature, the physical attractiveness of females, as opposed to males, is better defined, more well-known, and has higher agreement (Korthase & Trenholme, 1982).

Liggett reports extremely high concordance for physical attractiveness in ancient and in modern times. He also states that within contemporary times there is an accordance between persons of different countries. However, his attention is directed toward the physical attractiveness of females. The ideal physical attractiveness for a female during medieval times was described by Curry (see Liggett, 1974, p. 144). The description included hair that is blonde and golden, eyes that are sparkling bright and light blue, cheeks that are lily white and rose pink, white teeth, fingers that are white, long, and slender, small waist, and dazzling skin that is soft as silk.

Liggett (pp. 143–145) reports almost identical descriptions of the ideal physical attractiveness for females based on both a recent American survey by Cuber and a survey by his students. He also cites (p. 145) a modern British study that revealed further harmony pertaining to ideal physical attractiveness of females. The results of the British study included female faces with eyes that are large and spaced far apart, lashes that are long, nose that is small and slim, skin that is clear and smooth, high cheek bones, and a mouth that is medium to small in size with lips that are gentle and not too thick.

A final study cited by Liggett (p. 144) is a survey conducted in North America by Richard W. Brislin, an American psychologist. This research reported that because of high agreement among people, calculation of a "beauty score" is possible for every face. The highest beauty score involved a face of oval shape, clear complexion, large blue eyes, fine eyebrows, long lashes, straight diamond-shaped nose, mouth of moderate size, and ears that did not protrude or possess small lobes. For males, the highest beauty score involved a face of square shape, bushy eyebrows, and Roman nose. The highest beauty score was also achieved by the proper proportion of the central area of the face relative to the total facial area. This proportion component included a front view of the face which had the mouth width greater than the width of the cheeks, and the height of the forehead greater than the height of the chin.

Recognition and Memory

A final area of specific face research shifts emphasis away from definitions and dimensions. This research reports that the physical attractiveness of a face carries implications for the recognition and memory of that face. These differences are evidenced in research concerning reliability of physical attractiveness ratings, as well as research directly investigating face memory as a function of face physical attractiveness. The explanation of such data may exist in published literature that is not related to physical attractiveness research, but does deal with cognitive processes used with different strategies for facial memory (McKelvie, 1976; cf. Parkin & Hayward, 1983).

Sex of Face. The reliability of physical attractiveness ratings, as a measure of face recognition and memory, varies by sex of the face. Physical attractiveness ratings of female faces are more consistent in test–retest situations than corresponding ratings of male faces (Kerr & Kurtz, 1978). This inconsistency over time is in contrast to high agreement of physical attractiveness ratings between male and female judges. The reason for this difference may be due to the fact that both male and female judges look at, focus on, remember, and recognize female faces significantly more than male faces (Kenrick & Gutierres, 1980).

Sex of Judge. Recognition and memory of faces may also vary with the sex of the judge. A newspaper article reporting the work of Daniel Yarmey, a University of Guelph psychologist, stated that women were better than men in the recognition and memory of faces (Neubacher, 1978). Furthermore, this ability was especially pronounced when female faces were involved. A review of relevant research (McKelvie, 1981) revealed results that were not unanimous but which generally found female judges to be better at facial recognition and memory than were male judges. This same-sex effect was shown by McKelvie (1978) to be especially prominent for memory of female faces. The same pattern was again reported by McKelvie (1981) in a replication of the procedure in five experiments.

Time Spans. The relationship between facial physical attractiveness and memory of faces is reported for varying time spans between exposure and recognition. Faces of higher physical attractiveness were most memorable in an immediate, unanticipated recognition test (Cross et al., 1971). In a 2-hour time span, the faces of lower and higher physical attractiveness were recognized and remembered better than those of moderate levels (Fleishman, Buckley, Klosinsky, Smith, & Tuck, 1976). This latter study involved 24 subjects (12 males and 12 females) who were asked to rate the physical attractiveness of 35 photographed stimulus persons. Two hours later, subjects' recognition ability was assessed when the 35 rated photographs were randomly mixed with 10 previously unseen photographs.

Another study, using three time intervals, reported greater recognition and memory for the faces at the ends of the physical attractiveness continuum as opposed to the middle (Shepherd & Ellis, 1973). Slides of 27 female faces were presented to 36 subjects (18 males and 18 females). Recognition tests of these faces were then given immediately after the presentation, 6 days later and 35 days later. The authors reported that recognition scores decreased significantly for the moderate level of physical attractiveness but not for the faces of either high or low physical attractiveness. Contrary evidence was reported by one study with data suggesting that faces higher in physical attractiveness may be more difficult to remember (Light, Hollander, & Kayra-Stuart, 1981). However, this contrasting study concluded that "it is unclear why" (p. 275) the results obtained were inconsistent with other research. Furthermore, in light of this study's lack of an experimental research design the authors stated that "caution must be exercised in interpreting correlational data" (p. 275).

PHYSIQUE

Huge amounts of research on physique are discussed in both the medical literature and the psychological literature. In both these major categories, the emphasis is on an overweight physique. The medical research focuses on health whereas the psychological research focuses on the relationship between obesity and self-concept. The psychological research also deals with the interpersonal consequences of obesity, which is often represented as a stigma within our society. On the one hand, these three research categories are interdependent, but on the other hand, each of the three represents independent topics in its own right. A fourth category that deals strictly with the relationship between physical attractiveness phenomena and physique is probably similarly interdependent. There is also a fifth category that involves facial and body disfigurements. The reader interested in this latter research is referred to an article that discusses these characteristics within the context of stereotyping (Adams, 1982).

All this research is of interest, but the immediate focus is on physical attractiveness phenomena. Therefore, despite any common denominator among these five designations, only the research pertaining specifically to the relationship between physical attractiveness and physique is presented here. Omitted for the same reason is the interesting somatotype research on the perceived relationship between body type and personality.

Persons of both sexes hold distinct preferences of body type for both stimulus persons of the same sex and the opposite sex. The overwhelmingly favored physique is an average or moderate build. The overwhelmingly disliked physique is the obese or overweight whereas a mildly unfavorable view exists for the thin or underweight (Lavrakas, 1975; Lerner & Korn, 1972; Scodel, 1957; Stafferi, 1967; Wiggins, Wiggins, & Conger, 1968).

The above preferences for adults parallel those for children. Children of all ages, and as young as 5 years old, exhibit the same liking pattern for mesomorphic, ectomorphic, and endomorphic physiques. Children exposed to stimulus persons (either in photographs, line drawings, or descriptions) were asked which body type they preferred. The ectomorph is occasionally selected by girls (Staffieri, 1967, 1972). However, the pattern is that the endomorph is practically never selected, whereas the mesomorph is practically always chosen (Brenner & Hinsdale, 1978; Lerner & Gellert, 1969; Lerner & Korn, 1972; Lerner & Schroeder, 1971).

The collective research efforts regarding the body's role in determining physical attractiveness are analogous to research on the face's role. In both, efforts are needed to determine a hierarchy of importance and then to identify the dimensions that determine physical attractiveness for each component. However, the amount of research attention given to the face has been far greater than that given to the body. This discrepancy is probably justified in light of the importance of these two variables for determining physical attractiveness.

Hierarchy of Importance

Individual physique components are addressed through data collected by self-evaluations and evaluations by others. Collectively, there is agreement that different components vary in their importance for determining physical attractiveness. However, there is no such agreement for the actual hierarchy, that is, a ranking of importance is not yet identified for the specific components.

The quantity of self-evaluation research is much greater than the quantity of evaluations by others. Numerous articles report self-evaluation data assessing subjective importance of body components for evaluations of overall physical attractiveness (Berscheid, Walster, & Bornstedt, 1973; Lerner & Karabenick, 1974; Lerner, Karabenick, & Stuart, 1973; Mahoney, 1974; Rosen & Ross, 1968). However, the value of these respective data is questionable because identification of relative importance is not feasible when high intercorrelations exist between components and their dimensions.

The quantity of research using evaluations by others appears limited to one recent exploration (Budge, 1981). In this study data were collected for 44 different body components and analyzed through factor analysis. Those results pertaining to the physique are detailed in the following four paragraphs.

Males judging males produced six factors, of which three included body components. Factor 2 accounted for 7.6% variance with the following relevant factor loadings for body components: weight distribution (.92), weight (.89), trunk (.87), overall body appearance (.84), waist (.81), body build (.76), buttocks (.75), back (.65), and thighs (.60). Factor 3 accounted for 6.5% with relevant factor loadings of calves (.87), leg length (.73), knees (.71), leg shape (.69), ankles (.65), and thighs (.51). Factor 4 accounted for

5.8% with biceps (.86), shoulder width (.74), chest size (.74), wrists (.73), and arms (.63).

The sex dyad of male stimulus persons and female judges produced six factors, of which five included body components. Factor 1 accounted for 45.7% variance with only two body components near the lower end of the loadings, hands (.69) and foot size (.67). Factor 2 accounted for 14.2% with relevant factor loadings of overall body appearance (.97), weight distribution (.96), thighs (.96), trunk (.96), and weight (.95). Factor 4 accounted for 4.5% with waist (.76), buttocks (.75), body build (.68), neck (.60), and back (.60). Factor 5 accounted for 4.2% with biceps (.76), chest size (.72), shoulder width (.70), and arms (.60). Factor 6 accounted for 3.6% with leg length (.73) and height (.67).

Females judging males produced six factors of which four included body components. Factor 1 accounted for 52.4% of the total variance with waist (.95), weight (.93), body build (.91), back (.90), hips (.88), buttocks (.88), weight distribution (.87), overall body appearance (.85), trunk (.81), and thighs (.80). Factor 3 accounted for 5.9% with height (.65), leg length (.65), and knees (.60). Factor 4 accounted for 4.3% with fingers (.81), nails (.68), and hands (.49). Factor 5 with 3.4% included bust size (.58), posture (.54), ankles (.53), and calves (.51).

The sex dyad of female stimulus persons and female judges produced six factors of which three included body components. Factor 1 accounted for 76.2% variance with weight (.94), waist (.89), body build (.88), overall body appearance (.88), weight distribution (.87), hips (.84), buttocks (.83), trunk (.79), arms (.77), and thighs (.76). Factor 4 accounted for 5.2% with leg shape (.76), calves (.73), ankles (.67), knees (.64), foot size (.55), height (.51), and leg length (.50). Factor 5 accounted for 4% variance with nails (.67), fingers (.66), and hands (.57).

These data provided some interesting insights into the contributions that various body components make to physical attractiveness. Although a definite importance hierarchy does not emerge, face and weight components would certainly be at the top of such a ranking. A potential problem with these data is that global characteristics (e.g., overall body appearance and weight distribution) were analyzed with specific features (e.g., knees and leg length). Also, instead of reporting only data separated by sex, some aggregation by sex may have provided additional value for establishing an importance hierarchy of body components.

Component Dimensions

The role of physique as a component of physical attractiveness is a very distant second to the face. But like the face, physique is a component made up of many subcomponents. To increase understanding of the role of physique within physical attractiveness, scant research has gone beyond an importance hierarchy into the dimensions of each component. These efforts acknowledge the impossibility of identifying and qualifying all the subcomponents relevant to the physique, let alone overall physical attractiveness. Consequently, the authors have all used drawings instead of live stimulus persons or photographs of actual persons. The necessary trade-off in this procedure is less realism for greater experimental control. To further increase control, the drawings of the stimulus persons have presented the body with its face obscured.

Not all research pertaining to component dimensions applies specifically to physical attractiveness. Much of this research has focused on the relationship of body components and personality. Wiggins et al., (1968) assessed preferences of male subjects by using silhouettes of nude females. The manipulations of the stimulus persons were the size and shape of breasts, buttocks, legs, and overall shape. After the subjects indicated their preferences, they were administered a battery of personality inventories to assess differences among subjects who preferred certain dimensions. A similar study expanded the stimulus persons to include both males and females (Beck, Ward-Hull, & McLear, 1976). Profile silhouettes were again used to manipulate size of chest, buttocks, and legs. The most negative responses were given to male and to female stimulus persons with large buttocks. For male stimulus persons, the most physically attractive ratings were given to those with moderate chest size, moderate sized legs, and small buttocks. The least favorable ratings were given to those with large chests described as "Atlas-type."

An English study dispensed with components and examined the relationship between body type and assumed qualities (Stewart, R. A., Tutton, & Steele, 1973). The stimulus materials were photographs of actual female persons. These stimulus persons had their faces masked and their overall body somatyped as either endomorph, mesomorph, or ectomorph. The subjects were 25 males (with average age of 25.1 years) and 25 females (with average age of 23.8 years). Each subject was given a package of three stimulus persons that represented each of the three somatypes. The subjects were then asked to rank the female physiques from "most suiting" to "least suiting" on each of 15 concepts. The results were relatively neutral for the mesomorphs, positive for the endomorphs, and negative for the ectomorphs. The endomorph was ranked as liked best, most likely to be successful, and most likely to be a leader, whereas the ectomorph was liked least, was most likely to be a homosexual, and was most likely to be an alcoholic. The results did not yield a sex difference for any of the concepts or somatypes.

Body component preferences permit only indirect inference about physical attractiveness. Direct inference is allowed by other research that directly addresses the relationship between body component dimensions and physical attractiveness. One such study used detailed, front-view drawings in a stated attempt to maximize realism (Horvath, 1979). Production procedures were designed to permit extreme care in drawing the figures to comply with standard anthropometric mean values for dimensions and proportions. Eleven female drawings were used to present manipulations of (a) full figures with standard hip and waist, (b) standard waist with four different hip widths, (c) standard hip with four different waist widths, (d) narrower waist and hip combination, and (e) a wider waist and hip combination. Eleven male drawings were used to present manipulations of (a) four shoulder widths, (b) two waist widths, and (c) two hip widths. All 22 figures lacked facial features. Subjects (131 males and 229 females) did not rate the manipulations but were provided with a 9-point, labeled scale and "asked to rate drawings of male and female figures for attractiveness" (p. 147).

A variety of statistical analyses revealed several distinct relationships between ratings of physical attractiveness and component dimensions. Statistically, significant main effects were found for sex of the stimulus persons but not for sex of the judges. For male stimulus persons, ratings of higher physical attractiveness were positively influenced by greater shoulder width. An equally positive influence was revealed for the ratio of shoulder width to waist width, as opposed to the ratio of shoulder width to hip width. The author stated that physical attractiveness is positively influenced by slenderness of the male physique and that greater influence is provided by waist width than hip width.

For female stimulus persons, ratings of higher physical attractiveness were positively influenced by less waist width and less hip width. Although decreasing waist width produced higher ratings of physical attractiveness, lessening of the hip width did so only to a certain level. After a certain threshold, too small a hip width resulted in lower ratings of physical attractiveness than a slightly larger width. Within the range manipulated, physical attractiveness ratings increased as slenderness increased. Contrary to popular belief, greater curvedness of the female stimulus person was associated with lower ratings of physical attractiveness. The definition of curvedness used in this study was the ratio of hip width to waist width. Horvath, however, urged caution in further exploration with regard to these data pertaining to curvedness.

Cross-cultural research has investigated the question of dimensions among American and Israeli subjects (Gitter, Lomranz, & Saxe, 1982). Subjects were 30 male and 57 female students at Boston University and 45 male and 45 female students at Tel-Aviv University. Stimulus materials were cards with carefully drawn male figures without detailed faces. All figures were drawn by an artist who attempted identical front and side views. Thirty-two male figures were systematically drawn to present physique manipulations described as either somatic or postural. Three somatic body components involved two values each. These manipulations were (a) shape (defined as either Atlas or pillar), (b) neck (thick or thin), and (c) abdomen (presence or absence of a protruding abdomen). Two postural body components were also manipulated with two values each: (a) head (either held up or bent forward) and (b) shoulders (either held straight back or slouched forward). The subjects were instructed (by a same-sex experimenter) to rank order each of the figures on a dimension of more or less attractive.

A series of analysis of variance tests were performed on the data. No significant effects were indicated for the cross-cultural differences of the subjects, and only minor deviations were suggested for sex. Extensive interactions occurred among practically all combinations of the manipulated variables: abdomen, shoulder, neck, head, and body shape. Although the many interactions make summary statements difficult, the abdomen revealed a consistent powerful impact. This impact was that stimulus persons with a protruding abdomen were consistently evaluated as lower in physical attractiveness than a stimulus person without a protruding abdomen. In all experimental conditions, the male stimulus persons who were evaluated as least physically attractive had protruding abdomens whereas those evaluated as most physically attractive did not have the protruding abdomen.

HEIGHT

Physical attractiveness research has neglected the height of an individual. Such disregard is unfortunate because height is likely to influence perceptions of physical attractiveness. This influence of height is probably greater for males than for females. Maybe this neglect is part of a much larger societal disregard for discrimination based on height. John Kenneth Galbraith, the 6' 8" economist, is quoted in the *Christian Science Monitor* as saying that one of society's "most blatant and forgiven prejudices" is the bias in favor of height (Unger, 1977, p. 22). This bias, with its consequent positive relationship with physical attractiveness, is supported by Feldman's statement that, "American society is a society with a heightist premise: To be tall is to be good and to be short is to be stigmatized" (Feldman, 1971, p. 1).

To some degree the social implications of height are analogous to physical attractiveness. Generally, those of taller heights receive more positive attributions. Like physical attractiveness, perceptions of height can be influenced by nonheight factors. For example, estimates of a person's height increased as his status increased (P. R. Wilson, 1968) and as social distance increased (Koulack & Tuthill, 1972). Also, estimates of height were shown to correlate with perceptions of physical attractiveness for male stimulus persons (Lerner & Moore, 1974). Because of its possible role in determining physical attractiveness, and because of its visual physical characteristic, which is by itself important, this section presents specific research relevant to the height variable.

Subtle Prejudice

Society appears to have a subtle predisposition against shorter people and in favor of taller people. "Short People," a best-selling popular song (Randy Newman, 1978) reflected this unacknowledged bias associated with being short.

Whether the American press is viewed as shaping or reflecting society, it too plays an important role in attitudes about height. Keyes (1980) performed a quasi-content analysis to determine whether the press treats individuals differently as a function of their height. Descriptive writings by the press predominantly treat both males and females most favorably when they are taller as opposed to shorter. Words used to describe taller men are often "tall, handsome, and athletic" whereas shorter men are often "small, pallid, and bland." Words used for taller women are "tall, lithe, and supple" whereas shorter women are "short, wiry, and frenetic." Another example is that shorter women may be "cute and perky" but are never thought of as elegant. Keyes (pp. 25–29) presented a comprehensive, persuasive listing of vocabulary usages in our society which associates negative words with shorter people and positive words with taller people.

The significance of height is not a new development. References to the value of height can be cited throughout history and throughout cultures. Pitirim Sorokin (1927), a sociologist who analyzed many cultures, determined that

> correlation of tall stature with the upper social classes and low stature with the low social classes which exists in present civilized societies has also existed in the past and in the most different societies. (pp. 222–223)

Wall paintings in ancient Egypt reflected status by height, such that the more important the person the taller the figure. Anthropologists commonly find prehistoric tombs that have individual, taller skeletons in elegant crypts but multiple, shorter skeletons are found in common graves. Maybe not as blatant, but just as discriminatory, are the social messages contained in adages originating in more recent times. For example, we respect people who "sit tall in the saddle" but we "wouldn't stoop so low" as to "belittle a person."

Alteration

The wish for a miracle formula to transform a shorter person into a taller one is commonly acknowledged. The motivations for such hopes range from increasing social comfortableness to qualifying for occupations with height requirements. Even today, newspapers at times report ingenious attempts to achieve an increase in height. Although of low priority, medical researchers continue to search for a chemical combination which will induce growth under certain circumstances. It is interesting to note that the desire to be taller rather than shorter is no doubt a ratio of a million to one. Consequently, a plethora of folklore, stretching exercises, and magical potions have all attempted to meet the challenge. Where medical science has failed, physical means have substituted. To increase height, women often prefer higher heels, and men sometimes resort to the infamous risers placed adjacent to the heel. In addition, the apparel, cosmetic, and coiffeur industries all have their own prescriptions to alter height perceptions.

Techniques directed toward modifying perceptions of height cannot be dismissed. Generic perception research offers scientific studies which document that perception of objective measures can be altered through subjective factors such as personal motivations and values. For example, the size of coins are estimated as larger than the same size of nonmonetary discs (Bruner & Goodman, 1974), and people overestimate the size of cards in relation to the monetary values assigned to each (Dukes & Bevan, 1952). In similar procedures the height of a person may be affected. In fact, research has shown that comparable manipulations can produce perceptual accentuation of a stimulus person's physical height.

Accentuation

The same process of perceptual distortions for inanimate objects operates within the perception process pertaining to the height of people. Perception of a person's height is altered by assigning greater value or authority to that person. Important people in our society may be routinely perceived as taller than they are in reality. For example, a year after former President Carter entered office, college students were questioned about his height in comparison to that of former President Nixon (Keyes, 1980, p. 56). The reality is that Nixon is 2 to 3 in. taller than Carter, but 66% of the 47 subjects surveyed perceived Carter as the taller of the two men. Likewise, former President Johnson's first return to Washington after leaving office brought the comment from one long-time observer that he looked "less tall" than in the past (Keyes, 1980, p. 56). Similarly, Keyes (pp. 311–312) cited a number of specific instances in which movie and television stars appeared surprisingly shorter in personal face-to-face meetings. These latter observations were not empirically investigated but were informal observations of which formal research results offer confirmation and explanation.

Height is relative. Statistically, the average American male is 5' 9" tall and the average American female is 5' 3.6" tall (Abraham, Johnson, & Najjar, 1976, p. 2). However, judgments of height are based more on perception rather than reality. Consequently, the determinants of perceived height should be identified. It should be realized that only a mere 3 or 4 in. separate individuals considered short or tall. For example, males of 5' 8" are short whereas men of 6' 0" are tall.

Desires to alterate and accentuate height may be analogous to desires for enhancing physical attractiveness. Although both traits are visual, their similarities extend beyond appearance. Like facial physical attractiveness, physical height of an individual is not a neutral characteristic in our society. Its effects are subtle and pervasive with implications ranging from friendly social interactions to employment decisions. Therefore, the remainder of this section will illustrate that consequences due to height and physical attractiveness are at times simiilar.

Preferences

Variations in height may influence the amount of physical distance maintained by individuals. One study asked subjects to move toward stimulus persons until they felt uncomfortably close (Hartnett, Bailey, & Hartley, 1974). The manipulations involved 84 college students as subjects, and several stimulus persons who varied in height. The subjects remained twice as far from the 6' 3" stimulus person than the 5' 4" counterpart. This study in personal distance may explain why personal friends tend toward similar heights. Berkowitz (1969) measured the heights of 514 friendship dyads. The average differences in height were 2.76 in., which is significantly less than random pairing. In combination, these two studies logically suggested that the approach/avoidance of certain height differentials must naturally influence the acquaintance process and ultimately the development of friendships.

Height may influence romantic involvement as well as nonromantic interpersonal interactions. The height of a male appears correlated with the physical attractiveness of his romantic partner (Feingold, 1982b). Height of 72 college males was established through self-reports. Physical attractiveness of each subject and each subject's girlfriend was established by impartial, independent judges. Males who had partners more physically attractive than themselves averaged 2.6 in. more height than males who had partners who were less physically attractive.

An explanation for these interpersonal interactions based on height were offered in a doctoral dissertation done at Temple University (Portnoy, 1972). It concluded that being with others of dissimilar height causes doubts about oneself whereas being with others of similar height promotes positive feelings about oneself (pp. 49, 56).

If this observation is true, it may translate into unequal attention based on unequal heights. Keyes (1980, pp. 24–25) cited a newspaper experiment that reported height is served first. Apparently, a newspaper assigned two reporters to seek the help of various people who normally service the public. The reporters simultaneously asked for service in as identical a manner and appearance as possible, only their height differed—5′ 6″ versus 6′ 2″. The taller of the two was helped first in every situation. A car rental clerk stated that the tallness of the one customer demanded he be spoken to first. A waitress alleged that she never thought about it, but that she must be serving the taller customers first all the time. Some caution should be expressed here because the "experiment" may be somewhat more anecdotal than is allowed under typical scientifically controlled investigations.

Political Benefit

Admittedly, many factors determine the outcome of political campaigns. However, with all the subtle, and not so subtle, dynamics associated with height a few observations are in order. Although these cannot be empirically tested cause-and-effect relationships, the correlations between height and political outcomes are too great to be neglected. The height of our elected officials is reported to correlate with the electorate's attraction to him (Berkowitz, Nebel, & Reitman, 1971; Kassarjian, 1963; Ward, 1967). This relationship, between a politician's height and a politician's success, is captured in the following: "It is not by chance that every American president elected since at least 1900 has been the taller of the two major candidates" (Feldman, 1971, p. 2).

A notable exception to the relationship between height and politics was the 1976 presidential election of Jimmy Carter over Gerald Ford. Observation of news reports, as well as reports based on conversations with the staff personnel for Ford and Carter (Keyes, 1980, pp. 205–208), indicated that considerations of height played an important role in former President Carter's campaign. It was reported by Keyes, and others, that Carter was careful not to select a running mate who was taller than he. Likewise, Carter was adamant that the presidential debates, with the much taller Ford, be designed to minimize physical size comparisons. The Carter personnel wanted the candidates seated or the lecterns sufficiently far apart to minimize the likelihood of direct height comparisons. Through proper planning and utilization of communication technology, Carter was never seen by the electorate as shorter than his opponent. These precautionary measures may explain this exception among all the presidential contests since 1900. The following election pitted the former President Carter against Ronald Reagan who was both taller and acknowledged to be a master of mass communication. Thus, the decision of the 1980 election adds further support to the quote from Feldman.

The Senate is no exception to the benefits of height. In a personal communication, Senator Weicker was quoted as saying: "On balance, I would have to say it's an advantage to be tall" (Keyes, 1980, p. 218). Evidence from both the past and present support Senator Weicker's statement. In 1866, the average reported height of the U.S. Senate was 5' 10.5", which was well above the population average for that time (Hathaway & Foard, 1960). In 1916, the average reported height of state governors was 5' 11.2" and U.S. senators was 5' 10.6" (Gowin, 1917).

The heights of elected officials continue this pattern of being taller than the population mean (Keyes, 1980, p. 219). In 1978, based on self-reports, the average height of the U.S. Senate was 6' 0.33", which was 3.33 in. taller than the average height of the male population. The average height of 31 governors who responded to a questionnaire in 1978 was 6' 0.46", again well over the national population mean. In summation, it is difficult not to question the possible role of an office seeker's height on election outcomes.

Employment Benefits

The employment arena is not immune to the effects of height. Such a statement is certainly reasonable in light of the discussion of height and politics, as well as the more common role of height in everyday social functions. In response to the frequently asked question of how to get promoted, Gerald R. Roche (president of Heidrick & Struggles, Inc.) was quoted as saying, "The easiest way is to be born right and born tall" (Rockmore, 1978, p. 49). This quote appears accurate. Height is, unfortunately, correlated with employment decisions both at the time of application and later in compensation.

The Applicant

To investigate the relationship between height and hiring decisions, 140 actual sales managers were used as subjects (Kurtz, 1969). These sales managers, serving as recruits, were presented with a hypothetical situation involving two equally qualified applicants. The applicants were identical except that one was tall and the other short. The responses of these professional employment managers and recruiters included one affirmative recommendation for the shorter applicant, whereas 72% would have hired the taller. Later, in a personal comment after the publication of the research, Kurtz stated that his biggest response was from corporate personnel office who confirmed that his results accurately reflected reality.

Height certainly appears to be a factor in employment decisions before actual hiring. A quote by economist John Kenneth Galbraith in the *Christian Science Monitor*, although not empirical data, does lend introspective anecdotal support to hypotheses of preferential employment treatment. Mr. Galbraith, who stands 6' 8" tall, stated,

> My height gave me a range of opportunity that I would never have had otherwise, because people always remember the guy who stands high above the others when they are trying to think of somebody for a job. (Unger, 1977, p. 22)

The logical question to follow pertains to how this apparent bias in hiring is interpreted for those who do get hired.

The Employee

Once hired the discrimination continues. Despite the many factors that influence income, height is a factor difficult to ignore. A survey of University of Pittsburgh graduates compared starting salaries with heights of the graduates (Deck, 1968). Based on 91 graduates, this survey showed that taller persons (over 6 feet) received starting salaries 12% greater than those shorter (under 6 feet). A bonus for being *cum laude* translated into a 4.2% advantage whereas the bonus for being 6' 2" versus 5' 11" was 12.4%. The survey found salaries increased steadily up to 6' 2", after which they declined. In an unpublished follow-up study 3 years later, Deck concluded that employers with first choice get to pick the tallest candidates whereas those with lower salaries choose from among the shorter (Deck, 1971).

The results of other correlational data are consistent with this height/salary relationship. In the late 1930s, Provident Mutual Life Insurance Company found a high correlation between body height and policy value (Keyes, 1980, pp. 179–180). Even though life insurance coverage is not the same as income, it serves as an indirect measure.

Keyes (p. 180) reported a personal communication with a Merrill Lynch investment broker who confirmed the apparent influence of height on income. This study involved the work of labor economist Lee Benham taking a sample of 17,000 Army Air Corps cadets in 1943. After 12 to 20 years of service, taller persons made 8% more than shorter persons even after controlling for other possible factors. The investment broker concluded that, "We found a very definite income differential we could attribute solely to height" (Keyes, p. 181). A complementary, but unrelated, article reported a telephone poll of 1,067 Canadians ("Tall Men Make More Money," 1978). The poll showed men, who categorized themselves in the $25,000 income bracket, were an average of 3.7 in. taller than those in the bracket of $5,000 to $10,000.

Taller people are paid more, but they do not necessarily earn it. A doctoral dissertation at North Texas State University evaluated the sales records of life insurance personnel as a function of their height (Murrey, 1976). Samples companies appeared to have had a definite height preference in that the average height of salesmen was more than 1 1/2 in. above the national average for males. The erroneous belief of the sales managers was that taller salesmen do sell more. However, there was no significant difference in sales associated with height variations among this sample of salesmen.

PERCEPTUAL DISTORTIONS

Most of the physical attractiveness research has supported the stereotype that most everything beautiful is good. A relatively meager amount of research effort has reversed this focus to examine the notion that most everything good is also beautiful (Kaplan, 1978). In other words, the vast bulk of research has identified the specific impact that physical attractiveness has on various perceptions and attribution of individuals who possess differing levels of physical attractiveness. The small amount of research reported in this section reverses the direction by identifying the impact that attributions of nonappearance factors have on the perceptions of physical attractiveness. These experimental manipulations were not extensive but they did reveal that attributions of nonappearance characteristics distored perceptions of an individual's appearance. For example, people increased their estimates of another person's height as his status increased (Wilson, 1968) and as social distance increased (Koulack & Tuthill, 1972).

Academic Status

Early perceptual distortion research explored the effect of academic status on height. In 1964, Dannemaier and Thumin asked 46 nursing students to estimate the heights of various people with whom they were in contact. These people were the school's assistant director, an instructor, the class president, and a specific fellow student. Students overestimated the height of the school administrators and underestimated the height of fellow students. These authors concluded that a significant relationship exists between status and perception of a person's height.

Several years later, Wilson (1968) also dealt with perceptual distortions of physical height as a function of academic status. His hypothesis was that increases in academic status would increase the perception of the stimulus person's height. The procedure divided undergraduate students of an Australian university into five groups. These subjects were asked to estimate the height of the man which was presented to them. The presentations were identical for all five groups except for systematic changes of the same man's academic status. In all situations, the course director introduced the man as being from the Cambridge University psychology department. Status manipulations described him as either a student, demonstrator, lecturer, senior lecturer, or professor. After the stimulus person left the room, the course director asked the students to estimate the person's height to the nearest half inch. The course director, who was known to all the students, also asked them to estimate his own height. Height ratings of the course director were not significantly different between groups. Wilson's results did find that the stimulus person's mean estimated height was directly related to his academic status. His hypothesis was supported—increasing academic status produced increases in perceived height.

Academic status, as well as sex, was also used as an independent variable in investigating perceptual distortion of physical attractiveness (Lerner & Moore, 1974). The procedure was to introduce either a male or female to ten different undergraduate classes as either Tony Smith or Toni Smith, respectively. Both of these stimulus persons were 22 years old, white, and average height, weight, and physique for their age. Their physical attractiveness was average as rated earlier by independent judges. The male wore a jacket, tie, and slacks, and the female wore a dress. Neither of the stimulus persons was known by any of the subjects.

All groups of subjects (184 females and 117 males) were in similar rooms and given identical procedures. In each class the instructor introduced the experimenter as someone who wanted a few minutes of the class's time. The experimenter then passed out some data sheets that were placed face down. Subjects were informed that the experimenter wanted them to meet someone before explaining these sheets of paper. The experimenter then asked the stimulus person to enter the room, at which time he or she did so and remained standing at the front of the room for 15 seconds before leaving. During this time, the academic status was manipulated by introducing the stimulus person as either an undergraduate student, a graduate student, a recent master's degree graduate, a Ph.D. candidate, or a recent Ph.D. graduate. At all times, the stimulus person maintained the same behavior, position, and distance from the subjects.

After the stimulus person left the room, the subjects were told that this was a study on perceptual memory and that they were to rate anonymously the stimulus person with respect to several characteristics. Identical procedures were employed for all groups except for the academic status manipulations.

Manipulation of the status variable did not yield significant main effects on perceptions of physical attractiveness. However, an interaction involving physical attractiveness was reported for the lower status levels. At these levels, the female subjects rated the female stimulus persons higher in physical attractiveness than the male stimulus persons. Similarly, the female subjects rated the male stimulus persons higher in physical attractiveness than the female stimulus persons. Other than this interaction effect, this study did not indicate that differing levels of academic status distorted perception of a stimulus person's physical attractiveness.

Personality

Perceptions of physical attractiveness can be distorted by the personality (Gross & Crofton, 1977) and character (Bridges, 1981) of a stimulus person. Procedures identifying the relationship between physical attractiveness and perceptions of personality were reversed to assess the impact of personality (Gross & Crofton, 1977). To achieve this turnaround, photographs of female stimulus persons were first rated either high, low, or moderate in physical attractiveness. Descriptions of either a favorable, unfavorable, or neutral personality were attached to each photograph. After being presented with the stimulus materials, the subjects (69 males and 56 females) were asked to rate the physical attractiveness of the photographed female. The results indicated that for each level of physical attractiveness those persons attributed more favorable personalities were rated more highly in physical attractiveness than their counterparts.

Impact of character involved manipulation of sex-role orientation for both subjects and stimulus persons (Bridges, 1981). Using the Bem Sex-Role Inventory, subjects (43 males and 60 females) were classified as either sex-typed or androgynous. Stimulus materials were photographs of individual males and females, who were appropriately attributed the character of either a feminine female, masculine male, or an androgynous person. Subjects were presented with two opposite-sex stimulus persons (one sex-typed and one androgynous) and asked to indicate their liking and their ratings of physical attractiveness for each. This character manipulation did not affect the males' expressed liking for the female stimulus persons. However, the androgynous male stimulus persons were liked significantly better by female judges regardless of their own sex-role orientation. Notwithstanding the judges' or the stimulus persons' sex, character attributions of sex-type increased the ratings of the stimulus persons' physical attractiveness.

Attitudes

The impact of attitudes on perceptions of physical attractiveness can be divided into two categories. First, similarity of attitudes may be manipulated to include both quantity and quality. A huge amount of research exists pertaining to attitude similarity and liking (cf. Patzer, 1978). However, only one study appears directly related to attitude similarity and evaluations of physical attractiveness (Johnson, 1981). The study asked 67 subjects (ranging in age from 19 to 50 years) to rate the physical attractiveness of photographed stimulus persons. Experimental treatments assigned stimulus persons to conditions of either support or nonsupport for political candidates in a recent national election. Those persons who were supposedly aligned with the same political attitude as the subjects, were those rated highest in physical attractiveness. Other existing research is causal data that pertains to either the impact of physical attractiveness or to perceptions of attitude similarity (Insko et al., 1973; Mashman, 1978; Schoedel, Frederickson, & Knight, 1975) or correlational data between perceived physical attractiveness and perceived attitude similarity (Bailey & Schreiber, 1981; Black, 1974; Cavior, Miller, & Cohen, 1975).

The second category which has received some scant attention is the manipulation of a variety of attitudes. Banziger and Hooker (1979) manipulated attitudes pertaining to feminism. The subjects were 76 males whose attitudes were measured as they pertained to females who did or did not support feminism. Female stimulus persons were attributed attitude statements that either reflected a feminist or nonfeminist orientation. After being presented with the stimulus materials, the subjects used an 8-point scale to rate the physical attractiveness of the photographed stimulus persons. Female stimulus persons identified as profeminist, as opposed to nonfeminist, were rated higher in physical attractiveness by the male subjects identified as profeminist. The female stimulus persons identified as nonfeminist were rated higher in physical attractiveness by the male subjects identified as nonfeminist.

Another study involving attitudes manipulated sexual attitudes of stimulus persons and also measured sexual attitudes of the subjects (Patzer, 1975). Photographs of stimulus persons were used to perform two experiments that tested two main hypotheses. The first hypothesis was that sexual attitudes of a subject would affect attributions of sexual attitudes to stimulus persons when the only available information was the stimulus person's physical attractiveness. The second hypothesis dealt with ratings of a stimulus person's physical attractiveness when the only information available was his or her physical attractiveness and sexual attitudes.

To test these hypotheses the first experiment used 30 female subjects and the second experiment used 38. The independent variables in the first experiment were really blocking variables for the physical attractiveness of the stimulus persons and sexual attitudes of the subjects. The dependent variables were the stimulus persons' physical attractiveness ratings and attributed sexual attitudes. The independent variables in the second experiment included the stimulus persons' physical attractiveness and the sexual attitudes attributed to each stimulus person. Three levels of physical attractiveness were manipulated (low, moderate, and high) and four levels of sexual attitudes were manipulated (conservative, moderate, liberal, and unknown). The dependent variables were the physical attractiveness ratings given by the subjects for each of the stimulus persons as they were randomly paired with a sexual attitude.

Results of the first experiment were significant for the relationship between sexual attitudes of subjects and their attribution of sexual attitudes to the stimulus persons. These significant effects included:

1. Attribution or assumption of similar attitudes, that is, liberal subjects attributed liberal sexual attitudes whereas conservative subjects attributed conservative sexual attitudes.
2. Stimulus persons of lower physical attractiveness were attributed liberal sexual attitudes most frequently, regardless of the subjects own attitudes.
3. Stimulus persons of moderate physical attractiveness were attributed sexual attitudes similar to the subjects' own attitudes.
4. Stimulus persons of higher physical attractiveness were attributed moderate sexual attitudes by liberal subjects, whereas conservative sexual attitudes were attributed by the conservative subjects.

The second experiment revealed significance for both main and interaction effects. A general conclusion was that the additional information of a stimulus person's sexual attitudes does influence perceptions of his or her physical attractiveness. Subjects with knowledge of a stimulus person's sexual attitudes did perceive the physical attractiveness of that person differently from subjects without such information. Furthermore, subjects with different sexual attitude information perceived the physical attractiveness of the stimulus persons differently. Finally, the effects of different sexual attitudes were evident at each level of physical attractiveness but their effects were not the same at each of these levels.

Among the many significant effects was one of special interest pertaining to lack of information. When judging the physical attractiveness of the stimulus persons, the subjects gave the highest scores to those whose sexual attitudes were unknown. This finding may be explained by pointing out that this unknown sexual attitude category allows the subject to formulate his own precise idea of this stranger's sexual attitudes. In this way, the subject is able to form his ideal sexual attitude of the person and thereby raise the perception of physical attractiveness.

Behavior

As with assumptions of attitudes, assumptions of behavior also influence perceptions of physical attractiveness (Cavior & Howard, 1973; Felson & Bohrnstedt, 1979). Research in this area is extremely limited and appears to consist of only younger people. In an early study pertaining to juvenile deliquency social or antisocial behavior was attributed to stimulus persons (Cavior & Howard, 1973). Results revealed that such attributions of behavior distort perceptions of physical attractiveness. The physical attractiveness of the stimulus persons was rated significantly lower when paired with an attribution of antisocial behavior as compared to social behavior.

Later research used 416 subjects in the sixth and eighth grades (Felson & Bohrnstedt, 1979). The attributes investigated, which could possibly influence perceptual distortions, were behaviors pertaining to athletic and academic abilities. Data were collected through sociometric measures. The results demonstrated that the investigated variables of athletic and academic ability did influence perceptions of a stimulus person's physical attractiveness.

ASSOCIATION

In 1937, Waller referred to the external rewards of associating, or even being seen, with others who were physically attractive. Now, 45 years later, the rewards he spoke of are being identified and documented. One determinant of a person's physical attractiveness is the physical attractiveness of his or her associates. This association effect is produced regardless of the type of interpersonal relationship or the sex of the parties involved. The mere association with a person of lower physical attractiveness produces a negative social reaction (Sigall & Landy, 1973), whereas association with a person of higher physical attractiveness results in perceived social status that is positive (Bar-Tal & Saxe, 1974).

The physical attractiveness of females is affected by the physical attractiveness of their male partner (Strane & Watts, 1977). A female stimulus person was photographed with a male stimulus person who was either high or low in physical attractiveness. Sixty subjects (30 males and

30 females) presented with the stimulus pairings were asked to evaluate the female. Manipulations included eight bipolar adjective scales for the subjects to rate the female stimulus person within each of the experimental treatment conditions. Significant main effects were found for physical attractiveness but not for sex of judges. No significant interactions occurred between sex and physical attractiveness manipulations. The signifiant main effects indicated positive consequences for the female associated with a male of high physical attractiveness, and negative consequences for the female associated with a male of low physical attractiveness. Females paired with a male of higher physical attractiveness received more positive evaluations on all scales including evaluations of her own physical attractiveness.

Prestige

Physical attractiveness of a partner may be more powerful than the partner's status or prestige (Meiners & Sheposh, 1976; Sheposh, 1976). Sheposh (1976) paired the same female with male stimulus persons who were either high or low in physical attractiveness. The male stimulus person also underwent vocation manipulation as either a medical student or sales clerk. The 88 subjects (44 males and 44 females) were asked to evaluate the female after a photograph and information about the status of the male stimulus person were presented.

When the female was paired with a male stimulus person of higher physical attractiveness she was evaluated most positively. She was evaluated higher in her own physical attractiveness intelligence, self-confidence, friendliness, talent, likability, and excitement. The authors stated that manipulation of the status variable did not affect as many attributes as did the physical attractiveness manipulation, and that the female subjects were more affected by the physical attractiveness manipulation than were the male subjects.

Similar effects occurred when males were evaluated as a function of being paired with females (Meiners & Sheposh, 1976). The experimental treatments involving the male with a femal stimulus person of high physical attractiveness produced positive evaluations for the male. He was rated higher in physical attractiveness as well as more positive on other nonappearance attributes that were examined. Again, manipulation of the partner's intelligence has less impact than manipulation of the partner's physical attractiveness.

Intimacy

Association effects are not limited to platonic relationships. Sigall and Landy (1973) performed two very different experiments to assess the impact of a romantic partner whose physical attractiveness is either high or low. The first experiment involved a male stimulus person paired with a female of either low or high physical attractiveness. The pairings included a description of the association as either boyfriend (i.e., intimate relationship) or simply a male friend of the woman. The 56 subjects (28 males and 28 females) were asked to evaluate the male stimulus persons after being presented with one of the experimental treatment conditions. Romantic/intimate association accentuated both the positive and the negative impact of a partner's physical attractiveness. The male stimulus person was evaluated least favorably when paired as a boyfriend with a female stimulus person of low physical attractiveness. Conversely, the most favorable evaluations were given to the male stimulus person when paired as a boyfriend with a female stimulus person of high physical attractiveness.

The second experiment was similar to the first but did not use ratings by others. Instead, 40 subjects were selected to participate in a role-playing situation where each was paired with a female. Pairings involved either a female of low or high physical attractiveness who was described as either a girlfriend (i.e., intimate relationship) or simply a female friend of the male subject. The male subjects were then asked to evaluate how others would perceive them (the male subjects) based on their paired partner. Consistent with the results of the first experiment, the subjects indicated accentuated physical attractiveness impact due to a romantic association. The subjects believed they would be perceived most favorably when paired romantically with a female of high physical attractiveness and least favorably when paired romantically with a female of low physical attractiveness. These male subjects believed that the physically attractive female stimulus person would increase ratings of the subject's own physical attractiveness, as well as enhancing perceptions of his own intelligence, friendliness, confidence, talents, and excitingness.

Sex Effects

Interaction effects may occur when sex of stimulus persons are fully manipulated (Hartnett & Elder, 1973). Photographs of both males and females of either low or high physical attractiveness were paired and evaluated by 144 female subjects. The results revealed that a male of higher physical attractiveness was perceived most favorably when paired with a female of high physical attractiveness. Similar effects were revealed for the male of lower physical attractiveness. These latter effects were less dramatic, nevertheless, the male of lower physical attractiveness was perceived more favorably when paired with a female of high physical attractiveness.

Unexpectedly, the female of higher physical attractiveness was liked more and perceived to possess more favorable personal characteristics when associated with a male of lower physical attractiveness. The authors explained this last finding in terms of preferential advantages. Females of higher physical attractiveness may be perceived as exploiting their assets when associating with males of higher physical attractiveness. But females of higher physical attractiveness may be perceived as good persons with favorable personal characteristics when they associate with males of lower physical attractiveness. Unfortunately, this study did not fully manipulate the sex of judges so as to reverse the male and female roles.

Same-Sex

The association effects of a partner's physical attractiveness include same-sex peers. Earlier research reported in this section has involved the effect of physical attractiveness of a partner who is of the opposite sex to that of the stimulus person. Kernis and Wheeler (1981) appraised the effect of a same-sex situation within two pairing circumstances. The stimulus persons were males or females paired with a same-sex stimulus person of either low or high physical attractiveness. Pairings were presented as either associated (friendship relationship) or unassociated (merely in the presence of the stimulus person).

The procedure involved 159 subjects who evaluated the stimulus person after being exposed to one of the four experimental conditions. Results revealed an interaction between association and physical attractiveness. In the unassociated condition, the stimulus person was rated more positive when paired with a partner of low physical attractiveness. In the associated condition, the stimulus person was rated more positive when paired with a partner of high physical attractiveness.

CONTEXT

Research on interpersonal attraction documents that it is not immune from its environment. In a polluted atmosphere, strangers demonstrate greater liking for another as compared to a clean environment (Botton, Barry, Frey, & Soler, 1978). Adverse conditions can also promote the opposite effect where liking is decreased by heat (Bell & Baron, 1974; Griffitt & Veitch, 1971), crowding (Epstein & Karlin, 1975; Freedman, Levy, Buchanan, & Price, 1972), and noise (Bull, Burboge, Crandall, Fletcher, Lloyd, Rosenberg, & Rockett, 1972). Similarly, the physical attractiveness variable is not isolated from the context in which it is viewed. Evaluation of physical attractiveness is influenced by both the physical attractiveness of others surrounding the stimulus person and by factors unrelated to the person's physical attractiveness. The research identifying these influences are important because it emphasizes that in reality the physical attractiveness of a person is always exposed to factors external to the individual.

Past and Present

Physical attractiveness of a person exists within the context of the physical attractiveness of other individuals. It is evaluated in terms of both prior and current exposures to the physical attractiveness of other persons. A series of three studies were performed to explore how an individual's physical attractiveness was affected by the observer's prior exposure to others' physical attractiveness (Kenrick & Gutierres, 1980). The procedure involved 227 male subjects within both a naturalistic field setting and a controlled laboratory experiment.

The field experiment involved 81 subjects who were watching a popular television show with female actors of high physical attractiveness. These subjects were approached and asked to rate the physical attractiveness of a female stimulus person. The stimulus person was represented in a photograph that had been previously rated at a moderate level of physical attractiveness. Those subjects watching the actresses of high physical attractiveness rated the stimulus person significantly lower in physical attractiveness than did a comparable control group.

The second and third studies consisted of controlled laboratory experiments with 146 different subjects. An experimental group viewed a videotape of female stimulus persons of high physical attractiveness, but the control group did not view such a videotape. After an equal amount of time, both groups were asked to evaluate the physical attractiveness of an unrelated stimulus person. This second procedure produced the same pattern for evaluating a stimulus person lower in physical attractiveness after first observing stimulus persons of high physical attractiveness.

Physical attractiveness need not only be subjected to the observer's prior exposures to others but may also be evluated within the context of current exposures. Exploration of this specific relationship was performed by testing a general hypothesis pertaining to social stimuli and context effects (Melamed & Moss, 1975). This endeavor included two related studies, 140 subjects, and photographs of female stimulus persons. The subjects were asked to rate the physical attractiveness of the stimulus person while also viewing other stimulus persons of either high or low physical attractiveness.

Data revealed a contrast effect. Stimulus persons of moderate physical attractiveness were rated higher in physical attractiveness when within the context of others who were low in physical attractiveness. Similarly, stimulus persons of moderate physical attractiveness were rated lower in physical attractiveness when within the context of others who were high in physical attractiveness. These same contrast effects were consistent with a later study using three presentation conditions (Sugarman, 1980). The three conditions were successive viewing, simultaneous viewing, or absolute viewing of a stimulus person. The differences in physical attractiveness ratings were greatest in the simultaneous viewing conditions.

Musical Environment

Music is a common environmental factor of contemporary life. It is also an environmental factor in which an individual's physical attractiveness is possibly affected. An experiment was designed to test the effect of background music on physical attractiveness (May & Hamilton, 1980). The stimulus materials were photographs of males who were either high or low in physical attractiveness. The background music was either rock music (described as positive affect evoking), avant-garde music (described as negative affect evoking), or an experimental treatment of no background music. In addition to a consistent preferential evaluation of the stimulus person of high physical attractiveness, the differences in music produced variations of physical attractiveness ratings. The music condition described as evoking positive affect resulted in the highest ratings of physical attractiveness for the stimulus person.

Time Pressure

Threatened behaviors and possessions become more attractive (Wicklund, 1974). This experience of threat can be induced through decreasing time available to make a decision. In fact, as time available to make a decision decreases, differences in the values of alternatives become less distinct (Linder & Crane, 1970). Integrating these findings of threat, value, and time, a relationship emerges between physical attractiveness and time pressures. Inspection of this relationship was based on a hypothesis that the physical attractiveness of an opposite-sex stimulus person would increase as the time available to interact decreased (Pennebaker, Dyer, Caulkins, Litowitz, Ackreman, Anderson, & McGraw, 1979). Data were collected through a field study designed to identify the effect of decreasing decision time on perceptions of physical attractiveness. Subjects were 52 males and 51 females who were customers at three different bars. They were interviewed by same-sex interviewers at 3 1/2 hours, 2 hours, and half-hour before closing time. All interviews included evaluations of the physical attractiveness of opposite-sex customers. Although the data revealed no significant differences between males and females, the closing times produced divergent physical attractiveness ratings. The authors concluded that ratings of physical attractiveness did increase as time available to make a decision to interact decreased.

CONCLUSION

This chapter has presented not only an in-depth discussion of the major determinants of physical attractiveness but also a host of other factors that probably contribute to physical attractiveness. Some of these factors are characteristics of the stimulus person, whereas others are characteristics of the judge. The characteristics of the judges, which some research has addressed, included the judges own physical attractiveness (Tennis & Dabbs, 1975), their self-esteem (Graham & Perry, 1976), and manipulations of internal arousal based on heart-rate information (Woll & McFall, 1979). Even though stimulus persons are rated higher in physical attractiveness when associated with subject information pertaining to false increases in heart rate (Kerber & Coles, 1978), these studies have generally not produced data of meaningful value to the physical attractiveness phenomena.

Research with miscellaneous characteristics possessed by stimulus persons has also produced data of relatively dubious value to the physical attractiveness phenomena. These efforts have dealt with the relationship between physical attractiveness and the stimulus person's voice (Blood, Mahan, & Hyman,1979; Page & Balloun, 1978), first name (Garwood, Cox, Kaplan, Wasserman, & Sulzer, 1980), and eye features, such as gaze (Fugita, Agle, Newman, & Walfish, 1977; Kleinke, Staneski, & Berger, 1975), pupil size (Bull & Shead, 1979; Hicks, Pellegrini, & Tomlinson, 1978), and movement (Goldstein & Papageorge, 1980; McDowell & Zook, 1973). Body chemicals such as androstenol are even explored for their impact on perceptions of physical attractiveness (Black & Biron, 1982).

There are also variables that produce substantial temporary effects on perceptions of physical attractiveness, as, for example, the industries involved in clothes, cosmetics, and jewelry. Despite the obvious importance of these variables, social science research has really not given them notable attention with regard to the physical attractiveness phenomena. However, private interests within each of these industries have probably amassed impressive data pertaining to the relationship between physical attractiveness and body adornments.

Certainly, the demand for such adornments is caused, at least in part, by the desire of people to maximize their physical attractiveness. In fact, academic studies can be found that showed both cosmetics (Cash & Cash, 1982; Graham & Jouhar, 1981) and clothes (Hoult, 1954; Nielsen & Kernaleguen, 1976) influenced perceptions of personality and appearance. The early research on clothes was so specific as to indicate why certain styles were worn (Cunnington, 1941; McCullough, Miller, & Ford, 1977), as well as the impressions they made (Douglas & Solomon, 1983; Hamid, 1968, 1969; Silverman, S. S., 1945). There is no doubt that clothes, cosmetics, and jewelry can all have a significant influence on the physical attractiveness of an individual. However, the respective research on these adornments is not detailed here because it is outside the primary focus of this book.

Chapter 7

Persuasive Communication

ORIGINAL RESEARCH

Several years ago I contacted the three major networks regarding potential funding for research on the relationship between a communicator's physical attractiveness and the effectiveness of persuasive communication. The Director of Corporate Projects, at ABC television headquarters, responded with an item of personal curiosity. This television executive posed the question, "Should a government, a corporation, or other institution consider physical attractiveness factors in determining who should present a message?" Furthermore, he asked if the President of the United States should ask the Vice President or the Press Secretary or his wife or some other person to announce a new program? Another question posed by this executive was whether the major automobile makers should use different persons to announce a new car and to announce a major recall?

These questions were indirectly pursued through experiments which I conducted. These experiments, among others, will be discussed in this chapter, which departs somewhat from earlier chapters by concentrating on primarily one topic and in a manner normally associated with academic research journals. One purpose for this departure is to explain and examine the procedures often used in experimental research on the physical attractiveness variable. Another purpose is to consider two major factors that are prevalent in our society and which separately and together possess important implications for every person. A research project investigating the relationship between communicator physical attractiveness and persuasive communication effectiveness is now presented.

THE NEED

Both organizations and individuals concerned with survival must take a serious interest in the communication that flows from them to their audiences. Although the type of communication and the type of delivery medium varies, a substantial amount of communication from both profit and nonprofit organizations is persuasive communication delivered by a communicator. Regardless, if this persuasive communication is obvious commercial advertising or noncommercial public service announcements, the intent of the sponsor is information acquisition by its audience. Certainly, a primary concern for all such entities is to achieve persuasive communication effectiveness.

An antecedent to achieving persuasive communication effectiveness is the need for such practitioners to realize the milieu in which an individual functions. Individuals in today's society are literally drowning in a sea of information bidding for their attention. The consequence is that excessive information, which most of it becomes, is never perceived.

Such selective perception continues to increase in importance as the amount of excessive information continues to increase. Practitioners of persuasive communication must appreciate at least the rudiments of neurological processes. According to these processes an important function of the human brain is its works as a filtration system (Ornstein, 1972). In a normal individual, the filtration system will permit only limited amounts of information to be observed, perceived, and encoded into the mind. To describe this perceptual operation the phrase "cognitive economics" was coined (Mischel, 1979). Cognitive economics describes the fact that

> people are flooded by information which must somehow be reduced and simplified to allow efficient processing and to avoid an otherwise overwhelming overload. (Mischel, 1979, p. 741)

With this understanding, the objective of persuasive communication practitioners must be to identify techniques to permeate the individual's perceptual filters.

PERSUASIVE COMMUNICATION

The communication process can be viewed as *who* says *what* to *whom* through what *channels* and with what *effects* (Lasswell, 1948). Other authors have presented the communication process as an interaction of four major components: source, message, medium, and receiver (Engel,

Wales, & Warshaw, 1971). Research identifying the impact and roles that each of these four components has within persuasive communication is reviewed and summarized by McGuire (1969).

Source versus Communicator

Although all four components are shown to affect persuasion (see McGuire, 1969), the focus of current research is on the source, or more precisely, the communicator. The distinction here between source and communicator is important. In the above communication model, the source component is not necessarily the originator of the communication but may also be the sender or spokesperson for the source. This distinction may be of special interest to marketing communications (McCroskey, Larson, & Knapp, 1971) because hired spokespersons, rather than the sources themselves, usually communicate marketing messages to the receivers. Because of the distinction between communicator and source, the generalizations from one to the other should be viewed with caution.

Source Credibility

With this communicator–source distinction in mind, it may be said that, generally, the more credible the source is perceived to be, the greater will be the influence of the delivered persuasive communication (e.g., Choo, 1964; Hovland & Weiss, 1951). Source credibility is defined in the research in a number of ways, but the three most common dimensions are source expertise, source trustworthiness, and liking of the source (Britt, 1978; Byrne, 1971; Janis & Kelley, 1953; Miller and Basehart, 1969). Although the liking component receives some support for its role in source credibility, it is the two components of expertise and trustworthiness which are consistently cited.

Numerous factors affecting the source component have been investigated. One source factor, which has not been studied but which has both theoretical and empirical support for its influence on source credibility, is communicator physical attractiveness. Attribution theory, combined with empirical research documenting physical attractiveness phenomena, suggests that all three source credibility elements (trustworthiness, expertise, and liking) may be influenced by communicator physical attractiveness, which ultimately influences overall persuasive communication effectiveness.

PHYSICAL ATTRACTIVENESS

The relationship between persuasive communication and consumer attitudes toward a product (regardless of its definition) is of major interest to the users of such communication. One major issue here is the definition of effectiveness. The preference of many marketing practitioners to define persuasive communication effectiveness in terms of communication is not new (Boyd & Ray, 1971; Wolfe, Brown, & Thompson, 1962; Wolfe, Brown, Greenberg, & Thompson, 1963). Both practitioners and researchers continue to use measures such as recall, evaluation, perceptions, beliefs, and attitudes to assess effectiveness of persuasive communication efforts. Because the communicator, as perceived by the receiver, may influence the effectiveness of the persuasive communication, all available informational cues become important. One potentially powerful informational cue that may serve as the dominant feature in this communication setting is the physical attractiveness of the communicator.

Physical attractiveness is a relatively new topic of research attention which has produced substantial knowledge within a short time span. However, many aspects of the relationship between behavior and physical attractiveness are not yet understood. For this study, and consistent with existing research, physical attractiveness refers to facial appearance. Past research does not define physical attractiveness, but it is defined here as the degree to which a stimulus person's facial features are pleasing to observe. The author recognizes this definition is not necessarily adequate to fully capture the comlexity of the physical attractiveness construct. However, for lack of a definition, and assuming less-than-perfect information is better than no information, the intent is to provide a common reference standard among the raters.

Physical Attractiveness Phenomena

The importance of physical attractiveness in our lives may be succinctly stated in the proposition that "what is beautiful is good," a stereotype prevalent in today's society. Existence of this physical attractiveness stereotype is documented throughout the research presented in this book.

In short, the consequences of being physically attractive are positive, whereas the consequences of being physically unattractive are negative. Research consistently reports that people do not behave in a manner consistent with the adage You can't judge a book by its cover. Based merely on physical attractiveness, people do formulate comprehensive notions about an observed person. The findings of physical attractiveness research can be grouped into four broad generalizations:

1. Physically attractive people have greater social power than their counterparts (Mills & Aronson, 1965; Sigall & Aronson, 1969; Sigall, Page, & Brown, 1971).
2. All other things being equal, individuals of higher physical attractiveness are better liked than individuals of lower physical attractiveness (Byrne, 1971; Byrne, London, & Reeves, 1968; Walster et al., 1966).
3. Physically attractive people are perceived to possess more favorable personal and nonpersonal characteristics, including intelligence, personality traits, and success in life (Dion et al., 1972; Miller, 1970a; Nida & Nida, 1977).
4. Physically attractive people have more positive effects on other people and receive more positive responses from others, including influence attempts, work requests, and requests for help, than do people of lower physical attractiveness (Joseph, 1977; McGuire, 1969; Sternthal, 1972).

Measurement: Truth-of-Consensus

A popular fallacy appears to be that beauty is a unique assessment by each observer. Yet, even conceding that beauty may be subjective, perception of another person's physical attractiveness can be accurately predicted. Because no objective or absolute answer exists for the question of who is physical attractiveness or what determines physical attractiveness, researchers generally use the truth-of-consensus method to measure physical attractiveness. This method is based on the premise that judgments of physical attractiveness are necessarily subjective, and that such judgments are formed through gestalt principles of person perception rather than single characteristics. If a substantial number of judges rate a stimulus person as high or low in physical attractiveness, then, for research purposes, the stimulus person is interpreted to represent that level of physical attractiveness. However suspect this empirical approach to physical attractiveness may initially appear, it is consistent with broader issues of science. For example, an article dealing with the philosophy and history of science stated that scientific knowledge is necessarily "sanctioned largely by consensus" (Anderson, 1983, p. 25).

PHYSICAL ATTRACTIVENESS AND
PERSUASIVE COMMUNICATION

Existing research shows that the physical attractiveness variable plays an influential role throughout behavior and interpersonal relationships.

Specific research has shown that the physical attractiveness variable also holds considerable consequences for persuasive communication. It is clear that those higher in physical attractiveness are more effective in persuasive communication than those lower in physical attractiveness. Indirect manipulations such as sexiness support the role of communicator characteristics in persuasive communication (Alexander & Judd, 1978; Patzer, 1979b; 1982; Steadman, 1969). Direct confirmation of the value of physical attractiveness for marketing activities has involved industrial salespeople (Lamont & Lundstrom, 1977), mass media advertising (Patzer, 1983b), source credibility (Patzer, 1983a, 1983c), and general personal selling (Ronkainen & Reingen, 1979). More generic research on attitude changes also offers support for the relationship between physical attractiveness and persuasive communication effectiveness (e.g, Blass, Alperstein, & Black, 1974; Egaly & Chalken, 1975; Mills & Harvey, 1972; Sigall & Helmreich, 1969). The focus here is on communicator physical attractiveness, however, aspects of nonverbal communication are also relevant (Hemsley & Doob, 1978; Mehrabian, 1972; Scherwitz & Helmreick, 1973; Tankard, 1970). Findings pertaining to the relationship between physical attractiveness and persuasive communication are:

1. When the receiver knows a source's intent to influence or persuade, persuasive communication is more effective from a source of higher physical attractiveness than a source of lower physical attractiveness. But, when the source is low in physical attractiveness it makes no difference whether the intent to persuade is known or not known by the receiver (Mills & Aronson, 1965).

2. It appears that sources of higher physical attractiveness are more effective because the receivers experience greater liking for the physically attractive source. Persuasive communication is more effective when combined with a photograph of a physically attractive source than when no photograph of a source is used (Snyder & Rothbart, 1971).

3. Sources who are both physically attractive and expert result in greater persuasive communication effectiveness than their counterparts. No information about a source results in greater persuasion than a source who is either low in physical attractiveness or low in expertise (Horai, Naccari, & Fatoullah, 1974).

4. Influence attempts measured in terms of actual behavior indicate that those of higher physical attractiveness are more successful in persuasion than their counterparts. These effects, however, vary according to the sex of the individuals involved (Dion & Stein, 1978).

5. Based in part on Chaiken (1979), the positive effects of a

physically attractive source appear to be consistent across populations, ages, settings (laboratory and field studies), and interaction modes (print communication, print combined with recorded audio, and face-to-face). These positive effects are also consistent across measurement techniques (paper-and-pencil questionnaires and actual behavior observations).

6. When the research on physical attractiveness is conducted within a marketing context, with the focus being on the communicator (as opposed to the source as originator and communicator), the results are comparable to and supportive of other physical attractiveness research. A communicator of higher physical attractiveness enhances both the receivers' attitudes and evaluations pertaining to the product, as well as to the product's advertising (Baker & Churchill, 1977).

RESEARCH PROBLEM AND HYPOTHESES

The psychological research, which identifies physical attractiveness phenomena, suggests an urgent need to understand the function of this variable within both commercial and noncommercial applications of persuasive communication. This need was first alluded to over 30 years ago (Hovland et al., 1953) by proposing that one goal of communication research is to isolate factors that account for the effectiveness, or lack thereof, of persuasive communication.

People only process some of the information available to them. Consequently, the likelihood is high that a single informational cue acquires disproportionate weight in determining source credibility, and, ultimately, persuasive communication effectiveness. Given physical attractiveness phenomena, this single cue may well be source (or communicator) physical attractiveness.

The primary issue is that the effects of communicator physical attractiveness on the effectiveness of persuasive communication are not known. Therefore, the research problem (Patzer, 1980) was to design and execute a study to properly address this relationship. In addition to this broad question of effects, two empirical questions were addressed in this research. First, are communicators of different levels of physical attractiveness perceived differently with regard to source credibility characteristics? Second, what is the relationship between communicator physical attractiveness and persuasive communication effectiveness as measured in terms of receivers' recall, attitudes, beliefs, perceptions, and evaluations? In an attempt to more fully address these questions, an underlying concern of this research pertained to theoretical prediction and explanation.

The following hypotheses all share common theoretical underpinnings put forth by attribution theory. Throughout these hypotheses, attribution theory suggests that receivers attribute meaning to or infer meaning from what they observe (Heider, 1944). Therefore, combining knowledge provided by empirical research, attribution theory suggests that a variety of positive characteristics and variables will be attributed to those of higher physical attractiveness. Based on this combination of attribution theory and empirical knowledge, a variety of negative characteristics and variables will be attributed to those of lower physical attractiveness. Although numerous theories may be applicable, attribution theory is most relevant as a common thread throughout all the hypotheses.

Several aspects of the research design related to the hypotheses are clarified in this paragraph. Communicator physical attractiveness was measured (and operationally defined) through a consensus of judges by using mean rating values and standard deviation values. Persuasive communication effectiveness is a general term interpreted for each hypothesis to mean the extent of agreement with the hypothesized effect. Finally, no hypotheses were proposed for interaction effects although such hypotheses may be informative in future research.

> Hypothesis One. *Communicators of higher levels of physical attractiveness will be perceived more trustworthy and of higher expertise than communicators of lower levels of physical attractiveness.*

Attribution theory (Bem, 1972; Heider, 1944, 1946, 1958; Jones & Davis, 1965; Kelley, 1967, 1973) combined with the results from the physical attractiveness research is the basis of this first hypothesis. Receivers will use physical attractiveness as an informational cue about the communicator. With this information the receivers will attribute more positive personal characteristics, such as trustworthiness and expertise, to those communicators of greatest physical attractiveness.

> Hypothesis Two. *The greater the communicator's (manipulated) physical attractiveness the greater will be the receiver's liking for the communicator.*

First, attribution theory may be interpreted to suggest that receivers will infer personal characteristics about the communicators in a manner consistent with the physical attractiveness phenomena. Second, learning theory states that a response to a certain stimulus will generalize to similar stimuli (Lott, 1955; Staats, 1968; Staats & Staats, 1958). Hypothesis Two combines this learning theory concept with the empirical research that shows people experience the most liking for those of greatest physical attractiveness (Berscheid *et al.*, 1971; Byrne *et al.*, 1968). Loose interpretation of learning theory states that a liking of the physically attractive will persist or generalize to a variety of situations including a persuasive communication dyad with a communicator and receiver.

> Hypothesis Three. *Communicators of higher physical attractiveness will be most effective as measured by attitudinal components (i.e., cognitive, affective, and conative measures).*

Distraction theory (Festinger & Maccoby, 1964; Zimbardo, Snyder, Thomas, Gold, & Gurwitz, 1970) applied here states that a communicator of either high or low physical attractiveness reduces the receiver's ability to generate internal counterarguments. However, the effectiveness of persuasive communication will be greater when communicators possess high physical attractiveness rather than low physical attractiveness. The reason is that receivers will tend to focus attention on the high physical attractiveness and tend to shy away or direct their attention elsewhere when confronted with low physical attractiveness. The result will be that receivers pay increased attention to those lower in physical attractiveness. Consequently, distraction leading to reduction of internal counterarguments will be greater with the former than the latter.

The third hypothesis is also based on the combined effects of Hypotheses One and Two. The persuasive communication research literature (Britt, 1978; McGuire, 1969) identifies three major components of source credibility as trustworthiness, expertise, and liking. The result of Hypotheses One and Two is that source credibility, as defined by these three components, will vary directly with communicator physical attractiveness. Furthermore, because persuasive communication effectiveness is dependent on source credibility, the effectiveness of the persuasive communication will vary positively with these three source credibility variables.

> Hypothesis Four. *Receivers exposed to the persuasive communication of communicators of high physical attractiveness will respond with more positive and stronger beliefs than their counterparts.*

This fourth hypothesis is based on attribution theory, combined with results from both communications research and physical attractiveness research. Communications research suggests that two important elements of communicator credibility are perceived trustworthiness and perceived expertise. (Bettinghaus, 1968; Burgoon, 1974; Cronkhite, 1969; Hovland *et al.*, 1953; Wenburg & Wilmot, 1973). Physical attractiveness research suggests that the physically attractive are perceived to possess greater positive characteristics, such as trustworthiness and expertise, than their counterparts. Therefore, according to attribution theory, receivers will attribute higher trustworthiness and expertise to those communicators of high physical attractiveness. The result of these attributions is that the more credible communicators will be believed more and will influence the beliefs of receivers more.

> Hypothesis Five. *Recall of advertisement details or facts will be less with communicators of higher physical attractiveness than with communicators of lower physical attractiveness.*

This hypothesis is in opposition to the third hypothesis because the former is based on distraction theory whereas the latter is based on an opposing view of distraction theory. This hypothesis is based on what may be termed the distraction theory opposition (Haaland & Venkatesan, 1968; Peterson & Peterson, 1959) which argues that distraction lowers learning. Recall of advertisement details and facts appear to represent learning, and, as such, recall is expected to be less when distraction of the higher communicator physical attractiveness is presented.

> Hypothesis Six. *Perceptions of product quality, product price, and product uniqueness will be positively correlated with perceived communicator physical attractiveness.*

Consistency theory (Festinger, 1957; Heider, 1958; Osgood & Tannenbaum, 1955) suggests the predicted correlations of Hypothesis Six. The physical attractiveness research combined with the learning theory application of Hypothesis Two suggests receivers will view a communicator of higher physical attractiveness more positively than a communicator of lower physical attractiveness. Consistency theory states that the receiver will balance his or her attitudes, that is, move toward consistent attitudes for both the communicator and the product. Consequently, receivers will adjust their attitudes toward the product (quality, price, and uniqueness) to reflect their attitudes toward the product.

> Hypothesis Seven. *The effects predicted in Hypotheses One through Five will be a monotonic increasing relationship. In*

other words, persuasive communication using communicators of high physical attractiveness will be most effective followed by communicators of moderate physical attractiveness, and least effective will be communicators of low physical attractiveness.

Existing research has dealt with only the two extremes of physical attractiveness, neglecting to study the middle or moderate levels of the physical attractiveness continuum. Assuming the population represents a normal distribution of physical attractiveness, it is reasonable to predict that the greatest number of people (i.e., receivers of mass persuasive communications) are of moderate physical attractiveness. Therefore, it may initially appear that the communicator of moderate physical attractiveness will be most effective because the greatest number of receivers will identify with this communicator type. Furthermore, because of the similarity and trust, liking will probably be enhanced, resulting in greater source credibility and, ultimately, increased persuasive communication effectiveness.

Despite the intuitively appealing argument advanced in the preceding paragraph, three reasons exist for this seventh hypothesis to the contrary. First, the correlation between self-rated physical attractiveness and ratings of physical attractiveness by others is exceedingly low because people consistently self-rate their physical attractiveness much higher (Adams, 1977a; Patzer, 1975; Stroebe *et al.*, 1971). Second, the physical attractiveness phenomena appear to overpower any similarity effects that the moderate level of communicator physical attractiveness may represent. Third, no theory exists that suggests a different relationship than proposed in this hypothesis. In addition, several unpublished studies using three levels of physical attractiveness have all found a monotonic relationship between physical attractiveness and its effects (Joseph, 1977; Patzer, 1973, 1975). Finally, according to selected information processing theory, people seek out, tend to like, and are more attentive to stimuli that are moderately unfamiliar rather than totally unfamiliar to them (Berylne, 1960; Bexton *et al.*, 1954; Heron *et al.*, 1956).

RESEARCH METHODOLOGY

The research was performed in two major phases. The primary purpose of phase one was to obtain photographs of individauls who represented low, moderate, and high levels of physical attractiveness for each sex. Using the photographs obtained in phase one to test the hypotheses, the purpose of phase two was to investigate the influence of communicator physical attractiveness on audience attitudes. Furthermore, to explain this potential relationship, liking for the communicator and perception of communicator trustworthiness and expertise were also measured for each experimental treatment. All statistical analyses were performed with the SPSS standard (Statistical Package for the Social Sciences; Nie, Hull, Jenkins, Steinbrenner, & Bent, 1975), and SAS (Statistical Analysis System; Helwig & Council, 1979).

Overall Procedure

Subjects. The entire study involved 542 subjects: 120 in phase one, 30 in the pilot test, and 392 in phase two. All subjects were university juniors and seniors enrolled in introductory business courses. Although nonstudents may be desirable, responses from university students were justified for a number of reasons:

1. Discussions of external validity questions in business and other social science research often conclude that, dependent on the situation, college students are permissible subjects (Oaks, 1972; Permut, Michel, & Joseph, 1976).
2. The results of this study were intended to generalize to the consumer market. Consequently, university students were appropriate in several respects: (a) although college students may not allow generalization to a distinctly different behavior or an extremely different population, such as business decisions or industrial executives (Fromkin & Streufert, 1976, p. 428), they may well be appropriate for similar behavior by similar populations; (b) this research is one study among a much larger body that comprises many different behaviors and populations; and (c) the topic, or product advertised, is a product bought and used by the subjects, and is a product shown not to elicit different familiarity and usage responses between students and nonstudents (Shuptrine, 1975, p. 385).

Stimulus Persons. The stimulus persons were depicted in black-and-white photographs measuring 1½ in. by 2 in. To allow maximum control (i.e., achieve internal validity), each photograph was of a college senior in his or her early 20s taken from a university yearbook. These stimulus persons were selected because the photographs were the most standardized among the alternatives (e.g., snapshots or professional photographs from advertising and talent agencies). Photographs were used to control for extraneous variables inherent with live stimulus persons (i.e., speech and body language can differ between experimental treatments which would weaken internal validity).

Faces. The use of faces in marketing communications is especially appropriate because of the several properties a face represents. First, there are the comparisons of faces with other nonface stimuli, and, second, there are the comparisons of faces with other faces. In general, the cognitive processes involved with recognition of nonface pictures are qualitatively different from those use in recognition of face stimuli (Ellis, 1975; McKelvie, 1976).

Several studies indicated that faces possess properties not possessed by other possible stimuli that could be used in marketing communications, such as designs and verbal descriptions. Faces are more recognizable than other complex patterns, such as ink blots, photographs of snow crystals (Goldstein & Chance, 1971), houses, stick figures, or other designs (Yin, 1969). The multiple cues available in pictures are a better aid to recall than controlled nonvisual imagery (Bevan & Feur, 1977). This controlled imagery was also investigated by Hagiwara (1975). He reported that visual information served as a greater determinant of impression formation than did verbal information.

Specific faces were also shown to possess different properties than other faces (Fleishman *et al.*, 1976). Photographs of persons' faces, judged to be either high, moderate, or low in physical attractiveness, were later used in a recognition task. The faces rated low and high in physical attractiveness were recognized better than the faces of moderate physical attractiveness.

Faces differ in memorability. The characteristic which distinguishes a more memorable face from a less memorable face is the physical attractiveness of the face. Cross, Cross, and Daly (1971) found that faces judged earlier as high in physical attractiveness were recognized with greater frequency than those faces judged lower. Recent generic research has even identified variations in cognitive strategies for memory of faces (Parkin & Hayward, 1983).

Phase One

Subjects. A total of 120 subjects (60 males and 60 females) made the required judgments in phase one. All subjects were exposed to the same setting (i.e., furnishings, lighting, stimulus materials, verbal and written instructions, anonymity assurance, and experimenter).

Procedure. Eighty-four stimulus persons were presented to each judge. For each judge and for each task, the stimulus persons were randomized to counterbalance possible boredom and/or practice effects.

When the subject (judge) arrived, he or she was seated and given a letter of introduction followed by an instruction page. Verbal instructions and interactions between experimenter and subjects were minimized at all times and, when necessary, involved only brief clarification of judging mechanics (i.e., serious attempts were made to eliminate all potential experimental bias and/or demand characteristics).

Measurement Methods. To operationally define the physical attractiveness of communicators and to strengthen the physical attractiveness construct, two methods were used to measure physical attractiveness: a bipolar rating scale and an assimilation–contrast grouping method. These methods were replicated 2 weeks later, and no subjects who served in one method also served in the other.

To assure (convergent) validity, attempts were made to maximize differences between the two measurement methods. The bipolar rating scale method required subjects to view and rate only one stimulus person at a time, whereas the assimilation–contrast method required the subjects to view and group all the stimulus persons at the same time. The bipolar scale was a 7-point, labeled, continuum ranging from extremely low to extremely high physical attractiveness. For the assimilation–contrast method, judges were given all the photographs and asked to sort them into seven different groups that represented different levels of physical attractiveness. These judges were told to arrange (and rearrange), so that photographs within groups were comparable in physical attractiveness, and that photographs between groups were different (i.e., contrasted) in physical attractiveness. Sixty totally different subjects (30 males and 30 females) participated in each method, and stimulus persons were randomized for each subject and for each time.

Reliability Results. In light of Nunally's propositions (1967, p. 226), the reliability coefficients indicated that the measures of the physical attractiveness construct were very reliable for both the rating and grouping methods. Using Cronbach's Alpha Reliability Coefficients, the average coefficient for the rating method based on the male judges were .768, and .800 when based on the female judges. The average coefficient for the grouping method based on the male judges was .686, and .687 when based on the female judges.

Stimulus Person Selection. The data from the rating and grouping methods were used to select photographs of stimulus persons for the advertisement mock-ups. Selections were based on the means and standard deviations calculated by assigning numerical values, ranging from 1 to 7, to the scales. To minimize any unique characteristics or unique effects that a specific person might possess, multiple stimulus persons were chosen to represent each physical attractiveness level.

Using the judges' data, the mean scores and standard deviations for each stimulus person were calculated for each of the two methods and for each of the four judging periods. Next, the means representing the lowest, middle, and highest scores were grouped together for each stimulus person's sex. From each of these groups, those stimulus persons with the smallest standard deviations were selected to represent their respective level of physical attractiveness. Finally, t tests were performed to ensure that significant differences existed between the scores that were in different levels, and that no significant differences existed within each level. Stimulus persons were selected only (a) when no significant difference existed beween a stimulus person's mean scores from the test and retest of each method, and (b) when stimulus persons at different levels of physical attractiveness were judged significantly different at the .001 level of probability.

Because only stimulus persons who met the above criteria were selected, the number of stimulus persons for each physical attractiveness level could vary. The outcome was the same for both sexes; two stimulus persons for the moderate physical attractiveness level, and three stimulus persons for the low and high levels. Average statistics for male stimulus persons selected were (a) low physical attractiveness: $M = 1.28$, $SD = 0.53$, $M = 1.85$ $SD = 0.90$, $M = 1.90$ $SD = 0.85$; (b) moderate physical attractiveness: $M = 3.93$ $SD = 1.15$, $M = 4.07$ $SD = 1.12$; and (c) high physical attractiveness: $M = 4.86$ $SD = 0.96$, $M = 5.02$ $SD = 1.25$, $M = 6.08$ $SD = 0.85$. Average statistics of female stimulus persons selected were (a) low physical attractiveness: $M = 1.20$ $SD = 0.46$, $M = 1.91$ $SD = 0.87$, $M = 1.87$ $SD = 0.91$; (b) moderate physical attractiveness: $M = 3.89$ $SD = 0.99$, $M = 4.04$ $SD = 1.33$; and (c) high physical attractiveness: $M = 5.52$ $SD = 1.00$, $M = 5.56$ $SD = 1.11$, $M = 5.68$ $SD = 0.97$.

Pilot Test

When phase one was completed, 30 additional subjects were presented with the entire procedure for phase two. These pilot test data were not analyzed in the phase two analysis but were used to identify potential methodological problems. Because no problems were identified, and no changes appeared necessary, phase two was begun.

Phase Two

Subjects. A total of 392 subjects were involved in phase two. After the phase two data were collected, the questionnaire forms were scrutinized to identify potential bias. Results of these preliminary screening procedures are presented and explained in the introduction to the following section, Analyses and Results.

Stimulus Materials. Stimulus materials were black-and-white advertisement mock-ups printed on 8½ by 11 in. paper. Although an advertising professional aided in the copy and design, it was apparent that the advertisements were mock-ups. These advertisements consisted of either a male or a female communicator of either low, moderate, or high physical attractiveness, combined with the advertising message. As a control for physical attractiveness, a treatment consisted of an advertisement with no physical attractiveness information (i.e., no photograph of a communicator). The advertised product was a new, nonexistent, headache and minor pain reliever. Layout of the advertisement involved a boldface headline followed by a space for the communicator's photograph and then text under the photograph (see Figure 1).

Hand-held print advertisements, rather than projected slides and verbal messages, were used to allow for maximum individual receiver differences. This procedure permitted individual subjects to view the advertisement, read the copy, and process the information as long as desired (which approximates a normal print advertising setting).

Design. An experimental 2 × 2 × 4 factorial design was used. The

---

IT TOOK YEARS TO DEVELOP OUR NEW PAIN RELIEVER, BUT YOU WILL THANK US.

NOW, THE ULTIMATE PAIN RELIEVER IS JUST THAT: "ULTIMATE"

(communicator's photograph)

Being a————(communicator's sex) graduate of————(subject's university name), I know the headaches and minor pains that occur while being a student . . . and now there is relief.

ULTIMATE is a safe and strong non-prescription pain reliever that is perfect for both men and women. Independent laboratory chemical tests prove that its two safe ingredients (75% acetaminophen and 25% analgesic) reduce headache and minor pain in 98% of the population in twelve minues or less; and this strength is with no upset stomach in 99% of the population. ULTIMATE has also received the American Medical Association's seal of approval.

It is safe, fast, and effective. By relieving you of headache and minor pain, the ULTIMATE pain reliever is a refreshing, exhilarating experience.

ULTIMATE!!! . . . the pain reliever that brings you to life and life to you.

Figure 1. Sample Advertisement Mock-up

two independent variables were the sex of the communicator and the physical attractiveness level of the communicator, whereas the one blocking variable was the sex of the receiver. The dependent variables included a 7-point bipolar scale assessing subjects' perceptions of the communicator's expertise and trustworthiness as well as liking for the communicator if they were to meet. Questionnaires were randomly deleted to achieve equal cell sizes of 20 subjects per experimental condition. This number is more than sufficient according to Bruning and Kintz (1977) who stated that most factorial design experiments use 10 to 15 subjects per condition. The end result was 320 questionnaires that represented 20 subjects in each of the 16 experimental conditions.

Procedure. There were 14 sessions of 30 to 40 subjects per session. To minimize potential experimental bias and/or demand characteristics, all experimental treatments were administered within each session. Individual subjects were randomly assigned to an experimental treatment, controlling for equal cell sizes; however, after the screening for bias eliminated 31 total questionnaires, the cell sizes were no longer equal. Except for the manipulation of communicator physical attractiveness and communicator sex, all subjects were given identical research materials: (a) introduction letter, (b) written instructions, (c) advertisement mock-up, and (d) posttreatment questionnaire concerning the advertising, the product, the communicator, and the subject, as well as a postexperimental, open-ended question (to identify possible subject bias).

Caution to control for various subject roles and other experimental artifacts was closely followed as suggested by a number of researchers (e.g., Aronson & Carlsmith, 1968; Fromkin & Streufert, 1976; Rosnow & Aiken, 1973; Sawyer, 1975; Silverman, 1968; Venkatesan, 1967; Weber & Cook, 1972). The manipulation check was placed toward the end of the questionnaire, because the strongest causal inferences can be made when the dependent variable measures are taken before the manipulation check (Fromkin & Streufert, 1976). The subjects were permitted to view their advertisement as long as desired but were not given the questionnaire until after they had disposed of the advertisement so that it was not possible for a subject to refer back to the advertisement once they had begun the questionnaire. All subjects were exposed to the same setting (e.g., furnishings, lighting, stimulus materials, verbal and written instructions, anonymity assurance, and experimenter). Verbal instructions and interactions between experimenter and subjects were minimized at all times and, when necessary, involved only brief clarification about procedural mechanics (i.e., serious attempts were made to eliminate all potential experimental bias and/or demand characteristics). Finally, rather than mislead the subjects with a false explanation, all were simply asked to participate in a marketing communications study.

ANALYSES AND RESULTS

After the phase one data were collected, the questionnaire forms were scrutinzed to identify potential bias. This screening eliminated 31 questionnaires which contained either items not answered or responses to the postexperimental query that indicated a subject knew the purpose of the research. In addition to the above questionnaire eliminations, 41 questionnaires were randomly omitted to achieve equal cell sizes of 20 subjects per experimental condition.

Manipulation Check

The question designed as a manipulation check of the physical attractiveness variable asked the subjects to evaluate the physical attractiveness of the spokesperson for the product's advertising. Note that data from the four experimental control conditions, in which subjects were not exposed to a photograph of a communicator, were necessarily omitted from this analysis. This omission reduced the number of experimental cells from 16 to 12, and the total number of questionnaires from 320 to 240 only for analysis of the manipulation check.

Cell means were 2.21, 3.59, and 4.81 for the communicator of low, moderate, and high physical attractiveness, respectively. Analysis of variance showed no interaction effects and only one significant main effect due to physical attractiveness. The cell means were all significantly different from each other at the .05 level for both the Duncan and Tukey multiple comparison tests. Based on both the ANOVA (analysis of variance) summary table that indicated no interaction effects and the consequent multiple comparison tests, the physical attractiveness manipulation was totally successful.

Hypothesis One

The first hypothesis was supported. Communicators of higher levels of physical attractiveness were perceived more trustworthy and of higher expertise than communicators of lower levels of physical attractiveness. By asking the subjects to evaluate the trustworthiness and expertise of the spokesperson for the product's advertising, an assessment was made of the subjects' perception of the trustworthiness and expertise of the communicators used in the different experimental conditions. Table 3 presents the ANOVA results for trustworthiness. The cell means of ANOVA main effects for physical attractiveness, using trustworthiness scores as criteria, were 3.31 (low communicator physical attractiveness), 3.71 (moderate),

Table 3. Analysis of Variance Using Trustworthiness Scores as Criteria

Source of variation	SS	DF	MS	F	Pr>F
Main effects	45.41	5	9.08	6.03	0.000
Receiver sex (A)	0.11	1	0.11	0.08	0.785
Communicator sex (B)	2.45	1	2.45	1.63	0.203
Communicator physical attractiveness (C)	42.85	3	14.28	9.49	0.000
Two-way interactions	14.95	7	2.14	1.42	0.197
A × B	0.61	1	0.61	0.41	0.524
A × C	7.64	3	2.55	1.70	0.169
B × C	6.70	3	2.33	1.48	0.219
Three-way interaction A × B × C	1.14	3	0.40	0.25	0.860
Explained	61.50	15	4.10	2.72	0.001
Residual	457.68	304	1.51		
Total	519.18	319	1.63		

4.34 (high), and 3.84 (no photograph). Analysis of variance results for expertise are presented in Table 4. The cell means of ANOVA main effects for physical attractiveness, using expertise scores as criteria, were 3.20 (low communicator physical attractiveness, 3.45 (moderate), 3.88 (high), and 3.66 (no photograph). These tables show that the source of variation was due only to main effects of trustworthiness and expertise scores. The Duncan multiple comparison test indicated that all groups for trustworthiness were different at the .05 level except for the no-photo group and the moderate group. For expertise, both the Duncan and the Tukey tests indicated that only the low and high groups were significantly different at the .05 level of probability.

Hypothesis Two

To test the second hypothesis, the subjects were asked what their feelings would be toward the spokesperson for the product's advertising if they had the opportunity to meet the person. Based on the subjects' responses to this question, the second hypothesis was strongly supported. Communicator physical attractiveness had a significant effect on liking for the communicator, but no other main effects or interactions approached

Table 4. Analysis of Variance Using Expertise Scores as Criteria

Source of variation	SS	DF	MS	F	Pr>F
Main effects	21.67	5	4.33	1.98	0.081
Receiver sex (A)	0.90	1	0.90	0.41	0.521
Communicator sex (B)	0.70	1	0.70	0.32	0.571
Communicator physical attractiveness (C)	20.06	3	6.69	3.06	0.028
Two-way interactions	16.97	7	2.43	1.11	0.357
A × B	3.40	1	3.40	1.56	0.213
A × C	11.66	3	3.89	1.78	0.151
B × C	1.91	3	0.64	0.29	0.832
Three-way interaction A × B × C	10.61	3	3.54	1.62	0.185
Explained	49.25	15	3.28	1.50	0.102
Residual	664.02	304	2.18		
Total	713.27	319	2.24		

significance. Table 5 presents the ANOVA results. The cell means of ANOVA main effects for physical attractiveness, using liking scores as criteria, were 3.66 (low communicator physical attractiveness), 4.16 (moderate), 4.65 (high), and 4.06 (no photograph). Multiple comparison tests on the mean scores showed that all groups were different from each other except for the no-photo and moderate groups at the .05 level for the Duncan and the Tukey multiple comparison tests.

Hypothesis Three

The third hypothesis was supported. Communicators of higher physical attractiveness resulted in greater values for the affective, cognitive, and conative attitude components. Twelve items were designed to assess the affective, cognitive, and conative attitude components. These 12 items were the same as used by other authors involving advertising research (Baker & Churchill, 1977). However, rather than blindly use the same items as those authors reported, the data were subjected to several analyses. These statistical analyses were performed in an attempt to ensure that each attitude component was properly defined by the questionnaire items before executing the respective analysis of variances. These pre-

Table 5. Analysis of Variance Using Liking Scores as Criteria

Source of variation	SS	DF	MS	F	Pr>F
Main effects	43.07	5	8.61	13.28	0.000
Receiver sex (A)	0.70	1	0.70	1.08	0.299
Communicator sex (B)	0.70	1	0.70	1.08	0.299
Communicator physical attractiveness (C)	41.66	3	13.89	21.41	0.000
Two-way interactions	0.95	7	0.14	0.21	0.983
A × B	0.08	1	0.08	0.12	0.729
A × C	0.68	3	0.23	0.35	0.788
B × C	0.18	3	0.06	0.10	0.963
Three-way interaction A × B × C	3.51	3	1.17	1.80	0.146
Explained	47.52	15	3.17	4.89	0.000
Residual	197.15	304	0.65		
Total	244.67	319	0.77		

liminary analyses included (1) item-to-total correlations, (2) reliability coefficient alphas, (3) factor analysis, (4) inter-item correlation coefficients, and (5) multivariate analysis of variance. The three attitude components were believed, *a priori*, to be measured as follows:

1. Affective attitude component—interesting, appealing, impressive, attractive, and eye-catching.
2. Cognitive attitude component—believable, informative, and clear.
3. Conative attitude component—seek, try, and buy.

To test these *a priori* components, all the questionnaire items listed above, as well as the measure of the subjects' overall reaction to the advertising were subjected to the preliminary analyses.

Item-to-Total Correlations. The criteria used to make the judgments were based on the item-to-total correlations of questionnaire items within each of the components. Consistent with statistical recommendations (Nunnally, 1967, pp. 261–267), the selected items were those with the largest positive values that were above .50. These considerations were adhered to in selection of the questionnaire items for the affective, cognitive, and conative attitude components. In addition, natural groupings and substantial breaks were observed between the value of items selected and the value of items not selected to represent a specific component.

Reliability. The alpha reliability coefficient values were in agreement with the other preliminary analyses of the item definitions of each components. The SPSS computer program (Hull & Nie, 1979, p. 110–144) was used, and two values for alpha were reported for each component. For these questionnaire items, the alpha reliability coefficient was .83 for the cognitive component, .81 for the affective component, and .86 for the conative component, and the standardized item alpha reliability coefficient values were .93, .87, and .94, respectively. Although no standard of acceptable values appears to exist, the .80+ coefficient values obtained here seem to be exceedingly high in light of the few items which make up each component (Nunnally, 1967, pp. 210–211).

Factor Analysis. The items used to define each of the three attitude components corresponded with the results from the factor analysis of the data. The loadings on the three factors were obtained from the varimax rotated factor matrix. The eigenvalue of each of these three factors exceeded the minimum eigenvalue of 1.00. The cumulative percentage of variance explained by these three factors was 70.3.

Item Correlations. To further check the validity of each of the three attitude components, correlations were calculated for the items defining each respective component. The resulting correlations were statistically significant for all intracomponent items to at least the .0001 level of probability.

Multivariate Analysis of Variance. Multivariate analysis of variance was performed on each attitude component. The multivariate analysis indicated statistical significance at the .0001 level for each of the components, as well as statistical significance for the univariate analyses for all the items of each component.

Results of Preliminary Analyses. Although generally supportive of the *a priori* definitions, these preliminary analyses did suggest slightly different definitions for the affective and cognitive attitude components. Identification of the questionnaire items was based on the unanimous results of the preliminary analyses. The outcome of these analyses was that the attitude components were best represented by the following questionnaire items:

1. Cognitive attitude component—believable, impressive, and informative questionnaire items regarding the advertisement.
2. Affective attitude component—interest, appeal, attractive, eye-catching, and overall reaction questionnaire items regarding the advertisement.

3. Conative attitude component—try, buy, and seek questionnaire items regarding the advertised product brand.

The questionnaire item "clear" was not used in the definition of any of the three attitude components.

Cognitive Component. The cognitive component was tested through a procedure that initially averaged the appropriate questionnaire items identified by the results of the preliminary analyses (i.e., believable, impressive, and informative). This averaging produced one score for each subject which was then used in the analysis of variance for the cognitive component. The hypothesis that the communicator physical attractiveness would have a positive influence on the cognitive component was confirmed (Table 6). The cell means of ANOVA main effects for physical attractiveness, using cognitive component scores as criteria, were 3.52 (low communicator physical attractiveness), 3.79 (moderate), 4.87 (high), and 4.00 (no photograph). The Duncan multiple comparison test indicated that the only significant difference at the .05 level for the main effect of communicator physical attractiveness was between the high physical attractiveness group and each of the other three groups.

Affective Component. The affective component was tested through a procedure that initially averaged the appropriate questionnaire items

Table 6. Analysis of Variance Using the Cognitive Component Scores as Criteria

Source of variation	SS	DF	MS	F	Pr>F
Main effects	82.88	5	16.58	14.48	0.000
Receiver sex (A)	1.42	1	1.42	1.24	0.267
Communicator sex (B)	0.14	1	0.14	0.12	0.727
Communicator physical attractiveness (C)	81.32	3	27.11	23.68	0.000
Two-way interactions	28.97	7	4.14	3.62	0.001
A × B	1.71	1	1.71	1.49	0.223
A × C	15.97	3	5.32	4.65	0.003
B × C	11.29	3	3.77	3.29	0.021
Three-way interaction					
A × B × C	15.81	3	5.27	4.61	0.004
Explained	127.66	15	8.51	7.44	0.000
Residual	347.93	304	1.15		
Total	475.59	319	1.49		

identified by the results of the preliminary analyses (i.e., interesting, appealing, attractive, eye catching, and overall reaction). This averaging produced one score for each subject which was then used in the analysis of variance for the affective component. The hypothesis that communicator physical attractiveness would have a positive influence on the affective component was confirmed (Table 7). The cell means of ANOVA main effects for physical attractiveness, using affective component scores as criteria, were 2.66 (low communicator physical attractiveness), 3.02 (moderate), 4.50 (high), and 3.59 (no photograph). The Duncan multiple comparison test indicated that all the groups were significantly different from each other at the .05 level for the main effect of communicator physical attractiveness.

Conative Component. Finally, these preliminary analyses were used for the conative attitude component. The initial step was to average the appropriate questionnaire items identified by the results of the preliminary analyses, that is, try, buy, and seek. This averaging produced one score for each subject which was then used in the analysis of variance for the conative component. The hypothesis that the communicator physical attractiveness would have a positive influence on the conative component was supported (see Table 8). The cell means of ANOVA main effects for

Table 7. Analysis of Variance Using the Affective Component Scores as Criteria

Source of variation	SS	DF	MS	F	Pr>F
Main effects	160.77	5	32.16	32.73	0.000
Receiver sex (A)	5.36	1	5.36	5.46	0.020
Communicator sex (B)	2.42	1	2.42	2.46	0.118
Communicator physical attractiveness (C)	153.00	3	51.00	51.91	0.000
Two-way interactions	53.57	7	7.65	7.79	0.000
A × B	0.03	1	0.03	0.03	0.867
A × C	44.60	3	14.87	15.13	0.000
B × C	8.94	3	2.98	3.03	0.030
Three-way interaction					
A × B × C	25.53	3	8.51	8.66	0.000
Explained	239.88	15	15.99	16.28	0.000
Residual	298.68	304	0.98		
Total	538.55	319	1.69		

Table 8. Analysis of Variance Using the Conative Component Scores as Criteria

Source of variation	SS	DF	MS	F	Pr>F
Main effects	109.44	5	21.89	13.28	0.000
Receiver sex (A)	1.96	1	1.96	1.19	0.277
Communicator sex (B)	0.53	1	0.53	0.32	0.571
Communicator physical attractiveness (C)	106.96	3	35.65	21.64	0.000
Two-way interactions	49.24	7	7.03	4.27	0.000
A × B	3.98	1	3.98	2.42	0.121
A × C	32.82	3	10.94	6.64	0.000
B × C	12.44	3	4.15	2.52	0.058
Three-way interaction					
A × B × C	23.34	3	7.78	4.72	0.003
Explained	182.02	15	12.14	7.36	0.000
Residual	500.93	304	1.65		
Total	682.95	319	2.14		

physical attractiveness, using conative component scores as criteria, were 2.59 (low communicator physical attractiveness), 3.07 (moderate), 4.18 (high), and 3.35 (no photograph). The Duncan multiple comparison test indicated that, for the main effect of communicator physical attractiveness, the no-photo group and moderate group were not significantly different at the .05 level, but that each of these groups was significantly different from both the low and high groups. Similarly, the low and high groups were significantly different from each other for the main effect of communicator physical attractiveness.

Hypothesis Four

Preliminary Analyses

Eleven items (i.e., multiple measures) were designed to assess the influence of the experimental treatments on subject persuasion. These items dealt with subjects' beliefs about specific attributes of the product. Before testing the persuasion with analysis of variance, several preliminary analyses were performed to establish a persuasion measure or belief component.

The data subjected to these preliminary analyses involved seven belief items that were explicitly addressed in the advertisement, and four belief items that were not addressed in the advertisement. The addressed questionnaire items dealt with the beliefs that the advertised product (a) provided relief from headaches, (b) provided relief from minor pains, (c) was effective for both males and females, (d) was safe, (e) was strong, (f) worked fast, and (g) had the American Medical Association's seal of approval. The questionnaire items not addressed by the advertising dealt with beliefs about the advertised product's price, quality, uniqueness, and taste.

Because there was no *a priori* definition of the belief component to be used in the analysis of variance, factor analysis was first performed on all 11 belief questionnaire items. The varimax rotated matrix revealed that the factor loadings appropriate for the belief components were the questionnaire items regarding headache relief, relief from minor pain, effectiveness for both sexes, speed, strength, and safety. The results of this initial factor analysis indicated that those questionnaire items that were not addressed in the advertisement mock-up should be excluded from the belief component, again, based on the varimax rotated matrix. The criterion used for this factor analysis was a minimum eigenvalue of 1.00 for each factor. The eigenvalues were 4.32 and 1.49 for Factors 1 and 2, respectively. The cumulative percentage of variance explained was 52.9, represented by 39.3 for Factor 1 and 13.6 for Factor 2.

With these exclusions, a second factor analysis resulted in one factor. This second factor analysis clarified the appropriate questionnaire items for the belief component to be provides headache relief, provides relief from minor pain, effectiveness for both sexes, fast, and strong. Again, the criterion of a minimum eigenvalue of 1.00 was followed. The eigenvalue for this factor was 3.73, whereas the percentage of variance explained was 53.3. The eigenvalue and percentage of variance explained by a second factor was only 0.88 and 12.5, respectively.

The definition of items for the belief component indicated by factor analysis was supported by four additional analyses. First, the item-to-total correlations revealed high correlation values for all items making up the belief component. Second, the reliability coefficients alpha and standardized item alpha were .80555 and .91136, respectively, for the belief component items. Third, items within the belief component were all highly correlated to a statistical significance level of at least .0001. Finally, the multivariate analysis of variance revealed statistical significance for an overall communicator's physical attractiveness effect on the belief component at the .0084 level.

The criterion used with regard to the item-to-total correlations was to select the highest values once other minimum requirements were exceeded. Criterion used for determining the sufficient coefficient alpha values was based on the notion that a value of .80+ is exceedingly high for a component with only a few questionnaire items. (Both criteria are consistent with Nunnally, 1967, pp. 210–211, pp. 261–267.)

Analysis of Variance

The belief component was tested through a procedure that initially averaged the appropriate questionnaire items identified. These questionnaire items were (a) product provides relief from headache, (b) product provides relief from minor pains, (c) product is effective for both sexes, (d) product is strong, and (e) product is fast.

Results of the data analysis support the fourth hypothesis. Communicator physical attractiveness had a significant positive effect on the receivers' persuasion (as measured by beliefs). Analysis of variance results for the belief component are presented in Table 9. The cell means of ANOVA main effects for physical attractiveness, using belief component scores as criteria, were 5.49 (low communicator physical attractiveness), 5.81 (moderate), 6.01 (high), and 5.67 (no photograph). This table shows

Table 9. Analysis of Variance Using Belief Scores as Criteria

Source of variation	SS	DF	MS	F	Pr>F
Main effects	13.06	5	2.61	3.23	0.007
Receiver sex (A)	0.17	1	0.17	0.21	0.647
Communicator sex (B)	1.17	1	1.17	1.45	0.230
Communicator physical attractiveness (C)	11.71	3	3.90	4.82	0.003
Two-way interactions	13.22	7	1.89	2.33	0.025
A × B	2.35	1	2.35	2.90	0.089
A × C	4.26	3	1.42	1.75	0.156
B × C	6.61	3	2.20	2.72	0.044
Three-way interaction					
A × B × C	8.73	3	2.91	3.60	0.014
Explained	35.01	15	2.33	2.88	0.000
Residual	246.08	304	0.81		
Total	281.09	319	0.88		

that the source of variation was due only to the main effect of physical attractiveness scores. The Duncan multiple comparison test indicated that the low group was different than both the moderate and high groups and that the no-photo group was different than the high group. These differences were significant at the .05 level of probability.

Hypothesis Five

The fifth hypothesis was not supported by the results. Recall of advertisement details or facts, as manipulated in this study, was not significantly affected by communicator physical attractiveness. To measure recall, seven multiple choice questions were asked about specific details presented in the message of the advertisement mock-up. These seven questions were assigned one point each and the total correct were summed to produce a single score for each subject. This single score was then used in the analysis of variance to test the differences of recall due to the experimental treatments.

The analysis of variance (Table 10) revealed no main effects or three-way interaction effects. However, these results do indicate a two-way interaction between receiver sex and communicator sex. The cell means of ANOVA main effects for physical attractiveness, using recall scores as criteria, were 5.35 (male communicators with male receivers), 5.60 (male

Table 10. Analysis of Variance Using Recall Scores as Criteria

Source of variation	SS	DF	MS	F	Pr>F
Main effects	3.04	5	0.61	0.60	0.699
Receiver sex (A)	0.03	1	0.03	0.03	0.868
Communicator sex (B)	0.53	1	0.53	0.52	0.471
Communicator physical attractiveness (C)	2.48	3	0.83	0.82	0.485
Two-way interactions	8.80	7	1.26	1.24	0.280
A × B	4.28	1	4.28	4.27	0.041
A × C	1.33	3	0.45	0.44	0.725
B × C	3.18	3	1.06	1.05	0.371
Three-way interaction A × B × C	2.33	3	0.78	0.77	0.512
Explained	14.17	15	0.95	0.93	0.527
Residual	307.74	304	1.01		
Total	321.91	319	1.01		

communicators with female receivers), 5.45 (female communicators with female receivers), and 5.66 (female communicators with male receivers). The interaction was due to a higher recall when male and female receivers were confronted with a communicator of the opposite sex, rather than when confronted by a same-sex communicator.

Hypothesis Six

Three questions requested the subjects to indicate their beliefs about the price, quality, and uniqueness of the advertised brand in relation to other major brands. The first item requested the subjects to indicate their evaluation of the physical attractiveness of the spokesperson for the brand's advertising. Individual scores for each of these three questionnaire items were used to calculate correlation values for perceptions of communicator physical attractiveness with perceptions of each of these three product characteristics. This sixth hypothesis was not supported. Perceived product price (Pearson $r = .0088$; significance $= .434$) and perceived product uniqueness (Pearson $r = .0350$; significance $= .282$) were not correlated with perceived communicator physical attractiveness. Although perceived product quality was significantly correlated with perceived communicator physical attractiveness, the correlation was low. The weak, but statistically significant, correlation that did emerge was a correlation of .1084 (Pearson r) between perceived physical attractiveness and perceived product quality, which was significant at the .020 level.

Hypothesis Seven

The seventh hypothesis was confirmed to a large extent. In those hypotheses which exhibited significant effects, a monotonic increasing relationship was displayed with communicator physical attractiveness. These communicator physical attractiveness effects were illustrated by the mean score values related to Hypothesis One, for perceived trustworthiness and for perceived expertise. Likewise, the monotonic effects proposed in Hypothesis Two were evidenced. The hypothesized monotonic effects were also demonstrated in the mean scores related to the third hypothesis, the cognitive attitude component, the affective attitude component, and the conative attitude component. This relationship was evidenced again, for the fourth hypothesis which dealt with beliefs. Finally, the fifth hypothesis cannot be cited in either support or nonsupport of monotonic relationship because there were no significant correlation effects due to communicator physical attractiveness.

CONCLUSIONS

Overall, this study suggests that communicator physical attractiveness does have an effect on persuasive communication effectiveness. Furthermore, consistent with theoretical prediction and explanation, this effect seems to be monotonically increasing, such that, as communicator physical attractiveness increases, persuasive communication effectiveness also increases. Specifically, the major findings are:

1. A monotonic relationship exists between (manipulated) communicator physical attractiveness and perceptions of communicator trustworthiness, expertise, and liking, regardless of communicator sex and/or receiver sex.

2. Although some interaction effects occurred, the relationship between the effect of communicator physical attractiveness on the cognitive, affective, and conative attitudinal components is positive.

3. Recall of advertisement facts is not significantly different for different levels of communicator physical attractiveness.

4. Perceptions of product price, quality, and uniqueness do not correlate significantly with perceptions of communicator physical attractiveness.

5. The influence of communicator physical attractiveness on beliefs is monotonic, that is, as the communicator physical attractiveness increases, the receivers beliefs increase in agreement with the persuasive communication.

6. Low, moderate, and high communicator physical attractiveness produce negative, neutral, and positive effects on persuasive communication effectiveness, respectively. This observation is arrived at by first using the data obtained from the experimental control condition (no physical attractiveness information, i.e., no photograph), as a standard of comparison or norm. Then, the collected data for each of the experimental conditions of low, moderate, and high physical attractiveness are compared against this norm.

As suggested earlier, prior research has lacked a theoretical orientation. Two steps were involved in this study's attempts to correct this past situation. First, a theoretical foundation was used to develop each hypothesis. Then, after the theoretical hypotheses were developed, the hypotheses were scientifically tested.

Results of the data analyses suggest several theoretical implications. The first implication is actually a reverse benefit, meaning that the results of this study contributed to the tested theories (as well as the tested theories contributing to this study). One aspect related to the theoretical hypotheses was a high interdependence between the tested theories and the hypothesized effects. Prior to this study, the psychological theories cited here were untested in relation to their appropriateness for the physical attractiveness and persuasive communication relationship. Now, the ability of these four theories to explain and predict another behavioral phenomenon has received one confirmatory vote through the data of this study. This implication is also consistent with "philosophy of science throught" which indicates the need for "gradually increasing confirmation" (Carnap, 1953, p. 48) by accumulating empirical tests of a theory.

The second implication pertains to generalizations. Because the research was performed within a theoretical context, the results yield more than answers to only the empirical questions posed in this study and for this situation. The additional benefit is that these theories legitimize generalization to other situations related to the physical attractiveness and persuasive communication relationship. This extra benefit becomes clearer when the data analyses are viewed as tests of theory. These theories do not specify products, subjects, or situations, therefore, the fact they were confirmed here suggests similar outcomes will likely result with different products, subjects, and situations. The implication is that because these theories explained and predicted the tested hypotheses, they may also be relied on to explain and predict untested hypotheses, directly or indirectly, related to the immediate relationship.

The third theoretical implication involves the communication discussed earlier. The focus is on the communicator component of the communication process. By focusing on the source-as-communicator element, the issues surrounding the source as originator and/or communicator are minimized. However, because existing research has only addressed the source as originator and communicator, the discussion here must necessarily rely on that research. Therefore, the concept of source credibility is germane to this theoretical implication.

Although there is certainly no unanimous agreement about the determinants of source credibility, or even about the effect of source credibility itself, some summary assumptions are reasonable, justified, and worthwhile. First, source credibility refers to the attitude of receivers toward the source. Second, assuming source credibility has a positive influence in determining persuasive communication effectiveness, the next concern is what determines it. In general, source trustworthiness, source expertise, and liking for the source have all received substantial support as the major variables of source credibility.

Given these empirically based assumptions, communicator physical

attractiveness apears to play a substantial role in determining source/
communicator credibility. The data collected in this study found communicator physical attractiveness has a significant impact on all three of
the major determinants of source credibility. In other words, a monotonic
relationship exists between communicator physical attractiveness and
communicator trustworthiness (Hypothesis One), communicator expertise
(Hypothesis One), and liking for the communicator (Hypothesis Two).
These effects on variables within source credibility offer logical insight into
why communicator physical attractiveness influences persuasive communication effectiveness.

PRACTITIONER IMPLICATIONS

The need for the practitioner of persuasive communications to
understand communicator physical attractiveness was pointed out in the
opening section of this chapter. Because organizations make use of
substantial amounts of persuasive communication, often delivered through
communicators, it is important to understand the variables which influence
its effectiveness. It is therefore ironic to attempt separate treatments of the
contributions and implications for the theorist and the practitioner.

These two entities are so highly interdependent that information
important to the marketing theorist is also important to the marketing
practitioner, and vice versa. Although research seldom possesses this dual
purpose, the current research was conducted with an explicit focus on the
potential ramifications for both the theorist and the practitioner. Consequently, the above research and theoretical implications should be
considered as directly applicable to the practitioner. Separate discussions
are presented here because it is necessary to utilize the relevant theory to
present management implications derived from these theoretically oriented
findings.

In addition to the general theoretical findings, specific concerns of the
practitioner are also important. Two managerially relevant questions were
raised: (a) does communicator physical attractiveness affect source credibility, and (b) does communicator physical attractiveness influence recall,
evaluations, beliefs, and attitudes? The answer to both of these questions is
yes.

Communicator Effects. If the practitioner accepts the constructs of
trustworthiness, expertise, and liking as being major determinants of
source credibility, then, this current research provides clear results that
communicator physical attractiveness affects source credibility. The second
question is not so unanimously answered by the current research.

Communicator physical attractiveness, as studied here, was not shown to significantly influence recall of specific facts. Nor did perceptions of communicator physical attractiveness correlate significantly with perceptions of product characteristics not specifically addressed in the persuasive communication. On the other hand, communicator physical attractiveness was shown to significantly influence evaluations about the advertising and about the communicator, beliefs about the product, and the cognitive, affective, and conative attitude components.

Managerial Recommendations. This research does provide the marketing practitioner with specific decision-making aids in the area of persuasive communication. The implication for the practitioner is that the communicator physical attractiveness variable is not neutral but must be considered explicitly when designing persuasive communications. Physical attractiveness does influence perceptions of communicator characteristics, advertisement evaluations, attitudes, and beliefs.

These influences appear to be monotonically related to communicator physical attractiveness. In other words, when the experimental control condition of no physical attractiveness information is used as a norm, the low, moderate, and high levels of physical attractiveness produce corresponding effects. These corresponding effects may be described as either low, moderate, and high; or negative, neutral, and positive.

The conclusion for the designer of persuasive communications is that there apparently is no difference in effects between portraying a moderately physical attractiveness communicator or using a narrative-type persuasive communication without a communicator. Therefore, if the organization sending the persuasive communication can obtain only a spokesperson of moderate physical attractiveness, the organization's communication will be just as effective without portraying a spokesperson at all. Likewise, an organization's persuasive communication will be more effective if no communciator is portrayed rather than portraying a communicator of low physical attractiveness. Finally, if other factors are equal, persuasive communication effectiveness will be increased by presenting a communicator of high physical attractiveness rather than any other degree of physical attractiveness.

FUTURE RESEARCH

A scarcity of existing research on the communicator physical attractiveness and the persuasive communication effectiveness relationship provides an abundance of research opportunities. Much of the future research can be focused and based on the same four psychological theories used in the current study—attribution theory, learning theory, distraction theory, and consistency theory. Attribution theory, at this time, appears to be the one best theory to explain and predict the physical attractiveness and persuasive communication relationship. But future research should be directed toward identifying attribution theory or maybe another more appropriate theory as the general theory for this behavioral phenomenon. In the interim, these four psychological theories prompt relevant hypotheses to be tested.

In conjunction with the need for isolating the one best general theory, numerous empirical questions and issues should be dealt with. The investigations to be performed in future research can be based on these same theories in a manner similar to the current research. These impending issues focus on both main effects and interaction effects and should include variables associated with all major components of the communication process. For example, source-as-originator variables, such as the organization's own trustworthiness, expertise, liking, popularity, and prestige, can be investigated for potential interaction effects with communicator physical attractiveness. The medium variables such as print, television, and face-to-face interactions can be manipulated with communicator physical attractiveness and may be conducted within a consistency theory application. Despite procedural differences, the need to vary the medium variable is suggested by recent work indicating variances of effects between communication media (Chaiken & Eagly, 1983; Newman, 1983). The messages can be varied to study communicator physical attractiveness effects with persuasive communication that uses fear appeals, one-sided and two-sided messages, and conclusion-drawing presentations. Although no specific theory appears to address the receiver, different receiver variables such as demographics, psychographics, lifestyles, and personalities can be identified which may respond differently to communicator physical attractiveness. Finally, visual variables (such as communicator race, age, and clothes) and nonvisual variables (such as communicator education, religion, and reputation) can be varied within each communicator physical attractiveness level. In addition, both attribution theory and consistency theory appear applicable to the relation between communicator physical attractiveness and these other communicator variables.

THEORETICAL PROPOSITION

Persuasive communication is indispensible in contemporary society. Despite multitudes of definitions, motivations, circumstances, and objectives, its successful application is singularly vital for every individual and organization. The efforts explained in this chapter have begun to document an effective access to the receiver of these persuasive communication efforts. Specifically, a communicator's physical attractiveness may be utilized to efficiently pierce the perceptual screens inherent in the human mind. Synthesizing the material in this book prompts a proposition which formally stated is

> *The physical attractiveness of a communicator determines the effectiveness of persuasive communication, and ultimately, physical attractiveness of the communicator influences overall marketing outcomes.*

Modeling

The purpose of this proposition is to propose explanation, understanding, and prediction of the physical attractiveness variable. The comprehensive approach used here is consistent with Hunt's (1976, pp. 53–54) view pertaining to how deep marketing explanation chains should extend. An example is the current consideration of factors several times removed from the physical attractiveness and persuasive communication relationship. In other words, first, physical attractiveness is discussed resulting in the identification of determinants of physical attractiveness (e.g., liking, association, body type, etc.). Next, these determinants are discussed. Selecting liking as an example, the discussion identifies the determinants of liking (e.g., similarity of attitudes, environmental factors, etc.). Next, these latter determinants are discussed. Selecting similarity of attitudes as an example, the discussion identifies the determinants of similarity of attitudes (e.g., marital relationships, proximity, etc.). This procedure continues, creating or identifying variables at a geometric rate.

The importance of communicator credibility, and subsequently the communicator's physical attractiveness, is alluded to in the familiar AIDA (attention, interest, desire, and action) model of advertising. AIDA models a hierarchy of effects whereby people move through a series of stages from unawareness to awareness to liking to preference to the purchase decision (Colley, 1961; Lavidge & Steiner, 1961). This model clearly indicates that those who become aware and form a liking will ultimately (probably) be consumers of the product. Because attitude tends to indicate purchase behavior (Day, 1970), the implications for marketing strategy is to increase the probability of these early stages occurring in a manner advantageous to the party attempting the persuasive communication.

A number of sequential equations are used to illustrate this proposition of persuasive communication. These equations are used to help illustrate the linkages beween physical attractiveness and persuasive communication. Terms such as marketing, product, and organization are broadly defined but are still within the boundaries of accepted practice. For example, product represents anything for exchange, an organization reflects groups or individuals who may or may not be financially oriented, and marketing is any activity that facilitates exchange of the product.

The equations also need a preliminary note. First, there is an assumption of ego involvement on the part of the receivers. Second, for mathematical convenience, no negative numbers are illustrated. Consequently, mathematical properties equal to .5 are considered neutral, whereas values greater than .5 represent positive conditions and values less than .5 represent negative conditions.

Marketing

$$M = f(Pt \times Pe \times Pn \times Pd) \tag{1}$$

where M = marketing success/failure, Pt = product elements/decisions, Pe = price elements/decisions, Pn = promotion elements/decisions, and Pd = distribution elements/decisions.

The concept of the 4 Ps is well accepted. Therefore, the purpose of listing this function is to show where the physical attractiveness dimension ultimately fits into marketing. Intuitively this marketing function is multiplicative (with values ranging from -1 to $+1$; i.e., 0 to 1). Consequently, if any one of the elements is .5 or less than .5, the marketing effort will be worthless or even detrimental.

Assuming an organization has maximum values for price, product, and distribution (i.e., Pe, Pt, and Pd all equal 1, respectively), but has no promotion (i.e., Pn = .5), the marketing function would be worthless ($1 \times 1 \times 1 \times .5 = .5$). Or, worse yet, if the promotion has a negative value (Pn = .2) the marketing effort will have a negative effect on the entire organization, let alone having a negative impact on the chances of the product being accepted ($1 \times 1 \times 1 \times .2 = .2$). This example stresses the necessity of extending the explanation chains to include subcomponents which have an impact on each component. Furthermore, each subcomponent has a host of factors which influence its value. Because of this function's multiplicative property, any factor or combination of factors that influence the value of an element must be of concern. Regardless of what the contributing factor to the individual element is, if it affects the value of any one of the four major elements, its effect will ultimately be impacted upon the overall marketing effort.

These 4 Ps each represent a collection of microcomponents that can be expressed in equation form. Although only promotion is discussed here, the same scheme is applicable to product, price, and distribution. For example, the following discussion divides the global promotion element into numerous microcomponents illustrated through a series of equations. But first, because persuasive communication is such a major factor of promotion, it is probably acceptble to cautiously equate the two.

Promotion

$$Pn = Pc = Mc = Ad \tag{1a}$$

where Pn = promotion elements/decisions, Pc = persuasive communication elements/decisions, Mc = marketing communication elements/decisions, and Ad = advertising elements/decisions.

In marketing, promotion shares an interdependent relationship with the other Ps. However, to a large extent, marketing is communication. Persuasive communication is often used interdependently with the other Ps as well as an independent promotional technique. For example, price, product, and distribution are all influenced by promotion, but in turn they all influence and may be an integral part of promotion. Also, promotion or persuasive communication is used in personal selling as well as mass media advertising. Ultimately, the distinction between these different areas is not, and cannot, be well defined. Therefore, the terms promotion, marketing communication, persuasive communication, and advertising can all be used interchangeably to imply the attempts made by a marketer to influence the receiver. The next step is to identify the determining or influencing factors of persuasive communication.

Persuasive Communication

$$Pc = (S \times M \times Ch \times R) \tag{2}$$

where Pc = persuasive communication success, S = source or communicator elements/decisions, M = message elements/decisions, Ch = channel elements/decisions, and R = receiver element/characteristics.

Like the marketing function, persuasive communication consists of four broad elements in a multiplicative relationship. If one of these elements is .5 or negative (i.e., less than .5), the entire persuasive communication attempt will be zero or negative, respectively. For example, assume there is no message ($M = .5$) but the communicator, channel, and receiver are at maximum level ($S = 1$, $C = 1$, and $R = 1$). The outcome is no persuasive communication (1 × 1 × 1 × 5 = .5). Likewise, if there is no communicator (S = .5), but the message, channel, and receiver are at maximum there will still be no persuasive communication (1 × 1 × 1 × .5 = .5). Additionally, if the communicator in the latter illustration represents a negative value, where the receiver was somehow offended (S = .2), it does not matter if the other three elements are at maximum value (M, C, R, = 1, respectively), for the end result will be negative (1 × 1 × 1 ×.2 = .2). Now, instead of the persuasive communication being neutral, it has a negative impact on both the product and the organization, that is, the consumer's attitude will be negative rather than just neutral.

Given the example presented earlier, all factors are important. Although this discussion deals with only the source element, the same scheme is applicable for all four of the elements—message, channel, and receiver, as well as the source. Source credibility is the first determinant of the source which, for all practical purposes, is the same as the source.

Source

$$S = C = Sc \qquad (2a)$$

where S = source, C = communicator, and Sc = source credibility.

As this chapter documents, the source of the communicator of a persuasive communication is determined by several factors. However, all of these factors are normally viewed as source credibility. Consequently, the terms source and source credibility can be used interchangeably. The next step is to identify the function of source credibility.

Source Credibility

$$Sc = L(wE + wT) \qquad (3)$$

where Sc = source credibility, L = liking for the communicator, E = perceived expertise of communicator, T = perceived trustworthiness of communicator, and w = weight of physical attractiveness influence.

In this proposed source credibility function, the expertise and trustworthiness elements are additive whereas the liking element is multiplicative. This model can be logically demonstrated by varying one variable and holding the others constant. For illustrative purposes, only extreme values are used, however, more moderate values would be expected to yield results of corresponding magnitude. Also, the weight assigned each variable is likely to vary according to the situation.

The concern is not for the result when all elements are either negative

(A, E, T = .1, respectively) or all positive (A, E, T = +1, respectively), because the obvious occurs—outcomes are accordingly negative (.1 × .1 × .1 = .001) and positive (1 × 1 × 1 = 1). Concern arises if liking is actually multiplicative and expertise and trustworthiness are additive. Several logical examples can be posed to support this model.

Intuitively, it appears that if liking is very weak to the point of dislike (A = .1), it will make no difference as to how great the expert (E = 1) or how trustworthy (T = 1) the communicator. The outcome will be a communication that is ineffective. In fact, if this persuasive communication is presented, the receiver is likely to despise the entire effort, let alone the product (.1 × 1 × 1 = .1). On the other hand, if liking is strong (L = 1) and expertise and trustworthiness are not totally negative, the communication may still be effective. This situation reflects friends where one may have little, or even wrong, knowledge about a product, yet a receiver is influenced by this person. This equation appears to withstand the different values of the elements, however, it remains to be tested empirically.

The additive function of expertise and trustworthiness can be similarly illustrated by the above example. When liking is high (L = 1) for the communicator, who is also an expert (E = 1), effectiveness is high (1 × 1 = 1). However, maintaining the liking (L = 1) while dropping the expertise to nonexpert status (E = .5) does not reduce the persuasive communication accordingly. The trustworthiness element can be manipulated the same way. Again, intuitively, this additive function for expertise and trustworthiness is feasible, but it also remains to be empirically tested.

The substantial role of physical attractiveness in persuasive communication is suggested by equations 3 and 4 combined. First, liking serves as a major element in source credibility (equation 3), whereas equation 4 shows physical attractiveness as a determinant of liking. Second, existing physical attractiveness research supports the contention of equation 3, that is, physical attractiveness does influence a receiver's perception of another person's trustworthiness and expertise as well as a host of other potential determinants of source credibility.

Liking

$$L = (Pa + As + Cl + Ec) \qquad (4)$$

where L = liking, Pa = physical attractiveness, As = attitude similarity, Cl = common lives or lifestyles, and Ec = environmental conditions. The intent is not to propose an empirical test of this relationship, but

to illustrate that physical attractiveness plays a role in liking. Empirical
data do appear to support the additive relationship suggested among the
elements in Equation 4. Because the elements play greater roles in some
situations than others, the only addition that would be appropriate is to
place weights on each element.

This section can be summarized and concluded by combining the
subcomponent equations (3 and 4) with the initial broad marketing and
persuasive communication equations (1 and 2). In this way, the true
location and importance of the physical attractiveness and persuasive
communication relationship is illustrated.

Physical Attractiveness

$$Pa = (F, B, H, Co, At, Pd, \dots Pp) \tag{5}$$

where F = facial characteristics, B = body type or build, H = height
(primary male), Co = clothes, At = association with others, Pd = perceptual distortions, and Pp = previous and present exposures.

The possible divisions are infinite. Therefore, the final component to
be divided, in this discussion, is physical attractiveness itself. Although
there are more factors, research has expressly identified the above
determinants. The physical attractiveness model is simply listed as a
general function as opposed to assigning weights or mathematical relationships. Of course, each of these factors again represents a collection of
even smaller factors.

Summary

$$Pc = f\{[(wPa + wAs + wCL + wEc) \times (wE + wT)] \\ \times (M) (C) (R)\} \tag{6}$$

Equation 6 presents the persuasive communication function (equation
2) with the division of the source elements only. Ideally, the future will
advance the equations for the source and develop similar equations for the
message, channel, and receiver variables. Through this approach, the
physical attractiveness and persuasive communication relationship can be
realistically modeled.

$$M = f\{(Pt)(Pe)[(wPa + wAs + wCl + wEc)(wE + wT)](M) (C) \\ (R) (Pd)\} \tag{7}$$

Equation 7 presents the marketing function (Equation 1) with the division of the persuasive communication (promotion) element—actually, only the source element of promotion. Again, the proposal is to take each element of marketing and use a similar analysis to achieve a realistic understanding of marketing and physical attractiveness.

Finally, consumer behavior appears suitable to such analysis as indicated in Equation 8 (consumer behavior in response to persuasive communicator physical attractiveness):

$$Rr = [(C)\,(Dip)\,(Rpp)\,(Pag)] \tag{8}$$

where Rr = receiver response, C = cue the communicator serves, Dip = individual's drive for the specific product, Rpp = past experience with the product, and Pag = general inclination to different levels of physical attractiveness.

Rationale

This proposition is congruent with Zaltman's (1977) considerations for the process of model building: that is, the first step of model building is to select the variables which are relevant (p. 33). Correspondingly, this proposition has identified the relevant variables and then divided these broad components into subcomponents. Zaltman suggested that a second step would be to hypothesize the relationships between these variables. Again, this proposition incorporates this recommendation by assigning weights and proposing additive and multiplicative functions.

The purpose of the proposition, from the beginning, has implications for both pure and applied research. If this proposition can be viewed as a model and does benefit both the practitioner and the academician, it is then again in agreement with Zaltman (1977, p. 33), "One very important function of models in marketing is to assist both the researcher and manager in understanding market phenomena." Furthermore, this proposition recognizes that numerous factors may produce negative, positive, and neutral effects. To deal with this situation, weights and mathematical functions were assigned to the proposed relationships which is consistent with Blalock (1969, p. 44) who recommends that once variables are identified, a mathematical model should be proposed.

Finally, this proposition and its subsequent models are justified despite their extreme rudimentary condition. Ideally, this proposition should fully explain the relationship between marketing and physical attractiveness. Nevertheless, a beginning is proposed here to accomplish this explanation. Regardless of the lack of comprehensiveness at this time, it is not without worth because, "naturally, we would prefer all explanations to be complete, but the importance of partial explanations should not be minimized, especially in the context of discovery'' (Hunt, 1976, p. 54).

Chapter 8

Cultures and Societies

The picture is not pretty. Physical attractiveness touches practically every corner of human existence and it does so with great impact. The research thoroughly documents the advantages of higher physical attractiveness and the disadvantages of lower physical attractiveness. Preferential and detrimental treatment operates regardless of age, culture, or society. Overall, there is a bias in favor of those higher in physical attractiveness and against those lower profilerates.

Physical attractiveness is not a neutral characteristic. Despite contrary claims and intentions, people are not blind to this very visible characteristic. The importance of physical attractiveness may be inferred from a society's mass media. Regardless of whether the mass media reflects or shapes society, it provides a picture of society that is obsessed with physical attractiveness. For instance, in 1983, the mass media frequently broadcast a best-selling song with the lyrics "I admit I'm a slave to her beauty" (Bellamy Bros., 1983).

The physical attractiveness phenomena are subtle but their consequences are dramatic. Examples of this combination are revealed in everyday conversations where biased subtleties are expressed. Despite the honorable belief that we are all created equal, it just is not true for those of higher and lower levels of physical attractiveness. People of differing levels of physical attractiveness do not have equal opportunities in our society. Because of the inequities and subsequent consequences, physical attractiveness is pursued at all costs, even at the risk of losing mental and physical health.

Because many factors can influence perceptions of a person, why is physical attractiveness so uniquely important? Maybe it is due to the many relationships that exist between differences of physical attractiveness and perceptions of personal characteristics. Miller (1970a) concluded that with

225

all the positive expectancies for a person of higher physical attractiveness, it is not surprising that strong differential preferences influence behaviors.

The real answer may be that no other characteristic about a person is so readily apparent and observable as the single characteristic of physical attractiveness. Age and race may be exceptions because they are equally visible and recognition of discrimination based on these variables has culminated in respective legislation. But age and sex yield to easy definition through objective measures, whereas physical attractiveness remains an elusive, abstract construct that escapes corresponding discipline.

The immediate access to a person's physical attractiveness is perhaps why it has become such a potent informational cue. The perceptions of a person, based on this informational cue, go beyond the first impression. Physical attractiveness as an informational cue serves as both a gatekeeper and a continuous guardian. Qualities such as intelligence, wealth, and expertise may be more informative than physical attractiveness, but because such information is not so readily available it may never become known. Even when these characteristics become known they continue to be influenced, and often overpowered, by the person's physical attractiveness.

Scholarly thought about the complexity of physical attractiveness is not new. Philosophers of days past were similarly perplexed by the complexity of this human feature. For example, the paradox of subtle power associated with physical attractiveness seems to have been alluded to in Schiller's (1882) statement that physical beauty is a sign of a person's inner beauty. Regardless of the commentary, physical attractiveness certainly proffers opportunities for those fortunate enough to possess this characteristic, but not for others. Aristotle summarized the predicament in his statement that beauty is the greatest recommendation a person can offer (Cooper, 1932).

CROSS-CULTURAL CORROBORATION

The physical attractiveness phenomena are truly multicultural, for they are restrained by neither time nor geography. Published scholarly work from around the world documents the same basic findings that are consistent with the bulk of research conducted within the United States. Although the articles reporting research performed in foreign countries are not numerous, there are sufficient quantity and quality to reveal that the effects of physical attractiveness are not unique to the people of the United States in the twentieth century. In fact, the objective of increasing one's physical attractiveness, expressed through facial alterations, is evident in every time period, country, and culture throughout history (Liggett, 1974). Likewise, the extreme efforts expended to increase one's physical attractiveness is not limited to any specific population. Examples of painful facial treatments are endless, "all peoples, sophisticated as well as primitive, seem prepared to go through almost unbelievable suffering in the pursuit" (p. 46) of physical attractiveness. The benefits of physical attractiveness are what motivate the ideas that "beauty must be pursued at whatever price, because it confers on its possessor profound social influence, power and respect" (p. 46).

Reliability

Regardless of culture, judges agree on their ratings of physical attractiveness. A cross-cultural study compared the ratings of English, Chinese, and Indian female judges (Thakerar & Iwawaki, 1979). Each judge was asked to rate the physical attractiveness of modern Greek males. Although the different subject categories reflected different magnitudes of value for the physical attractiveness trait, there was significant agreement in the subjects' ratings of physical attractiveness. Research performed in South Africa yielded similar results through different procedures (Morse & Gruzen, 1976; Morse et al., 1974). The multicultural subjects consisted of 161 white South Africans and 262 Americans. The purpose of the research was to determine correlates and standards for judging physical attractiveness; however, it was disguised as a study pertaining to occupational choice. The two studies reported synonymous results for both (a) high agreement among the judges' ratings of physical attractiveness and (b) the standards or correlates used by the individual judges.

Informational Cue

Basic to physical attractiveness phenomena is the use of a person's physical attractiveness as an information cue, which apparently is not unique to current American culture. A review of three Russian studies on person perception indicates that physical attractiveness also serves as an informational cue among the Russian population (Panferov, 1974). The Russian article concluded that, before relationships are begun, physical attractiveness serves as an informational cue from which personal qualities are inferred.

A French study used 64 5- to 10-year-old French boys to investigate the notion of an informational cue (Coslin & Winnykamen, 1981). Although physical appearance was more the focus than physical attractiveness, the results were the same. Those youths lower in physical attractiveness, defined primarily as a function of dress, were attributed more negative acts whereas their counterparts were attributed more positive acts. Positive and negative acts were related to socially acceptable and unacceptable behaviors, respectively. A study with supportive results was performed in West Germany where expectations of another person differed according to physical attractiveness as defined by facial skin appearance (Bosse, 1976). Finally, a study conducted in India (Agarwal & Prakash, 1977) found women of higher physical attractiveness were perceived as more likely to have favorable attitudes toward feminist causes.

Ability

Ability or competence is accentuated as a function of higher physical attractiveness. In Belgium, 90 female high school students rated the creativity of writing attributed to one of five male college students (Lefebvre & McNeel, 1973). The experimental research design is unclear but the males apparently varied on a physical attractiveness continuum. The subjects rated the writing attributed to those of higher physical attractiveness as more creative than writing attributed to those of lower physical attractiveness.

A second foreign study involving evaluations of writing quality as a measure of ability was performed in England (Bull & Stevens, 1979). Subjects were presented with essays identical in content. The differences were the communication's form of either typing, good handwriting, or poor handwriting. Attached to each essay was a photograph of an assumed author who was either male or female of either high or low physical attractiveness. The responses of the subjects (48 teachers and 24 students) indicated that the evaluation of essay quality was influenced by the physical attractiveness of the author. Although the physical attractiveness manipulation did not reveal significant differences for the male authors, the essays evaluated most positively for the female authors were those representing high physical attractiveness.

The physically attractive may possess greater social powers in addition to receiving more positive perceptions. To test this notion, a cross-cultural study was performed to assess differences in the response of children to a smiling stranger (Alexander & Babad, 1981). The study used 485 second and third graders in Israel and 377 second and third graders in the United States. The conclusion was that smiling strangers elicited a similar behavior pattern that was not significantly different between the two cultures. However, smiling strangers of higher physical attractiveness received more smiling behavior responses than a smiling stranger of lower physical attractiveness regardless of culture.

Legal Process

In West Germany, a study pertained to the role of physical attractiveness within a legal, court setting (Piehl, 1977). The case is probably analogous to civil cases in that a traffic offense of questionable intention resulted in a street accident. This study is detailed in the section, Crime and Courts, of Chapter 3, which reports that offenders of higher physical attractiveness were given more lenient punishments than were given to offenders of lower physical attractiveness.

Helping Behavior

The physical attractiveness of help seekers is not a neutral variable, nor is it neutral for help providers. Researchers in Israel found that subjects sought more assistance from helpers who were lower in physical attractiveness but only when the help seekers and givers were of the same sex (Nadler, Shapira, & Ben-Itzhak, 1982). Explanations of this apparent reversal of the physical attractiveness phenomena can be interpreted as due to social distance and hesitation to approach those of higher physical attractiveness. With opposite sex dyads, the results were mixed. The male subjects sought more help from female providers of lower physical attractiveness, whereas female subjects sought less help from male providers of lower physical attractiveness.

Romantic Attraction

Romantic attraction is probably the aspect of physical attractiveness phenomena that is most open to speculation by the nonscientific population. American research on reciprocal interpersonal interactions focused on romantic attraction early in the development of physical attractiveness research. The role of physical attractiveness in romantic attraction is constant across cultures. An observational approach approximating a content analysis technique was used to examine the romantic attraction in India (Chakrabarti, 1974). Personal marriage advertisements for 200 male and 200 female advertisers were randomly selected from a major Indian newspaper. Content analysis revealed that the advertisers were generally middle class, highly educated, and of relatively high social status. As a reflection of the importance of physical attractiveness in courtship leading to marriage, the messages were searched for references to physical attractiveness. Advertisements seeking female partners referred to physical attractiveness 91% of the time as compared to 10% for equivalent counterpart advertisements. The authors concluded that the substantial references to physical attractiveness demonstrated that despite strong tradition, physical attractiveness plays an important role in courtship and marriage in India. Similarly, a 1983 *Wall Street Journal* article on marriages in Japan reported that "the men are all looking for good-looking women" (Lehner, 1983, p. 1).

Nonromantic Attraction

Interpersonal interactions are most frequently of a nonromantic nature and may be suspected to be less influenced by physical attractiveness than the romantic counterpart. This suspicion is not supported by research in any cultures. In West Germany, the impact of physical attractiveness was studied through a research design using photographs of individuals whose facial skin varied in health appearance (Bosse, 1976). To control for differences in the stimulus persons' physical attractiveness, due to nonskin factors, photographs of the same stimulus person were used. The experimental treatment was a natural photograph showing facial skin of low physical attractiveness in contrast to a retouched photograph presenting the same person with skin appearing high in physical attractiveness. Those of higher physical attractiveness were seen as more appealing and a smaller social distance was preferred. Another study which used 236 male and 255 female students in rural West Germany schools reported similar results (Kury & Bauerle, 1977). The research employed a sociometric questionnaire that asked the subjects to list three peers who represented positive characteristics and three peers who represented negative characteristics. Significant differences consistent with the physical attractiveness phenomena resulted.

Determinants

Physical attractiveness is influenced by physiology as well as psychology. A Japanese study manipulated feedback of physiological information (Inamori, 1979). Male subjects were presented with slides of nude females. The experimental treatment involved giving the subjects feedback which they believed to be their own heart rate; however, these feedback measures were manipulated regardless of the subjects actual heart rate responses. When subjects were given false information about an increase in their heart rate, the photographed stimulus persons were rated significantly greater in physical attractiveness than when either no rate change or a decrease in heart rate was given. A confounding factor in this study is that erotic appeal, which may be different than physical attractiveness, was possibly significant.

A study conducted in India did focus on a determinant of physical attractiveness (Kanekar, Mazumdar, & Kolsawalla, 1981). Subjects were

160 male and female Indian university students. The determinant explored was retaliation by a crime victim. Physical attractiveness manipulations were administered through verbal description as opposed to the typical procedure of utilizing visual stimuli. The data disclosed significant effects. Victims rated highest in physical attractiveness were the victims who did not retaliate, but the ratings of lower physical attractiveness were assigned to those victims who retaliated to an aggression. Consistently, negative views about the aggressor decreased as his physical attractiveness increased.

Cross-cultural comparisons were conducted for determinants of physical attractiveness for American and Israeli subjects (Gitter et al., 1982). The study, which is reported in detail in Chapter 6, focused on the influence of male body components in evaluations of physical attractiveness. Subjects were both males and females from both the United States and Israel. The authors reported extensive interactions between the body components, but no significant interactions were found between subjects representing the American and Israeli cultures.

Intrapersonal

The physical attractiveness phenomena hold implications for intrapersonal realities as well as interpersonal. A study of West German high school students investigated the relationship of actual personality possessed by individuals to different levels of physical attractiveness (Vagt & Majert, 1979). Subjects were 92 females and 115 males who self-rated their physical attractiveness and whose personalities were measured by standard testing procedures. Those subjects rated higher in physical attractiveness were better adjusted socially and had fewer problems than those rated lower in physical attractiveness. Congruent results were obtained from a study conducted in Japan (Lerner, Iwawaki, Chihari, & Sorell, 1980). The study involved 796 Japanese secondary and college students evenly divided between sexes. The Japanese students possessed lower self-esteem and expressed less favorable views of their physical attractiveness than their American counterparts. However, self-concept differences, as a function of physical attractiveness differences, were equivalent for both the American and Japanese cultures.

Subcultures

Within our own country, researchers have attempted to identify the effects of physical attractiveness among the diversity of populations located in the United States. These attempts reveal that the physical attractiveness phenomena extend beyond the general American culture into its subcultures. Despite the recent influx and increasing visibility of Asian Americans, the research attention is directed toward white, Hispanic, and black Americans. It is hoped that with future research attention will begin to address the growing Asian American population.

The physical attractiveness phenomena may be more powerful than ethnocentrism (Langlois & Stephan, 1977; Stephan & Langlois, 1980). Slides of second grade children were rated for physical attractiveness by 131 university students. The stimulus materials involved children described as either black, Anglo, or Mexican American. The data suggested that higher physical attractiveness is associated with the Anglo population. For example, the Anglo children were rated significantly higher in physical attractiveness than were parallel black children, regardless if the judge was black of Anglo. Although a tendency toward ethnocentrism was indicated by the Mexican-American adults, these subjects also rated the Anglo children highest when stimulus persons represented higher levels of physical attractiveness.

A 1982 article reported liking among black children to be significantly influenced by physical attractiveness (Reaves & Friedman, 1982). In a highly controlled study, 12 photographs were selected to represent different levels of physical attractiveness. The physical attractiveness of each child was rated previously by black adults, and then presented to 120 black children who served as the actual subjects. These 120 subjects were divided into groups of 40 five-year-olds, 40 seven-year-olds, and 40 nine-year-olds. Each subject was exposed to individual photographs of 12 different stimulus persons. A preference and affiliation questionnaire assessed liking by identifying the stimulus child for which the greatest liking was expressed. First, the results revealed high agreement between the physical attractiveness ratings of the black adults and the black children. Second, the results revealed that black children preferred to interact with and to be friends with those stimulus children of higher physical attractiveness. Other physical attractiveness research pertaining to cross-cultural examinations of responses by black and white persons has used young adults as subjects (McCullers & Staat, 1974; Wasserman, Wiggins, Jones, & Itkin, 1974). Regardless of ages, the physical attractiveness phenomena are significantly similar between black and white populations.

Physical attractiveness may be a more powerful variable than race between blacks and whites and between Hispanics and whites. Classroom misdeeds were attributed to children who were either black or white and either high or low in physical attractiveness (Marwit et al., 1978). These children were then evaluated by 60 student teachers and 137 practicing teachers who represented a wide range of education and age levels. The data revealed significant differences in evaluations for physical attractiveness levels but not for race differences. Children of higher physical attractiveness were evaluated more negatively than those of lower physical attractiveness. Although the data may initially appear contradictory to physical attractiveness phenomena, the authors interpreted the data to be consistent. The explanation was that teachers held higher expectations and subsequently gave greater attention to children of higher physical attractiveness. Therefore, equal misdeeds were more noticed and created a more negative response to children of higher physical attractiveness. The study pertaining to Hispanics and whites investigated a number of variables within a work setting (Mohajer & Steinfatt, 1982). Among the extensive and interactive results, it appears that physical attractiveness was an influential factor among working peers of different ethnic groups. In fact, the higher the physical attractiveness of either a Hispanic or white, the greater acceptability was expressed for choice of a stimulus person as a work partner regardless if the subject was Hispanic or white.

RESPONSE BY SOCIETY

The response to the physical attractiveness phenomena is paradoxical. Although societies adamantly loathe and deny the physical attractiveness phenomena, they implicitly endorse them by explicit exploitation. Three overall responses appear to exist within societies. First, there is the continual propagandism that permeates culture. Second, there is an awareness that leads to resistance and reaction. Third, there is an awareness that leads to compliance and action.

Promulgation

America is not unique. Promulgation of the physical attractiveness phenomena is worldwide, but the United States may be the leader. Americans are bombarded daily with implicit and explicit messages that decree the eminence of physical attractiveness. These messages run the gamut from blatant advertising to circumspect selection of employees.

Implicit messages begin during early formative years usually with the best of intentions. Nursery stories extol virtues of high physical attractiveness and the vices of low physical attractiveness. There is the ugly wicked witch, the gruff looking troll, and the (abnormal) ugly duckling. Parents praise looking good through proper dress and grooming, and they discourage and punish repugnant dress and behavior pertaining to the wrong appearance. In fact, some families even describe bad behavior as "acting ugly" or having an "ugly temper." Less obvious are the documented differences in voice, treatment, and attention that are given to children of differing physical attractiveness.

Reference groups may change but the message remains the same. Progression from childhood to adulthood normally includes transfer of reference powers from within the family to outside. This transition is not accompanied by a change in the physical attractiveness message.

The media now influences. Awareness of the physical attractiveness phenomena cannot be avoided by the multitude of continuous media presentations through music, television, film, and advertising. The winners, the stars, the heroes, and the successful are overwhelmingly those who are most handsome and most beautiful. Glamour products are associated with those higher in physical attractiveness, whereas the mundane—and the competing—products are aligned with persons of lower physical attractiveness.

Reaching the adult stage in life does not alter the significance of physical attractiveness. In fact, it is even increased due to the messages espousing the younger look of youth and beauty. A plethora of advertising delivers the notion that physical attractiveness is of extreme importance. Examples of these messages can be cited in all mass media. As a major aspect of modern life, advertising exploits this importance by offering the proper product to make a person thinner, younger, more beautiful, more loved, and subsequently happier.

From early adulthood onward, there is growing awareness of the power that physical attractiveness possesses in our world. The adult realizes the subtle, and often not so subtle, placement of those higher in physical attractiveness throughout the mass media. The person begins to observe the importance of physical attractiveness in employment of all types. To secure a position and to advance in that position, the person dresses and grooms accordingly. Soon it is apparent that the most visible employment positions are staffed by those of higher physical attractiveness. More than chance occurrence yields spokespersons for organizations, receptionists for companies, and other personnel in public contact to be those who are more physically attractive than other personnel. Formal employment requisites may directly or indirectly state appearance qualifications, whereas informal criteria can only be speculated.

The ultimate indoctrination is possessed and revealed within universally accepted nuances of our language. For example, national television sports commentators recently described poor and good tennis shots as "homely" and "attractive," respectively ("U.S. Open '83"); and a sports headline in a major city newspaper used the terms beauty and ugliness in describing positive and negative aspects of boxing, respectively (Hoffer, 1984). Furthermore, simply reading contemporary definitions of lower and higher physical attractiveness dramatically document divergent thought. Major dictionaries define ugly as displeasing to the eye, repulsive, and offensive in any way (Davies, 1982, p. 747). Conversely, "beauty" is defined as a quality that delights the senses or exalts the mind (Davies, p. 63), and "pretty" includes definitions of excellent and fine (p. 558).

Dramatic contrastive associations are also blatant in contemporary thesauri. Beauty is depicted in terms of loveliness, attractiveness, eye appeal, allurement, glamour, charm, grace, elegance, artistry, goddess, advantage, asset, strength, blessing, as well as handsome, radiant, excellent, superior, magnificent, first-rate, first-class, matchless, and unequaled (Urdang & LaRoche, 1978, p. 104). In contrast, ugly is characterized in terms of ill-favored, bad looking, homely, plain, unattractive, unlovely, unhandsome, unbeautiful, distorted, deformed, unsightly, blemished, disagreeable, unpleasant, distasteful, nauseating, sickening, disgusting, repulsive, offensive, obnoxious, dishonorable, disgraceful, corrupt, perverted, despicable, cruel, awful, sour, bad-tempered, ill-natured, raging, and threatening (Urdang & LaRoche, p. 1270). These words represent a sample of how explicit formal definitions reflect the socialization and acculturation of the physical attractiveness phenomena.

Reaction and Resistance

The physical attractiveness phenomena encounter relatively minute resistance. The resistance that does exist represents both passive and active reactions. Personal refusal to participate often constitutes the passive reactions. These personal rebellions are against conformity to the social dictates of physical attractiveness norms. Further, passive reaction is the denial to acknowledge that the physical attractiveness phenomena exist and certainly not within the individual himself or herself. This latter reaction may be socially desirable but unfortunately very harmful. Experimental research data have documented the preeminent influence of physical attractiveness regardless of individual conviction. Consequently, denial continues to sustain the very phenomena this ignorance attempts to dispel.

Active resistance is displayed by public opposition to the role that physical attractiveness holds within our society. This resistance is exhibited through legal proceedings and formal organizations. Although the goals are worthy, the impact is not yet significant. The legal actions are typically individual court cases against employers who discriminate based on physical attractiveness, which at present is predominantly a surrogate measure such as weight. Discrimination based on physical attractiveness is extremely difficult to remedy through legal means because of the inability to construct a standard definition of the variable (see "Bias Against Ugly People," 1983, "Now, a Drive to End Discrimination Against 'Ugly' People," 1976; "When an Authority Looks into the Problem of Ugliness," 1976).

A few resistance groups have organized formal groups. These groups typically address surrogate measures of physical attractiveness that can be quantified. Despite good intentions, their lack of financial means and organizational skills may partially explain why they have not met with success. However, two of the better organized groups appear to be the National Association to Aid Fat Americans (W. J. Fabrey, Chairman, personal communication, April 1983), and the Little People of America (M. E. Hansen, District Director, personal communication, August 1, 1983); aimed at obesity and shortness, respectively.

Compliance and Action

The overwhelming responses are acceptance and compatible action. These responses are consistent with a notion that the physical attractiveness phenomena are irreversible. Although all these actions exploit the physical attractiveness variable, the exploitations vary on a continuum ranging from negative to positive.

Negative

The negative end of the spectrum accepts the importance of physical attractiveness and explicitly capitalizes on it. The degree of explicitness may vary, but, regardless, the messages serve to encourage the existence of the physical attractiveness phenomena. One example is a relatively new talent agency called Uglies Unlimited. This agency was expressly formed to service advertising requirements that call for people of low physical attractiveness.

Less explicit is the entire range of mass media advertising. Regardless of product category, it is difficult not to recognize the messages stating the importance of physical attractiveness and how the right product can allow a person to attain this valued asset and all the accompanying benefits. However, these messages are not entirely negative, because attaining greater physical attractiveness allows the person greater confidence and a greater chance of success given the dynamics of the physical attractiveness phenomena. This success may evolve by the fact that the person's physical attractiveness is increased, or at least its perception, which in turn enhances the person's own mental well-being. The combination of more positive intrapersonal and interpersonal variables produces more positive outcomes in the individual's life.

Positive

Not all responses to the physical attractiveness phenomena are negative. Primarily, the more positive tend to be a blending of psychological and medical knowledge. Specifically, the medical practice of cosmetic surgery is applied in light of the psychological consequences of lower and higher physical attractiveness. The importance of physical attractiveness was alluded to by the plastic surgery profession several hundred years ago. Although the technology was limited relative to today's standards, in 1597 Gaspar Tagliocozzi wrote:

> We restore, repair, and make whole those parts of the face which nature has given but which fortune has taken away, not so much that they may delight the eye but that they may buoy up the spirit and help the mind of the afflicted. (Quoted in Maltz, 1946, p. 161)

Both the science of plastic surgery and motivations for plastic surgery have progressed. The technology has totally changed and is now commonly practiced on those within the normal spectrum of appearance. Today plastic surgery continues to address the relationship between physical appearance and psychological well-being, but often deals with realistic, minor modifications. However, plastic surgeons may not fully appreciate the importance of "gradations of physical attractiveness within the normal range" (Kalick, 1978, p. 247). Kalick proposes that the high rate of satisfaction with plastic surgery may be due to "the possibility that cosmetic surgery, by improving patients' appearance, directly enhances their social value to their peers, and thus enables them to gain greater social rewards" (p. 247).

Cosmetic surgery may be an alternative to psychotherapy. Those who request psychotherapy frequently have problems in interpersonal interaction. Given the dynamics of physical attractiveness phenomena, it is not unlikely that physical attractiveness plays a significant role within these difficulties. In fact, a number of authors have speculated that cosmetic plastic surgery can be a valuable supplement, if not a reasonable alternative, to psychotherapy (Cavior, 1970; Edgerton & Knorr, 1971; Gifford, 1972; Kalick, 1978; Linn, 1952; Macgregor, 1974).

Criminal Rehabilitation

Evidence of the recognition of the value of physical attractiveness is apparent in both psychiatric hospitals and penal institutions. Progressive psychiatric hospitals employ professional cosmetologists to help patients improve their physical attractiveness, and correctional facilities have progressed to employing physicians who specialize in cosmetic surgery. Correctional institutions in Florida, California, Georgia, and Virginia are currently attempting to aid prisoner rehabilitation through surgical improvements of physical attractiveness ("California Convicts Get Nose Beautified for Free," 1979; Cummings, 1981; "Fresh Faces," 1980). The study of actual inmates is difficult, but positive effects are suggested in studies in which follow-up data have been collected (Cavior & Howard, 1973; Cavior *et al.*, 1974). However, later correspondence with the facility administrators has indicated mixed results (L. G. Mercuri, Director, Temporomandibular Joint and Facial Pain, Medical College of Virginia, personal communication, June 1, 1983; and R. Stephens, Administrative Assistant to the Superintendent, Department of Corrections, California Institution for Men, personal communication, June 1, 1983).

Further support for cosmetic plastic surgery can be obtained from research showing a relationship between physical attractiveness and actual criminal behavior. Cavior and Howard (1973) found the physical attractiveness of juvenile deliquents is rated significantly lower than their nondelinquent counterparts. Based on this potential link between physical attractiveness and actual deviant behavior, another study conducted an experiment over a 3 year period (Kurtzberg, Safar, & Cavior, 1968). The subjects were 168 adult inmates in a New York City jail. After proper screening, these subjects were randomly assigned to one of four tretment groups involving cosmetic plastic surgery and social rehabilitation programs. The four treatment groups (i.e., experimental treatments) were (1) cosmetic surgery alone, (2) cosmetic surgery with social and vocational services, (3) social and vocational services without surgery, and (4) no cosmetic surgery and no social and vocational services. A follow-up study of the releases one year later showed the recidivism rate for those in conditions 1 and 2 to be significantly less than for those in either conditions 3 or 4. Furthermore, those receiving cosmetic surgery were identified as better adjusted psychologically and socially.

Recognition of physical attractiveness phenomena appears well-established. Even during times of intense decisions pertaining to budget alternatives, the medical doctor who directed the plastic surgery program at the Chino prison in California wrote:

> Indeed the program at the Chino prison is still in existence. It's interesting that it has survived despite some widespread publicity about irregularities in that

particular prison. The warden was let go amidst complaints that the prisoners were getting too many benefits and so forth. Our program stood up to the most rigid scrutiny as a valuable asset to their medical program. (B. M. Achauer, Division of Plastic Surgery, University of California at Irvine, personal communication, August 7, 1983).

Psychiatric Rehabilitation

Enhancement of physical attractiveness is strongly advocated by some professionals who work daily with psychological problems. W. Paul Jones, a private practitioner, has proposed cosmetic behavior therapy which "is a set of procedures used by the counselor that primarily focus on increasing the client's physical attractiveness" (W. P. Jones, 1980, p. 53). He suggested that a direct approach to increasing physical attractiveness may be more efficient than the indirect approaches employed in most personal growth therapies.

Dr. Jones presents an argument for a probable role that physical attractiveness possesses within interpersonal relationships. He feels that emphasis is justified even if physical attractiveness only influenced initial attraction. Physical attractiveness is then always a necessary attribute because without initial interaction there is no opportunity for later interactions. The argument is advanced by citing research that has asked people to indicate the traits they desire in a friend. Despite survey research that finds physical attractiveness listed toward the bottom (Hudson & Henze, 1969), experimental research shows it to be near the top as a determining factor in deciding to like another person (Dempsey & Zimbardo, 1978). Dr. Jones (p. 54) concluded that "regardless of the counselor's personal views, physical attractiveness does play a significant role in our society" and despite what people say,

the actual behavior of individuals suggest that all personality, temperament, and intellectual characteristics are, in fact, secondary to physical appearance in interpersonal attraction.

APPLICATIONS

The implications of the physical attractiveness phenomena are widespread. Similarly this knowledge yields applications throughout society. Consequences of the physical attractiveness phenomena can be immediate for professionals, such as attorneys and physicians, or delayed in the case of parents and clergy.

Operational manipulation of the physical attractiveness variable is probably analogous to the concepts of culture and subculture. Especially with the advent of modern communications technology, a standard

universal definition is enhanced. However, within this larger context there
are probably subcategories of the population who modify the general
physical attractiveness definition. Because the physical attractiveness
phenomena are not affected by these variations, the goal is to present high
levels of physical attractiveness as defined by local standards. The
reasoning is that evaluations of physical attractiveness by those impacted
on may be more effective than evaluations by the users. Implementation of
this strategy simply involves evaluation of physical attractiveness by those
affected. This notion is congruent with a principle of social reality that
states "if men define situations as real, they are real in their consequences"
(Thomas, 1928, p. 527).

Mass Media

Certainly the most visible application of the physical attractiveness
phenomena is in the mass media. At the same time, mass media are
important throughout all cultures and all societies. Regardless if the
sponsor represents the film industry, advertising industry, or the media
itself, every person is exposed to mass media in one way or another.
Because the medium is so powerful and influential, it is reasonable to
conclude that mass media applications of physical attractiveness phenomena cannot be neglected. Because of the impact of mass media, its
messages about physical attractiveness differences are very important. For
example, those higher in physical attractiveness tend to be the Hollywood
heroes, the purveyors of glamour products, and the media spokespersons.
As one illustration, few would deny the physical attractiveness of this
country's leading news anchorman (i.e., Dan Rather). However, it is not
possible to conclude if these applications represent the cause or the
effect.

Public mass media developments concur with the physical attractiveness phenomena. In September, 1983, unexpected management actions
replaced Roger Mudd as anchor for NBC national television news with
Tom Brokaw, a stereotypically more physically attractive person (Shales,
1983). Similarly, in 1983, ABC national television also promoted a person
of stereotypically high physical attractiveness (Peter Jennings) to the head
anchor position for their national news broadcasts (Henry, 1983).

Concern about appearance attributes of successful newscasters is not
new (Markham, 1968). However, in 1983, mass media news reports
appeared to confirm the reality of physical attractiveness phenomena
within this industry (Fink, 1983; Mayer, 1983). Moreover, physical
attractiveness, as a critical attribute for newscasters, was highlighted in a
1983 U.S. District Court case that received national attention (Fink, 1983;

Mayer, 1983). Outcome of that case was a one-half million dollar award, due in large part, for physical attractiveness discrimination ("Jury Awards Craft," 1983). The award represented the culmination of a $1.2 million lawsuit filed by a newscaster for a Kansas City television station. In the lawsuit, the plaintiff charged that she was dismissed from her position because a viewers' survey indicated she was perceived as physically unattractive (Fink, 1983). The defendant appealed the decision, but the plaintiff's retrial went again in her favor with an award of $225,000 for actual damages and $100,000 for punitive damages (Christine Craft is Awarded $325,000 in Retrial, 1984).

Legal System

The legal milieu is another major area of potentially great application. Like mass media, the legal system is one of the few integral artifacts of most all cultures and societies. The relevance of physical attractiveness includes the characteristics (of defendants and victims) discussed earlier as well as jury members and attorneys themselves. A related issue germane to the physical attractiveness phenomena is the valuation of physical attractiveness. What is the worth of diminished physical attractiveness in cases involving personal injury as in cases of burns and accidents? How is such value determined and quantified?

Entire volumes could be assembled that pertain to court cases involving physical attractiveness. Much of this legal activity centers on facial injury and the consequential awarding of damages. An appeals court action of a 1954 accident can be cited to illustrate the importance that the legal system places on physical attractiveness as represented by the face (*Carminati v. Philadelphia Transportation Co.*, 1962). On January 2, 1962 the Supreme Court of Pennsylvania heard an appeals case based on a claim of an excessive financial award. The case involved a 10-year-old girl who suffered a facial injury in a public transportation accident. The Supreme Court affirmed the lower court's verdict by ruling the judgment was not excessive.

The opinion of the appellate court was partially based on future humiliation and embarrassment that the child would experience even though the court record suggested that her physical attractiveness was not grotesque. This state Supreme Court ruled that the earlier verdict was not excessive because lower physical attractiveness does represent a loss that can be stated in economic terms. In writing its opinion the court quoted the conclusion of another court in a different case.

> The cosmetic appearance of this girl must be considered. . . . The jury was told, and it is not disputed, that her condition will be permanent. It cannot be doubted

that the minor plaintiff's chances for marriage and support by a husband have been greatly diminished, and this, too, is a factor which must be taken into consideration. (*Carminati v. Philadelphia Transportation Co.*, 1962, pp. 443–444)

Based, in part, on this conclusion, the Supreme Court calculated an amount per year multiplied by the life expectancy of the injuried party. The Supreme Court in this case delivered the following opinion (*Carminati v. Philadelphia Transportation Co.*, 1962, pp. 443–444):

> Jean Carminati, like every girl in the world, would want to be attractive. Untold hundreds of millions of dollars are spent annually in the United States by and for girls so that they may enter the temple of physical attractiveness. . . . The doors of this temple are perhaps sealed to Jean Carminati. She may have to wait at another tarrying point—the house of sympathy—for the man who will close his eyes and accept his life mate principally on commiseration and faith . . . because of her condition and appearance as the result of the accident of September 27, 1954, she has suffered an item which enters into the calculation of a compensable verdict.

EXPANDING PLIGHT

How and when the physical attractiveness phenomena began is irrelevant today. References to the importance of physical attractiveness can be found in early historical archives and throughout recorded history. Preferences and definitions have evolved, but the value of physical attractiveness has remained constantly high to the point of even increasing. What is relevant is the fact that physical attractiveness phenomena are established. Their firm grounding and acceptance suggests absolutely no future developments to diminish the importance placed on physical attractiveness.

Evidence that people in many societies are extremely interested in physical attractiveness is readily observable. Diet books top the best-sellers list, talk shows continuously host beauty experts, and health spas, exercise studios, and low calorie foods all soar in expenditures by those hoping to enhance their physical attractiveness. Extremes are so great that entire separate books now address specific body components of physical attractiveness such as thin thighs, beautiful bottoms, and flat stomachs.

If the trend continues, the significance of a person's physical attractiveness will continue to increase. Its prominence will advance throughout the population and subsequently be magnified through the mass media. Both negative and positive consequences associated with lower and higher physical attractiveness will be exaggerated in reality. Greater liabilities and assets will translate into more desperate searches to attain higher levels of physical attractiveness. Conventional methods (e.g., diets, body shaping, clothes, and cosmetics) will continuously multiply and be exploited.

Regardless of how physical attractiveness is defined, solutions will extend beyond conventional methods. Pharmaceutical compounds can be expected to assume increasing importance for altering surrogate measures of physical attractiveness such as weight and age. Despite their lack of effectiveness, there are already many remedies for people concerned about celluite. These remedies include wraps, blows, machines, chemicals, massages, and even a medical suction procedure to surgically remove cellulose ("Celluite: Fact, Fad, Fantasy"). General cosmetic surgery for only incremental improvement within the normal physical attractiveness range is now commonly accepted and growing in popularity. This cosmetic surgery currently represents the extreme actions taken in pursuit of greater physical attractiveness by individuals already within the normal range.

The medical limits of today may be transcended by scientific advancements of tomorrow. These advancements may allow greater authorship of a person's physical attractiveness. Although still in their early stages, our society already has recently developed procedures that allow access to the unborn. Current pregnancy tests permit valuable information about the health of unborn children. These technologies include both external and internal procedures. One external procedure is obstetric ultrasonography which uses ultrasound to evaluate the fetus. The patterns of sound waves yield "a realistic Polaroid picture" (Pagana & Pagana, 1982, p. 255) that identifies abnormal pregnancies. Internally, a transabdominal amniocentesis allows extraction of fluid from the amniotic cavity. Analysis of this fluid can also provide valuable information about unborn children. The accuracy and importance that medical science places on this procedure is illustrated in a recent textbook that states "if chromosomal or genetic aberrations are suspected, the test should be done early enough (14 to 16 weeks) to easily allow safe abortion" (Pagana & Pagana, 1982, p. 258).

Somewhere in the future, a variation of this prenatal information could be the parents' request for physical attractiveness with consequent decisions for appropriate action. Such abilities may not be too distant. Our technologies already permit visual observations of internal body parts. For example, the laparoscopy is a procedure in which "the abdominal organs can be visualized by inserting a fiberoptic scope through the abdominal wall" (Pagana & Pagana, 1982, p. 247). But even before the child is conceived, the foreseeable future will allow manipulations through genetic engineering. At the completion of this book, genetic engineering is not yet practical but is receiving substantial attention by the scientific and religious communities. Because it is theoretically possible, and is being demonstrated in laboratories, many books and articles are being published on the opportunities and ramifications of this process.

Physical attractiveness is a life and death issue. The first chapter of this book quoted Charles Darwin who long ago stated that physical attractiveness "is not the weal or woe of any one individual, but that of the human race to come, which is here at stake" (Darwin, 1872, p. 323). Over 100 years later, a recent national news story reported on a Daniel McKay being tried for murder in Chicago (Paul Harvey News, 29 June 1983). Dr. McKay was a 35-year-old veterinarian with a respectable practice in the Chicago area who was described by neighbors as the "nicest, most gentle person." He was in the hospital delivery rooom with his wife when he saw their newborn child had a cleft palet (which incidentally was correctable by surgery). The news account graphically reported: "when he saw their newborn son was imperfect, he immediately grabbed the baby and beat the infant's head on the floor until it was dead."

A futuristic society dominated by physical attractiveness is approaching. Technological advancements and recent human behavior provide signs that identify the emergence of dominance throughout an individual's life. It is evident that "from the moment of birth, good looking people enjoy big advantages, while less attractive individuals are penalized" ("America's Obsession With Beautiful People," 1982, p. 60). Despite societal concerns and ramifications, the importance of an individual's physical attractiveness is likely to continue to increase in magnitude. In fact, it is now reasonable to speculate that the physical attractiveness of even the unborn, and the unconceived, could be of significant consequence in a culture controlled by the physical attractiveness phenomena.

Chapter 9

Science and Theory

It is time to consider microissues of research in a perspective of larger macroissues. When such a larger perspective is taken, a problem with the physical attractiveness research becomes apparent. This problem is that knowledge about physical attractiveness remains scattered and fragmented after two decades of scientific query. Consequently, in an attempt to improve the situation, this final chapter discusses the relevance of science and theory for the study of physical attractiveness phenomena.

PHILOSOPHY AND HISTORY

The philosophy and history of science should not be overlooked as a possible source of valuable information. In fact, the philosophy and history of science suggests that the study of physical attractiveness phenomena needs to make a commitment to achieving increased scientific status. By so doing, greater progress will be made, and the problems associated with scattered and fragmented research findings should be alleviated. An initial step toward this commitment may be to begin the process of establishing the study of physical attractiveness phenomena as a scientific entity in itself. Such a movement will encounter resistance and will necessitate implications for actions, but the effort is justified.

One justification, for establishing the study of physical attractiveness phenomena as a science in its own right is that society in general will benefit. This consideration is somewhat self-serving, but it is not inconsistent with the philosophy and history of science. Based on similar utilitarian thought (Jones, Sontag, Beckner & Fogelin, 1977; Reagan, 1969), Anderson (1983, p. 27) stated that

> an important goal of any area of inquiry with scientific pretentions is to ensure that its knowledge base is widely dispersed through the greater society, so that this knowledge can be used to benefit society as a whole.

Commitment toward increasing scientific status is warranted in terms of both self-interest and altruism. In terms of self-interest,

. it is clear that societal resources tend to flow to those disciplines that produce knowledge considered valuable for the accomplishment of societal objectives. (Anderson, 1983, p. 27)

Simple observations of established sciences readily document that resources are allocated by society in a manner consistent with this quote. A recent account on medical research financing inquired why a specific physician received a research grant when to do so was somewhat unusual given the decrease in governmental funding. A director of the National Institutes of Health, Murray Goldstein, was quoted as saying that the particular physician received funding

both because the question he is asking is important and also because the . . . methodology he is using offers a new opportunity to find an answer. (Brooks, 1984, p. 1)

The implication is that support for the study of physical attractiveness phenomena could benefit from increased scientific status. However, less practical self-serving motives also exist. Some, within the philosophy and history of science (Jones *et al.*, 1977, Ravetz, 1971; Reagan, 1969), believe that researchers have special responsibilities to contribute knowledge that will "further society's goals and to enhance its citizens' quality of life" (Anderson, 1983, p. 27).

Papology

Increasing scientific status appears to be a needed and a desirable endeavor. However controversial, the appropriate step, may be to designate the study of physical attractiveness phenomena with a unique identification. To accomplish this task, to capture the essence of the research, and to communicate its scientific qualities in its own right, a new term is offered— *papology*. Papology (defined as the study of physical attractiveness phenomena) is used in the following discussion, as an accurate, concise expression which is also grammatically convenient.

Several factors support the designation, of papology, at this time. First, the accumulated knowledge represents a critical mass which is impressive in quantity and quality. This knowledge is also a cohesive unit centered around the unique properties of the physical attractiveness construct. Second, the study of physical attractiveness phenomena has borrowed tools and concepts from many disciplines, but it is now strong enough to reverse the flow of borrowing and the flow of information transfer. In other words, various segments of society may begin to use the resarch findings and applications in their own endeavors. Third, the term is broad enough to accommodate (a) the growing knowledge base, (b) research procedures that may emphasize either applied or basic research orientations, (c) theoretical developments, and (d) the applications by other segments of society. However, without being restrictive, the term lends a unifying thread to the diversity represented by the entire study of physical attractiveness phenomena. Fourth, other scientific specialties, as well as the general population, should be better able to comprehend and transmit the study of physical attractiveness phenomena. Finally, papology represents a move toward increased scientific status for the study of physical attractiveness phenomena. Inherent in this move are both benefits and requirements as well as resistance to change.

Resistance

Although human existence is uncontrollably metamorphic, change is usually resisted initially and then later accepted. Because a change is represented in the move toward increasing scientific status of the study of physical attractiveness phenomena (i.e., papology), it too is likely to be initially resisted. However, the benefits of increased scientific status are too great for researchers within papology not to accept. Likewise, because it may now seem incommodious to designate and define one term (such as papology) to communicate the study of physical attractiveness phenomena, initial resistance is probable. Yet, acceptance is also probable because such identification will be an efficient aid in the move toward increased scientific status.

Resistance to the increased scientific status may also be initially expressed on the basis of comparisons with the traditionally recognized sciences. But, these comparisons are not relevant because the line between a science and nonscience cannot be precisely determined. In other words, "the fact that 2,400 years of searching for a demarcation criterion has left us empty-handed, raises a presumption that the object of the quest is nonexistent" (Laudan, 1980, p. 275). This quote succinctly expresses the fact that the philosophy and history of science possesses no consensus for determining either a correct scientific method or a correct means for defining a science (Anderson, 1983). The result is that societal recognition defines and sanctions a science. Consequently, because these standards are subject to sociological evolvements, it is probably most important for papology to demonstrate why it deserves recognition as a science as opposed to displaying its use of the scientific method.

Three specific research issues could raise resistance to recognizing papology as a science. They are the reliability and validity of physical attractiveness measures, the subjectivity of the physical attractiveness variable, and the deviations in the research that may not always adhere to an ideal scientific method. However, none of these issues are actually detrimental given the philosophy and history of science.

Lack of attention given to the reliability and validity of measures, as cited in Chapter 2, is a serious methodological shortcoming. However, as papology continues to mature the remedy will be forthcoming. It is simply a matter of exerting extra time and effort to apply the relevant research technology that already exists elsewhere. Nevertheless, concern about measure reliability and validity does not diminish the scientific quest of papology. Even the natural sciences (Chalmers, 1976, pp. 28–30), as well as the behavioral sciences, experience measurement error. Such problems may decrease as a science matures, but the error associated with measure reliability and validity will never be eliminated.

No science can be entirely objective. Nevertheless, the subjective nature of physical attractiveness is likely to be questioned on the basis of a philosophy of science known as *logical positivism* (Brown, H. I., 1977; Passmore, 1967). Basic to this philosophy is verification theory which proposes that truth can only be identified if it can be empirically verified. Fortunately, examination of the philosophy and history of science reveals that such concerns are invalid. Despite early acceptance of logical positivism, it lost its recognition as the "received view" in the philosophy of science over 20 years ago. According to Anderson (1983, p. 19), this lost recognition combined with other developments in the philosophy and history of science, "call into question the claim that science is securely anchored by the objective observations of reality."

Papology has at times deviated from traditionally sacred methodologies of science. The construct at the center of the entire study of physical attractiveness phenomena remains devoid of definition. A ramification of this lack of definition is that judges provide subjective ratings that are not based on any common reference or standard. Furthermore, these ratings of physical attractiveness are assumed to be interval data that are then subjected to corresponding statistical manipulations, even though the ratings appear to be ordinal data. Finally, opposite to the desired sequence of theory driven research, physical attractiveness research has preceded theory.

Papology should not be denied scientific status because of these (admittedly serious) deviations from traditional scientific practices. In fact, such violations can be readily justified by examination of the philosophy of science. Lauden's (1977) distinction between scientific acceptance and scientific pursuit is relevant. He argued that acceptance of past methods will tend toward stifling progress. But subscription to the view of scientific pursuit represents belief in a dynamic evolving science that ultimately allows greater progress. Laudan's views applied to papology would justify breaks from traditional methodology. The explanation is that the pursuit of physical attractiveness knowledge should not be based on past scientific methods, but on those scientific methods that hold the greatest promise for future progress in the science.

No one within the philosophy and history of science suggests disregard for traditional scientific methods. But some do offer even greater support for creative scientific diversions that are carefully controlled. Feyerabend (1975) argued that scientific progress necessitates departures from the normally accepted practices. He also stated that unchallenged conformity to prior methodologies discourages valuable creativity in scientific investigations. According to Anderson (1983), the conclusion of Feyerabend (1978, 1981) and the conclusion of the cognitive tradition within the sociology of science are the same. Specifically, the greatest advances in the history of science have emerged when departures were made from the conventionally accepted practices of the time.

Implications for Actions

Increasing the scientific status of papology is not an unreasonable quest. But, the process necessary to attain this status involves implications that require substantial effort. Central to these implications is the need for papology to commit itself to programmatic research motivated by theory. Currently, there is neither a theoretical motivation within the research, nor is there a program to offer direction. This state of affairs exists despite indications by the philosophy and history of science that suggest the greatest scientific progress has emerged from such commitments. An incentive of papology should be the fact that "the established sciences can point with pride to the scientific problems they have solved and the exemplary theories which are their solutions" (Anderson, 1983, p. 28).

Subsequent to these commitments is the establishment of structure within papology. Creating a structured framework will not stifle advancements but will speed progress through a systematic organization of the current scatter and fragmentation. Ultimately, contributions to the growing knowledge of papology will be more efficient and more efficacious. Such structure may bring undue attention to an isolated study with research results that deviate from established knowledge. Regardless of such exceptions, the order will benefit papology more than be detrimental, because (according to Kuhn, 1962) a single anomaly has never upset an established theoretical framework.

Dissemination of knowledge is integral to the recognized sciences. In

its quest for increased scientific status, papology must recognize the
importance of disseminiating its knowledge base. Unfortunately, such
efforts are at this time restrained by two broad factors. First, researchers in
papology have failed to recognize this basic tenet of science, and so have
approached papology with a restrictive myopia. The myopic view exhibited
in the literature is that physical attractiveness research is conducted within
a vacuum that has little regard for other disciplines or the society at large.
Second, relevant audiences often perceive the knowledge base of papology
as either quixotic, unimportant, or commonsensical. The solution to these
attitudes is embraced within the serious commitment to increasing
scientific status for papology.

A general action implied here is the broadening of the perspective of
those who conduct research. By doing so, the knowledge base of papology
will be of greater interest to others. Papology should continue to identify
physical attractiveness phenomena because that in itself is valuable, but it
should also expand into supplemental realms of understanding, explanation, and application.

This move may initially appear to advocate applied research over basic
research, but it does not. The orientation remains strongly grounded in the
need to discover knowledge for the sake of knowledge because this
ultimately translates into knowledge for the good of others in society. In
fact, the shift in focus could provide opportunity for subspecialities within
papology. Philosophy and history of science shows that similar distinctions
have developed in other sciences without detriment (cf. Angelmar &
Pinson, 1975). The outcome could be either an applied research orientation,
a basic research orientation, or a combination of the two; possibly
analogous to the medical science discipline. Consequently, knowledge
about physical attractiveness could be better disseminated throughout
society and better utilized by societal institutions involved with science,
education, government, and policy making.

Pursuit of increased scientific status underlies these implied directives
for papology. Whatever actions are taken, the intent should be to meet the
objective of science, which, according to the philosophy and history of
science, is to solve problems that benefit society (Kuhn, 1970, 1977;
Laudan, 1977; Popper, 1962, 1972). The reality of this objective is that

> society tends to reserve full scientific legitimacy for those inquiry systems which
> are perceived to be operating in the higher interests of knowledge and general
> societal welfare. (Anderson, 1983, p. 27)

For papology to attain this status, it is expedient to use the more recognized
sciences for guidance. The eventual denouement is a self-perpetuating
cycle. In other words, a sequential ramification of enhancing scientific
status is greater acceptance of the knowledge base by all segments of

society which, in turn, is followed by greater societal resources for continuing development of papology.

State of Affairs

After two decades of scholarly investigation, the state of papology is respectable and, more specifically, the current knowledge base is substantial albeit scattered and fragmented. Nevertheless, papology is not unique. In fact, a presentation on another topic and in another discipline (Anderson, 1983, p. 28) provided several thoughts which have been interpreted and applied to the immediate discussion.

Scientific commitment, in its lexical meaning, appears weak. Typical studies do not really identify the problem attempting to be solved. Nor do the studies suggest that the answer being sought will provide any real significance to an important question or make a meaningful contribution toward the progress of papology.

The norm appears to be a preponderance of relationship studies. Both separately and collectively, research studies consist of manipulative exercises to discover if a dependent variable is related to the independent variable of physical attractiveness. Upon completion, there is little or no effort expended to conjoin the results with either established theory or with established research programs.

> This approach appears to be informed by an empiricist model of science which assumes that, if enough scattered facts (relationships) are gathered, they will somehow assemble themselves into a coherent body of theory. However, it should be clear that facts do not speak for themselves. (Anderson, 1983, p. 28)

Summary

Increasing the scientific status of the study of physical attractiveness phenomena appears desirable. Among the many implications for attaining this recognition, two characteristics of established sciences are illuminated as important criteria—exemplary theory and valued knowledge. In other words, inclusive of supporting ramifications, the requisite exists for a commitment toward "theory-driven programmatic research" that solves significant social problems.

The study of physical attractiveness phenomena does not fare well as a science, first, because there are methodological questions, and second, because it has not answered significant questions in society. These questions are best considered within the context of philosophy and history of science which show that established sciences gain recognition as a function of the product of their labor. Consequently, this third item may be most important because it represents the culmination of all other efforts. To aid future research, it is now appropriate to ask what the study of physical attractiveness phenomena has to show for its efforts. After this question is answered, the next step is to propose a true theory of physical attractiveness phenomena which will offer explanation, prediction, and empirically testable hypotheses. Finally, it is then appropriate to ask what answers the study of physical attractiveness phenomena should pursue in the future.

CURRENT KNOWLEDGE

The study of physical attractiveness phenomena has much to show for its efforts. It has provided answers to many microquestions which collectively allow speculation about major macroquestions. Answers to the many specific microquestions are not detailed here because to do so would be to duplicate what has already been stated in the first eight chapters of this book.

However, it is appropriate to mention several reasons why the value of these microquestions should not be minimized. First, many questions addressed by the research presented earlier in this book are of interest in their own right. Second, past answers to microquestions have produced a knowledge base from which future pursuits of additional microquestions can be launched. In fact, progress is recorded by the growing accumulation of such answers which continue to advance the frontiers of physical attractiveness knowledge. Finally, results from individual studies provide valuable building units. Together these units form the foundation on which periodic literature syntheses are analyzed for speculation about macroquestions (that are sometimes considered to be of greater value to society). Similarly, it is also these results which can be used retrospectively to analyze future developments in theory pertaining to physical attractiveness phenomena.

Macroquestions have not been answered, nor have they even received direct research attention. Yet, basic principles emerge when the collective research is analyzed. Foremost is the disclosure that physical attractiveness is not a neutral characteristic in anyone's life. Physical attractiveness is determined by many factors, it functions as an information cue, and it is associated with extensive stereotypes, assumptions, and expectations. Ultimately, physical attractiveness is the cause of phenomena that are pervasive, subtle, and incorporated into socialization processes. Furthermore, these phenomena are remarkably consistent throughout history and across cultures. Finally, although physical attractiveness is an abstract construct that still eludes definition, it is a variable that can be successfully studied through scientific research methodologies.

Macroquestions that possess greatest importance for society remain unanswered by the physical attractiveness research. Interpretation and commitment offer two explanations for this plight. First, great importance for society is somewhat of a value judgment. The research identified throughout this book, and associated with microquestions, could be judged as very valuable for society. Second, the greatest societal contribution will probably be associated with long-term commitments, both collectively and individually. Collectively, a theory-driven programmatic research orientation should aid solutions to questions of major societal importance. Individually, discovery of such information will probably be best accomplished by researchers who remain, long-term, with a personal program of research; as opposed to incipiently redirecting their efforts toward endeavors outside the study of physical attractiveness phenomena.

THEORY

A theory of physical attractiveness phenomena is necessary. Earlier discussion of the philosophy and history of science, the scatter and fragmentation of the knowledge base, and the need for theory-driven programmatic research, all summon development of a theory. Because much information is known about physical attractiveness phenomena, it is time to propose a theory that utilizes current knowledge to develop a comprehensive theory for generating future information.

The theory proposed here is an attempt to meet the needs of the study of physical attractiveness phenomena. First, it is consistent with the existing knowledge base. Second, it offers a logical understanding. Third, it meets the criteria of explanation, prediction, and testability. Especially important is the criterion that empirically testable hypotheses are suggested throughout the theory. Finally, it provides a comprehensive framework which organizes the current knowledge base and provides direction for theory-driven programmatic research in the future.

This proposed theory models a system. In general, the theory models the process and outcomes of units and subunits that interact in the system referred to as physical attractiveness phenomena. The proposed theory accounts for six major aspects of the system. These are

1. the consideration that many factors determine physical attractiveness,
2. the historical recognition of the importance of a physical attractiveness stereotype,

3. the extensive consequences associated with physical attractiveness phenomena,
4. the transmission of physical attractiveness phenomena between generations,
5. the gradual shifts that occur for preferred ideals of physical attractiveness, and
6. the role that society occupies within the physical attractiveness phenomenon.

According to the proposed theory, physical attractiveness phenomena are best represented by a skeletal causal loop. Within this circular structure are six units, all distinctly different and all occurring in a consistent successive pattern. These units, in sequential order, are: ascription, substratum, excrescence, illapse, impingement, and collectivism. Figure 2 illustrates the interaction process of these units as a recursive system (i.e., one-way causation). In other words, simultaneous feedback is not thought to operate, in any substantial manner, between the units. However, feedback and reciprocal causation is believed to occur within some units. Consequently, Figure 2 illustrates the presence of feedback and reciprocal causation between subunits that together comprise particular units.

Ascription

Ascription represents the identification and designation of an individual's physical attractiveness. It is comprised of two major subunits—the stimulus person and the evaluator. In turn, each of these two subunits consists of many characteristics. From the interactive process of this subsystem, a denomination of the stimulus person's physical attractiveness emerges.

Characteristics (i.e., determinants) affiliated with the stimulus person subunit can be categorized along a continuum with polar ends labeled controllable and uncontrollable. Bascially, the controllable determinants are those which are vulnerable to alteration, whereas the uncontrollable determinants are not (i.e., those genetic characteristics which are inherited through birth). Such a division is not precise, especially in the "gray area" where determinants may overlap. In fact, it is apparent that the stimulus person subunit is largely a function of controllable determinants because even the uncontrollable characteristics can often be modified.

Characteristics of the stimulus person subunit are primarily direct causal linkages with physical attractiveness. The exceptions, appear at this time, to be interpersonal and social status characteristics which are reciprocal with physical attractiveness. In other words, although interpersonal and social status factors are determinants of physical attractive-

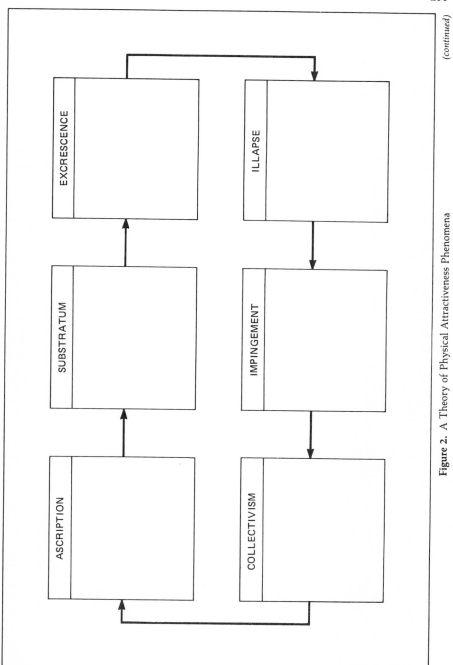

Figure 2. A Theory of Physical Attractiveness Phenomena

(continued)

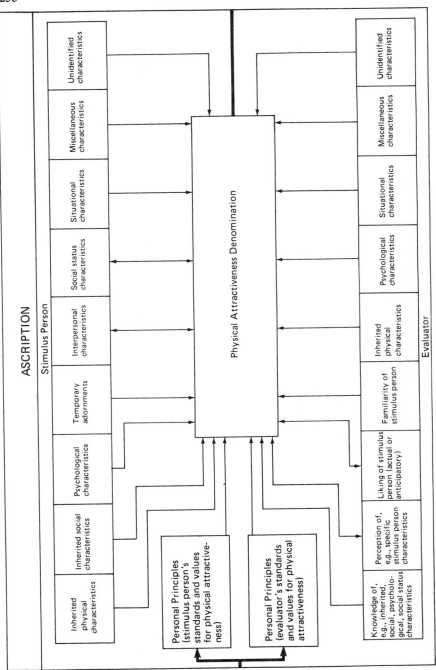

Figure 2. (continued)

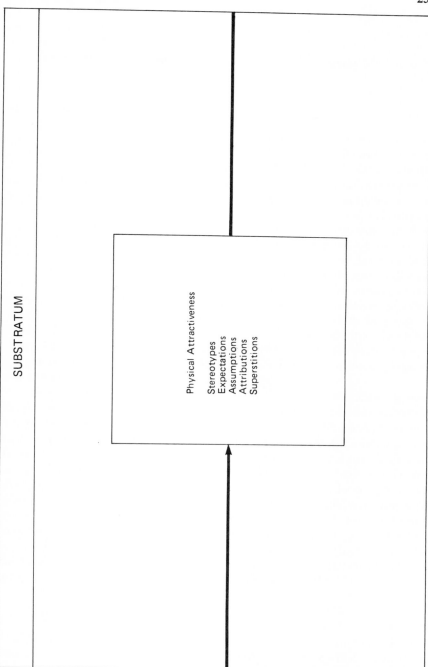

SUBSTRATUM

Physical Attractiveness

Stereotypes
Expectations
Assumptions
Attributions
Superstitions

(continued)

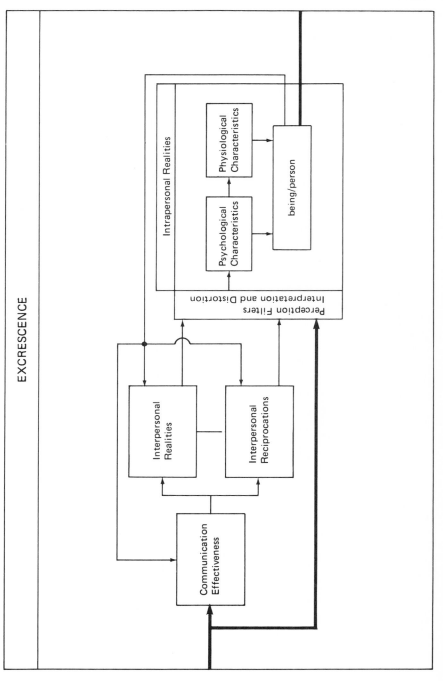

Figure 2. *(continued)*

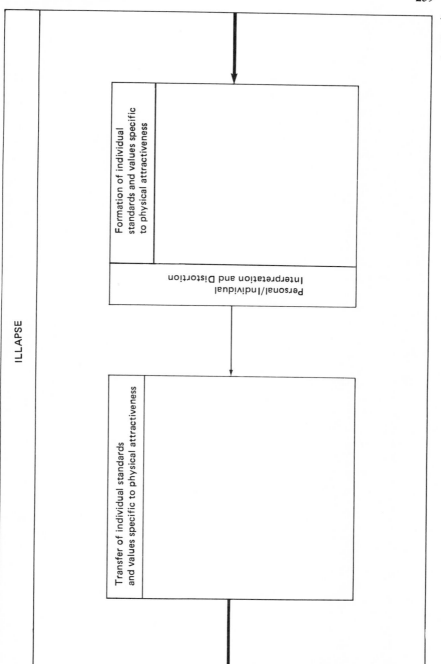

ILLAPSE

Formation of individual standards and values specific to physical attractiveness

Personal/Individual Interpretation and Distortion

Transfer of individual standards and values specific to physical attractiveness

(continued)

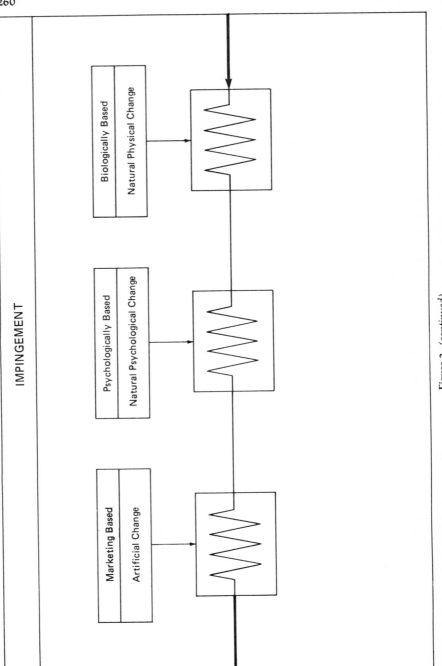

Figure 2. *(continued)*

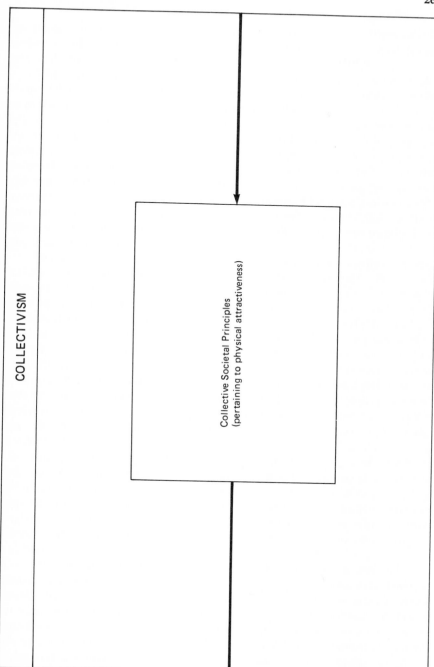

COLLECTIVISM

Collective Societal Principles
(pertaining to physical attractiveness)

ness, physical attractiveness also determines these two factors. Like the stimulus person, the evaluator subunit involves characteristics that are primarily direct causal linkages with physical attractiveness. The two exceptions here appear to involve a reciprocal relationship that physical attractiveness has between perceptions about specific stimulus person characteristics and feelings of (anticipatory) liking of the stimulus person.

Currently, nine labeled categories (which are inherited or innate and acquired or developed) make up the stimulus person subunit. At the same time, nine labeled categories comprise the evaluator subunit. However, there are several general properties that apply to each of these subunits independently. First, the specific labeled category that any one factor is placed in, may be open to debate for some factors. Second, some factors may actually be apropos to more than one category. Third, some factors within subunits may be interdependent, but this interdependence is not sufficient to justify an illustration of that relationship within the context of the ascription unit. Fourth, factors located in a specific category during one time period could conceivably be located in another category at some later time period.

Two additional components affect ascription of physical attractiveness denomination. These components are separate personal principles independently affiliated with the stimulus person and the evaluator. Personal principles are comprised of standards and values that specifically pertain to physical attractiveness. The standards are how an individual gauges physical attractiveness, and the values are the assigned worth or importance that the individual believes the physical attractiveness dimension possesses. Personal principles for stimulus persons affects the individual's judgment or gauge of physical attractiveness, and also affects efforts which the individual will expand to achieve higher levels. Similarly, personal principles for evaluators affect the judgment or guage of physical attractiveness, at the same time representing the believed importance of worth of different levels. These personal principles for both the individual stimulus person and the individual evaluator have direct causal linkage with the preceding collectivism unit. In other words, individual personal principles pertaining to physical attractiveness are largely the result of the general society's standards and values regarding physical attractiveness.

Although the ascription unit is well-developed, it is not complete and it still represents a fertile territory for future research. Consequently, an empty descriptive category ("unidentified characteristics") is placed within each of the two subunits. Future research efforts will idealistically expand the ascription unit with research that (a) provides additional factors within the labeled categories, (b) provides factors within the empty category, (c) identifies additional factors within each of the stimulus person and evaluator subunits, and (d) explores the personal principles associated with the stimulus person and the evaluator.

Substratum

The outcome of the ascription unit is a physical attractiveness denomination which may or may not be consciously recognized. Regardless of acknowledgment, or lack thereof, an individual's physical attractiveness is translated into a value within this substratum of the theory of physical attractiveness phenomena. In this unit, physical attractiveness is an information cue that invokes exhaustive stereotypes, expectations, assumptions, attributions, and superstitions.

Research results have consistently revealed a direct relationship between level of physical attractiveness and correspondent orientation within the substratum. In other words, research addressing this unit overwhelmingly concludes positive and negative associations with high and low physical attractiveness, respectively. Like ascription, the *substratum* unit of the theory is well developed, but it warrants additonal attention because of its extreme value as a link and foundation for a major portion of the physical attractiveness phenomena. Further research efforts will hopefull generate greater knowledge about the width and depth of these listed factors, as well as identifying extra factors. Continuing research is also desired for identifying the product (i.e., excrescence) of which this substratum unit underlies.

Excrescence

The *excrescence* unit represents extensive ramifications of the ascription unit via the substratum unit. Its illustration is complicated by the likelihood that both direct causal linkages and reciprocal relationships with feedback occur within this aspect of physical attractiveness phenomena. This excrescence section of the proposed theory consists of four subunits: communication effectiveness, interpersonal realities, interpersonal reciprocations, and intrapersonal realities. Within each of the subunits, there are numerous characteristics, and in the last subunit there is interaction between characteristics.

The likely sequential order or these subunits is first communication effectiveness, followed by interpersonal realities and interpersonal reciprocations similarly positioned, and last are the intrapersonal realities. Direct causal linkages run from the substratum directly to intrapersonal realities, whereas these causal linkages first pass through the communication effectiveness subunit before reaching the two interpersonal subunits. A direct causal linkage runs from interpersonal realities into interpersonal reciprocations, and direct causal linkages flow from each of these two interpersonal subunits into the intrapersonal realities subunit. However, reciprocal and feedback linkages also flow from the intrapersonal subunit, directly back into the one communication and two interpersonal subunits. These reciprocal feedback relationships are proposed because characteristics within a person (i.e., intrapersonal realities) are likely to be interactive with communication effectiveness, interpersonal realities, and interpersonal reciprocations.

Characteristics of the communication effectiveness subunit are persuasion, dissemination of information, and self-expression. Factors related to these characteristics include concepts such as information, education, and social power. Given many ways that communication can be defined, it is an essential and unavoidable artifact of the human race. Consequently, it appears that a communication subunit should be illustrated in a position that precedes the two interpersonal subunits. Two supplemental qualities of relevance are: (1) the fact that research results identify a relationship between communication effectiveness and the physical attractiveness variable, and (2) communication effectiveness, in one way or another, is an integral aspect of all the interpersonal characteristics.

The two interpersonal subunits are well-documented in the physical attractiveness research. Characteristics of the interpersonal realities include educational settings, social deviance, legal proceedings, and helping behavior. Although not all these specific characteristics possess a direct causal relationship with all interpersonal reciprocations, there certainly are substantial linkages, such as with romantic attraction, nonintimate liking, and employment dynamics.

The interpersonal realities subunit has a direct causal linkage from each of the two interpersonal subunits, as well as directly from the substratum unit. However, all these linkages pass through perceptual filters where the human processing interprets and distorts the information for the individual. Such distortion is the individual's reality of how he or she "chooses" to process incoming information. Characteristics within the intrapersonal subunit are psychological development, physiological effects, and the ultimate being or person.

Research in this area is not well-developed. Yet there are interesting indications that physical attractiveness may play a significant role within psychological development factors such as personality, interpersonal skills, and confidence. Scant research also suggests that physical attractiveness may be associated with physiological factors such as blood pressure; however, this relationship seems likely to be a function of the impact that physical attractiveness first has on psychological characteristics. The last characteristic is the entire being which admittedly is also a function of many factors unrelated to physical attractiveness. Because this theory is of physical attractiveness phenomena, the role of physical attractiveness is emphasized in this illustration. It is also logical that this entire being will interact with physical attractiveness which necessitates a linkage indicated from the being to each of the other three subunits. Finally, it is this total being who is involved most directly in the transfer process of physical attractiveness phenomena.

Although all four subunits are supported by relevant research, the attention has not been uniform for each. Consequently, the quantity of knowledge about each subunit varies. For example, the majority of efforts have focused on the interpersonal realities and interpersonal reciprocations. The subunits of intrapersonal realities and communication effectiveness are the recipients of substantially less magnitude, even though they are important elements of the subsystem within the excrescence unit. Future research should continue to refine the two interpersonal subunits, as well as more fully developing the communication subunit. But, most wanting is research attention for the interpersonal subunit which will explore the width and depth of its characteristics.

Illapse

The *illapse* unit represents the stage where the system begins the process of translating and transmitting physical attractiveness from an individual personal experience into a societal artifact. A formation subunit, followed by a transfer subunit, comprise the illapse. The direct causal linkage from the excrescence unit flows into the subunit labeled, in its entirety, "formation of individual standards and values specific to physical attractiveness." Within the illapse unit, the direct causal linkage then leads to the subunit labeled, in its entirety, "transfer of individual standards and values specific to physical attractiveness."

Standards and values both serve essential functions in the proposed theory of physical attractiveness phenomena. Standards are associated with the determination of physical attractiveness, whereas values are the worth associated with the physical attractiveness variable. In other words, standards are the measures of comparison that individuals use, consciously or subconsciously, to assess physical attractiveness. Standards alone are of little relevance, because the value's function serves to exaggerate or minimize the importance of physical attractiveness. Values are, then, the conscious or subconscious beliefs that an individual has about the importance or worth of physical attractiveness. It is this value's function that, because of its current intense magnitude, appears largely responsible for physical attractiveness phenomena which are pervasive and powerful.

Standards, and especially values, of the formation subunit appear to possess a direct causal linkage with the overall excrescence unit. Characteristics of this formation subunit include learning theory, life exposures and experiences, religious orientations, and physical attractiveness of a loved one such as spouse, child, or parent. Very strict adherence to most traditional religious orientations poses a unique influence on values (i.e., the beliefs about the importance of physical attractiveness). Another characteristic of this subunit is the notion that formation of standards and values are subjected to personal information interpretation and distortion within the individual before moving to the transfer subunit. Once formed, standards and values are linked directly with the transfer subunit. Characteristics of this subunit include socialization processes, fairy tales, folklore, and modeling of actions that specifically demonstrate standards and values of physical attractiveness.

Research has not addressed the illapse unit. The proposed subunits and subsequent characteristics are logical, but no direct confirmation exists. This void may be due to the difficulty of scientifically investigating the illapse link, at least through manipulations of typical experimental designs. However, despite the problems, it is important to begin conducting research endeavors that will provide empirical insight into this major unit of the proposed theory of physical attractiveness phenomena.

Impingement

Transferral of physical attractiveness standards and values is not unaffected or without error. To account for shifts in preferred ideals over time, the *impingement* unit is proposed to follow the illapse. This impingement unit is made up of natural and artificial changes which can be divided into three subunits that are either biologically based, psychologically based, or marketing based.

Modification of the standards and values pertaining to physical attractiveness appear influenced, if not caused, by change subunits that are primarily independent of each other. Biologically based change possesses the characteristics of evolution and random events to impose a natural modulation. Also natural is the psychologically based change that is characterized by the need for novelty, as identified in informational processing theory. Artificial change is marketing based. Alterations of the standards and values are forced into the system of physical attractiveness phenomena because of marketing motivations. Characteristics of this marketing subunit center around the mass media, fashion industries, and various marketing practices.

Research into the impingement area is lacking. Like the illapse, it is difficult to conduct experimental investigations. But, approaches used by other scientific disciplines can be utilized to provide knowledge about each of these three subunits, as well as exploration of this entire impingement unit. Each subunit offers opportunity for beneficial analyses. The marketing based subunit is especially large because capitalistic societies encourage excessive impingements. Observation of the biological changes and investigation into the psychologically based changes are equally interesting. The latter are especially intriguing because information processing theory possesses potential promise for explaining this stage of the physical attractiveness phenomena. Finally, the impingement unit is very susceptible to communication and the rapidly increasing developments in mass media technology carry implications for a new frontier of exploration.

Collectivism

The *collectivism* unit is the culmination of the illapse unit via the impingement unit. It is the collective societal principles pertaining to physical attractiveness. It represents the sum total of standards and values possessed by individuals. This total then becomes the cultural standard of physical attractiveness and the values that a culture places on physical attractiveness.

No doubt, the whole is greater than the sum of its parts, and this collectivism unit is an entity that changes slowly and is very powerful. Consequently, the cultural standards and values are likely to play an important function in determining physical attractiveness denomination. The upshot is that the loop is now completed, with the collectivism unit directly linked into the ascription unit. Furthermore, the collectivism unit yields specific impacts on the stimulus person and the evaluator. These specific linkages, within the ascription unit, are personal principles associated with the stimulus person and the evaluator. The collectivism unit substantially influences the standards and values which stimulus persons and evaluators hold with regard to physical attractiveness.

Some research has documented the shifts in ideal preferences of physical attractiveness. Although physical attractiveness phenomena have remained consistent over time, the standards used to gauge physical attractiveness have undergone minor but gradual change, which is logically explained by the impingement unit. Future research will hopefully expand this collectivism unit. This expansion can be pursued by defining the cultural standards and cultural values, measuring these principles over time, identifying additional relevant principles, and studying the precise linkage with characteristics within the ascription unit. Research that may provide substantial insight into the cultural standards and cultural values pertaining to physical attractiveness phenomena should also be pursued.

Conclusion

The intent of this proposed theory of physical attractiveness phenomena is to encourage theory-driven programmatic research. Benefits of such an approach were discussed earlier, and, certainly, one goal is the establishment of the study of physical attractiveness phenomena as a scientific entity in itself. It is hoped that this proposed theory provides the necessary conceptual framework to at least move toward the proper direction. Such a framework will allow greater progress, for

> when the individual scientist can take a paradigm for granted, he no longer, in his major works, attempt to build his field anew, starting from first principles and justifying the use of each concept introduced. (Kuhn, 1962, pp. 19–20)

Also, by establishing a theoretical and conceptual framework, the study of physical attractiveness phenomena may be more recognized and may attract an enduring group of first-rate adherents.

This proposed theory represents a realistic view of the current state of knowledge. However, it is a theory that, it is hoped, will generate specific hypotheses and subsequent empirical tests. In fact, as encouraged by Blalock (1969, p. 46), unnecessary detail for relatively minor relationships are intentionally omitted with the intent that greater focus on the physical attractiveness variable will permit greater testing of the theory. According to Carnap (1953, p. 48), ensuing research efforts are likely to produce gradual increasing confirmations or disconfirmations of the theory, and it is through this process that the greatest progress will ultimately be made in the study of physical attractiveness phenomena.

FUTURE RESEARCH QUESTS

Future endeavors in the study of physical attractiveness phenomena are infinite. Many macroquestions of social importance exist, as well as a plethora of microquestions. A sample of questions that call for answers are posed throughout this book. For example, summaries in Chapters 3, 5, and 7 present questions, as does the entirety of Chapter 2. Questions are also readily apparent with regard to units, subunits, characteristics, factors, and funtions of the proposed theory of physical attractiveness phenomena.

Fundamental questions that may be viewed as more important to society and subsequently to the study of physical attractiveness phenomena are plentiful. For example, how can the phenomena be minimized? Could challenging and attempting to restructure cultural standards and values pertaining to physical attractiveness be beneficial? What impact is due to our language nuances, beauty pageants, contemporary entertainment, and mass media advertising? Would voluntary changes, or government forced changes, in these impact areas control exaggerated physical attractiveness phenomena?

Implications pertaining to life cycle stages are of interest. For example, what affect does the current youth orientation have with regard to the aging of the baby boom generation? How are age and physical attractiveness related? Are child and spouse abuse someway a function of physical attractiveness? Does life expectancy differ as physical attractiveness differs? Does physical attractiveness have a relationship with lifelong illnesses, lifelong earnings, or lifelong variables of any type? What role, if any, does physical attractiveness have in the treatment of the dead and the dying?

Questions exist in the negative aspects of society. For example, what is the reality of victims and offenders in relation to physical attractiveness? What role does physical attractiveness hold in the lives of criminals, suicides, murders, and school dropouts? What is the relationship of physical attractiveness and those on death row, their victiims, and those associated with the respective legal proceedings? Does physical attractiveness play a role in divorce, infidelity, and depression? What is the role of physical attractiveness in failures in life, as well as successes?

Greater understanding is needed. An interdisciplinary approach could address the study of physical attractiveness phenomena. For example, what is the sociology of these phenomena? How does the mass media of a culture affect physical attractiveness phenomena? Does psychoanalysis provide relevant information? Can formal philosophy be applied? What insight can disciplines such as art and literature provide? What natural and social sciences are applicable to the study of physical attractiveness phenomena? What type of comparative analyses can be made between cultures, ages, and races, from the past, present and the future? Is formal content analysis a valuable research tool for this topic? How did the physical attractiveness phenomena originally begin, and why are they maintained from generation to generation?

Discrimination is important. How and why are physical attractiveness phenomena different for males and females? Why is more emphasis traditionally placed on the female? Of persons in authority, who and what type of person is most and least affected by physical atractiveness? How exactly do physical attractiveness phenomena affect providers of services, such as lawyers, physicians, teachers, professors, business persons, public contact service workers, and police?

What are the applications? Can use of physical attractiveness phenomena be exploited both in negative and positive ways? For example, can the relevant knowledge be used for treating mental illness or for use as unfair competition in industry? Can the knowledge be utilized by public policy makers? Should this knowledge be stressed in employment, laws, education, and other areas of potential discrimination? What discrimination actually occurs in the employment arena, and what are the actual job performance differences of those higher and lower in physical attractiveness?

Future uncontrollable developments also hold implications. For example, how will the developing technology in communications affect physical attractiveness phenomena? In light of developing societal events, does physical attractiveness play different roles for adults who are single, married, divorced, homosexual, and heterosexual? What implications are there for technological advancements in the areas of genetic engineering? What limit will the physical attractiveness phenomena eventually lead to and peak at, or will they continue to increase indefinitely? Are physical attractiveness phenomena relevant to the current interest in body building activity, by both males and females? What are the implications for an American population which pursues physical fitness for the primary purpose of physical attractiveness, as opposed to purposes of health? Are cultural values and cultural standards, specific to physical attractiveness, likely to change, and if so, in what direction?

A host of sociological and psychological questions invite answers. For example, are rural and urban Americans different in their response to and in their consequences of physical attractiveness phenomena? What is the effect of unrealistic pressures and expectations communicated by society, friends, and family? What are the differences in child-rearing practices among children and adults who differ in physical attractiveness? Is development of personality and intelligence affected? Which level of physical attractiveness is easiest and most difficult to remember, and why? Are certain levels of physical attractiveness more capable of penetrating the mental perceptual filters than other levels (e.g., to gain attention, to hold attention, and to have deliver a message)? Is physical attractiveness relevant to the fact that some persons who are very low in physical attractiveness become successful, whereas some who are very high do not succeed? Controlling for extraneous variables, what is the physical attractiveness level of vagrants? How can the public be made aware of the physical attractiveness phenomena? Can and should the physical attractiveness stereotype and corresponding phenomena be modified by forced means? What role do adornments such as cosmetics, jewelry, and clothing play? Exactly what is the extent of physical attractiveness effects within persuasive communication? What is the actual financial value of physical attractiveness, for example, in terms of injury, lawsuits, earning potential, and insurance accident claims? What are people willing to pay in terms of money and in effort to achieve higher physical attractiveness for themselves and loved ones?

Questions indirectly related to measurement present interesting directions for future research. First, the entire semantics used in the measurement of physical attractiveness (see Chapter 2) need to be more carefully manipulated and analyzed. Also, physical attractiveness itself must be defined. Also, physical attractiveness itself must be defined. Second, a ratio scale should be attempted which would establish a true, absolute zero point of physical attractiveness. Third, extraneous variables within physical attractiveness phenomena should be better considered. Fourth, verification of research results through observations or reality may be beneficial. Finally, a dual mission of the study of physical attractiveness phenomena should be explored in an attempt to identify the pros and cons of an applied research orientation, a basic research orientation, and/or a combination of these.

Manipulations need to be explained. First, the continuum typically studied should be extended past the current limits to include much lower levels and much higher levels of physical attractiveness. Also, instead of only two values, a third value (i.e., moderate level of physical attractiveness) should be regularly included, because this average level encompasses a major portion of our population and may consequently yield especially meaningful comparison. Second, careful control should be used to go beyond the face into other areas of physical appearance and physical attractiveness. Third, nonappearance characteristics should be considered as possible influential factors related to both the stimulus persons and the subjects. Fourth, positive and negative aspects of the very low levels and the very high levels of physical attractiveness should be investigated. For example, are the problems confronted by those very high in physical attractiveness analogous to those who are very gifted in other attributes? Also, what is the reality of such stereotypes as the "dumb blonde" and the "big hunk?" Finally, what is the extent, and at what level are those higher in physical attractiveness held in envy, which turns to contempt, which ultimately translates into higher physical attractiveness being a negative trait?

The lists of questions are infinite; regardless of whether they are considered microquestions or macroquestions. Therefore, without suggesting superiority of any one question over another, three general thrusts are now posed to conclude this discussion. First, pragmatic applications of the study of the physical attractiveness phenomena should be contemplated. Second, public policy makers should be aware of the knowledge base pertaining to physical attractiveness phenomena. Third, theory-driven programmatic research should be pursued in the future study of physical attractiveness phenomena.

References

Abbott, A. R., & Sebastian, R. J. (1981). Physical attractiveness and expectations of success. *Personality and Social Psychology Bulletin, 7*, 481–486.

Abraham, S., Johnson, C. L., & Najjar, M. F. (1976). *Height and weight of adults 18–74 years of age in the United States.* Washington, DC: National Center for Health Statistics, Public Health Service.

Adams, G. R. (1975). *Physical attributes, personality characteristics, and social behavior: An investigation of the effects of the physical attractiveness stereotype.* Unpublished doctoral dissertation, University of Pennsylvania, Philadelphia.

Adams, G. R. (1977a). Physical attractiveness, personality, and social reactions to peer pressure. *Journal of Psychology, 96*, 287–296.

Adams, G. R. (1977b). Physical attractiveness research: Toward a developmental social psychology of beauty. *Human Development, 20*, 217–240.

Adams, G. R. (1978). Racial membership and physical attractiveness effects on preschool teachers' expectations. *Child Study Journal, 8*, 29–41.

Adams, G. R. (1982). Physical attractiveness. In A. G. Miller (Ed.), *In the eye of the beholder: Contemporary issues in stereotyping.* New York: Praeger.

Adams, G. R., & Cohen, A. S. (1974). Children's physical and interpersonal characteristics that effect student–teacher interactions. *Journal of Experimental Education, 44*, 1–5.

Adams, G. R., & Cohen, A. S. (1976). An examination of cumulative folder information used by teachers in making differential judgments of children's abilities. *Alberta Journal of Educational Research, 22*, 216–225.

Adams, G. R., & Crane, P. (1980). An assessment of parents' and teachers' expectations of preschool children's social preference for attractive or unattractive children and adults. *Child Development, 51*, 224–231.

Adams, G. R., & Crossman, S. M. (1978). *Physical attractiveness: A cultural imperative.* Roslyn Heights, NY: Libra.

Adams, G. R., & Huston, T. L. (1975). Social perceptions of the middle-aged varying in physical attractiveness. *Developmental Psychology, 11*, 657–658.

Adams, G. R., & LaVoie, J. C. (1974a). The effect of student's sex, conduct, and facial attractiveness on teacher expectancy. *Education, 95*, 76–83.

Adams, G. R., & LaVoie, J. C. (1974b). *Attractiveness of the model and imitation.* Paper presented at the meeting of the Midwestern Psychological Association, Chicago, IL.

Adams, G. R., & LaVoie, J. C. (1975). Parental expectations of educational and personal-social performance and childrearing patterns as a function of attractiveness, sex, and conduct of the child. *Child Study Journal, 5*, 125–142.

Adams, G. R., & Read, D. (1983). Personality and social influence styles of attractive and unattractive college women. *The Journal of Psychology, 114*, 151–157.

Agarwal, P., & Prakash, N. (1977). Perceived physical attractiveness as related to attitudes toward women's liberation movement. *Indian Psychological Review, 15*, 31–34.

Ahrens, R. (1954). Beitrage zur Entvicklung des physiognomia—und mimikerkennes. *Zeitschrift für Experimentelle und angewandte Psychologie, 2*, 412–454.

Alexander, I. E., & Babad, E. Y. (1981). Returning the smile of the stranger: Within-culture and cross-culture comparisons of Israeli and American children. *Genetic Psychology Monographs, 103*, 31–77.

Alexander, M. W., & Judd, B. Jr. (1978). Do nudes in advertisements enhance brand recall? *Journal of Advertising Research, 18*, 47–50.

Allen, B. P. (1976). Race and physical attractiveness as criteria for white subjects' dating choices. *Social Behavior and Personality, 4*, 289–296.

Alley, T. R. (1981). Head shape and the perception of cuteness. *Developmental Psychology, 17*, 650–654.

America's obsession with beautiful people. (1982, January 11). *U. S. News & World Report*, pp. 60–61.

Ancker-Johnson, B. (1975). Physicist. *Educational Horizons, 53*, 116–121.

Anderson, P. F. (1983). Marketing, scientific progress, and scientific method. *Journal of Marketing, 47*, 18–31.

Anderson, R. (1978). Physical attractiveness and locus of control. *Journal of Social Psychology, 105*, 213–216.

Anderson, R., & Nida, S. A. (1978). Effect of physical attractiveness on opposite- and same-sex evaluations. *Journal of Personality, 46*, 401–413.

Andrew, R. J. (1963). Evolution of facial expression. *Science, 142*, 1034–1041.

Angelmar, R., & Pinson, C. (1975). The meaning of marketing. *Philosophy of Science, 42*, 208–213.

Aronson, E. (1969). Some antecedents of interpersonal attraction. In W. J. Arnold & D. Levine (Eds.), *Nebraska symposium on motivation*. Lincoln, NE: University of Nebraska Press.

Aronson, E., & Carlsmith, J. M. (1962). Performance expectancy as a determinant of actual performance. *Journal of Abnormal and Social Psychology, 65*, 179–182.

Aronson, E., & Carlsmith, J. M. (1968). Experimentation in social psychology. In G. Lindzey & E. Aronson (Eds.), *Handbook of social psychology*. (rev. ed., Vol. 2). Reading, MA: Addison-Wesley.

Associated Press. People "tend to lie" on voting question. 4 November 1981.

Athanasiou, R., & Greene, P. (1973). Physical attractiveness and helping behavior. *Proceedings of the 81st Annual Convention of the American Psychological Association, 8*, 289–290.

Bailey, R. C., & Price, J. P. (1978). Perceived physical attractiveness in married partners of long and short duration. *Journal of Psychology, 99*, 155–161.

Bailey, R. C., & Schreiber, T. S. (1981). Congruency of physical attractiveness perceptions and liking. *Journal of Social Psychology, 115*, 285–286.

Baker, M. J., & Churchill, G. A., Jr. (1977). The impact of physically attractive models on advertising evaluations. *Journal of Marketing Research, 14*, 538–555.

Balban, M. (1981). *Accuracy in self evaluation of physical attractiveness as a function of self esteem and defensiveness*. Unpublished doctoral dissertation, University of Southern Mississippi, Hattiesburg, MS.

Banziger, G., & Hooker, L. (1979). The effects of attitudes toward feminism and perceived feminism on physical attractiveness ratings. *Sex Roles, 5*, 437–442.

Bar-Tal, D., & Saxe, L. (1974). Effect of physical attractiveness on the perception of couples. *Personality and Social Psychology, 1*, 30–32.

Bar-Tal, D., & Saxe, L. (1976a). Perceptions of similarly and dissimilarly attractive couples and individuals. *Journal of Personality and Social Psychology, 33*, 772–781.

Bar-Tal, D., & Saxe, L. (1976b). Physical attractiveness and its relationship to sex-role stereotyping. *Sex Roles, 2*, 123–133.

Barocas, R., & Black, H. K. (1974). Referral rate and physical attractiveness in third-grade children. *Percentual and Motor Skills, 39,* 731–734.

Barocas, R., & Karoly, P. (1972). Effects of physical appearance on social responsiveness. *Psychological Reports, 31,* 495–500.

Barocas, R., & Vance, F. L. (1974). Physical appearance and personal adjustment counseling. *Journal of Counseling Psychology, 21,* 96–100.

Bassili, J. N. (1981). The attractiveness stereotype: Goodness or glamour? *Basic and Applied Social Psychology, 2,* 235–252.

Baumeister, R. F., & Darley, J. M. (1982). Reducing the biasing effect of perpetrator attractiveness in jury simulation. *Personality and Social Psychology Bulletin, 8,* 286–292.

Beck, S., Ward-Hull, C., & McLear, P. (1976). Variables related to women's somatic preferences of the male and female body. *Journal of Personality and Social Psychology, 34,* 1200–1210.

Beehr, T. A., & Gilmore, D. C. (1982). Applicant attractiveness as a perceived job-relevant variable in selection of management trainees. *Academy of Management Journal, 25,* 607–617.

Bell, P. A., & Baron, R. A. (1974). Environmental influences on attraction: Effects of heat, attitude similarity, and personal evaluations. *Bulletin of the Psychonomic Society, 4,* 479–481.

Bem, D. J. (1972). Self-perception theory. In L. Berkowitz (Ed.), *Advances in experimental social psychology.* New York: Academic Press.

Benassi, M. A. (1982). Effects of order of presentation, primacy, and physical attractiveness on attributions of ability. *Journal of Personality and Social Psychology, 43,* 48–58.

Bennetts, L. (1978, March 18). Beauty is found to attract some unfair advantages. *The New York Times,* p. 10.

Benson, P. L., Karabenick, S. A., & Lerner, R. M. (1976). Pretty pleases: The effects of physical attractiveness, race, and sex on receiving help. *Journal of Experimental Social Psychology, 12,* 409–415.

Berkowitz, L., & Frodi, A. (1979). Reactions to a child's mistakes as affected by her/his looks and speech. *Social Psychology Quarterly, 42,* 420–425.

Berkowitz, W. R. (1969). Perceived height, personality, and friendship choice. *Psychological Reports, 24,* 373–374.

Berkowitz, W. R., Nebel, J. C., & Reitman, J. W. (1971). Height and interpersonal attraction: The 1969 mayoral election in New York City. *Proceedings of the 79th Annual Convention of the American Psychological Association. 6,* 281–282.

Berlyne, D. E. (1960). *Conflict, arousal, and curiosity.* New York: McGraw-Hill.

Berscheid, E., & Walster, E. (1969). *Interpersonal attraction.* Reading, MA: Addison-Wesley.

Berscheid, E., & Walster, E. (1972). Beauty and the best. *Psychology Today, 5,* 42–46.

Berscheid, E., & Walster, E. (1974). Physical attractiveness. In L. Berkowitz (Ed.), *Advances in experimental social psychology.* New York: Academic Press.

Berscheid, E., Dion, K. K., Walster, E., & Walster, G. W. (1971). Physical attractiveness and dating choice: A test of the matching hypothesis. *Journal of Experimental Social Psychology, 7,* 173–189.

Berscheid, E., Walster, E., & Bohrnstedt, G. (1973). The happy American body: A survey report. *Psychology Today, 7,* 119–131.

Bettinghaus, E. (1968). *Persuasive communications.* New York: Holt, Rinehart, & Winston.

Bevan, W., & Feur, J. N. (1977). The facilitative role of imagery in episodic memory: Multiple cues or active construction? *Bulletin of the Psychonomic Science, 10,* 172–174.

Bexton, W. H., Heron, W., & Scott, T. H. (1954). Effects of decreased variation in the sensory environment. *Canadian Journal of Psychology, 8*, 70–76.

Bias against ugly people: How they can fight it. (1983, November 28). *U. S. News & World Report*, pp. 53–54.

Black, H. K. (1974). Physical attractiveness and similarity of attitude in interpersonal attraction. *Psychological Reports, 35*, 403–406.

Black, S. L., & Biron, C. (1982). Androstenol as a human pheromone: No effect on perceived physial attractiveness. *Behavior and Neural Biology, 34*, 326–330.

Blalock, H. M., Jr. (1969). *Theory construction.* Englewood Cliffs, NJ: Prentice-Hall.

Blass, T., Alperstein, L., & Black, S. H. (1974). Effects of communicator's race and beauty and of receiver's objectivity–subjectivity on attitude change. *Personality and Social Psychology Bulletin, 1*, 132–134.

Blood, G. W., Mahan, B. W., & Hyman, M. (1979). Judging personality and appearance from voice disorders. *Journal of Communication Disorders, 12*, 63–68.

Blood, R. O. (1955). A retest of Waller's rating complex. *Marriage and Family Living, 17*, 41–47.

Blood, R. O. (1956). Uniformities and diversities in campus dating preferences. *Journal of Marriage and Family Living, 18*, 37–45.

Bosse, K. (1976). Social situation of persons with dermatoses as a phenomena of interpersonal perception. *Zeitschrift für Psychosomatische Medizin und Psychoanalyse, 22*, 3–61.

Bower, T. G. R. (1977). *A primer of infant development.* San Francisco: Freeman.

Boyd, H. W., Jr., & Ray, M. L. (1971). What big agency men in Europe think of copy testing methods. *Journal of Marketing Research, 2*, 22–27.

Brenner, D., and Hinsdale, G. (1978). Body build stereotypes and self-identification in three age groups of females. *Adolescence, 13*, 551–562.

Brideau, L. B., & Allen, V. L. (1980). *Individual differences in nonverbal communication: Facial and vocal encoding skills* (Report No. MF01-PC02). Unpublished manuscript, 1980. (ERIC Document Reproduction Service No. ED 196 908).

Bridges, J. S. (1981). Sex-typed may be beautiful but androgynous is good. *Psychological Reports, 48*, 267–272.

Brigham, J. C. (1980). Limiting conditions of the "physical attractiveness stereotype": Attributions about divorce. *Journal of Research in Personality, 14*, 365–375.

Bringmann, W. G., & Abston, N., Jr. (1981, March 25–28). *The selection of patients for psychotherapy by college students.* Paper presented at the annual meeting of the Southeastern Psychological Association, Atlanta, GA.

Brislin, R. W., & Lewis, S. A. (1968). Dating and physical attractiveness: Replication. *Psychological Reports, 22*, 976.

Britt, S. H. (1978). *Psychological principles of marketing and consumer behavior.* Lexington, MA: Lexington Books.

Brooks, G. (1984, January 27). A physician treating Lou Gehrig's disease seeks a cure in the lab. *The Wall Street Journal*, pp. 1, 16.

Brophy, J. E., & Good, T. L. (1974). *Teacher-student relationships: Causes and consequences.* New York: Holt, Rinehart, & Winston.

Brown, H. I. (1977). *Perception, theory, and commitment.* Chicago, IL: University of Chicago Press.

Brown, T., & Eng, K. (1970). *The effects of race, physical attractiveness and value similarity on interpersonal attraction.* Unpublished manuscript, University of British Columbia, Vancouver.

Brundage, L. E., Derlega, V. J., & Cash, T. F. (1977). The effects of physical attractiveness and need for approval on self-disclosure. *Personality and Social Psychology Bulletin, 3*, 63–66.

Bruner, J. S., & Goodman, C. C. (1947). Value and need as organizing factors in perception. *Journal of Abnormal and Social Psychology, 42,* 33–44.

Bruning, J. L., & Kintz, B. L. (1977). *Computational Handbook of Statistics* (2nd ed.). Glenview, IL: Scott, Foresman.

Brunswik, E. (1939). Perceptual characteristics of schematized human figures. *Psychological Bulletin, 36,* 553.

Budge, H. S. (1981). *Dimensions of physical attractiveness: How others see us.* Unpublished doctoral dissertation, University of Utah, Salt Lake City.

Bull, A. J., Burboge, S. E., Crandall, J. E., Fletcher, C. I., Lloyd, J. T., Rosenberg, R. L., & Rockett, S. L. (1972). Effects of noise and intolerance of ambiguity upon attraction for similar and dissimilar others. *Journal of Social Psychology, 88,* 151–152.

Bull, R., & Shead, G. (1979). Pupil dilation, sex of stimulus, and age and sex of observer. *Perceptual and Motor Skills, 49,* 27–30.

Bull, R., & Stevens, J. (1979). The effects of attractiveness of writer and penmanship on essay grades. *Journal of Occupational Psychology, 52,* 53–59.

Burgoon, M. (1974). *Approaching speech communication.* New York: Holt, Rinehart, & Winston.

Burley, N. (1981). Sex ratio manipulation and selection of attractiveness. *Science, 211,* 721–722.

Byrne, D. (1961). Interpersonal attraction and attitude similarity. *Journal of Abnormal Social Psychology, 62,* 713–715.

Byrne, D. (1971). *The attraction paradigm.* New York: Academic Press.

Bryne, D., & Clore, G. L. (1970). A reinforcement model of evaluative responses. *Personality: An International Journal, 1,* 103–128.

Byrne, D., & Nelson, D. (1964). Attraction as a function of attitude similarity–dissimilarity: The effect of topic importance. *Psychonomic Science, 1,* 93–94.

Bryne, D., London, C., & Reeves, K. (1968). The effects of physical attractiveness, sex, and attitude similarity on interpersonal attraction. *Journal of Personality, 36,* 259–271.

Bryne, D., Griffitt, W., Hudgins, W., & Reeves, K. (1969). Attitude similarity–dissimilarity and attraction: Generality beyond the college sophomore. *Journal of Social Psychology, 79,* 155–161.

Byrne, D., Ervin, C. R., & Lamberth, J. (1970). Continuity between the experimental study of attraction and "real life" computer dating. *Journal of Personality and Social Psychology, 16,* 157–165.

Calhoun, L. G., Selby, J. W., Cann, A., & Keller, G. T. (1978). The effects of victim physical attractiveness and sex of respondent on social reactions to victims of rape. *British Journal of Social and Clinical Psychology, 17,* 191–192.

California convicts get noses beautified for free. (1979, August 21). *Roanoke Times and World News* (Virginia).

Campbell, D. R., & Fiske, D. W. (1959). Convergent and discriminant validation by the multitrait-multimethod matrix. *Psychological Bulletin, 56,* 81–105.

Cann, A., Siegfried, W. D., & Pearce, L. (1981). Forced attention to specific applicant qualifications: Impact on physical attractiveness and sex of applicant biases. *Personnel Psychology, 34,* 65–75.

Carminati v. Philadelphia Transportation Company, Atlantic Reporter 2d Series, 176 A.2d. 440 (1962).

Carnap, R. Testability and Meaning. (1953). In H. Feigel & M. Brodbeck (Eds.), *Readings in the philosophy of science.* New York: Appleton-Century-Crofts.

Carter, J. A. (1978). Impressions of counselors as a function of counselor physical attractiveness. *Journal of Counseling Psychology, 25,* 28–34.

Cash, T. F. (1980). Physical attractiveness: An annotated bibliography of theory and research in the behavioral sciences. *American Psychological Association: Catalog of Selected Documents in Psychology* (Ms. No. 2370). Washington, DC: American Psychological Association.

Cash, T. F., & Burns, D. S. (1977). The occurrence of reinforcing activities in relation to locus of control, success–failure expectancies, and physical attractiveness. *Journal of Personality Assessment, 41*, 387–391.

Cash, T. F., & Cash, D. W. (1982). Women's use of cosmetics: Psychosocial correlates and consequences. *Internal Journal of Cosmetic Science, 4*, 1–14.

Cash, T. F., & Derlega, V. J. (1978). The matching hypothesis: Physical attractiveness among same-sexed friends. *Personality and Social Psychology Bulletin. 4*, 240–243.

Cash, T. F., & Kehr, J. (1978). Influence of nonprofessional counselors' physical attractiveness and sex on perceptions of counselor behavior. *Journal of Counseling Psychology, 25*, 336–342.

Cash, T. F., & Salzbach, R. F. (1978). The beauty of counseling: Effects of counselor physical attractiveness and self-disclosures on perceptions of counselor behavior. *Journal of Counseling Psychology, 25*, 283–291.

Cash, T. F., & Soloway, D. (1975). Self-disclosure correlates of physical attractiveness: An exploratory study. *Psychological Reports, 36*, 579–586.

Cash, T. F., Begley, P. J., McCown, D. A., & Weise, B. C. (1975). When counselors are heard but not seen: Initial impact of physical attractiveness. *Journal of Counseling Psychology, 22*, 273–279.

Cash, T. F., Gillen, P., & Burns, S. D. (1977). Sexism and beautyism in personnel consultant decision making. *Journal of Applied Psychology, 62*, 301–310.

Cash, T. F., Kehr, J. A. Polyson, J., & Freeman, V. (1977). Role of physical attractiveness in peer attribution of psychological disturbance. *Journal of Consulting and Clinical Psychology, 45*, 987–993.

Cavior, H. E., Hayes, S. C., & Cavior, N. (1974). Physical attractiveness of female offenders: Effects on institutional performance. *Criminal Justice and Behavior, 1*, 321–331.

Cavior, N. (1970). *Physical attractiveness, perceived attitude similarity, and interpersonal attraction among fifth and eleventh grade boys and girls.* Unpublished doctoral dissertation, University of Houston, TX.

Cavior, N., & Boblett, P. J. (1972). Physical attractiveness of dating versus married couples. *Proceedings of the 80th Annual Convention of the American Psychological Association, 7*, 175–176.

Cavior, N., & Dokecki, P. R. (1971). Physical attractiveness self-concept: A test of Mead's hypothesis. *Proceedings of the 79th Annual Convention of the American Psychological Association, 6*, 319–320.

Cavior, N., & Dokecki, P. R. (1973). Physical attractiveness, perceived attitude similarity, and academic achievement as contributors to interpersonal attraction among adolescents. *Developmental Psychology, 91*, 44–54.

Cavior, N., & Howard, L. R. (1973). Facial attractiveness and juvenile delinquency among black and white offenders. *Journal of Abnormal Child Psychology, 1*, 202–213.

Cavior, N., Jacobs, A., & Jacobs, M. (1974). *The stability and correlation of physical attractiveness and sex appeal ratings.* Unpublished manuscript, West Virginia University, Morgantown.

Cavior, N., Miller, K., & Cohen, S. H. (1975). Physical attractiveness, attitude similarity, and length of acquaintance as contributors to interpersonal attraction among adolescents. *Social Behavior and Personality, 3*, 133–141.

Celluite: Fact, Fad, Fantasy. 20/20. *ABC*, 18 May 1983.

Chaiken, S. (1979). Communicator physical attractiveness and persuasion. *Journal of Personality and Social Psychology, 37*, 1387–1397.

Chaiken, S., & Eagly, A. H. (1983). Communication modality as a determinant of persuasion: The role of communicator salience. *Journal of Personality and Social Psychology, 45,* 241–256.

Chaikin, A. L., Gillen, B., Derlega, V. J., Heinen, J. R. K., & Wilson, M. (1978). Students' reactions to teachers' physical attractiveness and nonverbal behavior: Two exploratory studies. *Psychology in Schools, 15,* 588–595.

Chakrabarti, T. (1974). Attitudes reflected in matrimonial advertisements. *Australian and New Zealand Journal of Sociology, 10,* 142–143.

Chalmers, A. F. (1976). *What is this thing called science?* St. Lucia, Australia: University of Queensland Press.

Charlesworth, W. R. (1964). Instigation and maintenance of curiosity behavior as a function of surprise verus novel and familiar stimuli. *Child Development, 35,* 1169–1186.

Chess, S., Thomas, A., & Cameron, M. (1976). Sexual attitudes and behavior patterns in a middle-class adolescent population. *American Journal of Orthopsychiatry, 46,* 689–701.

Choo, T. (1976). Communicator credibility and communication discrepancy as determinants of opinion change. *Journal of Social Psychology, 64,* 1–20.

Christine Craft is awarded $325,000 in retrial of suit over loss of tv anchor job. (1984, January 14). *Los Angeles Times,* Part 1, pp. 1, 3.

Churchill, G. A., Jr. (1979). A paradigm for developing better measures of marketing constructs. *Journal of Marketing Research, 16,* 64–73.

Clifford, M. M. (1975). Physical attractiveness and academic performance. *Child Study Journal, 5,* 201–209.

Clifford, M. M., & Walster, E. (1973). The effect of physical attractiveness on teacher expectations. *Sociology of Education, 46,* 248–258.

Clifton, R. A., & Baksh, I. J. (1978). Physical attractiveness, year of university, and the expectations of student-teachers. *Canadian Journal of Education, 3,* 37–46.

Colley, R. H. (1961). *Defining advertising goals for measured advertising.* New York: Association of National Advertisers.

Coombs, R. H., & Kenkel, W. F. (1966). Sex differences in dating aspirations and satisfaction with computer-selected partners. *Journal of Marriage and the Family, 28,* 62–66.

Cooper, L. (Trans.). (1932). *The rhetoric of Aristotle.* New York: Appleton-Century-Crofts.

Corter, C., Trehub, S., Bonkydis, C., Ford, L., Celhoffer, L., & Minde, K. (1975). *Nurses, judgments of the attractiveness of premature infants.* Unpublished manuscript, University of Toronto, Ontario.

Coslin, P. G., & Winnykamen, F. (1981). A contribution to the study of the genesis of stereotypes: Attribution of negative or positive aspects as a function of dress and ethnic appearance. *Psychologie Française, 26,* 39–48.

Critelli, J. W. (1975). *Physical attractiveness in dating couples.* Paper presented at the meeting of the Midwestern Psychological Association, Chicago.

Critelli, J. W., & Waid, L. R. (1980). Physical attractiveness, romantic love, and equity restoration in dating relationships. *Journal of Personality Assessment, 44,* 624–629.

Cronkhite, G. (1969). *Persuasion: Speech and behavior change.* Indianapolis, IN: Bobbs-Merrill.

Cross, J. F., & Cross, J. (1971). Age, sex, race, and the perception of facial beauty. *Developmental Psychology, 5,* 433–439.

Cross, J. F., Cross, J., & Daly, J. (1971). Sex, race, age, and beauty as factors in recognition of faces. *Perception and Psychophysics, 10,* 393–396.

Crouse, B. B., & Mehrabian, A. (1977). Affiliation of opposite-sexed strangers. *Journal of Research in Personality, 1977, 11,* 38–47.

Cummings, P. (1981, February 11). New face gives Virginia prisoner hope for a better life. *The Richmond News Leader*, p. 13.

Cunnington, C. W. (1941). *Why women wear clothes*. London: Faber & Faber.

Curran, J. P. (1973). Correlates of physical attractiveness and interpersonal attraction in the dating situation. *Social Behavior and Personality*, 1, 153–157.

Curran, J. P., & Lippold, S. (1975). The effects of physical attraction and attitude similarity on attraction in dating dyads. *Journal of Personality*, 43, 528–538.

Dailey, C. A. (1952). The effects of premature conclusion upon the acquisition of understanding of a person. *Journal of Psychology*, 33, 133–152.

Dannenmaier, W. D., & Thumin, F. J. (1964). Authority status as a factor in perceptual distortion of size. *Journal of Social Psychology*, 63, 361–365.

Darwin, C. (1872). *The expression of the emotions in man and animals*. London: Murray.

Darwin, C. (1952). The origin of species by means of natural selection. The descent of man and selection in relation to sex (1871). In R. M. Hutchins (Ed.), *Great Books of the Western World* (Vol. 49). Chicago, IL: Encyclopedia Britannica.

Davies, P. D. (Ed.). (1982). *The American heritage dictionary of the English language*. New York: Dell.

Davis, G., Ellis, H., & Shepherd, J. (1977). Cue saliency in faces as assessed by the "Photofit" technique. *Perception*, 6, 263–269.

Day, G. (1970). *Buyer attitudes and brand choice behavior*. New York: Free Press.

Deck, L. P. (1968). Buying brains by the inch. *Journal of College and University Personnel Association*, 19, 33–37.

Deck, L. P. (1971). *Supplemental study*. Unpublished manuscript, University of Pittsburgh, PA. (Cited in Keyes, R. [1980]. *The height of your life* [pp. 178–179]. Boston, MA: Little, Brown.)

Deitz, S. R., & Byrnes, I. E. (1981). Attribution of responsibility for sexual assault: The influence of observer empathy and defendant occupation and attractiveness. *Journal of Psychology*, 108, 17–29.

DeMeis, D. K., & Turner, R. R. (1978). Effects of students' race, physical attractiveness, and dialect on teachers' evaluations. *Contemporary Educational Psychology*, 3, 77–86.

Dempsey, D., & Zimbardo, P. K. (1978). *Psychology and you*. Glenview, IL: Scott, Foresman.

Dermer, M., & Thiel, D. I. (1975). When beauty may fail. *Journal of Personality and Social Psychology*, 31, 1168–1176.

Dion, K. K. (1972). Physical attractiveness and evaluations of children's transgressions. *Journal of Personality and Social Psychology*, 24, 207–213.

Dion, K. K. (1973). Young children's stereotyping of facial attractiveness. *Developmental Psychology*, 9, 183–188.

Dion, K. K. (1974). Children's physical attractiveness and sex as determinants of adult punitiveness. *Development Psychology*, 10, 772–778.

Dion, K. K. (1977). The incentive value of physical attractiveness for young children. *Personality and Social Psychology Bulletin*, 3, 67–70.

Dion, K. K., & Berscheid, E. (1974). Physical attractiveness and peer perception among children. *Sociometry*, 37, 1–12.

Dion, K. K., & Stein, S. (1978). Physical attractiveness and interpersonal influence. *Journal of Experimental Social Psychology*, 14, 97–108.

Dion, K. K., Berscheid, E., & Walster, E. (1972). What is beautiful is good. *Journal of Personality and Social Psychology*, 24, 285–290.

Dipboye, R. L., Fromkin, H. L., & Wibeck, K. (1975). Relative importance of applicant sex, attractiveness, and scholastic standing in evaluation of job applicant resumes. *Journal of Applied Psychology*, 60, 39–43.

Dipboye, R. L., Arvey, R. D., & Terpstra, D. E. (1977). Sex and physical attractiveness of rates and applicants as determinants of resume evaluations. *Journal of Applied Psychology, 62,* 288–294.

Donley, B., & Allen, B. (1977). Influences of experimenter attractiveness and ego-involvement on paired-associates learning. *Journal of Social Psychology, 101,* 151–152.

Douglas, S. P., & Solomon, M. R. (1983). Clothing the female executive: Fashion or fortune. In P. E. Murphy & G. R. Laczniak (Eds.), *1983 American Marketing Association Educators' Proceedings.* Chicago: American Marketing Association.

Downs, A. C., & Walz, P. J. (1980, May). *Sex differences in preschoolers' perceptions of young, middle-aged, and elderly adults.* Paper presented at the annual meeting of the Western Psychological Association. Honolulu, HI.

Downs, A. C., & Wright, A. D. (1982). Differential conceptions of attractiveness: Subjective and objective ratings. *Psychological Reports, 50,* 282.

Driver, M. J. (1962). Conceptual structure and group processes in an inter-nation simulation. Part one: The perception of simulated nations. (RB62–15). *Educational Testing Service Research Bulletin.* (Cited in Schroder, H. M, Driver, M. J., & Streufert, S. [1967]. *Human Information Processing.* New York: Holt, Rinehart, & Winston).

Dukes, W. F., & Bevan, W. (1952). Size estimation and monetary value: A correlation. *Journal of Psychology, 34,* 43–53.

Dushenko, T. W., Perry, R. P., Schilling, J., & Smolarski, S. (1978). Generality of the physical attractiveness stereotypes for age and sex. *Journal of Social Psychology, 105,* 303–304.

Edgemon, C. K., & Clopton, J. R. (1978). The relationship between physical attractiveness, physical effectiveness, and self-concept. *Psychological Rehabilitation Journal, 2,* 21–25.

Edgerton, M. T., & Knorr, N. J. (1971). Motivational patterns of patients seeking cosmetic (esthetic) surgery. *Plastic and Reconstructive Surgery, 48,* 551–557.

Efran, M. G. (1974). The effect of physical appearance on the judgment of guilt, interpersonal attraction, and severity of recommended punishment in a simulated jury task. *Journal of Research in Personality, 8,* 45–54.

Efran, M. G., & Patterson, E. W. (1974). Voters vote beautiful: The effect of physical appearance on a national election. *Canadian Journal of Behavioural Science, 6,* 352–356.

Egaly, A., & Chalken, S. (1975). An attribution analysis of the effect of communicator characteristics on opinion change: The case of communicator attractiveness. *Journal of Personality and Social Psychology, 32,* 136–144.

Eibl-Eibesfeldt, I. (1970). *Ethology, the biology of behavior.* New York: Holt, Rinehart, & Winston.

Ekman, P. (1973). *Darwin and facial expression.* New York: Academic Press.

Elder, G. H., Jr. (1968). Achievement motivation and intelligence in occupational mobility: A longitudinal analysis. *Sociometry, 31,* 327–354.

Elder, G. H., Jr. (1969). Appearance and education in marriage mobility. *American Sociological Review, 34,* 519–533.

Ellis, H. D. (1975). Recognizing faces. *British Journal of Psychology, 66,* 409–426.

Engel, J. F., Wales, H. G., & Warshaw, M. R. (1971). *Promotional strategy* (rev. ed.). Homewood, IL: Richard D. Irwin.

Epstein, Y. M., & Karlin, R. A. (1975). Effects of acute experimental crowding. *Journal of Applied Social Psychology, 5,* 34–53.

Exline, R. V. (1971). Visual interaction—The glances of power and preference. In J. K. Cole (Ed.), *Nebraska symposium on motivation.* Lincoln, NE: University of Nebraska Press.

Fantz, R. L. (1966). Pattern discrimination and selective attention as determinants of perceptual development from birth. In A. H. Kidd & J. L. Rivoire (Eds.), *Perceptual development in children*. New York: International Universities Press.

Farina, A., Fischer, E. H., Sherman, S., Smith, W. T., Groh, T., & Mermin, D. (1977). Physical attractiveness and mental illness. *Journal of Abnormal Psychology, 86*, 510–517.

Fast, J. (1970). *Body language*. New York: Pocket Books.

Feeg, V. D., & Peters, D. L. (1979). *Children's physical appearance and adult expectations*. Paper presented at the annual meeting of the National Association for the Education of Young Children, Atlanta, GA.

Feild, H. S. (1979). Rape trials and jurors' decisions: A psycholegal analysis of the effects of victim, defendant, and case characteristics. *Law and Human Behavior, 3*, 261–284.

Feingold, A. (1982a). Physical attractiveness and romantic evolvement. *Psychological Reports, 50*, 802.

Feingold, A. (1982b). Do taller men have prettier girlfriends? *Psychological Reports, 50*, 810.

Feinman, S., & Gill, G. W. (1977). Females' response to males' beardedness. *Perceptual and Motor Skills, 44*, 533–534.

Feinman, S., & Gill, G. W. (1978). Sex differences in physical attractiveness preferences. *Journal of Social Psychology, 105*, 43–52.

Feldman, S. D. (1971). *The presentation of shortness in everyday life—height and heightism in American society: Toward a sociology of stature*. Paper presented at the meeting of the American Sociological Association, Washington, DC.

Feleky, A. M. (1914). The expression of the emotions. *Psychological Review, 21*, 33–41.

Felson, R. B. (1980). Physical attractiveness, grade and teachers' attributions of ability. *Representative Research in Social Psychology, 11*, 64–71.

Felson, R. B., & Bohrnstedt, G. W. (1979). "Are the good beautiful or the beautiful good?" The relationship between children's perceptions of ability and perceptions of physical attractiveness. *Social Psychology Quarterly, 42*, 386–392.

Festinger, L. (1957). *A theory of cognitive dissonance*. Stanford, California: Stanford University Press.

Festinger, L., & Maccoby, N. (1964). On resistance to persuasive communications. *Journal of Abnormal and Social Psychology, 68*, 359–366.

Feyerabend, P. (1975). *Against method*. Thetford, England: Lowe & Brydone.

Feyerabend, P. (1978). From incompetent professionalism to professionalized incompetence: The rise of a new breed of intellectuals. *Philosophy of the Social Sciences, 8*, 37–53.

Feyerabend, P. (1981). More clothes from the emperor's bargain basement. *British Journal of the Philosophy of Science, 32*, 57–94.

Fink, D. (1983, July 25). Looks count a lot in ratings race. *U.S.A. Today*, pp. 1D, 2D.

Finn, D. W. (1976). *An investigation of the differential effects of two dimensions of spokesman credibility as they interact with consumer involvement with brand choice*. Unpublished doctoral dissertation, University of Massachusetts, Amherst.

Fiser, I., & Fiserova, O. (1969). Beauty and cosmetics in ancient India. *New Orient, 5*, 92–94.

Fisher, S. (1973). *Body consciousness: You are what you feel*. Englewood Cliffs, NJ: Prentice-Hall.

Fleishman, J. J., Buckley, M. L., Klosinsky, M. J., Smith, N., & Tuck, B. (1976). Judged attractiveness in recognition memory of women's faces. *Perceptual and Motor Skills, 43*, 709–710.

Foder, N., & Gaynor, F. (Trans.). (1958). *Freudian dictionary of psychoanalysis*. Greenwich, CT: Greenwood Press.

Ford, C. S., & Beach, F. A. (1951). *Patterns of sexual behavior*. New York: Harper.

Freedman, D. (1969). The survival value of the beard. *Psychology Today, 3*, 36–39.

Freedman, J. L., Levy, A. S., Buchanan, R. W., & Price, J. (1972). Crowding and human aggressiveness. *Journal of Experimental Social Psychology, 8*, 528–548.

Fresh faces: Help for homely cons. (1980, December 8). *Time, 116* (23), 116.

Freud S. (1959). The future prospects of psychoanalytic theory. *Collected Papers* (Vol. 2). New York: Basic Books.

Friend, R. M., & Vinson, M. (1974). Leaning over backwards: Jurors' responses to defendants' attractiveness. *Journal of Communication, 24*, 1124–1129.

Fromkin, H. L., & Streufert, S. (1976). Laboratory experimentation. In M. D. Dunnette (Ed.), *Handbook of industrial and organizational psychology*, Chicago: Rand McNally.

Fugita, S. S., Agle, T. A., Newman, I., & Walfish, N. (1977). Attractiveness, self-concept, and a methodological note about gaze behavior. *Personality and Social Psychology Bulletin, 3*, 240–243.

Fugita, S. S., Panek, P. E., Balascoe, L. L., & Newman, I. (1977). Attractiveness, level of accomplishment, sex of rater, and the evolution of feminine competence. *Representative Research in Social Psychology, 8*, 1–11.

Garwood, S. G., Cox, L., Kaplan, V., Wasserman, N., & Sulzer, J. L. (1980). Beauty is only "name" deep: The effect of first-name on ratings of physical attraction. *Journal of Applied Social Psychology, 10*, 431–435.

Gergen, K. G. (1972). *The concept of self*. New York: Holt, Rinehart, & Winston.

Giffin, K. (1967). The contribution of studies of source credibility to a theory of interpersonal trust in the communication process. *Psychological Bulletin, 68*, 104–120.

Gifford, S. (1972). Cosmetic surgery and personality change: A review and some clinical observations. In R. B. Goldwyn (Ed.), *The unfavorable result in plastic surgery: Avoidance and treatment*, Boston: Little, Brown.

Gillen, B. (1981). Physical attractiveness: A determinant of two types of goodness. *Personality and Social Psychology Bulletin, 7*, 277–281.

Gillen, B., & Sherman, R. C. (1980). Physical attractiveness and sex as determinants of trait attributions. *Multivariate Behavioral Research, 15*, 423–437.

Gillmore, M. R., & Hill, C. T. (1981). Reactions to patients who complain of pain: Effects of ambiguous diagnosis. *Journal of Applied Social Psychology, 11*, 14–22.

Gitter, A. G., Lomranz, J., & Saxe, L. (1982). Factors affecting perceived attractiveness of male physiques by American and Israeli students. *The Journal of Social Psychology, 118*, 167–175.

Glasgow, R. E., & Arkowitz, H. (1975). The behavioral assessment of male and female social competence in dyadic heterosexual interactions. *Behavior Therapy, 6*, 488–498.

Glenwick, D. S., Jason, L. A., & Elman, D. (1978). Physical attractiveness and social contact in the singles bar. *Journal of Social Psychology, 105*, 311–312.

Goebel, B. L., & Cashen, V. M. (1979). Age, sex, and attractiveness as factors in student ratings of teachers: A developmental study. *Journal of Educational Psychology, 71*, 646–653.

Goffman, E. (1963). *Stigma: Notes on the management of spoiled identity*. Englewood Cliffs, NJ: Prentice-Hall.

Goldman, W., & Lewis, P. (1977). Beautiful is good: Evidence that the physically attractive are more socially skillful. *Journal of Experimental Social Psychology, 13*, 125–130.

Goldstein, A. G., & Chance, J. E. (1971). Visual recognition in memory for complex configurations. *Perception and Psychophysics, 9*, 237–241.

Goldstein, A. G., & Papageorge, J. (1980). Judgments of facial attractiveness in the absence of eye movements. *Bulletin of the Psychonomic Society, 15*, 269–270.

Gowin, E. B. (1917). *The executive and his control of men*. New York: Macmillian.

Graham, D., & Perry, R. P. (1976). Limitations in generalizability of the physical attractiveness stereotype: The self-esteem exception. *Canadian Journal of Behavioural Science. 8,* 263–274.

Graham, J. A., & Jouhar, A. J. (1981). The effects of cosmetics on person perception. *International Journal of Cosmetic Science, 3,* 199–210.

Gray, D. B., & Ashmore, R. D. (1976). Biasing influence of defendants' characteristics on simulated sentencing. *Psychological Reports, 38,* 727–738.

Griffitt, W., & Veitch, R. (1971). Hot and crowded: Influences of population density and temperature on interpersonal affective behavior. *Journal of Personality and Social Psychology, 17,* 92–98.

Gross, A. E., & Crofton, C. (1977). What is good is beautiful. *Sociometry, 40,* 85–90.

Guise, B. J., Pollans, C. H., & Turkat, I. D. (1982). Effects of physical attractiveness on perception of social skill. *Perceptual and Motor Skills, 54,* 1039–1042.

Haaland, G. A., & Venkatesan, M. (1968). Resistance to persuasive communication: An examination of the distraction hypothesis. *Journal of Personality and Social Psychology, 9,* 167–170.

Hagan, R., & Kahn, A. (1975). Discrimination against competent women. *Journal of Applied Social Psychology, 4,* 362–376.

Hagiwara, S. (1975). Visual versus verbal information in impression formation. *Journal of Personality and Social Psychology, 32,* 692–698.

Hamid, P. N. (1968). Style of dress as a perceptual cue in impression formation. *Perceptual and Motor Skills, 26,* 904–906.

Hamid, P. N. (1969). Changes in person perception as a function of dress. *Perceptual and Motor Skills, 29,* 191–194.

Hansell, S., Sparacino, J., & Ronchi, D. (1982). Physical attractiveness and blood pressure: Sex and age differences. *Personality and Social Psychology Bulletin, 8,* 113–121.

Hansen, F. (1972). *Consumer choice behavior: A cognitive theory.* New York: Free Press.

Hansson, R. O., & Duffield, B. J. (1976). Physical attractiveness and the attribution of epilepsy. *Journal of Social Psychology, 66,* 233–240.

Harrell, W. A. (1978). Physical attractiveness, self-disclosure, and helping behavior. *Journal of Social Psychology, 104,* 15–17.

Harrell, W. A. (1979). Physical attractiveness and public intimacy of married couples: An observational study. *Social Behavior and Personality, 7,* 65–75.

Harris, A. S. (1970). The second sex in academe. *American Association of University Professors Bulletin, 56,* 283–295.

Hartnett, J., & Elder, D. (1973). The princess and the nice frog: Study in person perception. *Perceptual and Motor Skills, 37,* 863–866.

Hartnett, J., & Secord, G. (1983). Physical attraction and its effects on the perception of extramarital affairs. *Perceptual and Motor Skills, 56,* 310.

Hartnett, J., Bailey, K. G., & Hartley, C. S. (1974). Body height, position, and sex as determinants of personal space. *Journal of Psychology, 87,* 129–136.

Hartnett, J., Gottlieb, J., & Hayes, R. L. (1976). Social facilitation theory and experimenter attractiveness. *Journal of Social Psychology, 99,* 293–294.

Hathaway, M. L., & Foard, E. L. (1960). *Heights and weights of adults in the United States* (Home Economics Research Report No. 10). Washington, DC: Human Nutrition Research Division, Agricultural Research Service.

Heider, F. (1944). Social perception and phenomenal causality. *Psychological Review, 51,* 358–374.

Heider, F. (1946). Attitudes and cognitive organization. *Journal of Psychology, 21,* 107–112.

Heider, F. (1958). *The psychology of interpersonal relations.* New York: Wiley.

Heilman, M. E., & Saruwatari, L. R. (1979). When beauty is beastly: The effects of appearance and sex on evaluations of job applicants for managerial and nonmanagerial jobs. *Organizational Behavior and Human Performance, 23,* 360–372.

Helwig, J. T., & Council, K. A. (Eds.). (1979). *SAS User's Guide.* Raleigh, NC: SAS Institute.

Hemsley, G. D., & Doob, A. N. (1978). The effect of looking behavior on perception of a communicator's credibility. *Journal of Applied Social Psychology, 8,* 136–144.

Henry, W. A. (1983, August 8) Weighing network anchors. *Time, 122,* 56.

Heron, W., Doan, D. K., & Scott, T. H. (1956). Visual disturbances after prolonged perceptual isolation. *Canadian Journal of Psychology, 10,* 13–18.

Hess, E. H. (1965). Attitude and pupil size. *Scientific American, 212,* 46–54.

Hicks, R. A., Pellegrini, R. J., & Tomlinson, N. (1978). Attributions of female college students to male photographs as a function of attractiveness and pupil size. *Perceptual and Motor Skills, 47,* 1265–1266.

Hildebrandt, K. A. (1980, April). *Parents' perceptions of their infant's physical attractiveness.* Paper presented at the International Conference on Infant Studies, New Haven, CT.

Hildebrandt, K. A. The role of physical appearance in infant and child development. In H. E. Fitzgerald, B. M. Lester, & M. W. Yogman (Eds.), *Theory and research in behavioral pediatrics* (Vol. 1). New York: Plenum Press.

Hildebrandt, K. A., & Fitzgerald, H. E. (1978). Adults' responses to infants varying in perceived cuteness. *Behavioral Processes, 3,* 159–172.

Hildebrandt, K. A. & Fitzgerald, H. E. (1979a). Adults' perceptions of infant sex and cuteness. *Sex Roles, 5,* 471–481.

Hildebrandt, K. A., & Fitzgerald, H. E. (1979b). Facial feature determinants of perceived infant attractiveness. *Infant Behavior and Development, 2,* 329–339.

Hildebrandt, K. A., & Fitzgerald, H. E. (1983). The infant's physical attractiveness: Its effect on bonding and attachment. *Infant Mental Health Journal, 4,* 3–12.

Hill, C. T., Rubin, Z., & Peplau, L. A. (1976). Breakups before marriage: The end of 103 affairs. *Journal of Social Issues, 32,* 147–168.

Hill, M. K., & Kahn, A. (1974). *Physical attractiveness and proximity in the attribution of success.* Paper presented at the meeting of the Midwestern Psychological Association, Chicago.

Hill, M. K., & Lando, H. A. (1976). Physical attractiveness and sex-role stereotypes in impression formation. *Perceptual and Motor Skills, 43,* 1251–1255.

Hobfoll, S. E., & Penner, L. A. (1978). Effect of physical attractiveness on therapists' initial judgments of a person's self-concept. *Journal of Consulting and Clinical Psychology, 46,* 200–201.

Hochberg, J. E. (1964). *Perception.* Englewood Cliffs, NJ: Prentice-Hall.

Hoffer, R. (1984 January 14). Beauty and ugliness: Mancini and Chacon figure to offer a little bit of both in title fight tonight. *Los Angeles Times,* Part 3, pp. 1, 10.

Hooper, E. M., Comstock, L. M., Goodwin, J. M., & Goodwin, J. S. (1980, May). *Patient characteristics that influence physician behavior.* Paper presented at the National Meeting of the American Federation for Clinical Research, Washington, DC.

Hopkins, K. A. (1980). Why do babies find faces attractive? *Australian Journal of Early Childhood, 5* 25–28.

Horai, J. (1976). The effects of sensation seeking, physical attractiveness of stimuli, and exposure frequency on liking. *Social Behavior and Personality, 4,* 241–246.

Horai, J., Naccari, N., & Fatoullah, E. (1974). The effects of expertise and physical attractiveness upon opinion agreement and liking. *Sociometry, 37,* 601–606.

Horvath, T. (1979). Correlates of physical beauty in men and women. *Social Behavior and Personality, 7,* 145–151.

Horvath, T. (1981). Physical attractiveness: The influence of selected torso parameters. *Archives of Sexual Behavior, 10,* 21–24.

Hoult, R. (1954). Experimental measurement of clothing as a factor in some social ratings of selected American men. *American Sociological Review, 19,* 324–328.

Hovland, C. I. & Weiss, W. (1951). The influence of source credibility on communicator effectiveness. *Public Opinion Quarterly, 15,* 635–650.

Hovland, C. I., Janis, I. L., & Kelley, H. H. (1953). *Communication and persuasion.* New Haven, CT: Yale University Press.

Huckstedt, B. (1965). Experimentelle Untersuchungen zum "Kindchenschema." *Zeitschrift für Experimentelle und angewandte Psychologie, 12,* 421–450.

Hudson, J. W., & Henze, L. S. (1969). Campus values in male selection: A replication. *Journal of Marriage and the Family, 31,* 772–775.

Hull, C. H., & Nie, N. H. (1979). *SPSS update: New procedures and facilities for releases 7 and 8.* New York: McGraw-Hill.

Hulse, F. S. (1967). Selection for skin color among Japanese. *American Journal of Physical Anthropology, 27,* 143–156.

Hunt, S. (1976). *Marketing theory: Conceptual foundations of research in marketing.* Columbus, OH: Grid.

Huston, T. L. (1973). Ambiguity of acceptance, social desirability, and dating choice. *Journal of Experimental Social Psychology, 9,* 32–42.

Huston, T. L., & Levinger, G. (1978). Interpersonal attraction and relationship. *Annual Review of Psychology, 29,* 115–156.

Illsley, R. (1955). Social class selection and class differences in relation to stillbirths and infant deaths. *British Medical Journal,* 1520–1524. (Cited in Lipset, S. M., & Bendix, R. [1959]. *Social mobility in industrial society.* Berkeley: University of California Press.)

Inamori, Y. (1979). Effects of false heart rate feedback on cognitive appraisal and physiological responses to emotional stimuli. *Japanese Psychological Research, 21,* 153–157.

Insko, C. A., Thompson, V. D., Stroebe, W., Shaud, K. F., Pinner, B. E., & Layton, B. D. (1973). Implied evaluation and the similarity–attraction effect. *Journal of Personality and Social Psychology, 25,* 297–308.

Irilli, J. P. (1978, March 27–31). *Students' expectations: Ratings of teacher performance as biased by teachers' physical attractiveness.* Paper presented at the annual meeting of the American Educational Research Association, Toronto, Ontario, Canada.

Izzett, R. R., & Leginski, W. (1974). Group discussion and the influence of defendant characteristics in a simulated jury setting. *Journal of Social Psychology, 93,* 271–279.

Jackson, D. J., & Huston, T. L. (1975). Physical attractiveness and assertiveness. *Journal of Social Psychology, 96,* 79–84.

Jacobson, M. B. (1981). Effects of victim's and defendant's physical attractiveness on subjects' judgments in a rape case. *Sex Roles, 7,* 247–255.

Jacobson, S. K., & Berger, C. R. (1974). Communication and justice: Defendant attributes and their effect on the severity of his sentence. *Speech Monographs, 41,* 282–286.

Johnson, R. W. (1981). Perceived physical attractiveness of supporters of Canada's political parties: Stereotype or in-group bias. *Canadian Journal of Behavioural Science, 13,* 320–325.

Jones, E. E., & Davis, K. E. (1965). From acts to dispositions: The attribution process in person perception. In L. Berkowitz (Ed.), *Advances in experimental social psychology.* New York: Academic Press.

Jones, W. H., Hansson, R. O., & Phillips, A. L. (1978). Physical attractiveness and judgments of psychopathology. *Journal of Social Psychology, 105* 79–84.

Jones, W. P. (1980). Cosmetic behavior therapy. *American Mental Health Counselors Association Journal, 2,* 53–58.

Jones, W. T., Sontag, F., Beckner, M. O., & Fogelin, R. J. *Approaches to ethics* (3rd ed.). New York: McGraw-Hill.

Joseph, W. (1977). *Effect of communicator physical attractiveness on opinion change and information processing.* Unpublished doctoral dissertation, Ohio State University, Columbus, OH.

Jourard, S. M., & Secord, P. F. (1954). Body size and body-cathexis. *Journal of Consulting Psychology, 18,* 184.

Jury awards Craft $500,000 in sex discrimination suit. (1983, August 9). *Minneapolis Star and Tribune,* II, pp. 1a, 7a.

Kaats, G. R., & Davis, K. E. (1970). The dynamics of sexual behavior of college students. *Journal of Marriage and the Family, 32,* 390–399.

Kahn, A., Hottes, J., & Davis, W. L. (1971). Cooperation and optimal responding in the prisoner's dilemma game: Effects of sex and physical attractiveness. *Journal of Personality and Social Psychology, 17,* 267–279.

Kalick, S. M. (1978). Toward an interdisciplinary psychology of appearances. *Psychiatry, 41,* 243–253.

Kanekar, S., & Kolsawalla, M. B. (1980). Responsibility of a rape victim in relation to her respectability, attractiveness, and provocativeness. *Journal of Social Psychology, 112,* 153–154.

Kanekar, S., Mazumdar, D., Kolsawalla, M. B. (1981). Perception of an aggressor and his victim as a function of physical attractiveness and retaliation. *Journal of Social Psychology, 113,* 289–290.

Kaplan, M. F. (1972). Interpersonal attraction as a function of relatedness of similar and dissimilar attitudes. *Journal of Experimental Research in Personality, 6,* 17–21.

Kaplan, R. M. (1978). Is beauty talent? Sex interaction in the attractiveness halo effect. *Sex Roles, 4,* 195–204.

Kaslow, F. W., & Schwartz, L. L. (1978). Self-perceptions of the attractive, successful female professional. *Intellect, 106,* 313–315.

Kassarjian, H. H. (1963). Voting intentions and political perception. *Journal of Psychology, 56,* 85–88.

Keating, C. F., Mazur, A., & Segall, M. H. (1977). Facial gestures which influence the perception of status. *Sociometry, 40,* 374–378.

Kehle, T. J., Bramble, W. J., & Mason, J. (1974). Teachers' expectations: Ratings of student performance as biased by study characteristics. *Journal of Experimental Education, 43,* 54–60.

Kelley, H. E. (1967). Attribution theory in social psychology. In D. Levine (Ed.), *Nebraska symposium on motivation.* Lincoln, NE: University of Nebraska Press.

Kelley, H. E. (1973). The process of causal attribution. *American Psychologist, 28,* 107–128.

Kenny, C. T., & Fletcher, D. (1973). Effects of beardedness on person perception. *Perceptual and Motor Skills, 37,* 413–414.

Kenrick, D. T., & Gutierres, S. E. (1980). Contrast effects and judgments of physical attractiveness: When beauty becomes a social problem. *Journal of Personality and Social Psychology, 38,* 131–140.

Kerber, K. W., & Coles, M. G. (1978). The role of perceived physiological activity in affective judgments. *Journal of Experimental Social Psychology, 14,* 419–433.

Kernis, M. H., & Wheeler, L. (1981). Beautiful friends and ugly strangers: Radiation and contrast effects in perceptions of same-sex pairs. *Personality and Social Psychology Bulletin, 7,* 617–620.

Kerr, B. A., and Dell, D. M. (1976). Perceived interviewer expertness and attractiveness: Effects of interviewer behavior and attire and interview setting. *Journal of Counseling Psychology, 23,* 553–556.

Kerr, N. L., & Kurtz, S. T. (1978). Reliability of "the eye of the beholder:" Effects of sex of the beholder and sex of the beheld. *Bulletin of the Psychonomic Society, 12*, 179–181.

Keyes, R. *The height of your life*. Boston: Little, Brown.

Kirkland, J., & Smith, J. (1978). Preferences for infant pictures with modified eye-pupils. *Journal of Biological Psychology, 20*, 33–34.

Kirkpatrick, C., & Cotton, J. (1951). Physical attractiveness, age, and marital adjustment. *American Sociological Review, 16*, 81–86.

Kleck, R. E. (1968). Physical stigma and nonverbal cues emitted in face-to-face interaction. *Human Relations, 21*, 19–28.

Kleck, R. E. (1969). Physical stigma and task interaction. *Human Relations, 22*, 53–60.

Kleck, R. E., & Rubenstein, C. (1975). Physical attractiveness, perceived attitude similarity, and interpersonal attraction in an opposite-sex encounter. *Journal of Personality and Social Psychology, 31*, 107–114.

Kleck, R. E., Ono, H., & Hastorf, A. H. (1966). The effects of physical deviance upon face-to-face interaction. *Human Relations, 19*, 425–436.

Kleck, R. E., Richardson, S. A., & Ronald, L. (1974). Physical appearance cues and interpersonal attraction in children. *Child Development, 43*, 305–310.

Kleinke, C. L., & Kahn, M. L. (1980). Perceptions of self-disclosers: Effects of sex and physical attractiveness. *Journal of Personality, 48*, 190–205.

Kleinke, C. L., & Staneski, R. A. (1980). First impressions of female bust size. *Journal of Social Psychology, 110*, 123–134.

Kleinke, C. L., Staneski, R. A., & Berger, D. E. (1975). Evaluation of an interviewer as a function of interviewer gaze, reinforcement, of subject gaze, and interviewer attractiveness. *Journal of Personality and Social Psychology, 31*, 115–122.

Kmiecik, C., Mausar, P., & Banziger, G. (1979). Attractiveness and interpersonal space. *Journal of Social Psychology, 108*, 277–278.

Kollar, M. M. (1974). The beautiful is rotten phenomenon: A negative stereotype of physical attractiveness. *Dissertation Abstracts International, 34* (9-B), 4632. (University Microfilms No. 74–77, 69)

Koopman, P. A., & Ames, E. W. (1968). Infants' preferences for facial arrangements: A failure to replicate. *Child Development, 39*, 481–487.

Kopera, A. A., Maier, R. A., & Johnson, J. E. (1971). Perception of physical attractiveness: The influence of group interaction and group coaction on ratings of the attractiveness of photographs of women. *Proceedings of the 79th Annual Convention of the American Psychological Association, 6*, 317–318.

Korabik, K. (1981). Changes in physical attractiveness and interpersonal attraction. *Basic and Applied Social Psychology, 2*, 59–65.

Korthase, K. M., & Trenholme, I. (1982). Perceived age and perceived physical attractiveness. *Perceptual and Motor Skills, 54*, 1251–1258.

Koulack, D., & Tuthill, J. A. (1972). Height perception: A function of social distance. *Canadian Journal of the Behavioural Sciences, 4*, 50–53.

Kramer, R. M. (1978, April 5–8). *Some determinants of commitment levels in premarital relationships*. Paper presented at the annual convention of the Rocky Mountain Psychological Association, Denver, CO.

Krebs, D., & Adinolfi, A. A. (1975). Physical attractiveness, social relations, and personality style. *Journal of Personality and Social Psychology, 31*, 245–253.

Kretschmer, E. (1925). *Physique and character*. New York: Harcourt, Brace.

Kuhn, M. H. (1972). Major trends in symbolic interaction theory in the past twenty-five years. In J. G. Manis & B. N. Meltzer (Eds.), *Symbolic interaction* (2nd ed.). Boston: Allyn & Bacon.

Kuhn, T. S. (1962). *The structure of scientific revolutions.* Chicago: University of Chicago Press.

Kuhn, T. S. (1970). *The structure of scientific revolutions* (2nd ed.). Chicago: University of Chicago Press.

Kuhn, T. S. (1977). *The essential tension.* Chicago: University of Chicago Press.

Kulka, R. A., & Kessler, J. D. (1978). Is justice really blind? The influence of litigant physical attractiveness on juridical judgment. *Journal of Applied Social Psychology, 8,* 366–381.

Kunin, C. C., & Rodin, M. J. (1982). The interactive effects of counselor gender, physical attractiveness and status on client self-disclosure. *Journal of Clinical Psychology, 38,* 84–90.

Kurtz, D. L. (1969). Physical appearance and stature: Important variables in sales recruiting. *Personnel Journal, 48,* 981–983.

Kurtzberg, R. L., Safar, H., & Cavior, N. (1968). *Proceedings of the 76th Annual Convention of the American Psychological Association, 3,* 649–650.

Kury, H., & Bauerle, S. (1977). The personality structure of popular and unpopular school children. *Psychologie in Erziehung und Unterricht, 24,* 244–247.

Lamont, L. M., & Lundstrom, W. J. (1977). Identifying successful industrial salesmen by personality and personal characteristics. *Journal of Marketing Research, 14,* 517–529.

Landy, D., & Aronson, E. (1969). The influence of the character of the criminal and his victim on the decisions of simulated jurors. *Journal of Experimental Social Psychology, 5,* 141–152.

Landy, D., & Sigall, H. (1974). Beauty is talent: Task evaluation as a function of the performer's physical attractiveness. *Journal of Personality and Social Psychology, 29,* 299–304.

Langlois, J. H., & Downs, A. C. (1979). Peer relations as a function of physical attractiveness: The eye of the beholder or behavioral reality? *Child Development, 50,* 409–418.

Langlois, J. H., & Stephan, C. W. (1977). The effects of physical attractiveness and ethnicity on children's behavioral attributions and peer preferences. *Child Development, 4,* 1694–1698.

Langlois, J. H., & Stephan, C. W. (1981). Beauty and the beast: The role of physical attractiveness in the development of peer relations and social behavior. In S. S. Brehm, S. M. Kassin, & F. X. Gibbons (Eds.), *Developmental social psychology: Theory and research.* New York: Oxford University Press.

Larrance, D. T., & Zuckerman, M. (1981). Facial attractiveness and vocal likeability as determinants of nonverbal sending skills. *Journal of Personality, 49,* 349–362.

Lasswell, H. D. (1948). The structure and function of communications in society. In L. Bryson (Ed.), *The communication of ideas.* New York: Harper & Row.

Laudan, L. (1977). *Progress and its problems.* Berkeley, CA: University of California Press.

Lefebvre, L. M., & McNeel, S. P. (1973). Attractiveness, cost and dependency in the exchange of unlike behaviors. *European Journal of Social Psychology, 3,* 9–26.

Lehner, U. C. (1983, July 29). For better or worse, arranged marriages still thrive in Japan. *The Wall Street Journal,* pp. 1, 12.

Lerner, R. M., & Gellert, E. (1969). Body build identification, preference and aversion in children. *Developmental Psychology, 1,* 456–462.

Lerner, R. M., & Karabenick, S. A. (1974). Physical attractiveness, body attitudes, and self-concept in late adolescents. *Journal of Youth and Adolescence, 3,* 307–316.

Lerner, R. M., & Korn, S. J. (1972). The development of body build stereotypes in males. *Child Development, 43,* 908–920.

Lerner, R. M., & Lerner, J. V. (1977). Effects of age, sex, and physical attractiveness on child–

peer relations, academic performance, and elementary school adjustment. *Development Psychology*, *13*, 585–590.

Lerner, R. M., & Moore, T. (1974). Sex and status effects on perception of physical attractiveness. *Psychological Reports*, *34*, 1047–1050.

Lerner, R. M., & Schroeder, C. (1971). Physique identification, preference, and aversion in kindergarten children. *Developmental Psychology*, *5*, 538.

Lerner, R. M., Karabenick, S. A., & Stuart, J. L. (1973). Relations among physical attractiveness, body attitudes, and self-concept in male and female college students. *Journal of Psychology*, *83*, 119–129.

Lerner, R. M., Venning, J., & Knapp, J. R. (1975). Age and sex effects on personal space schemata toward body build in late childhood. *Developmental Psychology*, *11*, 855–856.

Lerner, R. M., Orlos, J. B., & Knapp, J. R. (1976). Physical attractiveness, physical effectiveness, and self-concept in late adolescents. *Adolescence*, *11*, 313–326.

Lerner, R. M., Iwawaki, S., Chihara, T., & Sorell, G. T. (1980). Self-concept, self-esteem, and body attitudes among Japanese male and female adolescents. *Child Development*, *51*, 847–855.

Levinger, G. (1972). Little sand box and big quarry: Comment on Byrne's paradigmatic spade for research on interpersonal attraction. *Representative Research in Social Psychology*, *3*, 3–19.

Lewin, K., Dembo, T., Festinger, L., & Sears, P. S. (1944). Level of aspirations. In J. M. Hunt (Ed.), *Personality and the behavior disorders*. New York: Ronald Press.

Lewis, K. N., & Walsh, W. B. (1978). Physical attractiveness: Its impact on the perception of a female counselor. *Journal of Counseling Psychology*, *25*, 210–216.

Lewis, K. N., Davis, C. S., Walker, B. J., & Jennings, R. L. (1981). Attractive versus unattractive clients: Mediating influences on counselor's perceptions. *Journal of Counseling Psychology*, *28*, 309–314.

Liggett, J. (1974). *The Human Face*, New York: Stein & Day.

Light, L. L., Hollander, S., & Kayra-Stuart, F. (1981). Why attractive people are harder to remember. *Personality and Social Psychology Bulletin*, *7*, 269–276.

Linder, D. E., & Crane, K. A. (1970). Reactance theory analysis of predecisional cognitive processes. *Journal of Personality and Social Psychology*, *15*, 258–264.

Linn, L. (1952). Psychiatric aspects of plastic surgery. In L. Bellack (Ed.), *Psychology of physical illness*, New York: Grune & Stratton.

Lombardo, J. P., & Tocci, M. E. Attribution of positive and negative characteristics of instructors as a function of attractiveness and sex of instructor and sex of subject. *Perceptual and Motor Skills*, *48*, 491–494.

Lombroso, C. (1891). *The man of genius*. London: Scott.

Lorenz, K. (1943). Die angeborenen Formen möglicher Erfahrung. *Zeitschrift Tierpsychologie*, *5* 235–409.

Lott, B. E. (1955). Attitude formation: The development of a color-preference response through mediated generalization. *Journal of Abnormal and Social Psychology*, *50*, 321–326.

Lucker, G. W., Beane, W. E., & Guire, K. (1981). The idiographic approach to physical attractiveness research. *Journal of Psychology*, *107*, 57–67.

Lucker, G. W., Beane, W. E., & Helmreich, R. L. (1981). The strength of the halo effect in physical attractiveness research. *Journal of Psychology*, *107*, 69–75.

Lyman, B., Hatlelid, D., & Macurdy, C. (1981). Stimulus-person cues in first-impression attraction. *Perceptual and Motor Skills*, *52*, 59–66.

Macgregor, F. C. (1974). *Transformation and identity*. New York: New York Times Book.

Mahoney, E. R. (1974). body-cathexis and self-esteem: The importance of subjective importance. *Journal of Psychology, 88,* 27–30.

Mahoney, E. R., & Finch, M. D. (1967a). Body cathexis and self-esteem: A reanalysis of the differential contribution of specific body aspects. *Journal of Social Psychology, 99,* 251–258.

Mahoney, E. R., & Finch, M. D. (1976b). The dimensionality of body-cathexis. *Journal of Psychology, 92,* 277–279.

Mahoney, S. D. (1978, April 5–8). *The effects of physical appearance and behavior upon ratings of social attractiveness.* Paper presented at the annual convention of the Rocky Mountain Psychological Association, Denver, CO.

Maltz, M. (1946). *Evolution of plastic surgery.* New York: Froben Press.

Manz, W., & Lueck, H. (1968). Influence of wearing glasses on personality ratings: Cross-sectional validation of an old experiment. *Perceptual and Motor Skills, 27,* 7704.

Markham, P. (1968). The dimensions of source credibility of television newscasters. *Journal of Communication, 18,* 57–64.

Markus, S. (1977). Self schemata and processing information about the self. *Journal of Personality and Social Psychology, 35,* 63–78.

Maroldo, G. K. (1982). Shyness and love on a college campus. *Perceptual and Motor Skills, 55,* 819–824.

Martin, P. J., Friedmeyer, M. H., & Moore, J. E. (1977). Pretty patient—healthy patient? A study of physical attractiveness and psychopathology. *Journal of Clinical Psychology, 33,* 990–994.

Martinek, T. J. (1981). Physical attractiveness: Effects on teacher expectations and dyadic interactions in elementary age children. *Journal of Sport Psychology, 3,* 196–205.

Maruyama, G., & Miller, N. (1975). *Physical attractiveness and classroom acceptance* (Technical Report No. 75-2). Los Angeles: University of Southern California, Social Science Research Institute.

Maruyama, G., & Miller, N. (1980). Physical attractiveness, race, and essay evaluation. *Personality and Social Psychology Bulletin, 6,* 384–390.

Marvelle, K., & Green, S. K. (1980). Physical attractiveness and sex bias in hiring decisions for two types of jobs. *Journal of the National Association for Deans, Administrators, and Counselors, 44,* 3–6.

Marwit, K. L., Marwit, S. J., & Walker, E. (1978). Effects of student race and physical attractiveness on teachers' judgments of transgressions. *Journal of Educational Psychology, 70,* 911–915.

Marwit, S. J. (1982). Students' race, physical attractiveness and teachers' judgments of transgressions: Follow-up and clarification. *Psychological Reports, 50,* 242.

Mashman, R. C. (1978). The effect of physical attractiveness on the perception of attitude similarity. *Journal of Social Psychology, 106,* 103–110.

Mathes, E. W. (1975). The effects of physical attractiveness and anxiety on heterosexual attraction over a series of five encounters. *Journal of Marriage and the Family, 37,* 769–773.

Mathes, E. W., & Edwards, L. L. (1978). Physical attractiveness as an input in social exchanges. *Journal of Psychology, 98,* 267–275.

Mathes, E. W., & Kahn, A. (1975). Physical attractiveness, happiness, neuroticism, and self-esteem. *Journal of Psychology, 90,* 27–30.

May, J. L., & Hamilton, P. A. (1980). Effects of musically evoked affect on women's interpersonal attraction toward and perceptual judgments of physical attractiveness of men. *Motivation and Emotion, 4,* 217–228.

Mayer, J. (1983, May 25). TV anchor women never die, they get replaced by the young. *Wall Street Journal,* pp. 1, 21.

McClelland, D. C., Atkinson, J. W., Clark, R. A., & Lowell, E. L. (1953). *The Achievement Motive*. New York: Appleton-Century-Crofts.

McCroskey, J. C., Larson, C. E., & Knapp, M. L. (1971). *An introduction to interpersonal communication*. Englewood Cliffs, NJ: Prentice-Hall.

McCullers, J. C., & Staat, J. (1974). Draw an ugly man: An inquiry into the dimensions of physical attractiveness. *Personality and Social Psychology Bulletin, 1*, 33–35.

McCullough, E. A., Miller, M. F., & Ford, I. M. (1977). Sexually attractive clothing: Attitudes and usage. *Home Economics Research Journal, 6*, 164–170.

McDonald, P. J., & Eilenfield, V. C. (1980). Physical attractiveness and the approach/avoidance of self-awareness. *Personality and Social Psychology Bulletin, 6*, 391–395.

McDowell, K. V., & Zook, E. M. (1973, June). *Observers' assessments of the personalities of distance and looking norm violaters*. Paper presented at the meeting of the Canadian Psychological Association, Victoria, Canada.

McGuire, W. J. (1969). Nature of attitudes and attitude change. In G. Lindzey & E. Aronson (Eds.), *Handbook of social psychology*. Reading, MA: Addison-Wesley.

McGuire, W. J., & Padawer-Singer, T. (1976). Trait salience in the spontaneous self-concept. *Journal of Personality and Social Psychology, 33*, 743–754.

McKelvie, S. J. (1976). The effects of verbal labelling on recognition memory for schematic faces. *Quarterly Journal of Experimental Psychology, 28*, 459–474.

McKelvie, S. J. (1978). Sex differences in facial memory. In M. M. Gruneberg, P. E. Morris, & R. N. Sykes (Eds.), *Practical aspects of memory*. New York: Academic Press.

McKelvie, S. J. (1981). Sex differences in memory for faces. *The Journal of Psychology, 107*, 109–125.

McKelvie, S. J., & Matthews, S. J. (1976). Effects of physical attractiveness and favourableness of character of liking. *Psychological Reports, 35*, 1223–1230.

McWhirter, R. M. (1969). *Interpersonal attraction in a dyad as a function of the physical attractiveness of its members*. Unpublished doctoral dissertation, Texas Tech University, Lubbock, TX.

Mehrabian, A. (1972). *Nonverbal communication*. New York: Aldine-Atherton.

Meiners, M. L., & Sheposh, J. P. (1976, September 3–7). *Beauty or brains: Which image for your mate*. Paper presented at the annual conference of the American Psychological Association, Washington, DC.

Meiners, M. L., & Sheposh, J. P. (1977). Beauty or brains: Which image for your mate? *Personality and Social Psychology Bulletin, 3*, 262–265.

Melamed, L., & Moss, M. K. (1975). The effect of context on ratings of attractiveness of photographs. *Journal of Psychology, 90*, 129–136.

Mercado, P., & Atkinson, D. R. (1982). Effects of counselor sex, student sex, and student attractiveness on counselors' judgments. *Journal of Vocational Behavior, 20*, 304–312.

Michelini, R. L., & Snodgrass, S. R. (1980). Defendant characteristics and juridic decisions. *Journal of Research in Personality, 14*, 340–349.

Miller, A. G. (1970a). Role of physical attractiveness in impression formation. *Psychonomic Science, 19*, 241–243.

Miller, A. G. (1970b). Social perception of internal–external control. *Perceptual and Motor Skills, 30*, 103–109.

Miller, A. G., Gillen, B., Schenker, C., & Radlove, S. (1974). The prediction and perception of obedience to authority. *Journal of Personality, 42*, 23–42.

Miller, G. R., & Basehart, J. (1969). Source trustworthiness, opinionated statements, and response to persuasive communication. *Speech Monographs, 36*, 1–7.

Miller, H. L., & Rivenbark, W. (1970). Sexual differences in physical attractiveness as a determinant of heterosexual likings. *Psychological Reports, 27*, 701–702.

Miller, N., & Maruyama, G. (1981). Effect of targets' physical attractiveness on assumptions of similarity. *Journal of Personality and Social Psychology, 41,* 198–206.

Mills, J., & Aronson, E. (1965). Opinion change as a function of the communicator's attractiveness and desire to influence. *Journal of Personality and Social Psychology, 1,* 173–177.

Mills, J., & Harvey, J. (1972). Opinion change as a function of when information about the communicator is received and whether he is attractive or expert. *Journal of Personality and Social Psychology, 21,* 52–55.

Mims, P. R., Hartnett, J. J., & Nay, W. R. (1975). Interpersonal attraction and help volunteering as a function of physical attractiveness. *Journal of Psychology, 89,* 125–131.

Mischel, W. (1979). On the interface of cognition and personality: Beyond the person–situation debate. *American Psychologist, 34,* 740–754.

Mitchell, K. R., & Orr, F. E. (1976). Heterosexual social competence, anxiety, and self-judged physical attractiveness. *Perceptual and Motor Skills, 43,* 553–554.

Miyamoto, S. F. & Dornbusch, S. M. (1956). A test of interactionist hypotheses of self-conception. *The American Journal of Sociology, 61,* 399–403.

Mohajer, F., & Steinfatt, T. M. (1982, February 19–23). *Communication and interracial conflict: The role of disagreement, prejudice, and physical attraction on the choice of mixed race, mixed sex work-partners.* Paper presented at the annual meeting of the Western Speech Communication Association, Denver, CO.

Monahan, F. (1941). *Women in crime.* New York: Ives Washburn.

Moran, J. D. (1976). *Young children's conception of physical attractiveness as evidenced in human figure drawings* (Report No. MF01-PC01). Unpublished manuscript (ERIC Document Reproduction Service No. ED 196 538).

Morse, S. J., & Gruzen, J. (1976). The eye of the beholder: A neglected variable in the study of physical attractiveness? *Journal of Personality, 44,* 209–225.

Morse, S. J., Reis, H. T., Gruzen, J., & Wolff, E. (1974). The "eye of the beholder": Determinants of physical attractiveness judgments in the U.S. and South Africa. *Journal of Personality, 42,* 528–542.

Moss, M. K. (1969). *Social desirability, physical attractiveness, and social choice.* Unpublished doctoral dissertation, Kansas State University, Manhattan, KS.

Moss, M. K., & Page, R. A. (1972). Reinforcement and helping behavior. *Journal of Applied Social Psychology, 2,* 360–371.

Munn, L. (1940). The effect of a knowledge of the situation upon judgment of emotion from facial expression. *Journal of Abnormal and Social Psychology, 35,* 324–338.

Murphy, M. J., & Hellkamp, D. T. (1976). Attractiveness and personality warmth: Evaluations of paintings rated by college men and women. *Perceptual and Motor Skills, 43,* 1163–1166.

Murphy, M. J., Nelson, D. A., & Cheap, T. L. (1981). Rated and actual performance of high school students as a function of sex and attractiveness. *Psychological Reports, 48,* 103–106.

Murrey, J. H., Jr. (1976). *The role of height and weight in the performance of salesmen or ordinary life insurance.* Unpublished doctoral dissertation, North Texas State University, Denton, TX.

Murstein, B. I. (1972). Physical attractiveness and marital choice. *Journal of Personality and Social Psychology, 22,* 8–12.

Murstein, B. I., & Christy, P. (1976). Physical attractiveness and marriage adjustment in middle-aged couples. *Journal of Personality and Social Psychology, 34,* 537–542.

Nadler, A., Shapira, R., & Ben-Itzhak, S. (1982). Good looks may help: Effects of helper's physical attractiveness and sex of helper on males' and females help-seeking behavior. *Journal of Personality and Social Psychology, 42,* 90–99.

Napoleon, T., Chassin, L., & Young, R. D. (1980). A replication and extension of "Physical attractiveness and mental illness." *Journal of Abnormal Psychology, 89,* 250–253.

Nesdale, A. R., Rule, B. G., & McAra, M. (1975). Moral judgments of aggression: Personal and situational determinants. *European Journal of Social Psychology, 5,* 339–349.

Neubacher, J. (1978, October 1). Psychologist has case against Farrah Fawcett. *Roanoke Times & World News* (Virginia).

Newman, L. M. (1983). The effect of communication channels on consumers' responses to advertising. In P. E. Murphy & G. R. Laczniak (Eds.), *1983 American Marketing Association Educators' Proceedings.* Chicago: American Marketing Association.

Nida, S. A., & Williams, J. E. (1977). Sex-stereotyped traits, physical attractiveness, and interpersonal attraction. *Psychological Reports, 41,* 1311–1322.

Nie, N. H., Hull, C. H., Jenkins, J. G., Steinbrenner, K., & Bent, D. H. (1975). *SPSS: Statistical package for the social sciences* (2nd ed.). New York: McGraw-Hill.

Nielsen, J. P., & Kernaleguen, A. (1976). Influence of clothing and physical attractiveness in person perception. *Perceptual and Motor Skills, 42,* 775–780.

Novotny, M. A. (1977). *The effect of sex and attractiveness on mental illness pre-labeling.* Unpublished doctoral dissertation, Ohio State University, Columbus, OH.

Now, a drive to end discrimination against "Ugly" people. (1976, August 23). *U. S. News & World Report,* p. 50.

Nunnally, J. C. (1967). *Psychometric theory.* New York: McGraw-Hill.

Nunnally, J. C. (1978). *Psychometric theory* (2nd ed.). New York: McGraw-Hill.

Oaks, W. (1972). External validity and the use of real people as subjects. *American Psychologist, 27,* 959–962.

Ornstein, R. E. (1972). *The psychology of consciousness.* San Francisco: Freeman.

Orwell, G. (1949). *Nineteen eighty-four.* New York: Harcourt, Brace. (Cf. Howe, I. [1963]. *Orwell's nineteen eighty-four: Text, Sources, Criticism.* New York: Harcourt, Brace, & World).

Osgood, C. E., & Tannenbaum, P. H. (1955). The principle of congruity in the prediction of attitude change. *Psychological Review, 62,* 42–55.

Pagana, K. D., & Pagana, T. J. (1982). *Diagnostic testing and nursing implications: A case study approach.* St. Louis, MO: Mosby.

Page, R. A., & Balloun, J. L. (1978). The effect of voice volume on the perception of personality. *Journal of Social Psychology, 105,* 65–72.

Panferov, V. N. (1974). The perception and interpretation of personal appearance. *Voprosy Psikhologii, March–April,* No. 2, 59–64.

Paradise, L. V., Cohl, B., & Zweig, J. (1980). Effects of profane language and physical attractiveness on perceptions of counselor behavior. *Journal of Counseling Psychology, 27,* 620–624.

Parkin, A. J., & Hayward, C. (1983). The influence of trait and physical-feature-based orienting strategies on aspects of facial memory. *British Journal of Psychology, 74,* 71–82.

Passmore, J. (1967). Logical positivism. In P. Edwards (Ed.), *Encyclopedia of philosophy* (Vol. 5). New York: Macmillan.

Patzer, G. L. (1973). *Effects of sexual attitudes and physical attractiveness on heterosexual attraction.* Unpublished bachelor's senior project, Moorhead State University, MN.

Patzer, G. L. (1975). *Determinants of judgments of physical attractiveness and the attribution of sexual attitudes to strangers.* Unpublished master's thesis, Pittsburg State University, PA.

Patzer, G. L. (1978). *The physical attractiveness and persuasive communication relationship.*

Unpublished manuscript, Virginia Polytechnic Institute and State University, Blacksburg, VA.

Patzer, G. L. (1979a). *The moderate physical attractiveness hypothesis*. Unpublished manuscript, Virginia Polytechnic Institute and State University, Blacksburg, VA.

Patzer, G. L. (1979b). A comparison of advertisement effects: Sexy female communicator versus non-sexy female communicator. In J. Olson (Ed.), *Advances in consumer research* (Vol. VII). Ann Arbor, MI: Association for Consumer Research.

Patzer, G. L. (1980). *An experimental investigation of the relationship between communicator facial physical attractiveness and non-personal persuasive communication effectiveness in marketing*. Unpublished doctoral dissertation, Virginia Polytechnic Institute and State University, Blacksburg, VA.

Patzer, G. L. (1982). The effects of female nudity in advertising. In S. Achtenhagen (Ed.), *1982 conference proceedings: Western Marketing Educators' Association*. Los Angeles: Western Marketing Educators' Association.

Patzer, G. L. (1983a). Product perception as a function of communicator sex. In P. E. Murphy & G. R. Laczniak (Eds.), *1983 American Marketing Association Educators' Proceedings*. Chicago: American Marketing Association.

Patzer, G. L. (1983b). An experiment investigating the influence of communicator physical attractiveness on attitudes. In P. E. Murphy & G. R. Laczniak (Eds.), *1983 American Marketing Association Educators' Proceedings*. Chicago: American Marketing Association.

Patzer, G. L. (1983c). Source credibility as a function of communicator physical attractiveness. *Journal of Business Research, 11*, 229–241.

Pavlos, A. J., & Newcomb, J. D. (1974). Effects of physical attractiveness and severity of physical illness on justification seen for attempting suicide. *Personality and Social Psychology Bulletin, 1*, 36–38.

Pellegrini, R. J., Hicks, R. A., Meyers-Winton, S., & Antal, B. G. (1978). Physical attractiveness and self-disclosure in mixed-sex dyads. *Psychological Record, 28*, 509–516.

Pellegrini, R. J., Hicks, R. A., & Meyers-Winton, S. (1979). Situational affective arousal and heterosexual attraction: Some effects of success, failure, and physical attractiveness. *Psychological Record, 29*, 453–462.

Pellegrini, R. J., Hicks, R. A., & Meyers-Winton, S. (1980). Self-evaluations of attractiveness and perceptions of mate-attraction in the interpersonal marketplace. *Perceptual and Motor Skills, 50*, 812–814.

Pennebaker, J. W., Dyer, M. A., Caulkins, R. S., Litowitz, D. L., Ackreman, P. L., Anderson, D. B., & McGraw, K. M. (1979). Don't the girls get prettier at closing time: A country and western application to psychology. *Personality and Social Psychology Bulletin, 5* 122–125.

Peplau, L. A. (1976). *Sex, love, and the double standard*. Unpublished manuscript presented at the meeting of the American Psychological Association, Washington, DC.

Permut, S. E., Michael, A. J., & Joseph, M. (1976). The researcher's sample: A review of the choice of respondents in marketing research. *Journal of Marketing Research, 13*, 278–283.

Perrin, F. A. C. (1921). Physical attractiveness and repulsiveness. *Journal of Experimental Psychology, 4*, 203–217.

Peter, J. P. (1979). Reliability: A review of psychometric basics and recent marketing practices. *Journal of Marketing Research, 16*, 6–17.

Peterson, J. L., & Miller, C. (1980). Physical attractiveness and marriage adjustment in older American couples. *Journal of Psychology, 105*, 247–252.

Peterson, L. R., & Peterson, H. J. (1959). Short-term retention of individual verbal items. *Journal of Experimental Psychology, 58*, 193–198.

Pheterson, M., & Horai, J. (1976). The effects of sensation seeking, physical attractiveness of stimuli, and exposure frequency on liking. *Social Behavior and Personality, 4*, 241–247.

Piehl, J. (1977). Integration of information in the "courts:" Influence of physical attractiveness on amount of punishment for a traffic offender. *Psychological Reports, 41*, 551–556.

Piliavin, I. M., Piliavin, J. A., & Rodin, J. (1975). Costs, diffusion, and the stigmatized victim. *Journal of Personality and Social Psychology, 32*, 429–438.

Popper, K. (1962). *Conjectures and refutations.* New York: Harper.

Popper, K. (1972). *Objective knowledge.* Oxford: Clarendon.

Portnoy, S. (1972). *Height as a personality variable in a conformity situation.* Unpublished doctoral dissertation, Temple University, Philadelphia.

Powell, P. H., & Dabbs, J. M. (1976). Physical attractiveness and personal space. *Journal of Social Psychology, 100*, 59–64.

Power, T. G., Hildebrandt, K. A., & Fitzgerald, H. E. (1982). Adults' responses to infants varying in facial expression and perceived attractiveness. *Infant Behavior and Development, 5* 33–44.

Price, R. A., & Vandenberg, S. G. (1979). Matching for physical attractiveness in married couples. *Personality and Social Psychology Bulletin, 5* 398–400.

Rand, C. S., & Hall, H. A. (1983). Sex differences in the accuracy of self-perceived attractiveness. *Social Psychology Quarterly, 46*, 359–363.

Ravetz, J. R. (1971). *Scientific knowledge and its social problems.* New York: Oxford University Press.

Reagan, C. E. (1969). *Ethics for scientific researchers.* Springfield, IL: Charles C Thomas.

Reaves, J. Y., & Friedman, P. (1982). The relationship of physical attractiveness and similarity of preferences of peer affiliation among Black children. *Journal of Negro Education, 51*, 101–110.

Reis, H. T., Nezlek, J., & Wheeler, L. (1980). Physical attractiveness in social interaction. *Journal of Personality and Social Psychology, 38*, 604–617.

Reis, H. T., Wheeler, L., Spiegel, N., Kernis, M. H., Nezlek, J., & Perri, M. (1982). Physical attractiveness in social interaction: II. Why does appearance affect social experience? *Journal of Personality and Social Psychology, 43*, 979–996.

Rich, J. (1975). Effects of children's physical attractiveness on teachers' evaluations. *Journal of Educational Psychology, 67*, 599–609.

Rist, R. C. (1970). Student social class and teacher expectations: The self-fulfilling prophecy in ghetto education. *Harvard Educational Review, 40*, 411–415.

Robbins, P. R. (1962). Self-reports of reactions to fear-arousing information. *Psychological Reports, 11*, 761–764.

Robertiello, R. C. (1976). The myth of physical attractiveness. *Psychotherapy: Theory, Research, and Practice, 13*, 54–55.

Rockmore, M. (1978, January). *The American Way.* (Cited in Keyes, R. [1980]. *The height of your life.* Boston: Little, Brown, p. 177.)

Roff, M., & Brody, D. S. (1953). Appearance and choice status during adolescence. *Journal of Psychology, 36*, 347–356.

Ronkainen, I. A., & Reingen, P. H. Cognitive effects of the physical attractiveness stereotype in personal spelling. In N. Beckwith (Ed.), *The 1979 educators' conference proceedings.* Chicago: American Marketing Association.

Rose, R. M., & Levin, M. A. (1979). The crisis in stress research: A critical reappraisal of the role of stress in hypertension, gastrointestinal illness, and female reproductive dysfunction. *Journal of Human Stress, 5*, 4–48.

Rosen, G. M., & Ross, A. O. (1968). Relationships of body image to self-concept. *Journal of Consulting and Clinical Psychology, 32,* 100.

Rosenthal, R. (1971a). Teacher expectations and pupil learning. In R. D. Strom (Ed.), *Teachers and the learning process.* Englewood Cliffs, NJ: Prentice-Hall.

Rosenthal, R. (1971b). Teacher expectations and their effects upon children. In G. S. Lesser (Ed.), *Psychology and educational practice.* Glenview, IL: Scott, Foresman.

Rosenthal, R. (1973). The pygmalion effect lives. *Psychology Today, 7,* 56–63.

Rosenthal, R., & Jacobson, L. (1968). *Pygmalion in the classroom.* New York: Holt, Rinehart, & Winston.

Rosnow, R. L., & Aiken, L. S. (1973). Mediation of artifacts in behavioral research. *Journal of Experimental Social Psychology, 9,* 181–201.

Ross, J., & Ferris, K. R. (1981). Interpersonal attraction and organizational outcome: A field experiment. *Administrative Science Quarterly, 26,* 617–632.

Ross, M. B., & Salvia, J. (1975). Attractiveness as a biasing factor in teacher judgments. *American Journal of Mental Deficiency, 80,* 96–98.

Rotter, J. B. (1966). Generalized expectancies for internal versus external control of reinforcement. *Psychological Monographs, 80,* 1–28.

Rotton, J., Barry, T., Frey, J., & Soler, E. (1978). Air pollution and interpersonal attraction. *Journal of Applied Social Psychology, 8,* 57–71.

Rubenstein, C. (1983, January). The face. *Psychology Today,* pp. 48–55.

Rudolph, H. J. (1947). *Attention and interest factors in advertising.* New York: Funk & Wagnalls.

Runyan, W. M. (1980). The Life Satisfaction Chart: Perceptions of the course of subjective experience. *Internal Journal of Aging and Human Development, 11,* 45–64.

Rutzen, S. R. (1973). The social importance of orthodontic rehabilitation: Report of a five year follow-up study. *Journal of Health and Social Behavior, 14,* 233–240.

Salvia, J., Algozzine, R., & Sheare, J. B. (1977). Attractiveness and school achievement. *Journal of School Psychology, 15,* 60–67.

Santayana, G. (1936). *The sense of beauty.* New York: Scribners.

Sawyer, A. G. (1975). Demand artifacts in laboratory experiments in consumer research. *Journal of Consumer Research, 1,* 20–30.

Scherwitz, L., & Helmreick, R. (1973). Interactive effects of eye contact and verbal content on interpersonal attraction in dyads. *Journal of Personality and Social Psychology. 25,* 6–14.

Schiller, B. (1932). A quantitative analysis of marriage selection in a small group. *Journal of Social Psychology, 3,* 297–319.

Schiller, J. C. F. (1882). *Essays, esthetical and philosophical, including the dissection of the connexions between the animal and the spiritual in man.* London: Bell.

Schoedel, J., Frederickson, W. A., & Knight, J. M. (1975). An extrapolation of the physical attractiveness and sex variables within the Byrne attraction paradigm. *Memory and Cognition, 3,* 527–530.

Schooley, M. (1936). Personality resemblances among married couples. *Journal of Abnormal and Social Psychology, 31,* 340–347.

Schroder, H. M., & Suedfeld, P. (1971). *Personality theory and information processing.* New York: Ronald Press.

Schroder, H. M., Driver, M. J., & Streufert, S. (1967). *Human information processing.* New York: Holt, Rinehart, & Winston.

Schunk, M., & Selg, H. (1979). Sociometric status and the dimensions attractiveness, academic performance and aggressiveness in classrooms (correlations and group entropy). *Psychologie in Erzienhung und Unterricht, 26,* 267–275.

Schwartz, J. M., & Abramowitz, S. I. (1978). Effects of female client physical attractiveness on clinical judgment. *Psychotherapy: Theory, Research, and Practice. 15*, 251–257.

Scodel, A. (1957). Heterosexual somatic preference and fantasy dependence. *Journal of Consulting Psychology, 21*, 371–374.

Scott, W. C. (1973). The linear relationship between interpersonal attraction and similarity: An analysis of the "unique stranger" technique. *Journal of Social Psychology, 91*, 117–125.

Seamon, J. G., Stolz, J. A., Bass, D. H., & Chatinover, A. I. (1978). Recognition of facial features in immediate memory. *Bulletin of the Psychonomic Society, 12*, 231–234.

Secord, P. F., & Jourard, S. M. (1953). The appraisal of body-cathexis: Body-cathexis and the self. *Journal of Consulting Psychology, 17*, 343–347.

Secord, P. F., & Muthard, J. E. (1955). Personalities in faces: II. Individual differences. *Journal of Abnormal and Social Psychology, 50*, 238–242.

Secord, P. F., Dukes, W. F., & Bevan, W. (1954). Personalities in faces: I. An experiment in perceiving. *Genetic Psychology Monographs, 49*, 231–279.

Seligman, C., Paschall, N., & Takata, G. (1973). *Attribution of responsibility for a chance event as a function of physical attractiveness of target person, outcome, and likelihood of of event*. Paper presented at the meeting of the American Psychological Association, Montreal.

Seligman, C., Paschall, N., & Takat, G. (1974). Effects of physical attractiveness on attribution of responsibility. *Canadian Journal of Behavioural Science, 6*, 290–296.

Seligman, C., Brickman, J., & Koulack, D. (1977). Rape and physical attractiveness: Assigning responsibility to victims. *Journal of Personality, 45*, 554–563.

Shales, R. (1983, July 28). Ouster 'absolutely wrong,' Mudd says. *Minneapolis Star and Tribune, II*, pp. 1c, 7c.

Shanteau, J., & Nagy, G. F. (1979). Probability of acceptance in dating choice. *Journal of Personality and Social Psychology, 37*, 522–533.

Shapiro, H. L. (1947). From the neck up. *Natural History, LVI*, 456–465.

Sharf, R. S., & Bishop, J. B. (1979). Counselors' feelings toward clients as related to intake judgments and outcome variables. *Journal of Counseling Psychology, 26*, 267–269.

Shaw, J. (1972). Reaction to victims and defendants of varying degrees of attractiveness. *Psychonomic Science, 27*, 229–330.

Shea, J., Crossman, S. M., & Adams, G. R. (1978). Physical attractiveness and personality development. *Journal of Psychology, 99*, 59–62.

Sheldon, W. H. (1940). *The varieties of human physique: An introduction to constitutional psychology*. New York: Harper.

Shepherd, J. W., & Ellis, H. D. (1972). Physical attractiveness and selection of marriage partners. *Psychological Reports, 30*, 1004.

Shepherd, J. W., & Ellis, H. D. (1973). The effect of attractiveness on recognition memory for faces. *American Journal of Psychology, 86*, 627–633.

Sheposh, J. P. (1976). *The radiating effects of status and attractiveness of a male upon evaluations of his female partner*. Paper presented at the annual meeting of the Western Psychological Association, Seattle, WA.

Shettel-Neuber, J., Bryson, J. B., & Young, L. E. (1978). Physical attractiveness of the "other person" and jealousy. *Personality and Social Psychology Bulletin, 4*, 612–615.

Shuptrine, F. K. (1975). On the validity of using students as subjects in consumer behavior investigations. *Journal of Business, 48*, 383–390.

Sigall, H., & Aronson, E. (1969). Liking for an evaluator as a function of her physical attractiveness and nature of the evaluations. *Journal of Experimental Social Psychology, 5*, 93–100.

Sigall, H., & Helmreich, R. (1969). Opinion change as a function of stress and communicator credibility. *Journal of Experimental Social Psychology, 5,* 70–78.

Sigall, H., & Landy, D. (1973). Radiating beauty: Effects of having a physically attractive partner on person perception. *Journal of Personality and Social Psychology, 28,* 218–224.

Sigall, H., & Ostrove, N. (1973). Effects of the physical attractiveness of the defendant and nature of the crime on juridic judgment. *Proceedings of the 81st Annual Convention of the American Psychologial Association, 8,* 267–268.

Sigall, H., & Ostrove, N. (1975). Beautiful but dangerous: Effects of offender attractiveness and nature of the crime on juridic judgment. *Journal of Personality and School Psychology, 31,* 410–414.

Sigall, H., Page, R., & Brown, A. (1971). The effects of physical attraction and evaluation on effort expenditure and work output. *Representative Research in Social Psychology, 2,* 19–25.

Silverman, I. (1968). Role-related behavior of subjects in laboratory studies of attitude change. *Journal of Personality and Social Psychology, 8,* 343–348.

Silverman, S. S. (1945). *Clothing and appearance, their psychological implications for teenage girls* (No. 912). New York: Bureau of Publications, Teachers College, Columbia University.

Silvestro, J. R. (1982). Attractiveness and its effect on medical students' rank order for seeing patients. *Psychological Reports, 50,* 115–118.

Simmons, R. G., & Rosenberg, F. (1975). Sex, sex roles, and self-image. *Journal of Youth and Adolescence, 4,* 229–258.

Singer, J. E. (1964). The use of manipulative strategies: Machiavellianism and attractiveness. *Sociometry, 27,* 128–150.

Smith, E. D., & Hed, A. (1979). Effects of offenders' age and attractiveness on sentencing by mock juries. *Psychological Reports, 44,* 691–694.

Smith, G. H., & Engel, R. (1968). Influence of a female model on perceived characteristics of an automobile. *Proceedings of the 76th Annual Convention of the American Marketing Association,* 681–682.

Smith, P. A. (1962). A comparison of the sets of rated factor analytic solutions of self-concept data. *Journal of Abnormal and Social Psychology, 64,* 326–333.

Smits, G. J., & Cherhoniak, I. M. (1976). Physical attractiveness and friendliness in interpersonal attraction. *Psychological Reports, 39,* 171–174.

Snyder, M., & Rothbart, M. (1971). Communicator attractiveness and opinion change. *Canadian Journal of the Behavioural Sciences, 3,* 377–387.

Snyder, M., Tanke, E. D., & Bercheid, E. (1977). Social perception and interpersonal behavior: On the self-fulfilling nature of social stereotypes. *Journal of Personality and Social Psychology, 35,* 656–666.

Soble, S. L., & Strickland, L. H. (1974). Physical stigma, interaction, and compliance. *Bulletin of the Psychonomic Society, 4,* 130–132.

Solomon, M. R., & Schopler, J. (1978). The relationship of physical attractiveness and punitiveness: Is the linearity assumption out of line. *Personality and Social Psychology Bulletin, 4,* 483–486.

Sommer, R. (1969). *Personal space.* Englewood Cliffs, NJ: Prentice-Hall.

Sommers-Feldman, S., & Kiesler, S. (1974). Those who are number two try harder: The effect of sex on the attribution of causality. *Journal of Personality and Social Psychology, 6,* 846–848.

Sorokin, P. (1927). *Social and cultural mobility.* Glencoe, IL: Free Press.

Spence, J., & Helmreich, R. (1972). Who likes competent women? Competence, sex, role, congruence of interests, and subjects' attitudes toward women as determinants of inter-personal attraction. *Journal of Applied Social Psychology, 2,* 197–213.

Spitz, R. A., & Wolf, K. M. (1946). The smiling response: A contribution to the ontogenesis of social relations. *Genetic Psychology Monographs, 34,* 57–125.

Spreadbury, C. L., & Reeves, J. B. (1979). Physical attractiveness, dating behavior, and implications for women. *Personnel and Guidance Journal, 57,* 338–340.

Sroufe, R., Chaikin, A., Cook, R., & Freeman, V. (1977). The effects of physical attractiveness on honesty: A socially desirable response. *Personality and Social Psychology Bulletin, 3,* 59–62.

Staats, A. W. (1968). Social behaviorism and human motivation: Principles of the attitude-reinforcer-discriminative system. In A. G. Greenwald, T. C. Brock, & T. M. Ostrom (Eds.), *Psychological foundations of attitudes.* New York: Academic Press.

Staats, A. W., & Staats, C. K. (1958). Attitudes established by classical conditioning. *Journal of Abnormal and Social Psychology, 57,* 37–40.

Stafferi, J. R. (1967). A study of social stereotype of body image in children. *Journal of Personality and Social Psychology, 7,* 101–104.

Staffieri, J. R. (1972). Body build and behavioral expectancies in young females. *Developmental Psychology, 6,* 125–127.

Stapel, J. (1971). Sales effects of print ads. *Journal of Advertising Research, 11,* 32–36.

Starr, P. (1982). Physical attractiveness and self-esteem ratings of young adults with cleft lip and/or palate. *Psychological Reports, 50,* 467–470.

Steadman, M. (1969). How sexy illustrations affect brand recall. *Journal of Advertising Research, 9,* 15–19.

Stephan, C. W., & Tully, J. C. (1977). The influence of physical attractiveness of a plaintiff on the decisions of simulated jurors. *Journal of Social Psychology, 101,* 149–150.

Stephan, C. W., & Langlois, J. H. (1980). Physical attractiveness and ethnicity: Implications for stereotyping and social development. *Journal of Genetic Psychology, 137,* 303–304.

Sternglanz, S. H., Gray, J. L., & Murakami, M. (1977). Adult preferences for infantile facial features: An ethological approach. *Animal Behaviour, 25,* 108–115.

Sternlicht, M. (1978). Perceptions of ugliness in the mentally retarded. *Journal of Psychology, 99,* 139–142.

Sternthal, B. (1972). *Persuasion and the mass communication process.* Unpublished doctoral dissertation, Ohio State University, Columbus, OH.

Stewart, J. E. (1980). Defendant's attractiveness as a factor in the outcome of criminal trials: An observational study. *Journal of Applied Social Psychology, 10,* 348–361.

Stewart, R. A., Tutton, S. J., & Steele, R. E. (1973). Stereotyping and personality: I. Sex differences in perception of female physiques. *Perceptual and Motor Skills, 36,* 811–814.

Stohl, C. (1981). Perceptions of social attractiveness and communication style: A developmental study of preschool children. *Communication Education, 30,* 367–376.

Stokes, S. J., & Bickman, L. (1974). The effect of the physical attractiveness and role of the helper on help seeking. *Journal of Applied Social Psychology, 4,* 286–294.

Storck, J. T., & Sigall, H. (1979). Effect of a harm-doer's attractiveness and the victim's history of prior victimization on punishment of the harm-doer. *Personality and Social Psychology Bulletin, 5* 344–347.

Strane, K., & Watts, C. (1977). Females judged by attractiveness of partner. *Perceptual and Motor Skills, 45,* 225–226.

Stretch, R. H., & Figley, C. R. (1980). Beauty and the boast: Predictors of interpersonal attraction in a dating experiment. *Psychology: A Quarterly Journal of Human Behavior, 17,* 35–43.

Streufert, S., & Castore, C. H. (1968). Effects of increasing success and failure on perceived information quality. *Psychonomic Science, 11,* 63–64.

Stroebe, W., Insko, C. A., Thompson, V. D., & Layton, B. D. (1971). Effects of physical attractiveness, attitude similarity, and sex on various aspects of interpersonal attraction. *Journal of Personality and Social Psychology, 18,* 79–91.

Strune, K., & Watts, C. (1977). Females judged by attractiveness of partner. *Perceptual and Motor Skills, 45,* 225–226.

Suedfeld, P., & Streufert, S. (1966). Information search as a function of conceptual and environmental complexity. *Psychonomic Science, 4,* 351–353.

Sugarman, D. B. (1980). Perceiving physical attractiveness: The beauty of contrast. *Representative Research in Psychology, 11,* 106–114.

Sweat, S., Kelley, E., Blouin, D., & Glee, R. (1981). Career appearance perceptions of selected university students. *Adolescence, 16,* 359–370.

Tall men make more money. (1978, September 30). *Weekend Magazine, 28,* p. 3.

Tankard, J. W., Jr. (1970). Effects of eye position on person perception. *Perceptual and Motor Skills, 31,* 883–893.

Tanke, E. D. (1982). Dimensions of the physical attractiveness stereotype: A factor/analytic study. *Journal of Psychology, 110,* 63–73.

Taruiri, R. (1954). Person perception. In G. Lindzey & E. Aronson (Eds.), *Handbook of social psychology,* (Vol. II). Boston, MA: Addison-Wesley.

Taylor, P. A., & Glenn, N. D. (1976). The utility of education and attractiveness for females' status attainment through marriage. *American Sociological Review, 41,* 484–497.

Tedeschi, J. T., Schlenker, B. R., & Bonoma, T. V. (1975). Compliance to threats as a function of source attractiveness and esteem. *Sociometry, 38,* 81–98.

Tennis, G. H., & Dabbs, J. M. (1975). Judging physical attractiveness: Effects of judges' own attractiveness. *Personality and Social Psychology Bulletin, 1,* 513–516.

Terry, R. L. (1977). Further evidence on components of facial attractiveness. *Perceptual and Motor Skills, 45,* 130.

Terry, R. L., & Brady, C. S. (1976). Effects of framed spectacles and contact lenses on self-ratings of facial attractiveness. *Perceptual and Motor Skills, 42,* 789–790.

Terry, R. L., & Davis, J. S. (1976). Components of facial attractiveness. *Perceptual and Motor Skills, 42,* 918.

Terry, R. L., & Kroger, D. L. (1976). Effects of eye correctives on ratings of attractiveness. *Perceptual and Motor Skills, 42,* 562.

Terry, R. L., & Macklin, E. (1977). Accuracy of identifying married couples on the basis of similarity of attractiveness. *Journal of Psychology, 97,* 15–20.

Terry, R. L., & Zimmerman, D. J. (1970). Anxiety induced by contact lenses and framed spectacles. *Journal of American Optometric Association, 41,* 257–259.

Tesser, A., & Brodie, M. (1971). A note on the evaluation of a computer date. *Psychonomic Science, 23,* 300.

Thakerar, J. N., & Iwawaki, S. (1979). Cross-cultural comparisons in interpersonal attraction of females toward males. *Journal of Social Psychology, 108,* 121–122.

Thomas, W. I. (1928). *The child in America.* New York: Knopf.

Thornton, B. (1977). Effect of rape victim's attractiveness in a jury simulation. *Personality and Social Psychology Bulletin, 3,* 666–669.

Thornton, B., & Linnstaedter, L. (1975). *Effects of perceived attractiveness and sex-role interests on interpersonal attraction.* Unpublished manuscript, (ERIC Document Reproduction Service No. ED 134 896).

Thornton, B., & Linnstaedter, L. (1980). The influence of physical attractiveness and sex-role congruence on interpersonal attraction. *Representative Research in Social Psychology, 11,* 55–63.

Thornton, G. R. (1943). The effect upon judgments on personality traits of varying a single factor in a photograph. *Journal of Social Psychology, 18,* 127–148.

Thornton, G. R. (1944). The effect of wearing glasses upon judgments of personality traits of persons seen briefly. *Journal of Applied Psychology, 28,* 203–207.

Timmerman, K., & Hewitt, J. (1980). Examining the halo effect of physical attractiveness. *Perceptual and Motor Skills, 51,* 607–612.

Tompkins, R. C., & Boor, M. (1980). Effects of students' physical attractiveness and name popularity on student teachers' perceptions of social and academic attributes. *Journal of Psychology, 106,* 37–42.

Touhey, J. C. (1979). Sex-role stereotyping and individual differences in liking for the physically attractive. *Social Psychology Quarterly, 42,* 285–289.

Treisman, A. (1964). Selective attention in man. *British Medical Bulletin, 29,* 369–379.

Turkat, D., & Dawson, J. (1976). Attributions of responsibility for a chance event as a function of sex and physical attractiveness of target individual. *Psychological Reports, 39,* 275–279.

Turner, R. G., Gilliland, L., & Klein, H. M. (1981). Self-consciousness, evaluation of physical characteristics, and physical attractiveness. *Journal of Research in Personality, 15,* 182–190.

Udry, J. R. (1977). The importance of being beautiful: A reexamination and racial comparison. *American Journal of Sociology. 83,* 154–160.

Udry, J. R., & Eckland, B. K. (1983). *The benefits of being attractive: Differential payoffs for men and women.* Unpublished manuscript, University of North Carolina at Chapel Hill.

Unger, A. (1977, May 18). Galbraith turning economics to show biz. *Christian Science Monitor,* p. 22.

Unger, R. K., Hilderbrand, M., & Madar, T. (1982). Physical attractiveness and assumptions about social deviance: Some sex-by-sex comparisons. *Personality and Social Psychology Bulletin, 8,* 293–301.

Urdang, L., & LaRoche, N. (Eds.). (1978). *The synonym finder.* Emmaus, PA: Rodale Press.

U. S. Open '83. CBS National Sports Broadcast. 5 September 1983.

Vagt, G., & Majert, W. (1979). Relationships between physical attractiveness and kindness: Testing a prejudice. *Psychologische Beitrage, 21,* 49–61.

Vargas, A. M., & Borkowski, J. G. (1982). Physical attractiveness and counseling skills. *Journal of Counseling Psychology, 29,* 246–255.

Vaughn, B. E., & Langlois, J. H. (1983). Physical attractiveness as a correlate of peer status and social competence in preschool children. *Developmental Psychology, 19* 561–567.

Venkatesan, M. (1967). Laboratory experiments in marketing: The experimenter effect. *Journal of Marketing Research, 14,* 142–146.

Wagatsuma, E., & Kleinke, C. L. (1979). Ratings of facial beauty by Asian-American and Caucasian females. *Journal of Social Psychology, 109,* 299–300.

Wagman, M. (1967). Sex differences in types of daydreams. *Journal of Personality and Social Psychology, 7,* 329–332.

Waller, W. (1937). The rating and dating complex. *American Sociological Review, 2,* 727–737.

Walster, E., Aronson, V., Abrahams, D., & Rottman, L. (1966). Importance of physical attractiveness in dating behavior. *Journal of Personality and Social Psychology, 4,* 508–516.

Ward, C. D. (1967). Own height, sex, and liking in the judgment of the heights of others. *Journal of Personality, 35,* 381–401.

Wasserman, J., Wiggins, N., Jones, L., & Itkin, S. (1974). A cross-cultural study of the attribution of personological characteristics as a function of facial perception. *Personality and Social Psychology Bulletin, 1,* 45–47.

Waters, R. (1980, Spring). Beauty and job application. *Fairleigh Dickinson University Bulletin.*

Weber, S. J., & Cook, T. D. (1972). Subject effects in laboratory research: An examination of subject roles, demand characteristics, and valid inference. *Psychological Bulletin, 77,* 273–295.

Weiszhaar, O. (1978). *Sex drive, accentuation of physical attraction, and marital satisfaction.* Unpublished doctoral dissertation, University of Minnesota, Minneapolis.

Wenburg, J., & Wilmot, W. (1973). *The personal communication process.* New York: Wiley.

West, S. G., & Brown, T. J. (1975). Physical attractiveness, the severity of the emergency and helping: A field experiment and interpersonal simulation. *Journal of Experimental Social Psychology, 11,* 531–538.

When an authority looks into the problem of ugliness. (1976, August 23). *U. S. News & World Report,* pp. 51–52.

White, G. L. (1980). Physical attractiveness and courtship progress. *Journal of Personality and Social Psychology, 39,* 660–668.

Wicklund, R. A. (1974). *Freedom and reactance.* New York: Halsted.

Wiggins, J. S., Wiggins, N., & Conger, J. C. (1968). Correlates of heterosexual somatic preference. *Journal of Personality and Social Psychology, 10,* 81–90.

Wilson, D. W. (1978). Helping behavior and physical attractiveness. *Journal of Social Psychology, 104,* 313–314.

Wilson, G. D., & Brazendale, A. H. (1974). Psychological correlates of sexual attractiveness: An empirical demonstration of denial and fantasy gratification phenomena? *Social Behavior and Personality, 2,* 30–34.

Wilson, G. D., Nias, D. K., & Brazendale, A. H. (1975). Vital statistics, perceived sexual attractiveness, and response to risque humor. *Journal of Social Psychology, 95,* 201–205.

Wilson, P. R. (1968). Perceptual distortion of height as a function of ascribed academic status. *Journal of Social Psychology, 74,* 97–102.

Wolfe, H. D., Brown, J. K., & Thompson, G. C. (1962). *Measuring advertising results* (Business Policy Study No. 102). New York: National Industrial Conference Board.

Wolfe, J., Brown, F., Greenberg, S., & Thompson, G. (1963). *Pretesting advertising* (Business Policy Study No. 109). New York: National Industrial Conference Board.

Wolff, P. H. (1963). Observations on the early development of smiling. In B. M. Foss (Ed.), *Determinants of infant behaviour.* (Vol. 2). New York: Wiley.

Woll, S. B., & McFall, M. E. (1979). The effects of false feedback on attributed arousal and rated attractiveness in female subjects. *Journal of Personality, 47,* 214–229.

Women as bosses: The problems they face. (1983, July 11). *U. S. News and World Report,* p. 56–57.

Wylie, R. C. (1979). *Self-concept, Volume 2: Theory and research on selected topics.* University of Nebraska: University of Nebraska Press.

Wylie, R. C., & Hutchins, E. (1965). Schoolwork, ability estimates and aspirations as a function of socioeconomic level, race, and sex. *Psychological Reports, 2,* 781–808.

Yarbus, A. L. (1967). *Eye movements and vision.* New York: Plenum Press.

Yin, R. K. (1969). Looking at upside down faces. *Journal of Experimental Psychology, 81,* 141–145.

Young, J. W. (1980, May 18–23). *Willingness to disclose symptoms to a male physician: Effect of the physician's physical attractiveness body area of symptom, and the patient's self-esteem, locus of control and sex* (Reprot No. MF01-PC02). Unpublished manuscript presented to the annual meeting of the International Communication Association, Acapulco, Mexico. (ERIC Document Reproduction Service No. ED 198 588.)

Zajonc, R. B., & Brickman, P. (1969). Expectancy and feedback as independent factors in task performance. *Journal of Personality and Social Psychology, 11*, 148–150.

Zaltman, G. (1977). The structure and purpose of marketing models. In F. M. Nicosia & Y. Wind (Eds.), *Behavioral models of market analysis*. Hinsdale, IL: Dryden Press.

Zimbardo, P., Snyder, J., Thomas, J., Gold, A., & Gurwitz, S. (1970). Modifying the impact of persuasive communications with external distraction. *Journal of Personality and Social Psychology, 16*, 669–680.

Zlotlow, S. F., & Allen, G. J. (1981). Comparison of analogue strategies for investigating the influence of counselors' physical attractiveness. *Journal of Counseling Psychology, 28*, 194–202.

Index

Statistical analyses *(continued)*
   item-to-total correlations, 203, 208
   multivariate analysis of variance, 204
   Pearson product moment correlation,
      19–20, 24–25, 211
   reliability of measures, 19, 20, 22, 23
   t tests, 18, 197
   Tukey's multiple comparison, 200–202,
      205, 206, 209
Stereotype, 7–9, 14, 43, 98–99, 257, 263
Stimulus persons
   multiple, 18
Subtleness, 2, 7, 10, 13, 43, 134
Suicide, 45
Surgery, 237, 238

Theory
   attribution theory, 190, 192, 216
   consistency theory, 192, 216

Theory *(continued)*
   distraction theory, 191, 192, 216
   general discussion, 212–214, 223
   information-processing theory, 31, 266
   learning theory, 190–191, 216, 266
   marketing theoretical model, 216–224
   physical attractiveness phenomena
      theoretical model, 253–272
   verification theory, 248
Theory driven research. *See* Programmatic
   research
Truth of consensus procedure, 17, 187,
   190

Validity
   external, 39, 194
   internal, 39, 194–195
   See also Research measurement
Values. *See* Standards and values